FREEDOM FROM FEDERAL ESTABLISHMENT

FORMATION AND EARLY HISTORY OF THE FIRST AMENDMENT RELIGION CLAUSES

CHESTER JAMES ANTIEAU, S.J.D.

ARTHUR T. DOWNEY, LL.M.

EDWARD C. ROBERTS, LL.M

With the aid of PHILLIP M. CARROLL, LL.M., *and with the professional advice and assistance of* THOMAS H. O'CONNOR, PH.D., *Chairman of the Department of History, Boston College,* RICHARD L. DERRY, M.A., *Department of History, Boston College*

THE BRUCE PUBLISHING COMPANY
MILWAUKEE

Library of Congress Catalog Card Number: 64–25616

Preface

This is the initial publication of the Institute for Church-State Law of the Georgetown University Law Center. As the first step toward a fuller understanding of contemporary problems of church and state, the staff of the Institute has examined the history of church-state relationships in America during colonial times and the early years of independence.

The sole purpose of the study is to set forth the American experience and attitudes that are relevant to a clearer understanding of the religion clauses of the First Amendment. The authors offer no comment on recent Supreme Court decisions or judgment on the constitutionality of any aspect of modern church-state relationships. It should also be noted that the Institute offers no opinion in regard to the legal or historical validity of applying the First Amendment to the states through the Fourteenth Amendment. Such an investigation is beyond the range of this study.

The Institute for Church-State Law
Georgetown University Law Center
Washington, D. C.
March 1, 1963

Acknowledgments

The authors are greatly indebted to many librarians, archivists, historians, and correspondents for untold courtesies. They desire here to particularly express their thanks to: Dr. John Dawson, Director of Libraries, the University of Delaware, Newark, Delaware; Miss Virginia Shaw, Junior Archivist, Hall of Records of the State of Delaware, Dover, Delaware; Mr. Robert Costenbader of the Microfilm Reading Room of the Library of Congress, Washington, D. C.; Mr. John Dudley, Assistant Archivist of the Virginia State Library in Richmond, Virginia; Mr. David Rowland, Librarian of the Handley Library, Winchester, Virginia; Mr. Dan Youngblood, Assistant Librarian of the College of Charleston Library in South Carolina; Dr. Charles E. Lee, Director of the Archives Department of the State of South Carolina; Professor E. L. Inabinett and the staff of the Carolina Library at the University of South Carolina; Miss Virginia Rugheimer, Librarian of the Charleston Library Society in South Carolina; Mr. Joseph Jeffs, Librarian of Riggs Memorial Library of Georgetown University; Professor J. Harrison Boyles, Law Librarian of Georgetown University; Mr. Salvatore Costabile, circulation librarian of Riggs Memorial Library of Georgetown University; the personnel of the Maryland Collection of the Enoch Pratt Free Library in Baltimore; the personnel of the Virginia State Library in Richmond; the personnel of the Public Library in Wilmington, Delaware; the personnel of the Maryland State Archives in Annapolis; the personnel of the Rare Manuscript Room of the New York Public Library; the personnel of the Maryland Historical Society Library in Baltimore; the personnel of the social sciences collection of the Philadelphia Public Library; the personnel of the Virginia Historical Society, Richmond; the personnel of the Library of the Pennsylvania Historical Society in Philadelphia; the personnel of the New Jersey State Library, Trenton; the personnel of the public Library Trenton, New Jersey; the personnel of the Baptist Library and Boston Public Library at Boston, Massachusetts, of the Widener Library, of Harvard University at Cambridge, Massachusetts; and Mr. Paul V. Moynihan and his staff of the Bapst Library, at Boston College, Chestnut Hill, Massachusetts.

Our appreciation is also extended to the following firms and authors who have kindly allowed us to quote from their copyrighted materials: *The Life of Charles Carroll of Carrollton* by Kate Mason Rowland, G. P. Putnam's Sons, New York; *Commentaries on the Constitution of the United States* by Joseph Story, Little, Brown and Company, Boston; *Evolution of a Federalist* by William Loughton Smith, University of South Carolina Press, Columbia; *Jefferson on Religion in Public Education* by Robert M. Healy, Yale University Press, New Haven; *Catholics in the American Revolution* by Charles Metzger, Loyola University Press, Chicago; *Mitre and Sceptre* by Carl Bridenbaugh, Oxford University Press, New York; "Madison: On the Separation of Church and State," by Irving Brant, *William and Mary Quarterly,* Williamsburg; "How Far Does the Constitution Separate Church and State" by Lynfor A. Lardner, *American Political Science Review,* Washington, D. C.; *Religious Liberty* by Albert Dieffenbach, William Morrow and Company, New York; *A History of the South* by Francis Simkins, Alfred A. Knopf, Inc., New York; *Church and State in the United States* by Anson Phelps Stokes, Harper & Row, New York; *Protestant Crusade* by Ray Billington, Holt, Rinehart and Winston, Inc., New York; *The Relation of the State to Religious Education in Early New York, 1633–1825* by Charles Mahoney, Catholic University Press, Washington, D. C.

Our thanks are due to the excellent efforts of Mrs. Carol Franklin and Miss Peggy Coberly of the Institute Staff for their secretarial services.

The frequent aid and guidance of George Reed, Esquire, of the legal department of the National Catholic Welfare Conference, is greatly appreciated.

Lastly, the authors wish to acknowledge, with strong feelings of gratitude, the encouragement and guidance of the members of the Institute's advisory board: Paul R. Dean, Dean of the Georgetown University Law Center; the Reverend Charles M. Whelan, S.J., Professor of Law at Fordham University; and Doctor Heinrich Rommen, Distinguished Professor of Government at Georgetown University. The President of Georgetown University, the Very Reverend Edward B. Bunn, S.J., and the Academic Vice-President and Regent of the Law Center, Reverend Brian A. McGrath, S.J., are owed appreciation for their support and advice. The authors also wish to extend their appreciation to the Reverend F. William O'Brien, S.J., for his willingness to read the manuscript.

Introduction

"Congress shall make no law respecting an establishment
of religion, or prohibiting the free exercise therof. . . ."
— United States Constitution, First Amendment

Religious liberty and freedom in the United States are protected
by the First Amendment to the Constitution, directly in the case
of the Federal Government and indirectly in the case of the states,
by absorption of these religious guarantees into the Fourteenth
Amendment. Ratified in 1790, the First Amendment was a reflection on the situation in most of the colonies of early America,
where there was some relationship between church and state that
could be denominated "an establishment of religion." It seems from
the experiences of most of the Founding Fathers with "an establishment" that they believed such kind of governmental action was
undesirable. Accordingly, the Founding Fathers enunciated a consensus of their experience: that Congress should not make laws
"respecting an establishment of religion."

Unfortunately for their heirs of the democratic heritage, this
simple statement of policy has proved to be obscure in meaning.
Determination of the scope of the First Amendment's religion clauses,
therefore, requires recourse to the intent of the Founding Fathers
who sat in the First Congress that proposed this amendment, as
well as to the intent of the citizens of the states that ratified it
through their legislatures.* Inasmuch as men act in accordance

---

* The term "Founding Fathers" is incapable of exact definition. It is generally
applied to those persons who participated in the Philadelphia Convention of 1787,
which drafted the Constitution. It has also been applied to the members of the First
Congress who proposed the Bill of Rights. Members of the state legislative assemblies
that approved the Bill of Rights may also be included in the grouping. In order to
avoid confusion, the term will be qualified wherever possible by reference to the
particular group under discussion. It should be noted, however, that some leaders
of the era did not participate in any of these assemblies. Thomas Jefferson, for
example, was absent on diplomatic missions in Europe. Because this work would
not be complete without a discussion of the contributions that Jefferson and others
made to the advancement of constitutional thought in the period surveyed, their
statements and opinions will be consulted whenever they are found to illuminate the
problems surrounding the First Amendment.

with the events of their lives, the purpose of this study will be to set forth those historical facts relevant to the history of freedom of religion and the First Amendment. Thus the goal is to discover the presently unstated premises of experience which motivated the Founding Fathers to provide the First Amendment. In the process of the inquiry the following questions will be considered: What was an establishment of religion in colonial America? What was an establishment at the time of the drafting of the Constitution and the Bill of Rights? What practices were peculiar to an establishment of religion? Were they universal? What practices were condemned? Why were they condemned? Until these questions are answered in full detail, the premises of experience that motivated the adoption of the First Amendment will remain unknown, and the authors of the ban on laws "respecting an establishment of religion" will remain obscure.

There should be no doubt of the propriety of turning to the lessons of history in interpreting the United States Constitution. The Supreme Court has often endorsed the wisdom of ascertaining the views of the Founding Fathers in interpreting our Constitution. As early as 1819, the Court justified its conclusion by noting "that this idea was entertained by the framers of the American constitution."[1] Again, in 1872, the Supreme Court indicated that it was important to observe "the history of the times" surrounding the adoption of constitutional amendments.[2] Six years later, in an early case involving religion, the United States Supreme Court observed that "religion" was not defined in the Constitution, adding: "We must go elsewhere, therefore, to ascertain its meaning, and nowhere more appropriately, we think, than to the history of the times in the midst of which the provision was adopted."[3] Justice Black, speaking for the Court in 1947 in a case involving religion, indicated it was necessary to ascertain what was "in the minds of early Americans" when the First Amendment was adopted. The Court, he added, should concern itself with the "conditions and practices which they [the Founding Fathers] fervently wished to stamp out in order to preserve liberty for themselves and for their posterity." Accordingly, Justice Black concluded: "It is not inappropriate briefly to review the background and environment of the period in which that constitutional language [establishment of religion] was fashioned and adopted."[4] Most recently, in 1957, the United States Supreme Court in refusing to permit civilians to be tried by military tribunals, explained: "[T]he Founders had no intention to permit the trial of civilians in military courts. . . ."[5]

The wisdom and need of historical interpretation of our Constitution and its amendments have been generally acknowledged. The propriety of honoring the views of the men in the state ratifying conventions was attested to as early as April 6, 1796, by James Madison. He indicated in Congress that whenever it was necessary to go beyond the words of the Constitution to ascertain its meaning, "[w]e must look for it, not in the General Convention, which proposed, but in the State Conventions, which accepted and ratified the Constitution."[6] Again, in 1821, Madison stressed that the meaning of the Constitution is to be found "in the sense attached to it by the people in their respective State Conventions where it received all the authority which it possessed."[7] Three years later Madison underlined this thought when he wrote: "I entirely concur in the propriety of resorting to the sense in which the Constitution was accepted and ratified by the nation. In that sense is it alone the legitimate constitution."[8] Later in his life, Madison enlarged the scope of legitimate interpretive materials to be examined in constitutional adjudication, and listed them as follows:

1. The evils and defects for curing which the Constitution has called for and introduced;

2. The comments prevailing at the time it was adopted;

3. The early, deliberate, and continued practice under the Constitution.[9]

All these matters are surely the legitimate concern of any jurist intending a proper interpretation of the First Amendment. Further, as Conrad Moehlman has noted, competent historians have pointed out "that the Founding Fathers were deeply influenced by existing state constitutions as they framed the Constitution of the United States."[10] The practices in the United States at the time of the adoption of the First Amendment are clearly relevant to any study of what the community intended by, or extracted from, the religion clauses.

Accordingly, this study will first investigate the "conditions and practices which [the Founding Fathers] fervently wished to stamp out in order to preserve liberty for themselves and for their posterity," when they adopted the religion clauses of the First Amendment. To the majority of Americans the English heritage of the Established Church was to be rejected in its essentials. In England the establishment had been characterized by public endowment for the clergy of the Church of England, the presence of its prelates in the legislature, plus coercive power in the ecclesiastical courts.[11] Additionally, the Crown favored and protected the Church of England by the "Test Act" and the "Conventicle Act." The Test Act was passed "for preventing dangers which may happen from Popish recusants."[12] Under the provisions of the Act all civil and military officeholders were required to take oaths of allegiance and supremacy, to deny the doctrine of transubstantiation, to receive the sacraments of the Church of England, or to be subject to fine of five hundred pounds and disability to hold office. The Conventicle Act decreed punishment by imprisonment of every person above sixteen years of age present at a non-Anglican conventicle — described as "any meeting for religious worship at which five persons were present besides the household."[13] When the English settlers came to America, they brought with them such practices associated with the establishment. The first chapter of this work, therefore, sets forth in considerable detail establishment in colonial America, to highlight the practices considered anathema by the generation that won us independence and that institutionalized our constitutional protections for religious liberty.

"The history of the times," in the words of the Supreme Court, is narrated at length in Chapters Two, Three, Four, and Five to indicate thoroughly the aspects of "disestablishment" deemed necessary by the Founding Fathers to ensure religious liberty, the forms of accommodation between church and state which were thought permissible, the efforts of the community to protect religious liberty by the ban in the original Constitution upon religious test oaths, and the stated desires of the people for amendments to the federal Constitution on religion. The intention of those who proposed the First Amendment, noted so often as "highly persuasive" by the Supreme Court, is the subject of the sixth chapter. Obviously, not all members of the first House and first Senate had the same intention; moreover, it is almost impossible to ascertain the intentions of many members of the First Congress. Nevertheless, the ascertainable intentions of those who left behind a record of their wishes well deserve study. In order to throw further light upon the intentions of the members of the First Congress, this chapter also explores the meaning of the word "establishment" at the time of that assembly. Indeed, there are capable historians who consider the literal language of the Constitution and its amendments as the best evidence of the meaning of the document.[14] The views of those who ratified for the states in their legislatures, so emphasized by James Madison, are treated in the following chapter. "The comments prevailing at the time it was adopted," in the Madisonian language, also form part of Chapter Seven, and the subsequent chapter explores his rightful insistence upon the significance of the early practices in America under the First Amendment. Since the United States Supreme Court has so enthusiastically utilized the remarks made by

James Madison at other times and places about church-state relations as being relevant to, if not controlling of, First Amendment
interpretation, the views of other members of the First Congress are
set forth in Chapter Nine, to the extent that they can be ascertained.

In a study of what the American Founding Fathers intended
almost two hundred years ago, some words of caution may be in
order. First, a number of problems important to twentieth-century
America were naturally not anticipated by the Revolutionary generation. Thus their thinking, expressions, and acts are valuable only
insofar as they divulge a broad philosophy of church-state relations
which permits at best a calculated gamble as to how George Washington, for instance, would respond to the use of federal funds to
provide bomb shelters at church-related schools. Therefore, it is
necessary to examine carefully the documents relating to the Constitution and other original sources of the history during the era of
Constitution-making. Second, the impact of the views of certain of
our forebears upon the courts, and even upon this study, may be
far out of proportion to their significance at the time of the writing
of the Constitution simply because they have had capable biographers
or because their papers have been well preserved. It should also
be noted that many of the Founding Fathers had taken an oath of
secrecy at the Philadelphia Convention. Accordingly, they destroyed
many of their papers relating to the Constitution. Important leaders,
such as John Rutledge of South Carolina, later Chief Justice of the
United States, and Roger Sherman of Connecticut, a leader in the
First Congress, honored the oath and went to their graves without
a word of revelation.[15] Furthermore, the American struggle for
religious liberty and freedom from establishment was not the work
of one man — neither Charles Carroll of Carrollton nor James Madison. Therefore, historical understanding and proper constitutional
interpretation demand much wider appreciation of both the contributions and the intent of those hundreds of our Founding Fathers,
particularly those who served in the First Congress, as well as those
who participated in the Continental Congress, the federal constitutional convention, the state conventions that ratified the United
States Constitution, the state legislatures, and, last, the endless number of editors and pamphleteers who molded the American mind in
these directions. We must also bear in mind that a number of well-
known and well-publicized leaders of the time held highly personal
views which should not be automatically accepted as the dominant
view of their generation or even of their constituents.[16] Finally, even
as today's generation is sharply divided on many church-state problems so, too, the generation from 1776 to 1800 often held widely

disparate views — stemming at times from the religious faith of the individual, the part of the nation from which he had come, his economic status, and his political affiliations.

It is hoped that this study may recall to courts and scholars the legitimacy and the imperative necessity of understanding the First Amendment in the light of the struggles, the opposed evils, the practices, the utterances, and the aspirations of the generation that gave to us for perpetuity the religion clauses of this Amendment. Thus the heritage of the past may provide guidance to the problems of tomorrow, encouragement to strive for societal accommodations that are fair and just, and understanding of the problems of those who do not share the dominant religious beliefs.

Contents

FREEDOM FROM FEDERAL ESTABLISHMENT

CHAPTER ONE

Establishment in Colonial America

In molding the American heritage of liberty the period immediately preceding the American Revolution was of vital importance. For it was in the controversies between the royal government and the colonial citizenry that the fundamental concepts of American liberty were first set forth. Many of the grievances of the times dealt with the impairment of political rights, such as freedom of speech and taxation without representation. Consequently, one purpose of the Revolution in achieving independence was to secure these political rights. At the same time the desire to protect other personal rights contributed substantially to the break with Great Britain. Accordingly, at the time of the Revolution, there was a parallel movement to attain a more complete religious, as well as political, liberty.[1] This came to be known as the freedom from "an establishment" of religion. Basically, it dealt with the problem of religious liberty under some alliance between the church and the state, but many corollary ideas were encompassed within the term. Thus the expression, "an establishment," was not particular but generic, i.e., it was a shorthand expression which referred to an alliance with the following general characteristics:

1. A state church officially recognized and protected by the sovereign;
2. A state church whose members alone were eligible to vote, to hold public office, and to practice a profession;
3. A state church which compelled religious orthodoxy under penalty of fine and imprisonment;
4. A state church willing to expel dissenters from the commonwealth;
5. A state church financed by taxes upon all members of the community;
6. A state church which alone could freely hold public worship and evangelize;

1

7. A state church which alone could perform valid marriages, burials, etc.

In speaking of the struggle to be ' free from "an establishment" it is important to note that the relationship was far from uniform, varying widely from colony to colony. In some colonies only the Anglican Church was established; in others the local church, such as the Congregationalist, might be established, or a combination of churches might be established. In some colonies an established church was intended to make religious liberty more meaningful. On the other hand, an establishment could well be used to curtail political as well as religious liberty. Therefore, in speaking of the struggle against establishment, one should consider the *source* of the establishment and should observe the distinction between a local establishment, such as the Congregationalist in New England, and the establishment of the Church of England in the colonies. Opposition to an establishment in the Revolutionary period was largely directed against the Anglican Church as an instrument of royal tyranny, and not always against the local church, which was more directly amenable to the democratic process.[2]

Before proceeding to survey an establishment in colonial America, however, it would seem best to recall that the colonies were English possessions; their inhabitants Englishmen. It would not be surprising, therefore, to find that English customs and traditions permeated colonial life. This was in fact true in religious as well as political matters. And, although members of the local churches might dissent from the Church of England, many policies of the Anglican Establishment were shared in common by the various colonial churches. Accordingly, an examination of the structure of the Church of England would seem to be in order.

As its name indicates, the Church of England was as much a political institution as a religious one.[3] Like the new churches of the Reformation, it was founded on the principle later adopted by the settlement of Augsburg, *Cuis regio, eius religio,* that is, that the church was a national or state church and would henceforth represent all citizens of the state in the national aspect.[4] Such a monistic system could hardly be thoroughly "democratic," and in fact it was not. By establishing the Church of England, the Tudor rulers, Henry VIII and Elizabeth, had annexed the church to the state to make it "the highest department of the civil service of the pontiff-king."[5]

A necessary corollary to the system of the national state church was a need for unity which always reasserted itself in times of attack on either the monarchy or the church.[6] Flowing from this need for unity were two characteristics which came to distinguish an establish-

ment of religion: first, a preference to the members of the establishment and an exclusion of dissenters from their political rights; and,
second, a commingling of ecclesiastical and civil functions.[7]

The necessity of excluding dissenters from the political life of the
nation came from their frequent criticisms of the church. An attack
on the church was to a Tudor or a Stuart an attack on the divine
right of the king to rule and as flagrant a violation of the laws of
realm as the interference of the Pope had been. Blackstone in the
eighteenth century gave one of the clearest statements of the policy
in his *Commentaries:*

> He [the civil magistrate] is bound, indeed, to protect the established
> church; and, if this can be better effected, by admitting none but its
> genuine members to offices of trust and emolument, he is certainly at
> liberty to do so; the disposal of offices being a matter of favour and
> discretion.[8]

Accordingly, the famous Test and Corporation Acts were imposed.[9]
The method of exclusion was to introduce the articles of faith of
the Established Church into the oaths of office, such as a denial of
the doctrine of transubstantiation or an affirmance of the Trinity,
and to require as a prerequisite to holding office the taking of the
sacraments in the national church. The effect was to exclude the
religiously scrupulous dissenter who could not conscientiously affirm
these doctrines.[10]

The second characteristic, a commingling of ecclesiastical and
civil functions, was coordinate with the first as soon as religious
doctrines were used for civil purposes. More unfortunate was the
establishment of ecclesiastical courts to enforce the laws against
dissent. Often the courts of the star chamber and the Court of High
Commission had been used by the crown to dispense summary
criminal justice without a trial by jury.[11] By their very presence on
these courts the clergy of the Established Church made the term
"ecclesiastical courts" synonymous with established religion and
arbitrary government.[12]

In addition, the clergy of the Church of England soon came to be
directly involved in the political life of the nation. A legacy of the
Reformation had been the absolute privilege of the king to appoint
the bishops.[13] The important privileges attached to this office soon
made it an important source of political power. For example, the
bishops sat in the House of Lords; they also had strong influence over
the lower clergy and over many local civil offices, such as the town
clerk, by virtue of their power to appoint men to these positions.
James I had understood the function of the bishop as a supporter of

the government when he cried, "No bishop, no king!" With the development of the parliamentary system of government in the eighteenth century the bishopric was again utilized as a method of maintaining political power. Only those persons who would support the party in power had a chance of being appointed.[14] And as part of the price of the appointment the candidate was expected to bestow his own favors, the clerkships and benefices, on persons selected by the ministry.[15]

As the events portrayed in this chapter will indicate, many of the characteristics of the English establishment would be repeated in the colonies.

A State-Church Officially Recognized and Protected by the Sovereign

A fundamental characteristic of an established church has always been legislative sanction. The consequence of this sanction in England was the end of the church's independent existence and its submission to the civil authority of the state. To compensate for its loss the church received position and preference in the civil life of the nation. This pattern was repeated throughout the colonies. For example, the North Carolina Vestry Act of 1715 provided: "This province of North Carolina being a member of the Kingdom of Great Britain; and the Church of England being appointed by the charter from the crown to be the only Established Church to have public encouragement. . . ."[16] Nine years earlier the House of Assembly of South Carolina had effected the same policy by declaring that only those churches adhering to the doctrine and rubrics of the Church of England were to be eligible for public financial support.[17]

An establishment even permeated the form of government. The Southern colonies were divided into political subdivisions called parishes, which were in fact the principal organs of local government with the power to levy taxes.[18] This meant there could be no representation in the colonial legislature unless there was in each legislative district a church of the establishment.[19] On the local level members of the vestry conducted the affairs of the parish and chose the minister. But vestrymen were chosen only by members of the parish who, by exclusionary practices of tests and oaths, could only be practicing Anglicans. In Virginia the vestry was even less democratic Here the vestry was self-perpetuating with the power to fill vacancies. It became, in effect, what Sanford Cobb terms "a closed corporation."[20] In Massachusetts no man could be a freeman with the right to vote who was not a member of the Established Church, which was Congregationalist.[21] Thus, in its purest sense the Established

Church and its members were preferred to the exclusion of dissenters.

Perhaps the linking of the franchise to the state religion was part of the theocratic political theory shared by dissenters and members of the establishment alike. When Massachusetts dissenters were admitted to the franchise in the famous "Half-Way Covenant," under the theocratic notions that prevailed in the colony, they were allowed to vote only after being made members of the Established Church.[22] But the practice was altogether different in Georgia. Although the legislature in 1758 passed an act which established Anglican worship and divided the colony into parishes,[23] it nowhere defined the Church of England as the Established Church or as the official religion of the colony.[24] As events were to indicate, the omission was to be significant, for in practice the Church of England was never actually "established." As a result the franchise was extended to all alike.[25] As far as the franchise is concerned the same seems eventually to have been the case in South Carolina.[26]

The existence of a statute officially sanctioning the Church of England was not necessary, however, to the formation of an establishment. The change from the proprietary or charter colony to the royal colony brought with it the imposition of the royal governor who had a more direct link with the government and the English establishment. These men often sought to increase their power by using the Anglican Church as an instrument of civil policy. David Ramsey, the historian of the Revolution in the Southern colonies, writes: "[K]ings even more than proprietors, thought they had an interest in cementing the alliance between church and state, and connecting the altar with the throne."[27] Royal instructions offered many opportunities for the church party to influence colonial policy. Typically impressed upon the governor was the necessity for ensuring that God was worshiped according to rites of the Church of England and that the church be adequately supported.[28] The policy of the government as set forth in its instructions was to see that the Church of England was officially established by the provincial legislatures. The governors interpreted this advice as meaning that failure to achieve official establishment and support to the exclusion of other churches would be an affront to the government. For example, Governor Johnston of North Carolina addressed the House of Assembly in 1739, saying: "[That] there should be but two places where divine service is regularly performed is really scandalous. It is a reproach peculiar to this part of His Majesty's dominions which you ought to remove without loss of time."[29]

Such a situation easily led self-seeking men to think only of their political advantage. Lord Cornbury, governor of New York in the early eighteenth century, it is reported, "pandered" to the Church of England for his own private purposes.[30] In South Carolina, the attempts of the governor and Church party to exclude dissenters from the Legislature have been severely criticized as "making religion the stalking horse of political power."[31] Even the Reverend Dalcho, chronicler of the Episcopal Church in colonial South Carolina, writes that "their zeal . . . could not be prompted by any true love of religion . . . it merely arose from the *political considerations,* and from a desire to win the approbation of the authorities at home."[32] Because civil power had intimidated them, the clergy of the establishment on occasion distinguished themselves no more than did the royal governors. The address of the clergy to Governor James Glenn of South Carolina reveals their fault. On the occasion of his appointment they flattered him with the following address:

> Your Excellency's open Patronage and exemplary Practice of GOD's true Religion (the alone sure Foundation of Peace and Happiness of Society) and particularly as professed in the Church of England: Which cannot fail of happy and diffusive influence, for promoting the Interests of true Religion and virtue in general, and deriving the Blessing of GOD on Your Person and Government; & moreover, affording us Grounds to hope for your favorable Countenance and Encouragement towards the Church of England and her Clergy, in *particular.* . . .[33]

A more astonishing revelation of the uses of an establishment is found in an essay by the Anglican clergyman, the Reverend William Smith of New York. He was appalled at the idea of allowing all religions to be "equally favored by the Civil Power." He shuddered at "what a Scene of Confusion would thence arise . . . from such unbridled Liberty of Conscience." With perceptive insight into the political aspect of establishment he concluded:

> As to the Political Uses of national Establishments, he must indeed be a very shallow politician who does not see them. The Statesman has always found it necessary for the Purposes of Government, to raise one Denomination of religions above the rest to a certain degree. This favor'd denomination, by these means, becomes as it were the creature of the Government, thus enabled to turn the Balance and keep all in Subjection.[34]

More unfortunate connotations were often attached to the term "establishment" by the actions of members of the Established Church as they pressed forward with misdirected zeal. They were not content to win adherents on the strength of their own cause, but they proselytized in the territories with already settled churches. This became a factor of major importance in New England, which was overwhelmingly Congregationalist; in the back country of the two Carolinas, which was predominately Presbyterian; and in New York, which had a system of "multiple establishment," with equal privileges and benefits to all incorporated churches, except for the Roman Catholic.[35]

For the Anglican Church in the colonies the result was to bring down upon it the same charges that had been leveled at the establishment in England. Because of its close relationship with the royal government, it was viewed as both a department of state and an instrument of English tyranny.[36] For example in North Carolina during this period a struggle was occurring as the royal government attempted to impose an Anglican Establishment upon the staunch Presbyterians of that colony. Between 1754 and 1765 (the date of the last church legislation until the Revolution), Stephen Weeks records that the history of the colony is the story of "the stubborn resistance to church laws by the Dissenters, [and] the stubborn determination of the Churchmen to have an establishment."[37] In the minds of the dissenting colonists religion and politics fused. One authority writes that in New England from 1750 on "nearly every political maneuver was immediately interpreted as a device to gain influence and prestige for one or the other of the ecclesiastical groups."[38]

The fight against an establishment was, as it has been seen, largely a fight against an arbitrary, politically partisan state church. During the pre-Revolutionary period this was a struggle against the Church of England and not against the indigenous establishments of New England and New York. But one factor of the establishment remains to be clarified: the charge of "popery" that the colonists so often flung against the Church of England.[39] This would indeed seem to be a strange indictment against a Protestant church which was distinguished for its break from Rome. To understand the relationship observed by the colonists between Catholicism and the establishment it is necessary to recall the English heritage. Catholicism had traditionally been deemed an enemy of the state. The great propaganda machine of the government had accordingly created — with the aid of works such as Foxe's *Book of Martyrs*, a myth incredible to the modern mind.[40] But to these settlers there seemed to be a clear relationship between Roman Catholicism and arbitrary government.[41] In this context the epithets of the dissenters are understandable, and quite consistent with their opposition to tyrannical government.

Their action in repressing Catholics must also be understood.

When it is compared with the colonists general views on liberty, it is seemingly contradictory. However "colonial enmity towards popery and papists," writes Charles Metzger, "was in the best English Protestant tradition."[42] The Roman Catholic was looked upon as an enemy of the colonies as well as of the British Isles. With the French colonies of Quebec to the north, Louisiana to the west, and Spanish Florida to the south, the settlers were constantly kept aware of the threat of Catholic power.[43] Stern measures to repress the introduction of Catholicism into the colonies were enacted. The charters from the earliest days provided liberty of conscience for all inhabitants "except papists."[44] Disenfranchisement and economic burdens were imposed upon the Catholics.[45] Virginia in 1756 passed *An Act For Disarming Papists* which required that Catholics give up arms on the penalty of three months' imprisonment and a fine.[46]

There was rarely any sound factual basis for this "no-popery" legislation in the colonies, for Catholics were virtually nonexistent.[47] Billington concludes that for the most part it was "the inherited bigotry of the Protestant settlers [which] motivated their enactment of the papal statutes."[48] In the border colonies, however, there was genuine reason for the anti-Catholic policy. In Georgia, which had borders with Louisiana and Florida, a 1738 mutiny along the Spanish frontier was found to have been caused by soldiers in the pay of the Spaniards. One was found to be Irish and another confessed that he was a Catholic. The trustees of Georgia reacted by barring Catholics from immigrating into the colony.[49] Like its neighbor on the southern end of the colonies, New England found much to be concerned with in the actions of a foreign power on its border. The French colony of Quebec was a constant source of concern to New England. In 1647 and 1700, inspired by the belief that French Jesuits were proselyting among the Indians, instigating raids, and seducing away adherents to the English crown, Massachusetts passed a law declaring that "Jesuits, priests, and popish missionaries" found in the colony were subject to perpetual imprisonment and the death penalty if they escaped from their incarceration.[50] That there was no softening of the attitude toward the Catholics is indicated by their view of the French and Indian War, which Metzger reports, "became to them a crusade against French Papists."[51]

This crusade achieved a new intensity in 1774 with the passage of the Quebec Act. The terms of the act were seemingly noncontroversial, and they had been thought by the British Cabinet to be an act of statesmanship.[52] The Act stated:

And, for the more perfect security and ease of the minds of the inhabitants of the said province, it is hereby declared that his majesty's subjects in the said province of Quebec may have, hold, and enjoy the free exercise of the religion of the Church of Rome, subject to the King's supremacy . . . and that the clergy of the said Church may hold, receive, and enjoy their accustomed dues and rights with *respect to such persons only as shall profess the said religion.* Provided, nevertheless, that it shall be lawful for his majesty, his heirs, or successors to make such provision out of the rest of the said accustomed dues and rights for the encouragement of the Protestant religion and for the maintenance and support of Protestant clergy without the said province as he or they shall . . . think necessary and expedient. . . .[53]

The Act simply provided equality of religious opportunity for the Catholics and other settlers of the colony. Moreover, it recognized the principle of religious voluntarism by allowing the clergy and church of each denomination only such control and benefits as were coexistensive with the membership in the respective church. This was in the tradition of New England and New York. Thus, the provisions were distinct from those of the English establishment, based on an exclusionary preference for the state church.

The tumult which resulted in the colonies must have truly surprised the Ministry. Instead of lauding the Act as a measure of progress in providing liberty for religious dissent, the colonists denounced the Act as "sheer popery." Again they drew the equation between an establishment and arbitrary government. The people of Suffolk County, Massachusetts, protested that the Act was "dangerous in the extreme to the Protestant religion, and to the civil rights and liberties of all Americans."[54] In Georgia, Pastor Zubly of the Independent Church denounced the Act as an *unlawful combination* between the royal government and the Catholic Church whose purpose was to take away "trials in the vicinage and taxation only by representation."[55] In South Carolina the relationship seemed equally clear. The preamble to the Constitution of 1776 declared that

the Roman Catholic religion (although before tolerated and freely exercised there) and *an absolute government* are established in that province, and its limits extended through a vast tract of country so as to border on the free Protestant English settlements, with design of using a whole people differing in religious principles from the neighboring colonies, and subject to arbitrary power, as fit instruments to overawe and subdue the colonies.[56]

Thus, at the outbreak of the Revolution the colonists saw an establishment as a department of the state which was seeking to serve the ends of this world and not the next. Because of its close association with the royal government, it often meant an instrument to impose a tyrannical and irresponsible regime on the colonies. Whether the instrument was the Church of England or Roman Catholicism made little difference.

A State Church Whose Members Alone Were Eligible to Vote, Hold Office, and Practice a Profession

The colonial heritage of an establishment was often characterized by interference with the personal liberties of dissenters. The purpose of the restrictions was to maintain the dominance of the establishment. Hence, members of dissenting sects were curtailed in the exercise of the basic political and economic rights of voting, holding office, and practicing a profession, such as teaching or preaching.

The right of private association was often infringed. A central issue in the fight against the Anglican establishment was the right of presentation of a minister. In the Church of England, and other hierarchical churches, this process had been traditionally reserved to the bishop.[57] This right was intended to serve the purposes of ecclesiastical discipline, although in practice it often became a device of political patronage.[58] Understandably, this claim on the part of the establishment came into immediate conflict with the congregational nature of the colonial churches, which insisted upon placing this right in the hands of the elected church vestry. This had been the practice in New England.[59] As other dissenting sects immigrated to the colonies the vestry system of presentation became widespread. It is found even in the Episcopal churches of South Carolina which had an Anglican Establishment.[60] In New York under the Act of 1693 a majority of the incorporators were allowed to select the pastor.[61] In Georgia the power of presentation was exercised in behalf of the settlers by the trustees, who admitted to the colony all ministers of good character of the Anglican, Presbyterian, Lutheran, and Moravian Churches.[62]

The importance of the vestry system was that it tended toward "disestablishment" for the reason that it was in opposition to the centralized authority, which in turn, was the usual characteristic of an establishment.[63] Thus the Bishop of London and his colleagues made repeated efforts to have the sole right of presentation to orders evolve upon them. The colonist, however, would have no outside influence in his religious affairs. The Georgia trustees met the problem by refusing to appropriate the land for the churches, denominated as glebe lands, since this action would have vested the fee in the minister for life subject to defeasance only by removal of the bishop of London. Because long periods of time were required for action, the trustees preferred to retain to themselves the ability to act.[64] Hence, they were able to remove the Anglican clergyman, Thomas Bosomworth, for his immoral conduct.[65] South Carolina had attempted to provide a "congregational" solution to the problem in the Church Act of 1704, which provided for a lay commission of twenty parishioners with power to remove an offending clergyman. Because the Act was opposed by the High Church, Queen Anne disallowed it.[66] Thereafter, the power seems to have been exercised by the governor or by the bishop's representative. The establishment seems to have prevailed. A 1706 act granting land to the French settlement on the Santee River provided that "no payment for the support of a minister shall commence before the arrival in the province of a minister sent by the Right Reverend Father in God, Henry, Lord Bishop of London, or his successor."[67] However, on the basis of available South Carolina records there seems to have been no unusual controversy over exercise of the right.

In North Carolina, on the other hand, the story is one of repeated conflict between the royal governor demanding the right of presentation be placed in the bishop of London and the legislature which refused to take it from the vestry of the church. The Assembly in 1741 passed an act which placed the sole right of presentation in the vestry, but the British Privy Council disallowed it as "incompatible with the rights of the Crown and ecclesiastical jurisdiction."[68] All subsequent acts were disallowed on the same ground.[69] In New York the experience of the dissenter was especially bitter. Under the terms of the Act of 1693 each church was free to choose its own minister. Later, both Governor Andros and Lord Cornbury contended that the Church of England alone had been established, and they claimed for themselves the right to induct ministers into the churches. So far did they press their claim that they even rejected duly elected Protestant ministers and placed Anglicans in their place.[70]

Control of the ministry was only one aspect of an establishment. Control of the education of the ministry was equally a part of the monopoly of the state church. This meant that the schools, the training ground for future clergymen, must not be allowed to teach doctrines subversive to the good order and safety of the state church. In England control was imposed through the Schism Act which required all schoolmasters to be licensed by a bishop of the Church of England.[71] The significance of this licensing system to religious and educational liberty lay in the fact that virtually all education at this time was entrusted to the churches. In the colonies, religion and education were often commingled so as to be indistinguishable, and teachers were frequently ministers, catechists, or lay readers.[72] The curriculum was largely the three R's and the Bible.[73] Thus, control of the schools would give the established church a monopoly on education and the ability to damage the churches' ministerial education programs.

It should not be thought, however, that all restrictions on paper would in fact work to the detriment of religious and educational freedom. Local restrictions were often harmless in fact because they were nothing more than the desire of a religiously homogeneous community to have the local teacher represent their general moral viewpoint. Thus, in Massachusetts the laws required merely that a teacher be religious. The fact that most communities were largely Congregationalist meant that the teacher chosen by them would be of that faith.[74] In New York where the Dutch were settled, King's College provided a professor of divinity of the Reformed Dutch Protestant Church for the instruction of candidates for the ministry in that particular denomination.[75]

In breaking the state-church monopoly, any accommodation to local interests was opposed to an establishment. Accordingly, throughout the eighteenth century in the colonies, the Anglican Church Party made systematic attempts to gain control of the colonial educational system. Sometimes it was by infiltration, as the apostacy of the rector of Yale, Reverend Timothy Cutler, demonstrated, and by the repeated attempts by the Anglicans to gain control of King's College.[76] Generally it was by the more direct means of requiring a teaching license from the royal governor or from the bishop of London. In colonial Virginia only those who were certified by the Archbishop of Canterbury could teach.[77] In New Jersey the governor used his licensing power to stifle dissenters' schools.[78] The royal government of North Carolina required a license from the Bishop of London for all teachers and repeatedly denied efforts of dissenters to have their own schools.[79] When the Assembly granted a charter to Queen's Museum, a school of Presbyterian origin, the charter was disallowed by the Board of Trade, which declared:

> We think it our duty to submit to your Majesty, whether it be advisable for your Majesty to add encouragement to toleration by giving royal assent to an establishment, which in its consequences promises with great and permanent advantages to a sect of Dissenters from the Established Church who have already extended themselves over that Province in very considerable numbers.[80]

The Board's recommendation was accepted and the King repealed the charter in 1773.[81] According to Stephen Weeks, the result was that "there was less freedom of education in North Carolina in 1773 than in 1673."[82] The danger of any monopoly of education was apparent to the leaders of the times. Thus in 1770, Henry Laurens, soon to be president of the Continental Congress, urged Benjamin Elliot to beware of the extremes and avoid "the snare of having *all* within the pale of the Church of England."[83]

The monopolistic tendency of an establishment had even more important political ramifications. It meant that in order to hold office or exercise the franchise a citizen often had to subscribe or to pay allegiance to the state church. The exclusion was maintained either by the parish system of government, or through the religious test, or as in South Carolina through overwhelming financial aid to the Established Church.[84] No matter what system was used, the inevitable result was an unfair accretion of political power to the members of the Church Party.

One method of maintaining the dominance of the establishment was by setting up theocratic units of political government, which required adherence to the Established Church. For example, in England the parish church, to which only Anglicans could belong, had certain civil duties, such as providing for the relief of the poor, which gave it the right to tax the inhabitants.[85] In New England this English heritage, plus a Calvinist political philosophy, led to the erection of essentially theocratic units of local government. The most extreme example was the New Haven colony where a man had no legal existence outside the church, which was the only system of local government.[86] In the early days of Massachusetts it had been required that a man be a member of the Established Church — the Congregationalist — in order to vote and hold office, but with the Charter of 1691 these religious distinctions were removed. It was no longer necessary for a person to belong to a church in order to exercise the franchise or hold office.[87] Thus, during the eighteenth century, a measure of disestablishment had begun in New England since civil and religious functions had begun to be separated from the church and the local government.

The experience of the colonies to the South was similar. Where the Anglican Church was established, the parish had been designated as the local system of government. By and large these parishes carried out the basic functions of local government as well as affairs of the church.[88] In Virginia, the self-perpetuating vestrymen set the tax rates for the relief of the poor, appointed church wardens, presented the minister to the government, and provided glebes at the expense of the parish.[89] They also exercised the very important civil functions of setting tax rates for the support of the minister, making presentments to the court for violations of the laws against drunkenness, swearing, and fornication; and they maintained the public records of births, deaths, and marriages.[90] The civil functions of the parish in South Carolina were extensive. The parish was the political subdivision of representation in the Assembly and church wardens were the ex-officio managers of elections.[91] It was the district of the constable,[92] and it was also a highway district for the maintenance of the roads.[93] In North Carolina, in addition to the standard powers of relieving the poor and supporting the Established Church, the vestry was instructed to procure a standard of weights and measures.[94]

The distinctive and objectionable feature of this system was that in theory only members of the Established Church could belong to it and have a share in determining its politics even though actions of the parish vestry might bind all persons living within its geographical zone. The key to the presence or absence of objection to the parish lay in its operation. When persons were actually excluded from political rights, this system brought forth natural resentment. But where the franchise and the right to hold office had no religious restrictions in practice, as was the case in Georgia, there was no establishment. From the lack of protest over the system in Georgia after the Act of 1758 establishing the Anglican Church it is perhaps reasonable to agree with Strickland that "it is natural to suppose that dissenters were frequently chosen . . . thus [the settlers] were able to continue the type of local government they had had since the original settlement."[95] A similar situation seems to have existed in South Carolina in the last half of the eighteenth century. Dissenters and Jews alike seem to have voted and held office, even though the Anglican Church was officially established.[96]

Of greater exclusionary potential was the use of the test oath to bar persons with religious scruples from voting or holding office. Since the oath was regarded as essentially a religious act,[97] it could be used to disseminate religious doctrine. Persons conscientiously dissenting from these doctrines or those scrupulous of formal swearing could be effectively excluded from the legislative halls.[98]

At the threshold of the eighteenth century there began a slow but progressive movement to free dissenters from the burden of the political exclusions of the establishment. The rate of progress was not always rapid, especially in the colonies, where royal governors stubbornly resisted the more. For example, in 1701 the Quakers had to petition John Nanfan, the governor of New York, in order to be permitted to make an affirmation instead of a formal oath as they had been customarily required to do under the Act of 1691 entitled "an Act to ease people that are scrupulous in Swearing."[99] Apparently the government relented, but in 1733 the Quakers again petitioned the government for relief from a denial of the right to vote on the ground that they could not take the oath. This time the attorney general of the royal government completely disenfranchised them by interpreting the same Act as applying only to witnesses giving evidence in court or to jurymen. According to his interpretation, the election laws of the province required every elector without exception to take the oath.[100]

In South Carolina the Church party was equally as reactionary, but much less successful. In the Church Act of 1704 they had attempted a direct exclusion of all dissenters from the Assembly.[101] This attempt failed when the Act was disallowed by the Queen. The Church Act of 1706 seemingly excluded only Catholics through the use of an oath of allegiance and supremacy.[102] Dissenters and scrupulous persons continued, as they had by "ancient law and custom" of the state,[103] to swear according to their profession by holding up their hand. This right was affirmed by an act of the Assembly in 1717. However, in 1721 choleric Governor Francis Nicholson, who had recently spent unhappy days as governor of Virginia, cajoled the Assembly into repealing the Act of 1717 and demanded the hard and fast rule of swearing on the Evangelists. Pleas of the dissenters were dismissed by the Governor even though influential men, such as Charles Pinckney (father of General Charles Cotesworth Pinckney, uncle of Governor Charles Pinckney), protested the practice as "an act of exclusion . . . as much as if it were such in set terms."[104]

In North Carolina the royal government attempted to disenfranchise the dissenters with disqualifying oaths. However, the stubborn dissenters of that colony would not be readily tyrannized. Contrary to the expectations of the government they qualified and became vestrymen in the parishes. They then proceeded to disregard all ecclesiastical functions and to carry out only the civil functions of the parish.[105] In Rowan County they adopted different tactics. Here they refused even to qualify; thus they obstructed the government because there was no one to constitute the vestry.[106] The practice of refusing to go to the polls became so widespread that the Vestry Act of 1764 required that all qualified electors (except Quakers) must appear at the polls and vote for the vestrymen or pay a fine of twenty shillings.[107] Stephen Weeks records that in Presbyterian North Carolina the law "was regarded with the bitterest hostility."[108]

During the colonial period there were a few signs of progress toward a fuller religious liberty. Maryland had imposed test oaths in the middle of the seventeenth century, but by 1724 it was willing to allow Quakers the right to make an affirmation.[109] Similar privileges were granted to them in Pennsylvania in 1725; in 1743 to all other dissenters; and finally in 1772 to all other persons.[110] And occasionally the tests were disregarded by the Jews who were able to vote and hold office in several local legislative bodies. But for them true political equality was not to come until after the Revolution.[111]

Furthermore, even beyond the denial of the right to vote and hold public office, there were other disqualifications of those who were not members of the establishment, particularly Catholics. Thus in Virginia "popish recusant convicts" were denied the opportunity to serve as witnesses. A Catholic was subject to indictment and conviction when he refused to take the oaths of supremacy or abjuration, and balked at taking the sacraments with the Church of England.[112]

A State Church Which Compelled Orthodoxy Under Penalty of Fine and Imprisonment

If an established church meant that dissenters might be coerced into support of the state church through various economic and political disabilities, so it meant too that citizens might be compelled to render allegiance by positive command of law. Such a law would require all members of the community under threat of severe fines and punishment to attend services and to adhere to doctrines of the established church. The effect of such a law is to "establish" articles of faith. This policy no doubt had its origin in the English experience. Blaskstone, for example, disapproved of persecution, but he warned that "care must be taken not to carry this indulgence into such extremes as may endanger the national church: there is always a difference to be made between toleration and establishment."[113] Accordingly, he approved the English laws which fined persons for not attending the Church of England and the laws against "popish recusants" who were a danger to the safety of the state.[114] In a somewhat different light were the Sabbath laws which made Sunday a day of rest for all. Blackstone found in these no relationship to an establishment. He declared that the period of quiet would humanize "by the help of conversation and society, the manners of the lower classes."[115]

That a system of morality should be enshrined in the statute books was typical of the thinking of the colonists. Most probably these people believed that they elevated the holiness of their religion by placing harsh "earthly" penalties on moral transgressors. The New Haven theocracy compelled attendance at divine worship under pain of a five-shilling fine for absence.[116] South Carolina passed a Sabbath

Law and a Law Against Blasphemy which provided for imprisonment of transgressors.[117] In the Blasphemy Act of 1723 Maryland
provided that offenders would be bored through the tongue and fined
twenty pounds or imprisoned for six months. For a second offense
the offender was to be branded in the forehead with the letter B
and fined forty pounds or be imprisoned twelve months, and for a
third offense he was to suffer death without benefit of clergy.[118] In
Virginia by an act of 1705 any person brought up in the Christian
religion who doubted the being of God, the Trinity, and similar
dogmas, could be punished on the first offense by incapacity to hold
office, on the second by inability to sue, to receive legacies and
devices, etc., or by three years of imprisonment.[119]

It must be noted, however, that the mere existence of these statutes
is no sure indication that the penalties were meted out with literal
severity. Although there were instances of enforcement, which seem
astonishing to the contemporary world, it is not unreasonable to assume that there were violators of the law who were never prosecuted.
Virginia, for example, had many severe ecclesiastical laws. Persons
failing to attend services at, or to have their children baptized in,
the Established Church were subject to penalties of fines and
whipping.[120] Cobb reports one instance of the enforcement of the
law in 1722 when a group of Quakers, who resisted the baptism
requirement, were flogged.[121] On the other hand, from 1650 until the
time of the American Revolution members of the Roman Catholic
Brent family not only practiced their religion openly but also held
prominent public offices.[122]

In the late colonial period these strictures began to ease, probably
because people began to realize that the laws had not improved the
general morality. When an attempt was made to introduce a blasphemy law in New Jersey to place restraints on deists, the assembly
rejected the bill on the second reading.[123] In 1770 Connecticut
removed penalties from dissenters who refused to attend the Established Church. But the struggle for liberty was not complete because
the indulgence was conditioned on the requirement that they meet
"together by themselves on said day for the public worship of God
in a way agreeable to their conscience."[124]

The undesirability of the stringent colonial practices was recognized by some of the founders of the new nation who were later
to have an important role in the drafting of the Constitution. Thus,
in 1773 on the eve of Revolution, Charles Carroll of Carrollton
wrote: "I am as averse to having religion crammed down my throat
as to a proclamation."[125]

A State Church Willing to Force Dissenters From the Commonwealth

Because religious and political homogeneity were thought necessary and desirable to the continuity of the state, the state church of an establishment found it necessary to impose religious orthodoxy on dissenters not only by excluding them from the franchise and holding public office or by placing heavy fines and harsh punishments, but also by banishing religious and political dissenters from the community. Article Ninety-Five of John Locke's *Fundamental Constitutions* epitomized the belief of the early colonial period with its provision that "no man shall be permitted to be a freeman . . . or to have any estate or habitation, that doth not acknowledge a God; and that God is publicly and solemnly to be worshipped."[126]

A number of the English colonies had adopted similar views and practices. Virginia by statute declared the Quakers an "unreasonable" and "turbulent" sect that should be driven out of the colony. Pressures were also applied to force certain ministers out of New England.[127] Massachusetts proved intolerant by banishing the Quakers.[128] It was in this same colony that the most famous example of this practice occurred when Roger Williams, the founder of Rhode Island, was expelled, as was Anne Hutchinson.[129] Ironically, even Rhode Island, the fountainhead of religious liberty in New England, found it expedient to banish on religious grounds Samuel Gorton, a refugee from Massachusetts.[130] According to the statute books, it also excluded Jews until 1762 and Roman Catholics until 1783.[131] Connecticut, distinguished for the liberality of her franchise law, passed an exclusionary law against Quakers in 1656 that remained in force until repealed by Queen Anne in 1705. Subsequently, by the Act of 1742 the Assembly decreed that "foreign" and "strange" preachers could be deported.[133]

In certain cases there need not have been an actual threat to the purity of religious doctrine to justify the exclusions. "Popery" always suggested stern countermeasures. For example, as tension rose along the French Canadian border, Virginia passed a law excluding "popish priests."[134] Maryland, along with her neighbor to the South, passed laws forbidding Catholics to have arms — a circumstance likely to discourage life on the frontier.[135] In order to keep out Catholics, Maryland placed a tax of twenty pounds on Irish immigrants who came to the colony to act as servants. Before there was any ground for fearing French power in New England, Massachusetts had in 1647 and 1700 declared that Jesuits would be expelled from the colony.[136] In 1743, when the first rumbles of the conflict that presaged the French and Indian War began, that colony turned against the Moravians, who, because of their use of a foreign language and foreign dress, were accused of being in consort with the Jesuits. Acting on such irrational fear, the colony drove them out.[137]

The Southern colonies were no more reasonable in this respect. In 1774, in reaction to the Quebec Act, the anti-Catholic custom of Pope Day was revived in Charleston, South Carolina.[138] In 1775 a quarrel among two Catholics and a Huguenot was magnified into a "miniature Guy Fawkes plot."[139] Through the machinations of a secret committee composed of leading citizens such as William Henry Drayton, Arthur Middleton, and C. C. Pinckney, a tactic "without precedent in South Carolina" was ordered when the committee voted to tar and feather the Catholics and to have them deported.[140] Georgia, a haven for a multiplicity of Protestant sects including Quakers, hired a special immigration agent to make sure that no Catholics would board the Georgia-bound ships in Europe.[141] So successful was this policy that the largest number of Catholics reported in Georgia up to the time of the Revolution was four.[142] However, actual experience was always a mitigator, as the case of the Virginia Brents indicates. At first Georgia also forbade Jews to enter the colony, but they arrived at Savannah in the middle of an epidemic which their doctor quelled and, as a result of this help, the governor allowed them to remain. In the hope that they would leave, the trustees refused to grant them land or the privilege of becoming freeholders.[143] They made themselves indispensable, however, and remained in the colony until the threat of war with Spain made them flee before the specter of the Inquisition.[144]

As had been the experience in New England, so also in Georgia the imminence of war brought with it interference with the rights of conscience. The victims were again the Moravians. When they refused to bear arms in keeping with the pacifist nature of their religion, the other settlers were outraged and threatened to kill them and burn their houses if they refused to give aid. The trustees of the colony attempted to placate the settlers by requesting that the Moravians hire substitutes to serve in place of their freeholders. At the same time, the trustees refused to allow them to maintain missionaries among the Indians because, it was said, that this would harmfully reflect upon the English Church, making it appear as though it had no good men to send to the Indians.[145] Frustrated in their mission work and faced with a financial burden for hiring substitutes, the Moravians joined their brethren in Pennsylvania.

It should be noted that the burden placed on the Moravians, Quakers, and other conscientious objectors was not necessarily the product of establishment of religion. In the frontier areas of the colonies it was generally considered that every freeholder had a primary duty to take up arms in defense of the community. Representative of this view is the statement on the departure of the Moravians attributed to Lord Egmont, a trustee of the Georgia Colony: "It were to be wished they had never gone, for though they be a very religious and painstaking people, yet that principle of not fighting is a very bad one in a new erected colony."[146] Many of the colonies, however, were willing to grant an exemption to the conscientious objector. Because the exemption was deemed a mere "privilege" and not a right, it was often burdened with requirements that the objector render nonmilitary service or pay a sum of money to hire a substitute.[147]

Although the burden of money payments or even the failure to obtain an exemption might not be considered the result of an establishment, it seems that a discriminatory system of exemption was. For example, North Carolina for many years granted no general exemption from military duty except to ministers of the Anglican Church, the Established Church of that colony. Presbyterian ministers were eventually added to the list, but Baptist and Quaker ministers were ignored. Stephen Weeks concludes that the injustice lay not in the failure to exempt Quakers generally from military service but "in the fact that their preachers were not exempted from this duty as clergymen of the establishment were."[148]

A State Church Financed and Endowed by Taxes Upon All the Members of the Community

State encouragement to education and religion were a prominent feature of the colonial period. Sometimes this encouragement was made by direct appropriations from the government. In most colonies, lands, known as glebes, were granted to support the church. Sometimes it was done by paying the salary of the ministers, a service often performed by the Society for the Propagation of the Gospel. Tax exemptions were frequently given to the churches and to the ministers. Fees and taxes might be earmarked for the support of religion, as in South Carolina and Georgia where a tax on liquor and drinking houses was directed to be used for religious purposes.[149] The right to hold a public lottery, an especial privilege tantamount to direct grant, was occasionally given. More often encouragement and support were given to religion by conferring the taxing power on a local governmental unit. This was true where the parish system was used, or in the New York corporate church, or in the New England town. The power to tax frequently included the power to sue and to distrain property in order to collect the tax.[150]

But this encouragement and support of religion did not itself mean that the state or colony had "established" a religion. The important distinction between encouragement and establishment lay in the presence or absence of the facts of exclusion and preference which gave the government a coercive power over its citizens. Typical of the concept of financial establishment is Locke's *Fundamental Constitution*. Although it was never entirely put into effect in the Carolinas, it was representative of the thinking of the time and had great persuasive force in formulating policies of the royal governors. Section Ninety-Six deals with the encouragement of religion in the following manner:

> As the country comes to be sufficiently planted and distributed into fit divisions, it shall belong to the parliament to take care for the building of churches, and the public maintenance of divines, to be employed in the exercise of religion, according to the Church of England; which being *the only true and orthodox, and national religion of all* the King's dominions, is so also of Carolina; and, therefore, *it alone shall be allowed to receive public maintenance by grant of parliament*.[151]

This attitude stubbornly persisted in supporters of an establishment until the time of the Revolution. In 1765 Governor Tryon of North Carolina declared:

> If I have pointed any consequences that are likely to attend the continuance of the neglect of our religion, I hope no persons of a different persuasion will imagine that I am an enemy to toleration. I profess myself a warm advocate for it in the fullest sense of his majesty's indulgence, yet I must inform them that I never heard of toleration in any country made use of as an argument to exempt Dissenters from bearing their share of the support of the established religion.[152]

That dissenters from the Established Church should resent such exclusions and preferences was a frequent phenomenon in the eighteenth-century colonial society which was developing a system of democratic government. The argument of the excluded churchmen was fundamentally one of distributive justice. Taxation without representation deprived the colonists of "their rights as Englishmen" and "in time . . . deprived them of liberty and property altogether," wrote Pastor John J. Zubly, Presbyterian minister of Savannah, in 1769.[153] In 1775 the Reverend Isaac Backus had unsuccessfully petitioned the Massachusetts Assembly to relieve the Baptists of paying taxes for

the Congregationalists. He declared: "Is not all America now ap-
pealing to heaven against the injustice of being taxed where we are
not represented, and against being judged by men who are interested
in getting away with our money? And will heaven approve of your
doing the same thing to your fellow servants?"[154] Southern dissenters
were in agreement. The Reverend William Tennant of South Carolina
summarized their objections in 1777:

> But that which shows much of the injustice and oppression of the
> present establishment, is the tax which it makes all other denomina-
> tions pay to the support of the religion of one. It puts its hand into
> the pocket of nine denominations, all equally pretending to the merit
> of good subjects and citizens, to bestow upon one and support its
> dignity.
>
> Sir! is this consistent with our first notions of justice and equality?
> . . . [The] treasury is the equal property of all denominations in the
> State, and it comes out of the treasury, it comes in effect out of their
> pockets.[155]

The injustice was greater when members of the establishment
constituted only a minority of the inhabitants. This was the opinion
expressed by the settlers of Prince Frederick Parish in the Pee Dee
region of South Carolina when they unsuccessfully petitioned the
Assembly to be allowed to set up their own parish and pay taxes
only to support their own church.[156] That the amount of the tax
was small in many cases made no difference to the dissenting
colonists who viewed the unrepresentative tax as the symbol of the
invasion of their liberty of conscience.[157] The citizens of Rowan
County in North Carolina said that "it was their opinion every one
ought to pay their own clergy, and what the law required was
restraint."[158]

Preferential support of religion had serious practical effects beyond
its intrusion into the rights of conscience. The Established Church
became in effect an endowed church. Its ministers were granted the
security of a superior income and its churches were kept in repair.
Distrusting the aristocratic pretensions of the Church of England in
Boston, the colonists had dubbed Apthorp House the "Bishop's
Palace" — the most leveling epithet in the colonies if one is to judge
by similar names given to the governor's "Palace" in Williamsburg
and Tryon "Palace" in North Carolina. Of greater concern to the
dissenters was the effect on the laity. The overwhelming advantages
of membership in the Established Church could not but influence the
minds of the younger members and coerce them to join the dominant
church. All dissenting churches suffered politically under an estab-

lishment. Dr. Leah Townsend observes: "As an inevitable result of establishment, which gave provincial support to the Anglican churches and placed them and their members in a favored position, the Anglicans secured a monopoly of public offices."[159]

The fight against an establishment, i.e., "disestablishment," was, therefore, a struggle to end the exclusions and preferences in favor of the state church and to institute the principle of religious voluntarism. The people of Mecklenberg County, North Carolina, expressed the principle well when they instructed their delegates to the Halifax Convention of 1776: "That in all times hereafter no professing Christian of any denomination whatever shall be compelled to pay any tax or duty towards the support of the clergy or worship of any other denomination."[160] The actions taken in the various colonies during the colonial period demonstrate that a measure of this variety "disestablishment" occurred when preferential support was abolished.[161] For example, Congregationalism had traditionally been the established religion in New England. All citizens of the early Massachusetts towns had been required to pay taxes for the support of an "orthodox" minister who would always be a Congregationalist.[162] But the Charter of 1691 removed the legal protection of the Congregational Church by theoretically tolerating all Christian denominations other than Roman Catholic.[163] The Quakers first won the right to be free of taxes for the support of their own church.[164] Then, in 1727, in an unusual position for them, the Episcopalians took up the banner of the "dissenter" from the "Established Church." As a result of their campaign they were allowed to pay their taxes to the support of their own church. The Baptists were accorded equality in 1729.[165]

Connecticut moved forward with Massachusetts in allowing the dissenters to pay taxes only to their own church. In the first quarter of the eighteenth century as the Connecticut Congregationalists came under the influence of the views of Ezra Stiles, they espoused religious voluntarism,[166] but they were slow to grant equal liberty to the Anglicans whom the colonists believed were attempting to curry favor with the English government. Not until 1727 were the Anglicans placed on a seemingly equal basis with the Congregationalists. But they were forced to file a certificate of religious intention with the town clerk.[167] As it had occurred in Massachusetts, similar privileges were accorded shortly thereafter to the Baptists and Quakers.[168] The next step toward disestablishment in Connecticut was taken in 1770 when all dissenting ministers received the benefit of the general exemption from taxation that had been accorded to ministers of the Established Church.[169] In New Hampshire the major breakthrough of early days had been the recognition that a town could hire a dissenting minister.[170] This colony also instituted the liberal policy of granting land to the "first settled church" in new areas. This grant was made without prejudice, although the dominance of the Congregationalist faith had meant in Connecticut, as it had in the rest of New England, that most of the churches would be in fact Congregationalist.[171]

It is to New York and Georgia, however, that we must look for the policy of nonestablishment encouragement in its fullest development. Since 1693 New York had adhered to a system of multiple establishment, which can best be described as "quasi-establishment." Upon incorporation, each church was granted land by the state and for its support it was allowed to tax the property of its members. This system theoretically allowed all denominations, except Roman Catholics, to share equally in the benefits of legal encouragement.[172] Georgia had developed a similar system. There the policy of the trustees and the royal government alike had been one of equality of all denominations. Land for glebes had been granted freely to churches of all sects without discrimination.[173] Dissenters merely had to apply to the governor and Council.[174] And even after 1758, when the colony had been divided into parishes for the purposes of civil government, dissenters had not been excluded from voting or from becoming members of the vestry.[175] There were even indications that the Presbyterians might be allowed to have their own church separate from the Anglicans in St. George's Parish.[176] Strickland concludes that under the circumstances the Church of England "can hardly be said to have been established."[177] When practices in New York and Georgia contrasted with those in other colonies, such as South Carolina, the relationship between preference and establishment and equality and nonestablishment becomes clearer. There the royal government was willing to grant land to only the Anglican Church. What few parcels of land that were given to dissenters went mainly to the Huguenots, and then they were hedged with restraints designed to give the royal government a strong coercive influence in the settlers' religious affairs.

A State Church Which Alone Could Hold Public Worship and Evangelize

Another general characteristic of establishment in colonial America was that only the Established Church could freely and legally hold public services and seek converts. Sometimes this policy was effected by an outright ban on the activities of dissenters, or by requiring that all religious adhere to an orthodox liturgy and canons of faith, or by the imposition of licensing requirements which gave the civil power ecclesiastical jurisdiction.[178] The effect in each case was to place restrictions on the religious exercises and activities of the dissenting sects.

Virginia provides many examples of the intolerance of an Established Church. Although the Toleration Act of 1689 was supposedly in force in the colonies, Presbyterians, who had been granted religious liberty through their adherence to the Westminster Confession, were persecuted and jailed for worshiping in public. Not until 1753 when they secured an opinion from the attorney general in England, that the Act applied to the colonies, were they allowed freedom of worship.[179] The spirit of general intolerance of dissent was hardly to be removed by this event, for Eckenrode reported that Baptists, unprotected by a parliamentary law, were being imprisoned as late as 1775 in Virginia for daring to preach in public.[180]

To the north, Maryland was not outdone by her neighbor. In 1649 public exercise of worship for Protestants was placed on a sufferance basis, while public celebration of the Mass was absolutely forbidden.[181] In 1700 the Book of Common Prayer was made standard in the Established Church.[182] Thus, with this standard to impose upon the ministry, Governor Sharp was able to maintain his political power through a skillful and adroit use of his investiture powers.[183] However, after 1702 it was generally true that all dissenters except Quakers and Roman Catholics had freedom of worship. The Quakers finally obtained complete freedom in 1724. During this same period, Catholics were increasingly persecuted. For example, in 1704 "An Act to Prevent the Growth of Popery" imposed a fine of fifty pounds or six months' imprisonment upon any "popish bishop or priest" who exercised his functions in public. A second offense brought transportation to England for punishment. The only worship service permitted was within the limits of a "private family of Romish communion."[184]

The problem of evangelizing was also being dealt with in other colonies at this time. In Georgia the Moravians had been denied the right to place missionaries among the Indians.[185] They met the same fate in Connecticut and in New York. The policy in these two states seems to have been based on the belief that the Moravians were a subversive element. In Connecticut they were accused of having Jesuits among them.[186] In New York they were forbidden to preach to the Indians and were required to register their churches.[187]

In the Southern colonies, interference with the dissenters' free exercise of religion followed as a matter of course from the establishment of the Church of England in the early days of the colonies. When South Carolina passed the Church Act of 1704, a major requirement to vote or hold office was attendance at the Church of England at stated times in the year and reception of the sacrament of communion according to her rites.[188] In other actions, the Assembly gave grants to the Huguenots which were contingent on the use of the Book of Common Prayer in translation.[189] Even the grants to Presbyterians were made on the conditions that the minister occupying the land profess, teach, and use the doctrine of the Church of Scotland and subscribe to the Westminster Confession.[190] Thus, in effect, a doctrine had been permanently established by the Legislature, for the members of the church were not free to change the articles and could be ejected from their holdings should they desire to change their theological views.

Under an establishment which had the special protection of the government, freedom of worship was not always infringed by direct force. Indirect obstruction flowed from the official agencies of the Established Church. This was often the case of the Anglican missionary group, the Society for Propagating the Gospel in Foreign Parts. Under the terms of its charter it was supposed to aid ministers and Christianity in those parts of the colonies where no church or ministers were found, but it frequently proselyted in settled areas and directly interfered with the activities of the dissenters. In 1715 Cotton Mather observed:

> In the more southern colonies their missionaries . . . unaccountably neglect the paganizing plantations, but chose to screw themselves in where a Presbyterian church is gathered; and if a Presbyterian makes a sally to do good in any of the aforesaid plantations, they will presently follow him, to persuade the people that all his ministrations are but nullities.[191]

So objectionable were its interferences throughout the colonies that George Howe records "it soon came to be regarded . . . as a society for propagating the *Episcopacy* in foreign parts."[192]

With this history of the commingling of the ecclesiastical and civil jurisdictions, it is not remarkable that the leaders in the fight against the tyranny of the English government demanded an end to the establishment of articles of faith and the interference with the free exercise of their religion by an Established Church with civil authority. The Mecklenberg Convention in North Carolina spoke from a long heritage of oppression when it instructed its delegates in September, 1775, to oppose "any particular church or set of clergymen being invested with power to decree rites and ceremonies and to decide in controversies of faith to be submitted to under the influence of penal laws."[193] They were also to oppose the "establishment of any mode of worship to be supported to the opposition of the rights of conscience."[194] And they declared fervently "that all professing Christians shall enjoy the free and undisturbed exercise of religion, and may worship God according to their consciences without restraint except idolatrous worshippers."[195]

A State Church Which Alone Could Perform Valid Marriages, Burials, Etc.

The connection of the state with the church, and the official sanction that the Established Church derived therefrom, brought with it many privileges for the favored church and many corresponding disabilities of dissenters. Ministers of the establishment frequently had the sole prerogative of solemnizing legal marriages. In Virginia, for example, the law declared children illegitimate unless the parents had been married by a Church of England minister.[196]

In the other colonies the attempt to obtain conformity was made by placing burdens on dissent. New York fined Quakers for marrying according to their own rite.[197] In Georgia the government policy was more liberal. Lutheran and other dissenting clergy were allowed to marry their church members provided that they obtained licenses from a magistrate.[198] They could also marry persons outside their sect if no Anglican minister was available.[199] The most dismal record in the colonies is found in North Carolina. In the early days of the colony all sects, including the Quakers, were allowed to marry either before their own minister or before a magistrate.[200] In 1741, however, the right to perform marriages was restricted to the clergy of the Church of England,[201] until 1766 when Presbyterian ministers were allowed the right to marry the members of their church.[202] Full recognition of dissenters continued to be denied until 1778 when all ministers were granted the power to perform legal marriages.[203]

Under a colonial establishment other privileges were accorded to the favored church. Fees for performing public duties, such as the registration of births and deaths, were assigned exclusively to the clergy of the establishment.[204] In North Carolina the Anglican clergyman could demand and receive fees for marrying and burying even though the service might have been performed by dissenting ministers.[205] Although Georgia was generally a liberal colony where religious freedom was involved, her history does provide one outstanding example of the intolerance of the established clergy. In 1769, an Anglican clergyman, Samuel Frink, sued a dissenter,

Joseph Gibbons, for three shillings, six pence for tolling the bell of the public meeting house while a funeral was being held at a dissenter church. He also instituted an action to recover his fee from a ship's captain who had buried his Presbyterian mate according to that faith.[206]

Outright disabilities on dissenters were also imposed as a part of an establishment. In Georgia, Jews were at first forbidden to hold land as freeholders and Catholics could not inherit land.[207] When a bill was introduced into the Commons House of the Assembly to set aside part of the Savannah Common as a burying ground for dissenters, the Anglicans successfully opposed it as an attack on the *"Privileges* of the Establishment."[208] A similar fate met a bill for granting a burying ground for the Jews.[209] The result was that dissenters had no suitable place for a graveyard and the Jews were forced to bury their dead on their own property.[210]

The most exasperating disability in many colonies was the denial of incorporation to dissident churches. Dissenters desired corporate status so that church property and funds might be vested in a continuing legal entity. The alternative to incorporation — placing title to the property in a trustee — was most unsatisfactory. Under the latter system, the congregation could only take indirect action in regard to their property by requesting a court of equity to compel their trustee to act, a task which was not always easy. The congregations were also exposed to the dangers of losing their property through indiscretion of the trustees.[211] In addition, when a trustee died, there was the danger of losing the property to the claims of his heirs, and the expense and inconvenience of setting up a new trust.[212]

Some colonies allowed corporate status. Pennsylvania and Delaware both had granted incorporation to Protestant churches in the first half of the eighteenth century,[213] but South Carolina, Virginia, and Maryland repeatedly denied incorporation to dissenting churches despite the well-known difficulties of the trustee system in those colonies.[214] New York theoretically granted corporate status to all Protestant churches on an equal basis, but control of the government by Anglicans had meant discrimination against Protestants other than those of the Church of England.

The importance of the denials of these rights and privileges should not be overlooked in an assessment of an establishment. For example, Carl Bridenbaugh declares that in New York "no local issue gave rise to more sectarian bitterness than the decision of the Governor's Council, acting under the relentless prodding of the Episcopal clergy, to deny incorporation to the Presbyterian Church."[215]

Allowing the Anglican clergyman, Samuel Frink, to sue for burial fees impinged on religious liberty, declared Presbyterian Pastor Zubly of Savannah, Georgia: "Free exercise of religion" meant that dissenters "should not be taxed for it."[216] Giving the exclusive privilege of performing marriages to one set of clergy was equally objectionable. The effect of such practices in the minds of the colonists was to make religious dissent burdensome and humiliating; it placed a premium on ecclesiastical conformity. In short, it was religious persecution.[217]

Thus, by the time of the American Revolution, an important term was to be included in the vocabulary of patriots: "establishment of religion." This was a shorthand expression which conveniently summed up the denials of full religious liberty that had resulted from a political and religious alliance. But the expression had no constant or absolute meaning, for religious conditions varied from colony to colony. It might mean that religious liberty was being curtailed; on the other hand, a member of a New England Church might believe that an establishment had made his religious liberty more meaningful by giving the church the protection of the law. Moreover, while the views of the royal government or the political necessity of an establishment had undergone little change, establishments in fact were frequently modified so as to allow the greater exercise of religious liberty on the part of colonial citizens. This expansion of religious freedom was summed up in the corresponding shorthand expression "disestablishment." Like the principal term, its cognate had various meanings depending on the context in which it was being used. As the statements of American patriots were to indicate, the context of the terms would be all-important.

The Struggle in the States for Equal Religious Liberty and Freedom From Established Churches — the Period From Independence Until Ratification of the Bill of Rights

The American Revolution initiated a period of liberty. With the dissolution of political bonds with Great Britain, there was little to hinder implementation of the ideas of freedom that the colonists had come to hold dear. The new era also meant that religious liberty could be better *secured* by "disestablishing" those churches which had restricted religious freedom through an alliance with the state. Although disestablishment was a parallel movement to the American Revolution,[1] it was not necessarily a radical movement.[2] The significance of the relationship of the "disestablishment" movement to the American Revolution was that the relaxation of the tension of British rule allowed the patriots not only to preserve the existing rights of the colonists but also to accelerate the implementation of the principles of religious liberty.

It is important to observe that the patriot's ideas of religious freedom or "disestablishment" had begun their development long before the Revolution. Modifications of colonial establishments had frequently been made in accordance with them. "Disestablishment" tended to be a selective and pragmatic process which sought to remove those privileges of the Established Church which had been unduly restrictive of religious and political liberty. The very fact of change itself would seem to negate the idea that there was a great vested interest to destroy[3] or that a revolutionary approach was dictated by the situation. Thus the process of "disestablishment" became largely a question of political power. When the patriots took control of the sovereign power of the state, the establishment began to fade.

Thus the term "disestablishment" generally meant the securing of religious liberty. An examination of the history of the times indicates that the Founding Fathers sought to attain this end by securing the following objectives:

1. An equal opportunity to hold public office and exercise political rights, regardless of religious beliefs;

2. An end to taxes for the support of a particular religious faith to which the taxpayer did not subscribe;

3. Termination of laws requiring dissenters to attend services of the dominant faith;

4. Equal economic opportunities for dissenters and an end to advantages and preferences possessed by the members of the dominant faith;

5. An end not only to "exclusive establishments," such as Anglican or Congregationalist, but also to "multiple establishments," such as Protestantism; and

6. Toleration and equal opportunity to practice a faith, so long as it did not jeopardize the equal rights of others or imperil the common good.

The first of these — the contest for an equal opportunity to hold public office and exercise political rights, regardless of religious belief — is detailed in Chapter Four, in connection with the ban upon religious test oaths in the United States Constitution.

The Struggle to Be Free From Taxes for the Support of a Particular Religion to Which the Taxpayer Did Not Subscribe

The support of religion with tax funds had been a prominent feature of the colonial establishment. Sometimes this had been the accidental result of the imposition of civil duties on the local church unit. For example, in Virginia the parish collected taxes from all persons within the geographic unit. Part of the money collected was used to carry the civil duties of the parish, such as poor relief and the keeping of public records; the remainder was used for support of the church. Throughout the colonial era dissenters had continually protested this inequity. In New England a different system was employed. There the tax system was utilized as a means for channeling the individual property owner's taxes to his own church. In the early days of the New England colonies all persons had been required to pay a tax to the Congregationalist Church. However, as the number of sects increased, dissenters had been allowed to pay the tax to their own church. In effect, the system had become a tax rebate for members of the favored churches. Since all dissenters had not been granted the privilege, there was some discontent among them over the partiality of the system.

When independence was declared, a relaxation of political restrictions on all liberties soon followed. Accordingly, the numerous dissenting sects seized the opportunity to oppose the unfairness of the contemporary tax systems. Perhaps the most colorful protests were found in Virginia. There the parish system had been tightly linked to the repressive aims of the Established Church and the royal government. Bitterness of Virginia dissenters was increased by the fact that the government had never yielded the slightest to their pleas.

The first move toward abolition of the unfair system came very shortly after the signing of the Declaration of Independence. On October 24, 1776, a "Memorial of the Presbytery of Hanover, Virginia," voiced the objections of the Presbyterians to paying taxes for the support of the Episcopal Church. "There is no argument in favor of establishing the Christian religion but what may be pleaded with equal propriety for establishing the tenets of Mahomet."[4] The memorial recognized the fact that multiplicity of sects made it undesirable to use the tax system to support any religious worship. It requested that dissenters be "exempted from all taxes for the support of any church whatsoever, farther than what may be agreeable to their own private choice or voluntary obligation." "It is well known," explained the Presbyterians, "that in the frontier countries . . . the dissenters have borne the heavy burthens of purchasing glebes and supporting the Established clergy, where there are very few Episcopalians either to assist in bearing the expense or to reap the advantage. . . ." Such large taxes to support establishment, they argued, were "violations of their natural rights."[5]

Apparently memorials such as this were effective in educating the Legislature, for on November 19, 1776, the Committee of the Whole of the House of Delegates of the first independent General Assembly of Virginia

> Resolved, That so much of the petitions of the several dissenters from the church established by law within this Commonwealth, as desired an exemption from all taxes and contributions whatever towards supporting the said church and the ministers thereof, or towards the support of their respective religious societies in any other way than themselves shall voluntarily agree is reasonable.[6]

On the thirtieth of that month, Thomas Jefferson drafted a bill which provided that no one could of right be forced to support a church to which he did not belong, and which exempted dissenters from forced contributions to the support of the Anglican Church.[7]

Acknowledging within that same year the just claims of the non-Anglicans, the Virginia Legislature exempted dissenters from having to support the *Church Established* after January 1, 1777. The statute provided that "all dissenters of whatever denomination, from the said church [Episcopal] shall . . . be totally free and exempt from all levies, taxes and impositions whatever, towards supporting and maintaining the said church, as it is now or hereafter may be established."[8] It can be seen that when the Virginians used the word "established" they had reference to the *one* church — the Episcopalian. This continued to be the view of the Virginians throughout the infant period. Expanding the scope of the above statute, the Virginia General Assembly on December 11, 1779, enacted: "That so much of the act entitled — 'An Act for the Support of the Clergy, and for the regular collecting and paying the Parish Levies,' and of all and every other Act or Acts providing salaries for the Ministers, and authorizing the vestries to levy the same, shall be, and the same is hereby repealed."[9]

Thomas Jefferson objected to the impositions of taxes for the support of ministers. Jefferson's *Act Establishing Religious Freedom,* drafted in 1777 but not enacted until 1785, provided: "That to compel a man to furnish contributions of money for the propagation of opinions which he disbelieves, is sinful and tyrannical." It continued "that even the forcing him to support this or that teacher of his own religious persuasion, is depriving him of the comfortable liberty of giving his contributions to the particular pastor, whose morals he would make his pattern, and whose powers he feels most persuasive to righteousness. . . ."[10] (It should be noted that the "teacher" referred to is the "pastor" or minister of a church.)

In 1783 the citizens of Jefferson's Albemarle County repeated these admonitions to their representatives in General Assembly in the following instructions for the contemplated state constitution:

[W]e could not be said to enjoy an equal share of freedom in religious matters, if the people of one persuasion were obliged, besides maintaining their own Ministers, to contribute to the maintenance of the Ministers of another, the members of another, the members of which were only to contribute to maintain their own; that unless every body was obliged to be of that Church (which would immediately destroy the liberty of Religion) such laws would signify, that those who by the dictates of conscience are called to another persuasion, ought to have no Ministers, or if they would have them, they ought not to maintain them, which way of reasoning could not be heard with any degree of patience.

You might even ask, what would be the consequence, if the Presbyterians, who are supposed to form already more than one-third of our Community, or the Annabaptists, or the people of any other denomination were to become more numerous than any other in the State, were to have a majority in the Legislative body, and should think of obliging those of the Episcopal Church to contribute to the maintenance of their own Ministers.

Such a question must make every one withdraw from the thought of promoting so bad, and so dangerous a president, a president diametrically opposite to Liberty; to that liberty, which we are bound to one another to maintain unstained, to that dear liberty, for which we now submit ourselves and families to so many heavy inconveniences; to that sacred liberty, to whose Altar we are now making a sacrifice of our lives and fortunes.[11]

That same year Jefferson's draft of a constitution for his native state sought to protect religious liberty with the provision that: "The general assembly shall not have power . . . to abridge the civil rights of any person on account of his religious beliefs . . . or to compel him to contributions. . . ."[12]

By 1784, therefore, considerable progress had been made in Virginia in the fight to be free from taxes for the support of a religion to which the taxpayer did not subscribe. It should be noted, however, that the parishes continued to perform some public services. The vestries in that state — required by law to be composed of Episcopalians — were still levying taxes for poor relief upon the members of all faiths.[13]

Protests of the dissenters continued even though the Established Church had been effectively abolished. Their attacks on privileged positions revealed a change in approach. Rather than a defense of liberty, they often were tinged with strong sectarian rivalry. In 1786, objections were lodged with the Virginia Legislature to the policy which allowed the former Established Church to retain the glebe lands purchased with funds from taxes that had been levied upon the entire community. On August 5 of that year the General Committee of the Baptists of Virginia resolved to submit a petition to the General Assembly urging that the public property which had been vested by law in the Protestant Episcopal Church be sold and the money applied to public use.[14]

In South Carolina also protests were raised over the payment of taxes to the Established Church. The matter had not been raised when the temporary Constitution of 1776 had been written, because of lack of time. In an effort to establish a working plan of government the writers of the document had inserted a clause continuing in force all laws and resolutions of the colony until repealed by the

Legislature.[15] However, after the initial period of organization had been completed, the leaders of the state began to compose a stronger fundamental charter to serve the needs of the state.

During the legislative session of 1777 disestablishment was first proposed. Although there was little true opposition to the measure, some persons urged that the matter be delayed until the assembly had more time to consider it. At this point the Assembly allowed the Reverend William Tennant, a Presbyterian minister, to speak in behalf of disestablishment. Almost singlehandedly, the Reverend Tennant carried the Assembly in favor of disestablishment. His stirring speech undoubtedly silenced the lingering doubts of the delegates. The thrust of his argument was that a religious establishment operates to restrict liberty.

> My first, and most capital reason, against all establishments is, that *they are an infringement of Religious Liberty.*
>
> Religious establishments, *as far as they operate,* do interfere with the rights of private judgment and conscience: in effect, they amount to nothing less, than the legislature's taking the conscience of men into their own hands, and taxing them at discretion. . . .
>
> Its chief characteristics are, that it makes a legal distinction between people of different denominations; equally offensive, it taxes all denominations for the support of the religion of one; it only tolerates those that dissent from it, while it deprives them of sundry privileges which the people of the establishment enjoy. . . .

One of Tennant's major concerns was the undemocratic method of levying taxes.

> The law vests the officers of the Church of England with power to tax not only her own people, but all other denominations within the bounds of each respective parish, for the support of the poor: an enormous power! which ought to be vested in no one denomination, more than another. Greater distinction still! where there are parishes the law throws the whole management of all the rights of freemen, into the hands of Church officers exclusively.
>
> And why all this inequality? Why does the law thus favour one, and bear hard upon every other denomination of Christians? The reason is only to be found in the spirit of the times when this unequal establishment was framed, and in the Machiavelian policy of the British government: which ought not any longer to take place in this country.
>
> But that which shows much of the injustices of the present establishment, is the tax which it makes all other denominations pay to the support of religion of one. It puts its hands into the pocket of nine

denominations, all equally pretending to the merit of good subjects and citizens, to bestow upon one and support its dignity.

Sir! is this consistent with our first notions of justice and equality? And here, it matters not whether the religious tax is equally levied upon the people at large, or whether it is paid by a general duty. That treasury is the equal property of all denominations in the State, and [if] it comes out of the Treasury, it comes in effect out of their pockets.[16]

As a result of Reverend Tennant's powerful arguments the new Constitution of 1778 made no provision for payment of ministers from parish funds, thereby placing the support of religion on an equal and voluntary basis. The undemocratic restriction on parish office-holding was removed by declaring eligible "every white man, and no other person, who acknowledges the being of a God, and believes in a state of future rewards and punishments."[17] The parish henceforth would be a civil unit of government having no religious functions. Since the purpose of the separation of functions had been to further religious liberty, the Constitution also extended the privilege of corporate status to all Protestant religious societies, a benefit which had previously been the exclusive right of the Anglican parish with its mixed duties.[18]

The danger of a *de facto* establishment was seen by some in the various attempts to provide aid to the churches. In Maryland, when it appeared to many in 1783 that some Protestant Episcopal ministers were readying a bill to have the state finance religion, the adherents of other faiths generally feared this was a covert attempt to reconstruct the old Established Church, the Anglican or Episcopal. Reverend Patrick Allison — the first pastor of the First Presbyterian Church of Baltimore — feared that if the bill passed, the Episcopal Church "will in effect become the church of Maryland." It was "giving preference to one denomination" that Allison objected to, as he asserted: "All possible descriptions of Christians are equally entitled to the countenance and favour of government." The legislators, according to Allison, could not have "conferred on [their church] the smallest preference or distinction, which was withheld from, or denied to, any of the rest."[19] Apparently it was not aid to religious activity in general that the Reverend Allison found unacceptable, but discriminatory aid to *one church* — the Episcopalian. Allison was seemingly on sound constitutional ground, for the Maryland Declaration of Rights of 1776 provided "[N]or ought any person to be compelled to frequent or maintain or contribute, unless on contract, to maintain any particular place of worship, or any particular ministry."[20]

The early constitutions and declarations of rights of some other states recognized the right to be free from taxation for support of another church. The 1776 Delaware Declaration of Rights, for example, stated "that no man ought or of right can be compelled to attend any religious worship or maintain any ministry contrary to or against his own free will and consent. . . ."[21] In similar words, the Pennsylvania Constitution of 1776 provided "that no man ought or of right can be compelled to . . . erect or support any place of worship, or maintain any ministry, contrary to, or against his own free will and consent."[22] Although as far back as the New Jersey Fundamental Constitution of 1683 that colony had declared that all persons acknowledging "the one Almighty and Eternal God" could not be compelled to "frequent and maintain any religious worship, place or ministry whatsoever,"[23] the New Jersey Constitution of 1776 more particularly specified that

> no person shall ever . . . under any pretense whatever, be compelled to attend any place of worship, contrary to his own faith and judgment; nor shall any person . . . ever be obligated to pay tithes, taxes, or any other rates, for the purpose of building or repairing any other church or churches, place or places of worship, or for the maintenance of any minister or ministry, contrary to what he believes to be right, or has deliberately or voluntarily engaged himself to perform.[24]

The New York Constitution of 1777 first generalized "that the free exercise and enjoyment of religious profession and worship, without discrimination or preference, shall forever hereafter be allowed;[25] it then added that "all such parts of the said common law, and all such of the said statutes and acts aforesaid, or parts thereof, as may be construed to establish or maintain any particular denomination of Christians or their ministers . . . are repugnant to this constitution . . . and they are hereby abrogated and rejected."[26] Under this Constitution, therefore, "establish" was an alternative for "maintain any particular denomination." This interpretation was confirmed seven years later when the New York Legislature amended the Charter of Trinity Episcopal Church in the following manner: "So much of the charter [of Trinity Church] . . . as relates to the induction of the rector by the governor . . . and to the collecting and levying a sum of dollars upon the City of New York for the use of the rector or incumbent . . . are hereby repealed and annulled."[27] As Jefferson's act for protecting religious liberty had sought to prevent the harmful effects of educational monopoly by "teachers," who were actually ministers of the establishment, so also the Georgia Constitution of 1777 ordained that no one had to support religious teachers except those of his own profession.[28] In their 1789 Constitution the Georgians reworded the proposition to read: "All persons shall have the free exercise of religion, without being obliged to contribute to the support of any religious profession but their own."[29] Similarly, the North Carolina Constitution of 1776 provided that no person was obliged to pay toward the support of a faith or a ministry "contrary to what he believes to be right."[30]

A strong degree of religious liberty prevailed during the late colonial period in Rhode Island. Dissenters were not taxed for the support of any other church; this practice continued during the years of statehood. Connecticut dissenters received comparable protection under an Act of May, 1777. That law exempted "those Persons in this State, commonly styled Separates, from taxes for the support of their established Ministry and building and repairing Meeting Houses."[31] This exemption was extended in 1784 to cover all Christians who attended a church other than the state church.[32]

Similarly, dissenters in New Hampshire benefited by the 1784 State Constitution which provided that "no portion of any one particular religious sect or denomination, shall ever be compelled to pay towards the support of the teacher or teachers of another persuasion, sect or denomination."[33]

However, as events portrayed in this chapter will indicate, this provision did not immediately bring relief. In New England, for example, taxes not otherwise directed by certificate system continued to be paid to the Established Church. The Massachusetts situation is typical. In the Massachusetts General Court that sat as a constitutional convention in 1778, there was a movement to declare illegal the taxing of a person for support of a religious instruction he did not attend, but limited strength of the proponents of the measure resulted in its failure.[34] The people, however, desired safeguards for religious liberty. Later that year the proposed constitution was rejected by a vote of nearly five to one — largely because of the absence of the bill of rights and unsatisfactory religious provisions. Numerous opinions were offered as to what specific proposals should have been included. The Warren Baptist Association, for example, opposed the Constitution and demanded assurance "that ministers shall be supported only by Christ's authority, and not at all by assessment and secular force."[35] On the other hand, the proposed Constitution was defended by the Congregationalist minister, Philips Payson, as conducive to virtue.[36] The debate continued as the people of Mendon in

Worcester County on May 21, 1778, made known their belief that "there is no man in this world would think that he is used with Christian wage if compelled by laws made by man to support a worship that is not agreeable to the dictates of his own conscience and way of thinking in matters of religion; and that the said plan ought not be approved."[37]

As the Massachusetts dissenters made their influence felt at the polls, their lot improved markedly. Under the adopted 1780 Constitution, members of any church other than the Established Congregationalist Church were able to indicate for the first time which church should be benefited by their taxes; but those who had no local church of their faith, or belonged to no church, were still taxed for the maintenance of the Congregationalist Church which continued as the dominant faith of the community.[38] The system generally seems to have worked satisfactorily even though it did occasionally break down. In the same year, for example, John Murray of Gloucester sued to recover money paid in that town by his Universalist parishioners. Distinguished men opposed each other in the litigation: Murray was represented in the suit by the famous liberal and future governor of Massachusetts, James Sullivan; the state's case was argued by Theophilus Parsons, future Chief Justice of the state and one of the authors of the state's constitutional clause acknowledging rights to dissenters. The state argued that the Universalists — with their doctrine of universal salvation — did not come under the provision of the Constitution which granted exemptions to those who supported "teachers of piety, religion and morality." Despite instructions to bring in a verdict for the state, the jury found for Murray. Thus the people of Gloucester demonstrated that although an establishment might exist in theory, it would be successful in practice only to the extent that it was not considered unfair by the community. The Murray decision was soon widely noted throughout Massachusetts.[39]

The system adopted by the Legislature for directing an individual's tax money to his church also could be unsatisfactory in practice. Under the Massachusetts practice, "certificates of dissent" had to be filed in order to direct the tax to a church other than the Congregationalist. Universalists and Baptists objected strongly to the requirement which, they alleged, subordinated them to the Established Church in violation of Article II of the Declaration of Rights which guaranteed no subordination. A 1781 test case arose in Attleborough: the Baptist Elijah Balkom refused to pay the tax for the Congregational Church and was arrested. Losing in the lower court, Balkom appealed to the county court where the state was represented by

Robert Treat Paine, attorney general of the state and one of the drafters of Article Three of the State Constitution.[40] Judgment was given for Balkom. Elsewhere in the state, however, the certificate system was maintained for many years afterward.[41] The Legislature even granted additional powers to the community for the purpose of aiding religion. Under the Act of 1786, the parish meetings were authorized to

> grant and vote such sum or sums of money as they shall judge necessary for the settlement, maintenance and support of the ministers or public teachers of religion; for the building and repairing of houses of worship, and all other necessary parish or precinct charges, to be assessed on the polls and property within the same as by law provided. And the inhabitants of each respective parish and precinct are hereby declared to be a body corporate.[42]

But discontent with the discriminatory provisions of the 1780 Massachusetts Constitution and unfair practices prevailing thereunder were expressed from time to time. The people of Bellingham desired better safeguards of religious freedom and an end to the ministerial taxes.[43] And the Baptists of New England sent their most forceful representative, the Reverend Isaac Backus, to the 1787 federal constitutional convention in Philadelphia. He informed the members of that assembly that "we claim and expect the liberty of worshipping God according to our consciences, not being obliged to support a ministry we cannot attend."[44] In 1789, dissenters from the Massachusetts Establishment won a significant victory in the town of Pittsfield. The townspeople in financing a new meeting house offered Baptists and Episcopalians the return of taxes paid by them so that they could be paid over to their own ministers. This was not satisfactory to the dissenters who carried their case to the state Supreme Court. The Court then ruled for the first time that on presentation of a certificate that they had paid taxes to their own church, dissenters were exempt from any further religious taxation on the part of local governments. The decision gave legal recognition to the idea of religious voluntarism. This principle soon had wide acceptance and contributed largely to the breakdown of the compulsory support of the Established Church, because of the many minor sects granted the certificate without payment of any tax.[45]

The representatives of the colonies in the Continental Congress recognized the injustice of having dissenters and Catholics pay taxes for the Established Churches. When the Congress sent to Canada Benjamin Franklin, Charles Carroll of Carrollton, and Samuel Chase, these emissaries were instructed to make it clear to the northern neighbors that after independence all Americans will "be totally exempt from the payment of any tythes or taxes for the support of any religion."[46]

In summary, it would seem that Founding Fathers of the United States of 1789 understood that freedom of religion for all required freedom from an establishment to the extent that a person was not to be subject to a taxing system that favored an Established Church to which he did not subscribe.

The Struggle to Be Free From Laws Compelling Dissenters to Attend Services of the Established Church

Shortly after independence was declared, members of faiths other than the Established Anglican and Congregationalist effectively persuaded the majority of the American community to constitutionalize bans upon compulsory worship in an alien creed. Thomas Jefferson expressed his opposition to "the impious presumption of legislators and rulers, civil as well as ecclesiastical, who being themselves but fallible and uninspired men, have assumed dominion over the faith of others, setting up their own opinions and modes of thinking as the only true and infallible, and as such endeavoring to impose them on others. . . ."[47] He put his words into action. A 1776 resolution submitted by Jefferson to the Virginia House of Burgesses forcefully impressed upon his colleagues in that body that it was improper to punish any person for "forbearing to repair to church."[48] In June of the same year, Jefferson's draft constitution for Virginia contained a clause to the effect that "all persons shall have full and free liberty of religious opinion; nor shall any be compelled to frequent or maintain any religious institution."[49] The Virginia Declaration of Rights enacted June 12, 1776, declared "that religion, or the duty which we owe to our Creator, and the manner of discharging it, can be directed only by reason and conviction, not by fear or violence; and therefore all men are equally entitled to the free exercise of religion. . . ."[50] This pronouncement was particularized on December 5, 1776, when the Virginia House resolved "that all and every act or statute, either of the Parliament of England or of Great Britain, by whatever title known or distinguished, which renders criminal the maintaining any opinions in matters of religion, forbearing to repair to church, or the exercising any mode of worship whatsoever, or which prescribes punishment for the same, ought to be declared hence forth of no validity or force within this Commonwealth."[51]

Most of the other states soon joined Virginia in freeing men from obligations of attending churches other than their own. The Maryland Declaration of Rights of 1776 announced: "[N]or any person to be compelled to frequent . . . any particular place of worship. . . ."[52] And the Delaware Declaration of Rights, adopted September 11, 1776, provided: "[T]hat no man ought or of right can be compelled to attend any religious worship . . . contrary to or against his own free will and consent. . . ."[53] With almost identical language, the Pennsylvania Constitution of the same year stated: "[N]o man ought or of right can be compelled to attend any religious worship . . . contrary to, or against, his own free will and consent."[54] The community, however, might still demand respect for a religious observance, but some scrupulous persons did object that they were being compelled to violate the dictates of their consciences. For example, the Pennsylvania Quakers protested that they were unable to obey the day of prayer and fasting decreed by the Continental Congress for May 17, 1776, and they opened their stalls and shops on that day to express their defiance of the so-called human ordinances. Almost immediately, a crowd gathered and demanded the conscientious "friends" to close their shops for the day. Some respected the wishes of the crowd and did no more business, but other more stubborn shopkeepers were compelled by stones to cease what the townspeople thought was disrespectful conduct.[55]

Thus when the members of the First Congress of the United States assembled in 1789, it was understood in the land that freedom of religion demanded that the federal government should never force adherents of all faiths to attend services of an Established Church as a prerequisite to the exercise of civil rights. They knew, however, that the community felt free to demand respect for and to protect expressions of religious sentiment shared by the community.

The Struggle for Equal Economic Opportunities for Dissenters and an End to Advantages and Preferences Possessed by the Members of the Dominant Faith

Establishment was anathema to most Americans of the Revolutionary generation because of the unfair advantage possessed by the Established Church with the concomitant discriminations against other faiths. However, in the movement to secure religious liberty, not all aspects of the prejudicial establishment were removed. Traces of political, economic, and even communicative discriminations lingered on from the colonial well into the constitutional period.

The demand for equality and an end to preference was presented with vigor, especially in Virginia. As early as August, 1775, the

Baptists of Virginia had resolved to circulate a petition to the General Assembly asking that the church establishment be abolished, and religion left to stand upon its own merits, and that all religious societies should be equally protected in the peaceable enjoyment of their own religious principles and modes of worship.[56] After 1776 the Baptists of that state specifically attacked that part of the establishment that permitted only ministers of the Anglican Church to perform marriages and conduct burial services. The struggle against this particular aspect of establishment was officially won in Virginia on December 16, 1784.[57]

The Baptists were not alone in inveighing against preference. The members of the Presbytery of Hanover in Virginia in 1776 indicated they opposed establishment because of its unfair advantages to one sect. The Presbyterians entreated the Assembly

> that all laws now in force in this Commonwealth which countenance religious dominations may be speedily repealed, that all and every religious sect may be protected in the full exercise of their several modes of worship, and exempted from the payment of all taxes for the support of any church whatever, farther than what may be agreeable to their own private choice, or voluntary obligation.[58]

Another petition to the general Assembly of Virginia, dated October 16, 1776, reads: "A petition of dissenters . . . that having long groaned under the burthen of an ecclesiastical establishment, they pray that this, as well as every other yoke, may be broken, and that the oppressed may go free, that so, every religious denomination being on a level, animosities may cease. . . ."[59] This stirring of religious freedom was reflected in the official state documents. The *Journal of the House of Delegates of Virginia* for October 22, 1776, noted the receipt of "Two petitions from dissenters from the Church of England . . . praying that every religious denomination may be put upon an equal footing."[60] The same *Journal* for November 1, 1776, records the arrival of another "Petition from dissenters . . . praying that every religious denomination may be put upon an equal footing, independent of another."[61] With these dissenters Thomas Jefferson was fully agreed that society should give no preeminence in law to any one religious sect over others.[62]

As early as 1776 Madison was positing his opposition to establishment upon its inequalities. In the Virginia convention of that year, he urged adoption of a clause providing: "No man, or class of men, ought on account of religion to be invested with peculiar emoluments or privileges, nor subject to any penalties or disabilities, unless under color of religion the preservation of equal liberty and the existence of the State are manifestly endangered."[63] When adopted the Virginia Declaration of Rights of 1776 expressed the principle slightly otherwise. It reads: "That no man, or set of men, are entitled to exclusive emoluments or privileges from the community, but in consideration of public service. . . ."[64]

As late as 1784 the Virginia dissenters were still struggling for equality before the law. This is indicated in a "Memorial of the Presbyterian Clergy" to the Virginia House of Delegates on May 26, 1784: "An entire and everlasting freedom from every species of ecclesiastical domination, and full and permanent security of the inalienable rights of conscience and private judgment, and an equal share of the protection and favor of government to all denominations of Christians were particular objects of our expectation."[65] Largely because it denied equal freedom of religion, James Madison the following year opposed the Virginia bill for religious assessments. "All men," he wrote, "are to be considered . . . as retaining [in the language of Article Sixteen of the Virginia Declaration of Rights] an 'equal title to the free exercise of Religion according to the dictates of conscience.' "[66]

In Maryland, Catholics and other dissenters fought to end a variety of discriminations — communicative, economic, and political. Charles Carroll of Carrollton in his communication with "Antillon" — Daniel Dulany, conservative member of the Established Church in Maryland — said of his correspondent: "He will not allow me freedom of thought or speech."[67] It is interesting to note that while Dulany became a neutralist Tory, Carroll fought and sacrificed for independence. In Maryland, financial favoritism of the Church of England came to an end with the Maryland Declaration of Rights of 1776. Thereafter public authorities were prohibited from assessing any sum of money or quantity of tobacco for the vestrymen or church wardens.[68] John Carroll frequently stressed that the essence of religious liberty lay in understanding that there should be no preference to any one sect and that all religions should be equal before the law.[69] Writing in the December, 1787, Supplement to the *Columbian Magazine* of Philadelphia, he observed:

> Thanks to genuine spirit and Christianity, the United States have banished intolerance from their system of government, and many of them have done the justice to every denomination of Christians, which ought to be done to them in all, of placing them on an equal footing of citizenship, and conferring an equal right of participation in national privileges, Freedom and independence, acquired by the united efforts and cemented with the mingled blood of Protestant and Catholic fellow-citizens, should be equally enjoyed by all. . . .

who that remembers our cordial unanimity in rejecting the claims of foreign oppression, could imagine that any of us would impose on fellow-soldiers and citizens the degrading mark of distrust, or the galling yoke of inferiority?[70]

And, little more than a year later, Bishop Carroll wrote to Mathew Carey, the editor of Philadelphia's *American Museum*

After having contributed in proportion to their numbers, equally at least with every other denomination, to the establishment of independence, and run every risk in common with them, it is not only contradictory to the avowed principles of equality in religious rights but a flagrant act of injustice to deprive them [the Catholics] of those advantages to the acquirement of which they so much contributed.[71]

Since John Carroll was familiar with the discriminations of Anglican Maryland against Catholics, it seems that he may have been thinking of economic as well as political disadvantages, when he wrote that Americans during the Revolution had "associated into one great national Union, under the express condition of not being shackled by religious tests."[72]

In South Carolina the Reverend William Tennant was equally active in protecting religious liberty. Speaking before the Constitutional Assembly of 1777, the Presbyterian minister entered a moving plea in behalf of equal rights of conscience, which led to the disestablishment of the Anglican Church. Like John Carroll he saw the danger in any state-established orthodoxies. In his address he declared:

We contend that no legislature under Heaven has a right to interfere with the judgment and conscience of men, in religious matters, if their opinions and practices do not injure the State. . . . The State may give countenance to religion, by defending and protecting all denominations of Christians, who are inoffensive and useful. The State may enact good laws for the punishment of vice, and the encouragement of virtue. *The State may do anything for the support of religion, without partiality to particular societies, or imposition upon the rights of private judgment.*

Thus the problem was that through preferential aid to religious groups the state could "buy up" the rights of the unfavored groups.

But when the legislative authority of the State sets itself up as a judge in church controversies, and proceeds to lay hardship upon the professors of one, while it lavishes its bounties on the other, and that while both are equally useful and inoffensive — I say, in this, it not only mistakes the proper objects of legislation, but is charge-

able with manifest injustice. No legislature upon earth has a right
to do such a thing. . . .

The significance of this prejudicial method was that it could achieve
the same result of an establishment without the imposition of formal
tests or burdens.

> On all hands it will be acknowledged, that those establishments are
> of this which lay heavy penalties upon those who refuse to conform
> to them. . . . Of the same nature, though differing somewhat in the
> degree of their cruelty, are those establishments, which incapacitate
> subjects, who differ from the speculative opinions of the State. Judg-
> ment and conscience, in these matters, is, or *ought to be,* as inde-
> pendent of our [the legislature's] will, as our height or colour. They
> are formed by the circumstances of the time in which we live, by
> the manner of our education, by the capacity of our mind, and the
> degree of evidence. Would not that prince be esteemed a cruel tyrant,
> who should ordain, that every man of six feet high, and of a sandy
> complexion, should be excluded from the rights of citizens? An
> assembly of two hundred senators, who could ordain, that good
> citizens should be deprived, on account of their inoffensive opinions,
> would be two hundred times as cruel.

When some members of the Assembly declared that an established
church worked no prejudice since anyone could join it, Reverend
Tennant scornfully dismissed the argument:

> Sir! You may say that the doors of the established church are open
> equally to all denominations, and that all may equally enjoy the
> benefit of it. I have never heard of such an argument. . . .

He added:

> It would be extremely natural to ask, how a rational dissenter can
> enjoy the benefit of the establishment? The only answer that I can
> give to such a question is a very short one. *He must do it at the
> expense of his own private judgment and conscience.*[73]

The result of this speech was a constitutional clause guaranteeing
to Protestant churches (there were virtually no others in the state
at the time) "equal civil and religious privilege."[74]

Throughout the other original states there was continual ferment
for an end to preference. The struggle generally succeeded and the
early state constitutions attempted to end establishment in this
sense. Thus the Delaware Constitution of 1776 provided: "There
shall be no Establishment of any one Religious Sect in this State
in Preference to another. . . ."[75] After making a similar declaration
in her Constitution of 1776 that there should be "no Establishment
of any one religious . . . denomination in preference to any other,"[76]

North Carolina proceeded to bring her laws into conformity with the new Constitution. The repressive Vestry Act of 1768 had been allowed to expire by limitation in 1773.[77] In 1778 the privilege of performing marriages was granted to all ministers alike,[78] and persons objecting to the taking of an oath — Quakers, Moravians, Mennonites, and Dunkards — were allowed to make an affirmation.[79] In 1787 James Iredell could note with satisfaction the religious balance in his state at the time the people were debating whether to ratify the federal Constitution: "Happily, no sect here is superior to another."[80] In Connecticut two years later the General Assembly passed "An Act Securing Equal Rights and Privileges to Christians of every Denomination in this State."[81] Although absolute equality was not achieved, the act was the beginning of modification of the Connecticut Establishment which would eventually lead to equal religious liberty. Speaking warmly of conditions under the New Jersey Constitution of 1776, the author of "Remarks on Liberty of Conscience" in 1778 said: "How amiable the intrenching, with the sanction of an ordinance, immutable and irrevocable, the sacred rights of conscience; and renouncing all discrimination between men, on account of their sentiments about the various modes of church government, or the different articles of their faith!"[82]

Old prejudices did not die easily even with the new spirit. In the New York Constitutional Convention of 1777, John Jay tried to have the Assembly adopt a clause forbidding Roman Catholics to hold lands or enjoy civil rights until they had taken an oath disavowing "foreign allegiance." His efforts were defeated in the convention, 19 to 10,[83] in favor of a clause that guaranteed religious liberty "without discrimination or preference."[84] Another article of the same document expressly abrogated all laws and parts of law, common or statute, which "might be construed to establish or maintain any particular denomination of Christians or their ministers."[85] In that same year, John Jay — then Chief Justice of the state and later Chief Justice of the United States — spoke with pride of the new state Constitution because under it "no preference [is] given to one sect to the prejudice of others.[86] To implement the above articles of the state Constitution, the New York Legislature in 1784 enacted a law "to carry into full effect those parts of the constitution" dealing with "all acts of the legislature of this State while a colony and all parts thereof which may be construed to establish or maintain any particular denomination of Christians or their ministers." The act declared:

In order to remove all doubts which may arise in the minds of any persons with respect to the continuance in force and effect of [such

laws, which] do also declare or imply a pre-eminence or distinction
of the said Episcopal Church or Church of England over all other
churches, and other religious denominations [it thereby enacted that]
the said acts . . . as do imply such pre-eminence and distinction, be
. . . absolutely abrogated . . . as inconsistent with and repugnant to
the constitution. . . . And it is hereby further declared that nothing
in this act contained, shall in any wise be construed or understood
to give any kind of pre-eminence or distinction to the Episcopal mode
of religious worship within this State but that an universal equality
between every religious denomination according to the true spirit of
the Constitution towards each other shall forever prevail.[87]

Favoritism and preference for one sect over others remained
throughout this period. In Massachusetts and New Hampshire the
picture was somewhat different; voices of protest were heard in both
these states, but in light of the jury verdicts in favor of the dissenters
— discussed earlier in this chapter — it is doubtful that the populace
approved such discriminations.

In these states, as in Virginia, the Baptists were particularly active
in demanding an end to preferences. It was "impartial liberty" of
religion for all men, which the Baptist spokesman Reverend Isaac
Backus demanded on April 6, 1780, in "An Appeal to the People
of the Massachusetts State Against Arbitrary Power."[88]

Thus, on the basis of available evidence, it would seem that when
the First Congress met in 1789, the overwhelming consensus of the
land accepted the proposition that any aspect of establishment that
denied equal religious liberty to others should be forever outlawed.
The period 1776 to 1789 was characterized throughout the United
States by a demand for absolute religious equality. The language of
the state constitutions adopted during this period indeed firmly
indicates that establishment meant preference and for this reason
was to be banned. Statements of the leaders of the times indicate that
religious freedom was guaranteed and disestablishment had occurred
when all religious groups were granted equal status before the law.
This was the policy on the federal level also. When on September 14,
1787, in the Federal Constitutional Convention, James Madison and
Charles Pinckney of South Carolina moved to clothe Congress with
a power to establish a university, they immediately added that "no
preferences or distinctions should be allowed on account of religion."[89] James Wilson supported the motion, but it was not passed
because Gouverneur Morris convinced the convention that the
congressional power over the district was ample to there establish a
university.[90] Other statesmen were agreed that in the Federal Government no *one* sect should receive legal preference. In endeavoring

to put to rest the fears of his fellow Virginians, Governor Edmund Randolph spoke these words in the Virginia convention that ratified the United States Constitution:

> How many different sects will be in Congress? We cannot enumerate the sects that may be in Congress. And there are so many now in the United States that they will prevent the establishment of any one sect in prejudice to the rest, and will forever oppose all attempts to infringe religious liberty.[91]

Charles Carroll shared the concern of his contemporaries during these years. Later in life he wrote to a Protestant minister: "To obtain religious as well as civil liberty I entered zealously into the Revolution and, observing the Christian religion divided into sects, I founded the hope that no one would become so predominant as to become the religion of the state. . . ."[92]

The "Multiple Establishment"

When the constitutional assemblies of the time were considering the problems of religious liberty, one often-proposed method of disestablishment was the enactment of a system of "multiple establishment." Instead of abolishing the colonial church-state system *in toto,* this system would remove the harmful effects of the colonial establishment by admitting the dissenting churches to the same privileges and protection that the colonial Established Church had enjoyed. In this respect it had many features in common with the New England "quasi-establishment" prior to the Revolution. Generally, in practice the term embraced any one of four possibilities:

a) The combination of two or more sects, such as the Episcopal and Congregationalist;

b) Preference of all Protestant sects over non-Protestant faiths;

c) Favoritism of all Christian sects over non-Christian; or

d) Legal recognition and enforcement of a body of doctrine recognized by more than one sect.

The statesmen of the time who proposed the system were probably motivated by the laudable ideal of securing greater religious freedom by extending state protection of religion. Unfortunately, they did not realize that the failure to extend legal equality to all religions could operate to abridge the rights of the excluded sects or denominations in the same way that the establishment of a single church had. It soon became apparent to many leaders in the states that the proposed systems of multiple establishment would not guarantee full religious liberty. In addition, the minority sects opposed the system vigorously because they feared the possibility of a merger or alliance of presently Established Churches, e.g., the Episcopal and the Congregationalist, to the detriment of all other faiths. Some Americans even opposed the establishment or governmental favoritism of Christianity over other religions. However, as the history of the times indicates, the views of this latter group did not prevail for many years to come.

The practice of the multiple establishment was fairly widespread in the states. Just as some of the New England states during this period were willing to establish or favor the Congregationalists at the expense of other worshipers, so too, other states were willing to establish or favor Protestantism. Protestantism, for example, was recognized as the official religion in South Carolina. The 1778 Constitution of that state decreed that "the Christian Protestant religion shall be deemed, and is hereby constituted and declared to be the established religion of this State."[93] In other states, Protestantism was preferred by constitutional clauses restricting public office to such believers; this was true of New Jersey's 1776 Constitution, which remained in force until 1844.[94] And the 1779 state convention in New Hampshire submitted a constitution which would have preferred Protestantism.[95] Even though the people rejected this, the later 1784 New Hampshire Constitution left in effect the old colonial law which favored Protestantism. This Constitution further empowered the Legislature to authorize the towns "to make adequate provision, at their own expense, for the support and maintenance of public Protestant teachers of piety, religion and morality."[96] Such preference of Protestantism did not escape criticism by the people of New Hampshire. Thus, in a protest drawn by General John Sullivan, the town committee of Durham in 1783 pointed to the constitutional incongruity:

> It is somewhat singular that a Bill of Rights should declare that every individual has a natural and inalienable right to worship God according to the dictates of his own conscience, and at the same time exclude every denomination of Christians except Protestants from being supported and protected by law, and even from holding any office in the State.[97]

Favoritism of Protestants prevailed not only in New Hampshire, but also in nine other of the thirteen states. John Carroll, writing in 1785 to the Papal Nuncio in Paris, stated: "Catholics are indeed tolerated everywhere but so far it is only in Pennsylvania, Delaware, Maryland and Virginia that they enjoy equal advantages with their fellow citizens."[98] In May of 1789, when it was known that the

First Congress of the United States would discuss proposals for a bill of rights, there appeared in the *Gazette of the United States* (which was published in New York, during the time Congress was assembled there) a letter by a still unknown writer, "E. C." It contained a subtle overture to the Congress that it prefer Protestantism under the national law. The suggestion elicited a memorable response from John Carroll who informed "E. C." and his readers that all Americans were entitled to freedom from such an establishment under "the great principle of religious freedom" and "the sacred rights of conscience before the state."[99] Except in Rhode Island, the New England states throughout this period established and favored one or more Protestant sects. Connecticut's religious liberty in 1784 was limited to Protestants under an "Act for Securing the Rights of Conscience."[100]

Where Protestantism was not officially established or preferred, dominant religious sentiment of the community in the states during the immediate post-Revolutionary period was reflected by an inclination to prefer or favor Christianity occasionally at the expense of other religions. Thus, under Maryland's Declaration of Rights of 1776, "only persons professing the Christian religion"[101] were entitled to religious freedom. In 1781 the Maryland Legislature ordained that public officials would have to subscribe a declaration of belief in the Christian religion,[102] and it was not until 1826 that Jews were permitted to hold public office in that state.[103] In Pennsylvania, too, Jews were apparently victims of a Christian preference, according to a memorial presented on December 23, 1783, to the Pennsylvania Council of Censors. It complained "that the tenth section of the frame of this government deprives the Jews of the most eminent rights of freedom, by disabling them to be elected by their fellow-citizens to represent them in the general assembly, or hold any civil office in the state. . . ."[104]

In Virginia in 1785 when it appeared to James Madison that the Presbyterians were willing to endorse a bill for general assessments, he criticized them, saying that they "seem as ready to set up an establishment which is to take them in as they were to pull down that which left them out."[105] Cobb is correct in stating that the effect of the bill "would have been to establish Christianity as the religion of the state,"[106] since it excluded all but the Christian sects. It might even have excluded some Protestants who did not adhere to the majority view of Christian theology. For example, Baptists might question the doctrine of the Trinity; Quakers denied the Incarnation. Thus it is more than plausible that Madison opposed the bill primarily for this reason.[107] In addition and because it might well have become an opening wedge to enable the state to prefer a single sect, such as the Episcopalian, Madison expressed his opposition thereto in these words from his *Remonstrance:*

> Who does not see that the same authority which can establish Christianity in exclusion of all other religions may establish with the same ease any particular sect of Christians in exclusion of all other sects. That the same authority which can force a citizen to contribute three pence only of his property for the support of any one establishment may force him to conform to any other establishment in all cases whatsoever. . . .[108]

This attempt to prefer Christian sects over Jews and all others also roused the opposition of many other Virginians, including the Baptists, Quakers, Presbyterians, the few Catholics, and many Methodists.[109] This combination resulted in the bill's failure. Since the proposed bill was defeated mainly through the efforts of the Baptists and Presbyterians, their objections are of special relevance. The Baptists had readily joined Madison in indicating their displeasure because religions such as the Jewish were excluded. "The exclusion of any religion from the assessment plan . . . ," said the Baptists, "made what should have been a state support of morality for the benefit of society a discriminating religious measure."[110] On August 13, 1785, the General Committee of the Baptist Church in Virginia

> RESOLVED, that it be recommended to those counties which have not yet prepared petitions to be presented to the General Assembly against the engrossed bill for a general assessment for the support of the teachers of the Christian religion, to proceed thereon as soon as possible; that it is believed to be repugnant to the spirit of the Gospel for the Legislature thus to proceed in matters of religion; that the holy Author of our religion needs no such compulsive measure for the promotion of His cause; that the Gospel wants not the feeble arm of man for its support; that it has made, and will again through divine power make its way against all opposition; and that should the Legislature assume the right of taxing the people for the support of the Gospel, it will be destructive to religious liberty.[111]

For some time the Presbyterians indicated their opposition to the state establishing or favoring Christianity by law. Thus the members of the Presbytery of Hanover in 1776 had expressed their objections to "establishing the Christian religion."[112] In their memorial of October 24 of the same year, the Presbyterians added that "there is no argument in favoring of establishing the Christian religion but what may be pleaded with equal propriety for establishing the tenets of Mahomet."[113]

The bill for a general assessment was also opposed by the Virginia Presbyterians, the Baptists, and other dissenters because of fear that the bill would set a precedent which would later allow the Legislature to resume the preference of the Episcopalians. The Presbyterians at their convention of August 13, 1785, prepared a memorial opposing the assessments, which reasoned: "If the Assembly have a right to determine the preference between Christianity, and the other systems of religion that prevails in the world, they may also, at a convenient time, give a preference to some favoured sect among Christians."[114]

Thus the opposition of the other Christian sects in Virginia, except the Episcopalian, to the proposed bill can best be understood with a realization of vivid memory of the distasteful conditions ten years previous when the colonial government had an established Anglican Church. This was the situation elsewhere in America. Opposition to state help to religion was voiced, not because general help was an "establishment," but rather because of a fear that it presaged a return to a single, preferred, exclusive Established Church. Reflecting contemporary sentiments in 1785, John Carroll wrote to an English friend that the Catholics of Maryland would join all other dissenters in opposing the exercise of the power clearly granted in the state constitution to the legislature to levy a general tax for the support of the Christian religion. He declared: "We have all smarted heretofore under the lash of an established church and shall therefore be on our guard against every approach to it."[115]

The South Carolina view on multiple establishment was somewhat different. There was no fear in that state that the Episcopal Church might misuse a common privilege to surreptitiously regain its undemocratic powers. The common belief seems to have been that there was no danger where all religions were treated alike and the franchise was unrestricted by religious tests. In this sense multiple establishment was a method to provide a fuller religious liberty. Hence, it was actually a species of disestablishment. For this reason it appeared to some that "multiple establishment" was a contradiction in terms. Speaking before the Constitutional Assembly of 1777, the Reverend William Tennant attacked the proposal as being facetiously offered: "Sir! it is impracticable in this State to establish all denominations . . . it is only thrown out to amuse us." He further argued:

> This, Sir! may operate as a scheme of division, but in practice it must appear equally absurd and impossible. Absurd, *as the establishment of all religions would be no establishment at all.* It would destroy the very end of an establishment, by reducing things just to the same state they would be in without it.

He then rejected the system as unworkable. By some misunderstanding he believed that under multiple establishment each church would have transferred to it the discharge of the civil functions of government over its respective parishioners. This overlapping of innumerable jurisdictions, he declared, "would prove the means of everlasting strife." Furthermore, the expense of such a system would be "insupportable." He concluded with a warning against the lurking dangers of inequality, stating:

> But to admit the establishment of a few dissenting churches, in preference to all others, as a means to make them acquiesce! It is too big with injustice to procure the consent of an honest man. Let us all have equal privileges or nothing. *Equality or Nothing!* ought to be our motto.

> In short, every plan of establishment . . . must operate as a plan of injustice and oppression; and therefore Sir! I am utterly against all establishments in this State.[116]

The Assembly, nevertheless, did proclaim a system of multiple establishment in South Carolina. The Constitution of 1778 declared that "the Christian Protestant religion shall be deemed and is hereby declared to be, the established religion of this State. . . ."[117] Although the Reverend Tennant ostensibly had opposed such a system he soon gave his approbation to it, since the Constitution of 1778 provided that "all denominations of Christian Protestants in this State, demeaning themselves peaceably and faithfully, shall enjoy equally religious and civil privileges."[118] Two months after his great speech before the General Assembly, he explained that his earlier position had been based on a misunderstanding. In the notes to a reprint of the speech he said that he had "had reference in this position and in all others of this nature, to an establishment of Parishes, with legal boundaries, and those supported out of the public treasury." He further stated:

> He has the pleasure to find, that a general establishment, or rather incorporation of all denominations is now thought of, and likely to be adopted, which while it makes all parties happy, is not liable to the above objection. The plan he refers to, leaves only the incorporation of the Church of England standing, and opens the door to the equal incorporation of all denominations — while not one sect of Christians in preference to all others, but Christianity itself is the established religion of the State.[119]

Thus it seems that the South Carolina system of multiple establishment was intended to promote the best interests of the religious denominations in that state which were all Protestant. Since there were no Roman Catholics and few Jews, their omission from the privileges in the Constitution probably was accidental and was not designed to suppress their congregations. But the South Carolina law did lay a snare for future generations by prescribing a religious test for the privilege of incorporation and for church membership. The members of the church were required to make the following declaration before a charter could be issued:

1st.   That there is one eternal God, and a future state of rewards and punishments.

2d.   That God is publicly to be worshipped.

3rd.   That the Christian religion is the true religion.

4th.   That the holy scriptures of the Old and New Testament are of divine inspiration, and are the rule of faith and practice.

5th.   That it is lawful and the duty of every man being thereunto called by those that govern, to bear witness to the truth.[120]

Reflecting the South Carolina fear of Roman Catholicism, the Constitution required that members of the Legislature be of the Protestant religion.[121] The qualifications for an elector specified a "free white man, and no other, who acknowledges the being of a God, and believes in a future state of rewards and punishments. . . ."[122]

The tests probably caused no trouble when first proposed since most Protestants could agree with them and since there was almost no non-Protestant minority in the state. There is evidence that they were not enforced against Jews.[123] But it should be noted that the Protestant Establishment lasted only a few years. In the Constitution of 1790 all religions were admitted to civil benefits and privileges without preference.[124] Thus it might be argued that South Carolina in 1790, by granting equality to all religions, in effect had established all religions. Far from operating to abridge the rights of conscience in the manner of the old colonial establishment, as the Reverend Tennant suggested, the establishment of all religions would operate to promote liberty.

Nevertheless, to many in this generation of rapid change, the multiple establishment did not hold out a bright hope for the achievement of equal liberty. Although a multiple establishment might be an improvement over the unitary establishment, the multiple establishment continued to prejudice those groups excluded from its benefits. Moreover, this power to set up a multiple establishment implied the ability to prejudice any person because of his religious belief. To many of the leaders of the time it was imperatively desirable to deny the political state the power to impose religious doctrine upon the community. This generation could clearly and quickly recall unfortunate results of most colonies to impose particular religious doctrines upon all. Even though the law might be passed with good intentions of encouraging religion, in practice it could become an instrument for persecution. For example, colonial Virginia had required all citizens to have their children baptized as infants. Quakers, however, did not believe in infant baptism. When the pacifist nature of the Quakers caused them to become unpopular for refusing to take up arms in defense of the colony, state officials were able to persecute the Quakers and to drive them out of the colony by enforcing the law requiring infant baptism.[125] Independence had not brought an automatic abolition of these doctrinal laws. Even after independence the Delaware Constitution of 1776 demanded of every public official a declaration of belief in the doctrine of the Trinity.[126]

But the American consensus was beginning to endorse the new laws that made it impossible for the governments to impose doctrine upon unwilling citizens. Thus, in 1777, the New York leader, John Jay, praised the then recently adopted New York Constitution because under it "no opinions are dictated, no rules of faith prescribed. . . ."[127] That this view prevailed up to the time of the federal Bill of Rights is illustrated by the debates on the proposed religion amendment in the First Congress. Representative Elbridge Gerry of Massachusetts stated on the floor that the early proposal "would read better if it was, that no religious doctrine shall be established by law."[128] There is some reason to believe this is what the Senate intended to accomplish by banning establishment, as indicated in Chapter Six, *infra*. The United States Supreme Court, a hundred years later, speaking through Justice Field, agreed with this interpretation, saying: "The First Amendment to the Constitution . . . was intended . . . to prohibit legislation for the support of any religious tenets, or the modes of worship of any sect."[129]

If the members of the First Congress shared the memories, the experiences, and the desires of their contemporaries — and there is no evidence that they did not — in preventing establishment they would have aimed to outlaw not only favoritism of one sect, but also to make impossible favoritism of two or more sects at the expense of other faiths, preference of all Christian sects over the non-Christian, and any attempt by the government to impose a body of religious doctrine upon the citizens of the United States.

*The Struggle for Toleration and an Equal Opportunity
to Practice One's Faith*

As early as the first meeting of the Continental Congress in
Philadelphia in 1774 there were American overtures that our repre-
sentatives acknowledge the right of all religious groups to toleration.
The Baptists delivered a memorial to the Congress, stating in part:

> The free exercises of private judgment, and the unalienable rights of
> conscience, are of too high a rank and dignity to be submitted to the
> decrees of councils, or the imperfect laws of fallible legislators. The
> merciful Father of mankind is the alone Lord of Conscience. Estab-
> lishments . . . cannot create Christians. . . . Happy in the enjoyment
> of these undoubted rights, and conscious of their high import, every
> lover of mankind must be desirous, as far as opportunity offers, of
> extending and securing the enjoyment of these inestimable blessings.

The memorial reached its logical conclusion:

> [W]e claim and expect the liberty of worshipping God according to
> our consciences, not being obliged to support a ministry we cannot
> attend, while we demean ourselves as faithful subjects.[130]

The colonial experience in exiling religious groups such as
Quakers and Moravians ended with the victorious conclusion of the
American Revolution. Thenceforth, all dissenters were tolerated
and permitted to reside where they willed. By 1783 Catholics were
allowed to settle in many more states. In that year John Carroll
wrote to a friend in Rome:

> You are not ignorant that in these United States our religious system
> has undergone a revolution, if possible, more extra-ordinary than our
> political one. In all of them a free toleration is allowed to Christians
> of every denomination, and particularly in the states of Pennsylvania,
> Delaware, Maryland and Virginia, a communication of all civil rights
> without distinction or diminution is extended to those of our religion.[131]

Recalling the frequent colonial impediments to full and free practice of religious faith, the Founding Fathers shortly after independence provided constitutional protection for the rights of toleration
and public worship. Some state constitutions acknowledged that the
right belonged not only to Protestants, but also to Catholics, Jews,
and all mankind. The Virginia Bill of Rights of 1776, drafted by
Mason and slightly modified by Madison, provided

> That religion, or the duty we owe to our Creator, and the manner of
> discharging it, can be directed only by reason and conviction, not by
> force or violence, and therefore all men are equally entitled to the

free exercise of religion according to the dictates of conscience, and that it is the mutual duty of all to practice Christian forbearance, love and charity towards each other.[132]

According to Thomas Jefferson, shortly after the adoption of the Bill of Rights a committee of the House listened to petitions to abolish spiritual tyranny, and finally the House passed a law to

> repeal the laws which rendered criminal the maintenance of any religious opinions (other than those of the Episcopalians), the forebearance of repairing to (Episcopal) Church, or the exercise of any (other than the Episcopal) mode of worship.[133]

Those ringing words, however, did not reach their full import in Virginia, for it was only two years later that the prominent Baptist preacher, Jeremiah Walker, was taxed with prison charges for his confinement in a Virginia jailhouse — for preaching.[134]

Henry Melchior Muhlenberg, writing on September 16, 1776, indicated that any draft of a plan for government in Pennsylvania should provide that "every religious part and persuasion shall, without distinction, have equal freedom to believe and teach what it pleases according to its so-called conscience or judgment."[135] All faiths were protected under New Jersey's Constitution of 1776 which provided "that no person shall ever in this colony be deprived of the inestimable privilege of worshipping Almighty God, in a manner agreeable to the dictates of his own conscience."[136] An unknown writer, reflecting on the New Jersey Constitution, in January of 1776 authored "Remarks on Liberty of Conscience," wherein he observed: "In contrast with this spiritual tyranny [British Establishment] how beautiful appears our catholic constitution, in disclaiming all jurisdiction over the souls of men; and securing by law, never to be repealed, the voluntary, unchecked moral suasion of every individual; and his own self-directed intercourse with the Father of Spirits, either by devout retirement, or public worship, of his own election."[137]

At this time, however, a move to abolish all religious distinctions was too bold. The result was that many states established Christianity. The right to freedom of religious worship was acknowledged only for Christians in their constitutions and declarations of right. Thus the Maryland Declaration of Rights in 1777 gave religious liberty only to those "persons professing the Christian religion.[138] As restrictive as was this grant of religious toleration, it was nevertheless a considerable improvement for Catholics who enthusiastically appreciated their improved lot. Father Joseph Mosley of Halbot County, Maryland, wrote on October 4, 1784: "The toleration here granted by the Bill of Rights has put all on the same footing, and has been of great service to us."[139] The same year, the Reverend John Carroll observed: "If we have the wisdom and temper to preserve [religious and civil liberty], America may come to exhibit a proof to the world, that general and equal toleration, by giving a free circulation to fair argument, is the most effectual method to bring all denominations of Christians to a unity of faith.[140] Similarly, the 1776 Delaware Declaration of Rights declared that "all persons professing the Christian religion ought forever to enjoy equal rights and privileges."[141] And as late as in the Constitution of 1818, the people of Connecticut were still willing to give only to Christians "equal powers, rights and privileges."[142]

In such states, Jews and non-Christians throughout this period sought legal recognition of their right to worship publicly. Shortly after independence, there were some individuals who were agreeable to denying Catholics the right to worship publicly. For example, during the discussions in the 1777 New York State Constitutional Convention it was proposed to grant to all mankind the free exercise of religious profession and worship. To this, however, Jay wanted to append:

> except the professors of the religion of the Church of Rome, who ought not to hold lands in, or be admitted to a participation of the civil rights enjoyed by members of this State, until such time as the said professors shall appear in the supreme court of the State, and there most solemnly swear, that they verily believe in their consciences, that no pope, priest, or foreign authority on earth, has power to absolve the subjects of this State from their allegiance to the same. And farther, that they renounce, and believe to be false and wicked, the dangerous and damnable doctrine, that the pope, or any other earthly authority, has the power to absolve men from sins described in and prohibited by, the Holy Gospel of Jesus Christ; and particularly that no pope, priest or foreign authority on earth, has power to absolve them from the obligation of this oath.[143]

Warmly debated, Jay's proposal was rejected by the convention, 19 to 10. It is interesting to discover the same Jay, later that year serving as Chief Justice of New York speaking with fulsome praise of the recently adopted Constitution because under it "every man is permitted to consider, to adore, and to worship his Creator in the manner most agreeable to his conscience."[144] Perhaps he had been hurriedly reeducated by his brethren in the constitutional convention.

The parallel inclination in New York and other states to allow only Protestants freedom of worship was repeated in Massachusetts.

The proposed Constitution of 1778, for example, would have provided: "The free exercise and enjoyment of religious profession and worship shall forever be allowed to every denomination of Protestants within this State." This was rejected by the people of Massachusetts.[145] The famous "Essex Result" drafted by Theophilus Parsons represented the views of the citizens in Essex County who objected to the proposed constitution because of its general vagueness. On the matter of religious freedom it declared that "the rights of conscience are not therein clearly defined and ascertained; and further, because the free exercise and enjoyment of religious worship is there said to be allowed to all the protestants of the State, when in fact, that free exercise and enjoyment is the natural and uncontrolable right of every member of the state."[146] Similarly, a letter in the *Boston Gazette* of September 6, 1779, demanded full civil liberties without religious qualification and complete freedom of conscience for all Christians."[147] When a state constitutional convention was called for Massachusetts in 1779, the people of Pittsfield instructed their delegates as follows:

> That every man has an unalienable right to enjoy his own opinions in matters or religion, and to worship God in that manner that is agreeable to his own sentiments without any control whatsoever, and that no particular mode or sect of religion ought to be established, but that every one be protected in the peaceable enjoyment of his religious persuasion and way of worship.[148]

In comparable language the people of Gorham (then in Massachusetts; now in Maine) instructed their delegates to the constitutional convention of 1779 to see "that no restriction be made on any profession of Christianity or denomination of Christians, but all equally entitled to protection of the laws."[149]

Although legal impediments to public worship — at least of Christians — were generally being removed during the period from independence to the Bill of Rights, there lingered some individual resistance to equal rights of worship for all. For example, in 1785 when it was announced in Philadelphia that a Protestant Episcopal Academy would soon be opened, opposition was soon expressed, apparently from Presbyterian sources. To this opposition a thorough defense was published which, in the words of Henry Muhlenberg, demonstrated that

> [A]ccording to the new form of government, every religious party has complete freedom to erect and develop its own schools; that for example the Quakers and Lutherans have had schools for fifty years,

which have not harmed, but rather benefited the republic; and, that, according to the new state constitution, no religious party may or can have a monopoly over the others.[150]

The years 1776 to 1789 were marked, then, in the American states by attempts to rid the states of the most hated aspects of religious establishment which infringed on religious liberty. Although perfect freedom was not everywhere available even by 1789, dissenters from the Anglican and Congregationalist churches generally succeeded in safeguarding their religious liberty. This was accomplished in many ways: by terminating legal obligations to support the state church; by securing recognition of their legal right to remain in the community regardless of their religious views; by ending all laws requiring dissenters to attend services of the Church Established; by securing equal opportunities and eliminating most of the preferences and advantages of the former state churches; by resisting attempts to establish Protestantism as the religion of the state; and by securing equal opportunity to worship publicly.

Because the legislators in the First Congress were men of the times and had participated in the molding of state policies throughout this period, it is reasonable to conclude, therefore, that the policies of their states on religious freedom would influence them in their task of achieving guarantees of religious liberty under the new Federal Government. As events related in the next chapters will indicate, the policies are of especial significance in an interpretation of the First Amendment.

Areas of Church-State Accommodation in America During the Period From Independence Until the Bill of Rights

Although the generation of the Founding Fathers opposed religious discrimination, evidence of the period 1776 to 1789 indicates that the American Founding Fathers approved government aid and encouragement to religious institutions in many ways. The period abounds in examples of accommodation of the interests of the church and the state. This may be termed a "nonestablishment" of religion to indicate the lack of prejudice to religious liberty. Because the representatives in the First Congress were well versed in public affairs these practices were surely known to them when they proposed the religion clauses of the First Amendment.

The most significant forms of governmental co-operation with religion were these:

a) Publicly owned lands were made available to religious faiths and to their affiliated religiously oriented educational institutions.

b) Public funds were provided for religious sects and to their church-related educational institutions.

c) Tax exemptions were given to religious denominations and to the affiliated religiously oriented educational institutions.

d) States aided in the financing of church construction as well as the erection and maintenance of church-related schools, by authorizing the conduct of lotteries by religious faiths.

e) Governmental units employed and paid chaplains in their conventions, legislatures, and armed forces; prayers were publicly read.

f) Christianity received protection in all the states through statutes punishing blasphemy.

g) Christianity received protection through statutes punishing those who labored on Sunday.

h) Governmental officials frequently proclaimed days of thanksgiving to the Deity, fasting, and prayer.

i) The state was generally agreeable to bestowing legal status and rights upon religious bodies through incorporation.

j) Ministers of religion were permitted to participate in governmental affairs.

The Grant of Government Land to Churches and Church-Related Educational Institutions

During the colonial period virtually all the colonies had given glebes to the churches even though they had been acquired from taxes imposed upon the entire community. Once independence was declared, the dissenters voiced their dissatisfaction. Thus, on October 24, 1776, the Virginia Legislature received a memorial from the Presbytery of Hanover stating that "the dissenters have borne the heavy burdens of purchasing glebes & supporting the established clergy," and requesting that the practice cease.[1] Nevertheless, the democratically elected Virginia Legislature agreed that such lands should be retained by the Episcopal Church. In October, 1776, the General Assembly of Virginia adopted a statute to the effect that "there shall in all time coming be saved and reserved to the use of the church by law established the several tracts of glebe land already purchased," as well as the other properties of what was now coming to be known as the Protestant Episcopal Church.[2] There is evidence that the State of Virginia also granted land to church-operated colleges and academies during the period of 1776 to 1789.[3] With such a heritage, therefore, it is likely that the representatives of Virginia in the First Congress were cognizant of the willingness of their constituents to have the government encourage the public institution of religion by grants of land.

It would also seem probable that representatives of other states would have been similarly affected for there is evidence from a number of states that during the period from 1776 to 1789 the people were willing to have the state aid these public institutions by the grant of land. In South Carolina, as in Virginia, glebe lands had been given by the government to the Anglican Church during colonial times. Title in the church was confirmed by the 1778 Constitution of South Carolina which provided that "the churches, chapels, parsonages, glebes, and all other property now belonging to any societies of the Church of England, or any other religious societies, shall remain and be secured to them forever."[4] The Legislature of that state on a number of later occasions passed acts granting to churches lands that had, or would have, escheated to the state.[5] This action would seem to be in the nature of a grant since the title was in the state due to a failure of heirs to take the land. In Georgia, too, tax funds had been used in colonial times to provide glebe lands for the Anglican Church; and title in that church to these lands was recognized by the Georgia Legislature.[6] A number of academies maintained by religious organizations in Massachusetts were the recipients of state aid, mostly in the form of grants of land.[7] New Castle Academy, a Presbyterian institution, received land on June 13, 1782, under grant from the state of Delaware.[8] Similarly, the Pennsylvania Legislature extended aid to education by the grant of state-owned lands. In 1786, for example, the Pennsylvania legislature granted ten thousand acres of land to the trustees of Dickinson College; whose trustees were required to be clergymen "of any Christian denomination."[9] The following year the same Legislature granted ten thousand acres of public land to the Academy of the Protestant Episcopal Church in the city of Philadelphia.[10] Also in 1787, another ten thousand acres of state land were granted to the German College and Charity School in the borough and county of Lancaster, which institution was under the management of Lutheran, Reformed, and Calvinist trustees.[11] The next year the Pennsylvania Legislature aided the Lutherans in operating their charity school in Philadelphia by the grant of five thousand acres of land.[12] In 1789 the German Reformed Congregation in the city of Philadelphia was the recipient of a similar legislative grant of five thousand acres for the use of their free school.[13]

The New York Legislature in 1786 passed an act providing that the suveyor-general should mark out in all the unappropriated lands in the state one lot for "gospel and schools," and that the lots so marked shall be "reserved for and applied to, promoting the gospel and a public school" in these townships. The law further provided that letters patent could be given to Samuel Kirkland "in trust for any minister of the gospel, who may hereafter for the time then being be employed by the Oneida Indians to preach the gospel among them."[14] As in the other states, the people of Connecticut were equally willing to aid religion by the grants of public land. Thus, in 1785–1786, the Connecticut Legislature provided that proceeds from the sale of land in the Western Reserve be divided among the various churches, at the same time reserving in each township 500 acres for the support of the ministry, 500 acres for the support of schools, and 240 acres of "good ground" to the first minister to settle there.[15]

While the states were aiding religious institutions with the grant of public land, so also was the Continental Congress, the then central organ of government for the Confederation. On May 9, 1787,

Samuel Parsons petitioned Congress to sell certain lands in each township of the Northwest Territory.[16] The memorial was referred to a committee, which included James Madison. On July 23, 1787, the Congress authorized the sale of the land with the following provision attached: "The lot N29 in each township or fractional part of a township to be given perpetually for the purposes of religion."[17] It is interesting to note that there is no record of dissent by Madison.[18]

The Donation of Public Funds to Churches and Church-Related Schools

The Revolutionary War Years had produced in Virginia, as elsewhere, a certain amount of dissolute behavior. Consequently, the leading citizens saw the need for more, rather than less, religion in the life of the community. Accordingly, as early as October 22, 1779, the Virginia House received a petition from the people of Essex reading: "The great confusion and disorder that hath arisen, and is likely to continue in this county on account of Religion, since the Old Establishment has been interrupted, convinces us of the great and absolute necessity there is for the Legislative body of this State, to take it under their most serious consideration. . . . A general Assessment for the support of Religious worship would be most agreeable to your petitioners."[19] The Legislature did not respond with a general assessment for religious purposes. Nevertheless, accommodation of the interests of the church and the state was a regular feature of life in Virginia. One particular place where the interests united was in providing for relief of the poor. Until 1784 the vestries in Virginia, which were required by law to be composed of Episcopalians, continued to perform their public duty of poor relief by levying taxes upon members of all denominations.[20]

In 1784 the Committee of Religion of the Virginia Legislature reported out a considerable number of petitions from the people on behalf of a general assessment.[21] Typical was the petition from Amelia County which read:

> That your Petitioners have with much concern observed a general Declension of Religion for a number of years past, occassioned in Part, we conceive by the late war, but chiefly by its not being duly aided and patronized by the Civil Power; that should it decline with nearly the same rapidity in the Future, your Petitioners apprehend consequences dangerous, if not fatal to the Strength and Stability of Civil Government. . . . Were all Sense of Religion rooted out of the Minds of Men, scarce anything would be left on which human laws would take hold. . . . Your Petitioners therefore think that those who

legislate, not only have a right . . . but as they wish to promote the
Virtue and Happiness of their Constituents and the Good People of
the State in general; as they wish well to the strength and Stability
of Government, they ought to aid and patronize Religion. . . . And
as every man of the State partakes of the Blessings of Peace and
Order . . . [so] every man should contribute as well to the support
of Religion, as that of Civil Government; nor has he any Reason to
complain of this, as an Encroachment upon his religious liberty, if
he is permitted to worship God according to the dictates of his
Conscience.[22]

However, in the language of James Madison, "the friends of the
measure did not choose to try their strength in the House."[23] In
October of that year the Presbyterians sent a communication to the
General Assembly indicating their acceptance of the principle of
general assessments.[24] Madison wrote to James Monroe on April
12, 1785, telling how the Episcopalians and the clergy of the Presbyterian Church were in favor of such a general assessment. The
Presbyterians, in Madison's words, "seem as ready to set up an
establishment which is to take them in as they were to pull down
that which shut them out."[25] Madison added: "I do not know a
more shameful contrast than might be found between their memorials
on the latter and former occasion."[26] Madison's "Memorial and Remonstrance" was highly influential in stirring opposition to the
proposed bill. This came largely from the Baptists, from Presbyterian
laity, and from the few Catholics and Quakers in the state,[27] all
of whom feared another attempt to finance the Episcopal faith. The
proposal was defeated in the Assembly,[28] although there were a great
many leading Virginians who favored the bill. Richard Henry Lee,
for one, wrote to James Madison on November 26, 1784:

[T]he experience of all times shows Religion to be the guardian of
morals — and he must be a very inattentive observer in our Country,
who does not see that avarice is accomplishing the destruction of
religion, for want of a legal obligation to contribute something to its
support. The Declaration of Rights, it seems to me, rather contends
against forcing modes of faith and forms of worship, than against
compelling contributions for the support of religion in general.[29]

George Washington wrote to George Mason in 1785: "Although
no man's sentiments are more opposed to any kind of restraint upon
religious principles than mine, yet I confess, I am not among the
number of those who are so alarmed at making men pay toward
the support of that which they profess."[30] John Marshall, Patrick
Henry, Edmund Pendleton, Robert Carter Nicholas, Joseph Jones,
Benjamin Harrison, Richard Bland Lee, Philip Barbour, and Henry

Tazewell were all in favor of the assessment.[31] Although the Virginia
Legislature thus refused to aid religion generally, the same Assembly
did indicate its willingness in 1787 and 1790 to aid in the financing
of the Transylvania Seminary by providing it surveyor's fees from
the Kentucky District.[32]

During colonial times, Maryland had a long record of church
taxes to support the Anglican communion.[33] When Marylanders
adopted their Declaration of Rights in 1776, they found it quite
consistent with their understanding of religious liberty to provide
that:

> [T]he legislature may, in their discretion, lay a general and equal
> tax for the support of the Christian religion, leaving to each indi-
> vidual the power of appointing the payment over of the money
> collected from him, to the support of any place of worship or minis-
> ter, or for the benefit of the poor of his own denomination, or the
> poor in general of any particular county.[34]

The vote in the Maryland Constitutional Convention was 48 to 18
in favor of this clause. Among those of the majority were Charles
Carroll of Carrollton, Samuel Chase, William Paca, and Charles
Carroll the barrister.[35] In 1782 a considerable number of Episcopal vestries throughout the state petitioned the Legislature to lay
a common and equal tax for the support of religion. The requests
were not honored. In May of the following year, Governor William
Paca recommended that the Legislature consider providing for adequate support of the Christian religion.[36] Accepting this overture on
January 8, 1784, the Maryland House of Delegates resolved that it
was advisable and proper for the General Assembly to levy a tax
for the support of all Christian societies in the state, with preference for none.[37]

Non-Episcopalians, who well remembered the use of funds in
colonial Maryland to favor the Established Church, were suspicious
of Episcopal desire for state funds. In a letter of February 27,
1785, to an English friend, John Carroll reported that the Presbyterians, Methodists, and Quakers in the state had misgivings that
the Maryland Declaration of Rights provision would be used primarily to aid the Protestant Episcopal Church. Because of this
possibility, Carroll said that the Catholics would join in opposing
the contemplated law which would levy a general tax for the support of religion. "We have all smarted heretofore under the lash of
an established church," he wrote, "and shall therefore be on our
guard against every approach to it."[38] The Reverend Patrick Allison,
pastor of the First Presbyterian Church in Baltimore, was outspoken

in his opposition to any legislation that seemed intended to finance the Episcopal Church alone. He recalled how "the land had been previously disgraced and distressed by a most absurb and iniquitous religious establishment," and pointed out that "former legislatures have even dared to declare one Christian denomination established in our ill-fated land."[39] *The Maryland Gazette or Baltimore Advertiser* during early 1785 carried many letters and articles which expressed opposition to the bill.[40] The proposed enactment was soundly defeated later in 1785.[41] Although there was no general aid to religion in that state during the immediate post-Revolutionary period, there were instances of state financial aid to both churches and church-related schools. Thus in 1784 the state had given to an Episcopal institution — Washington College — £1250, the marriage license fees received by state officials on the eastern shore, and sundry other license fees and fines.[42] Again, on May 27, 1788, the Maryland General Assembly had appropriated £742 for the building of a church in Annapolis, partly in compensation for materials taken by the Council of Safety during the war.[43] There is further evidence of grants to other institutions of learning which, though not denominationally controlled, were strongly religious in orientation.[44]

In the 1784 Georgia Assembly a bill was introduced to promote religion and piety by granting aid in the construction of churches and schools.[45] It was not enacted during that session, but the following year the General Assembly by a vote of 43 to 5 passed a similar measure entitled: "An act for the establishment and support of the public duties of religion."[46] This law declared the regular establishment and support of the Christian religion to be one of the most important objects of the Legislature. Whenever thirty heads of families in each county joined together, a minister was to be chosen by them, and four pence on every £100 of valuation of property owned by the church members was to be returned from the state general tax to the county for the support of religion.[47]

Throughout the period 1776 to 1789 there was a rather general belief in Massachusetts that the state could and should aid religion. In 1776 the Reverend Samuel West of Dartmouth had pointed out that laws for "maintaining public worship and decently supporting the teachers of religion [are] absolutely necessary for the well-being of society."[48] Four years later the Massachusetts Constitution of 1780 was ratified. It provided, in part: "As the happiness of a people, and the good order and preservation of civil government, essentially depend upon piety, religion and morality . . . the legislature shall from time to time authorize and require the several towns and parishes . . . to make suitable provision, at their own

expense, for the institution of the public worship of God."⁴⁹ Under
this Constitution an Act of 1786 authorized local communities to
grant and vote money for the settlement and maintenance of ministers and teachers of religion.⁵⁰ For many years thereafter, taxpayers
who belonged to no recognized church were required to pay for
the support of the state Congregational Church.⁵¹ Furthermore, the
Massachusetts Legislature gave financial aid to a number of religious
academies during the last quarter of the eighteenth century.⁵²

The Established Church continued in Connecticut until 1818
and, throughout the period 1776 to 1789, all persons who could
not prove that they were contributing to other recognized churches
were taxed to provide the state with funds to finance the Congregationalist State Church.⁵³ If there was understandable opposition in
Connecticut during this period to financially favoring the Congregationalist Church, there was no outspoken opposition to the state
financing all religions. In the *Connecticut Courant* for September 11,
1788, for example, a writer suggested a solution to the church-
state dilemma. He wrote:

> Allow me to propose a general and equitable tax collected from all
> the rateable members of a state, for the support of the public teachers
> of religion, of all denominations, within the State. . . . Let a moderate
> poll tax be added to a tax of a specified sum on the pound, and levied
> on all the subjects of a state and collected with the public tax, and
> paid out to the public teachers of religion of the several denomina-
> tions in proportion to the number of polls or families, belonging to
> each respectively, or according to their estimates.
> 1. It would be equitable.
> 2. It would be for the good order of the civil state.
> 3. All ought to contribute to such a religious education of the people
>   as would conduce to civil order.
> 4. It would promote the peace in towns and societies.⁵⁴

This letter had wide circulation throughout the states and was reprinted fully in *The American Museum* of 1789.⁵⁵

Of especial interest are the practices of Rhode Island. This state
had no Established Church, but its various communities strongly
believed in the encouragement of religion. The town of Barrington,
for example, went so far, as to pay an official town minister from
public funds.⁵⁶ Schools were generally under the control of religious
organizations. The charter of Rhode Island College gave complete
control to members of the Baptist faith, but allowed representation
on the faculty to the Quakers, Congregationalists, and Episco-
palians.⁵⁷ Funds totaling £4280 were granted the College by the
town of Providence.⁵⁸ Elsewhere in New England, the establish-

ments survived in Vermont until 1807, in New Hampshire until 1819, and in Maine until 1820.

In the Middle States — New York, New Jersey, and Pennsylvania — there were no constitutional prohibitions upon state financial aid to religion or church-related schools without preference, albeit the available evidence does not justify a conclusion that such a practice flourished. The views of some citizens may have been reflected in an unsigned article entitled "On the Establishment of Free Schools in Philadelphia and Surrounding Counties," which appeared in *The American Museum* for 1787. After stating that the children in all the free schools should be "carefully instructed in the principles of the Christian religion," the author continued:

> [T]he children of parents of the same religious denomination should be educated together, in order that they may be instructed with the more ease in the principles and forms of their respective churches. By these means the schools will come more immediately under the inspection of the ministers of the city, and thereby religion and learning to be intimately connected. After the experience we have had of the advantages derived by the Friends, from connecting their schools and church together, in forming the morals of their youth, nothing further need be added in favour of this part of the plan.

> Fourthly, let the money raised by the support of these schools, be lodged in the hands of the city treasurer, to be appropriated in the following manner: let a certain number of persons of each religious society, be appointed trustees of the free schools of their respective churches; and let a draught, signed by the president of a quorum of these trustees be a voucher to the treasurer to issue three or four pounds a year for every scholar who is educated by them.[59]

It is clear that the "free schools" to be financed by state tax funds under this proposal were schools of "the respective churches."

During the post-Revolutionary years support of the public institutions of religion was recognized by South Carolina as a duty of the state.[60] In Charleston, an "Orphan House" was established with appropriations from the municipal treasury; appended to the home was a church where divine services were regularly held.[61] In Delaware there is no proof presently available that religious institutions were receiving state funds in the period 1776 to 1789. Such support is likely, however; for it is well established that at a later date the state was providing financial aid to "Sabbath schools" and other institutions of learning operated by various religions.[62]

Inasmuch as there was relatively little legislative aid to education prior to the American Revolution, it would seem appropriate to examine the reasons for the quantitative increase in the grants and appropriations to the schools. It should be noted that this aid was not given in order to initiate a system of public education as it is known today. During early years of independence there was no concept of state-supported, free public education.[63] The main reason for the increase seems to have been that the destruction of the schools in the Revolution required the states to revive the institutions of learning that had formerly served their citizens.[64]

Problems of establishment do not seem to have concerned the legislatures. Of course, the schools of the time differed from modern school systems in several ways. During this, as well as the colonial period, education was strictly local and generally private. Only a few schools were supported by taxation, and this was always local. Such schools were mostly located in New England, although other states did have some tax-supported paupers' schools.[65] Another difference was that these schools had retained the religious orientation that had been characteristic of education in the colonial period.[66] The curriculum emphasized the three R's and religion; ministers were frequently the teachers.[67] The tax-supported schools followed the pattern. And in New England, where the community was small and religiously homogeneous, the tax-supported school was in fact operated for the benefit of the Congregationalist church members with a large influence residing in the Congregationalist ministers.[68]

Thus it seems that the aid was extended without regard to the school's status as private or tax-supported. Of course, where there was an Established Church, eligibility for these grants could depend on the school's affiliation with the denomination or denominations that had been officially sanctioned by the legislature. But this distinction would seem to have been predicated upon the preference given to the Established Church and not upon status of the school as private or tax-supported. The important thing to the state legislatures was meeting the needs of education. As Edward W. Reisner observed:

> At a time before the distinction between public and private education had taken on a political significance, public funds were frequently used to aid private academies, even though maintained by religious denominations. At a time when educational destitution was the common condition, public authorities were favorable to any institution that provided the increase of educational facilities.[69]

There were also occasions when the legislative bodies would undertake to pay propagators of religion, such as missionaries. This occurred even where there was establishment of religion. Apparently the legislators believed that the appropriation of public funds to advance a public purpose concurrent with that of a religious institution was proper, desirable, and not a feature of the undesirable establishment of religion.

Even with the severely limited powers possessed by the Continental Congress from 1774 to 1788, there is evidence that this body was willing to use tax money to aid the public institutions of religion. For instance, as early as July 12, 1775, the Continental Congress appropriated $500 for "Dr. Wheelock's Seminary in New Hampshire" — later to become Dartmouth College. The next year the appropriation was repeated, and in 1780 the Congress granted $5000 to the same institution.[70] The *Journal of the Continental Congress* reported this minute for December 20, 1775: "Resolved, That orders be drawn on the Treasurers, in favor of the Rev. Mr. Elihu Spencer and the Rev. Mr. Alexander MacWhorter, who have undertaken to go to North Carolina, for the sum of one hundred and twenty dollars each, being three months' advance, they to be accountable."[71] The Congress undoubtedly hoped that these ministers would stir the revolutionary spirit of the North Carolinians, but the Reverend Spencer indicated he was to "preach and converse for some time among those people."[72] On another occasion, early in 1776, White Eyes, a Delaware chief, was introduced in the Continental Congress. The presiding officer responded with words of welcome: "We are pleased that the Delawares intend to embrace Christianity. We will send you, according to your desire, a minister and a schoolmaster to instruct you in the principles of religion and other parts of useful knowledge."[73] Apparently in response to this promise, the Continental Congress authorized the Commissioners for Indian Affairs to employ "for reasonable salaries, a minister of the gospel" to work among the Delaware Indians preaching and teaching.[74] Later on, however, the congressional attitude changed. When, on June 1, 1785, the Roman Catholic inhabitants of New York presented a petition for an Indian mission to the Continental Congress, it was dismissed because "matters of this kind being more proper in the opinion of your Committee for the consideration of the State in which the petitioners may reside."[75] The probable reason for the rejection lies in the fact that the Congress at that time could no longer command the states' allegiance as it had in time of war. Moreover, it was during this period that the Congress was most aware of its limited governing powers. The Annapolis Convention was soon to confirm the fact of congressional apprehension.

Tax Exemptions

Since tax exemptions are generally considered a matter of legislative grace rather than a right, their existence is evidence of a positive legislative effort to aid a religious organization in serving the public interest. The existence of state tax exemptions for churches and church-related educational institutions during 1776–1789 does not appear with any frequency in the statutes, charters, and other available public records of the period. The explanation is probably — as Zollman theorizes — that in all states having established churches after the Revolution, the properties of the state church were in effect public property and "could not but be exempt from taxation."[76] However, even in the states with established churches, tax-exemption statutes have been discovered. For example, from 1702 until 1821 Connecticut law provided that

> all lands, tenements and hereditaments, and other estates that either had been given or hereafter to be given and granted by the General Assembly, colony, or by any town and village or particular person or persons for the maintenance of the ministry of the Gospel . . . school of learning . . . be exempted out of the general list of estates, and free from the payment of rates.[77]

Furthermore, a Massachusetts statute of 1781 imposing a poll tax, real and personal property tax, provided, "nevertheless, that the following persons, viz. settled Ministers of the Gospel are not to be assessed for their polls or Estates."[78]

Rhode Island[79] policies on taxation were in accord with those of its neighbors. In 1764 the charter of Rhode Island College had exempted all of its property from taxation.[80] Beginning in 1789 the General Assembly exempted all real estate granted or purchased for religious or educational uses.[81] When an excise tax was placed on horses and carriages in 1786, ministers, instructors in colleges, and masters of grammar schools were declared exempt from the tax.[82]

The general policy of exemptions was evidenced also in the South. Virginia records indicate that in 1777 the Legislature of that state exempted religious societies and educational institutions from taxes.[83] On April 12, 1787, it was reported in the South Carolina press that clergymen were exempted from a Charleston tax on occupations and professions.[84] Seven days later, the press carried language of a state tax law exempting "churches or buildings for divine worship or free schools" from taxation.[85] The South Carolina Legislature, the following year, exempted from taxation "lands whereon any churches or other buildings for divine worship, or free schools, are erected."[86] Similarly, the Georgia press in 1789 indicated that "all lands or other property vested in commissioners or trustees for public use," which included religious and charitable uses, should not be subject to taxation.[87]

Authorization of Lotteries to Finance Churches and Schools

The people of a number of American states during the 1776 to 1789 period believed it was proper for the states to aid the cause of religion and religious education by authorizing churches and church-related schools to conduct lotteries to produce funds for building and maintenance. The significance of the practice lies in the fact that the conducting of lotteries was a privilege not generally available to citizens; hence, such legislative interest and favor was a form of governmental aid to religion and church-related education.

During the 1780's there were a number of legislative authorizations by Virginia to both churches and church-related academies to finance their operations by lotteries.[88] Churches in New Jersey, throughout the same period, petitioned the New Jersey Legislature for authority to conduct lotteries,[89] and the Legislature generally acquiesced. Thus, on March 15, 1786, the Legislature authorized the Presbyterian Church in New Brunswick and the First Presbyterian Church in Elizabethtown to conduct lotteries.[90] The Pennsylvania Legislature was as ready to aid both churches and religiously oriented educational institutions by permitting lotteries.[91]

There were relatively fewer lotteries at this time authorized by New England legislatures for the financing of churches. It is known that in May of 1787 the Congregational Church of Greenwich was granted permission by the Connecticut Legislature to conduct a lottery to build a parsonage.[92] Two years later, the permission was renewed.[93] There is also evidence of a request by the town of Middleboro to the General Court of Massachusetts in 1784 for permission to conduct a lottery to support the minister, but no action appears to have been taken.[94] The paucity of lotteries in some states is to be explained in part by the Puritan opposition to all forms of gambling, but even more so by the fact that in all New England states but Rhode Island there was full public support of religion. In Rhode Island local communities might make provision for financial support, but the state legislature often supplemented the local efforts. For example, the General Assembly authorized lotteries for the Baptist Church at Warren in 1767 and for the Baptist Church at East Greenwich in 1774.[95] There is also evidence in the New England states of legislative authorization to denominational educational institutions to conduct lotteries. For example, Harvard College was a frequent beneficiary of such lotteries.[96] In 1767 and in 1796 lotteries were authorized for Rhode Island College, which was under the control of the Baptists of that state. And, in 1791, after several years of effort, Congregationalist-controlled Dartmouth College persuaded the New Hampshire Legislature to authorize the conduct of a lottery.[97]

Chaplains; Public Prayers

The attitude of the American Founding Fathers favoring accommodation of church and state is further illustrated by the general practice in both the federal and state governments of utilizing and compensating chaplains. Chaplains of various faiths regularly served in constitutional conventions, legislative assemblies, the armed forces, and hospitals.

In the colonies' earliest deliberative body, prayers were a regular feature. In 1774 when Caleb Cushing moved that the sessions of the first Continental Congress be opened with prayer, there were some objections, primarily on the ground of the diversity of religious sentiments of the members. To these objections Samuel Adams responded: "I am not a bigot. I can hear a prayer from a man of piety and virtue, who is at the same time a friend of his country." Adams then diplomatically proceeded to nominate not a Congregationalist but an Anglican clergyman, Jacob Duche, who was chosen.[98] Thus, the Continental Congress opened on September 6, 1774, with a prayer by Reverend Duche, following the resolution of the previous day.[99] Later events were to prove that Duche was hardly "a friend of this country": he became a Tory. However, before his change in allegiance became known he resigned his post on October 17, 1776, and on that date the Congress "Resolved, that Mr. President be desired to return the thanks of this House to Mr. Duche, for the devout and acceptable manner in which he discharged his duty during the time he officiated as Chaplain to it; and that one hundred and fifty dollars be presented to him as an acknowledgment for the House for his services."[100] To remedy the absence of a chaplain, a resolution of the Congress of December 21, 1776, authorized that two chaplains be appointed.[101] The *Journal* of the Congress notes the election of Reverend Daniel Jonas as chaplain in 1784,[102] and in 1788 provision was made by the Continental Congress for an annual salary for the chaplains "not to exceed three hundred dollars."[103]

Chaplains for various troops and hospitals had been named by the Continental Congress. Thus, on July 17, 1778, the Congress "Resolved, that the Reverend James Francis Armstrong be appointed Chaplain of the Second Brigade of Maryland Forces."[104] On another occasion the Continental Congress elected the Presbyterian minister, Elihu Spencer, chaplain for the hospital in the Middle Department.[105] The states joined in providing chaplains for the troops during the Revolution and paying them out of public funds.[106] In 1776 the Reverend Andrew Hunter was appointed by New Jersey as chaplain for three battalions of New Jersey Troops.[107]

The state conventions and legislatures regularly utilized and remunerated chaplains during the period from independence until the Bill of Rights. The Maryland Convention of 1776 for instance resolved that a certain Mr. Lendrum read prayers before the convention.[108] On July 17, 1776, the Pennsylvania Convention, assembled in Philadelphia,

> Resolved, That the Reverend Mr. William White be requested to perform Divine Service To-morrow Morning Before this Convention, that we may jointly offer up our Prayers to Almighty God to afford us his Divine Grace and Assistance in the important and arduous Task committed to us: and to offer up our Praises and Thanksgiving for the manifold Mercies and the Peculiar Interposition of his special Providence in Behalf of these injured, oppressed and insulted United States.[109]

The Virginia House of Delegates in 1777 employed the Reverend James Madison, a Protestant Episcopal clergyman, to read prayers to them every morning. The practice of paying chaplains was continued by that body throughout the century.[110] The New York Convention, called on June 17, 1788, to deliberate ratification of the United States Constitution, ordered that "the Business of this Convention be opened every Morning with Prayer, and that Mr. Duane and Mr. G. Livingston be a committee to wait on the Gentlemen of the Clergy, in the Precinct of Poughkeepsie, and request them to make such arrangements among themselves, that one of them may attend daily for that purpose."[111] The following year, on July 7, 1789, the Legislature of New York "ordered, that a committee wait on the Clergy of the City of Albany, and request of them to make such arrangements among themselves, as that one of them may attend, to open the business of the house each morning, with prayers."[112] Although Rhode Island did not employ chaplains in its Legislature, the General Assembly of that state evidently thought that public prayer was a practice which should be encouraged. On December 7, 1780, and on November 28, 1782, the General Assembly proclaimed "a day of public prayer and thanksgiving . . . to celebrate the praises of our Divine Benefactor."[113]

New Jersey presents an extensive picture of the practice of public prayer. The provincial Congress of New Jersey, which sat from the fourth to the twenty-eighth of October, 1775, had their daily sessions opened with prayer; a minister of the Presbyterian Church in Trenton, the Reverend Spencer, was the first official chaplain of that body.[114] The 1776 New Jersey Convention was opened with prayer on June 11, and the following day it is noted that proceedings were "opened with prayer, pursuant to the standing order of the house."[115] Similarly, when the New Jersey Convention — called to ratify the United States Constitution — assembled on December 11, 1787, the sessions were opened by the prayers of Reverend James Armstrong, pastor of the Presbyterian Church in Trenton.[116]

There were other occasions for prayer. When the surrender of Cornwallis was announced in Trenton on October 27, 1781, the governor, Council, Assembly, and citizens went in procession to the Presbyterian church where Reverend Spencer preached a sermon.[117] Again, on April 15, 1783, when peace with Great Britain was concluded, a divine service was conducted by Dr. Spencer at the Trenton Court House.[118] Six years later the same Legislature addressed President Washington as follows:

> We have reason to adore the Divine Providence, in raising up for us a Leader and Ruler, so perfectly suited to our situation and circumstances, and sincerely believe, that great and important as your Services have been you will not derive more honor therefrom, than from your humility and self-denial, in modestly ascribing all, as you have constantly done, to the power and wisdom of the Most High. We earnestly Pray, that the same kind Providence, which hath conducted you with so much honor to yourself, and such unspeakable felicity to the Public Office, at last crown you with that palm of Victory, which is promised to those, who by Divine assistance shall finally prove to be more than conquerors.[119]

Shortly after independence, the State of Maryland had promulgated a form of public prayer which so disturbed the clergy of the Church of England that many of them left the state.[120]

In the federal constitutional convention in Philadelphia, according to James Madison, "Dr. Franklin made the proposition for a religious service in the Convention. . . ." Franklin moved that "henceforth prayers imploring the assistance of Heaven, and its blessings on our deliberations, be held in this Assembly every morning before we proceed to business, and that one or more of the Clergy of this City be requested to officiate in that Service."[121] Franklin had prefaced his motion with the remarks:

> In this situation of this Assembly (which had been for some time deadlocked in the struggle between the small and large states), groping as it were in the dark to find political truth, and scarce able to distinguish it when presented to us, how has it happened, Sir, that we have not hitherto once thought of humbly applying to the Father of lights to illuminate our understandings? In the beginning of the contest with G. Britain, when we were sensible of danger we had daily prayer in this room for the divine protection. — Our prayers, Sir, were heard, and they were graciously answered. . . . And have we now forgotten that powerful friend? or do we imagine that we no longer need his assistance? I have lived, Sir, a long time, and the longer I live, the more convincing proofs I see of this truth — *that God Governs in the affairs of men.* . . . I also believe that without his concerning aid we shall succeed in this political building no better than the Builders of Babel: We shall be divided by our little partial local interests, our projects will be confused, and we ourselves shall become a reproach and a bye word down to future ages. And what is worse, mankind may hereafter from this unfortunate instance, despair of establishing Governments by Human wisdom and leave it to chance, war and conquest.[122]

Franklin's motion was seconded by Mr. Sharman,[123] although the records of the Convention indicate no vote was ever had on the motion.[124] Shortly thereafter Mr. Randolph of Virginia proposed that a sermon be preached on the fourth of July "and thenceforward prayers be used in the Convention every morning." Franklin seconded this motion, but there seems to have been no vote on it.[125]

Aid to Christianity by Punishment of Blasphemers

Blasphemy had been a serious offense throughout the colonies. The use of the power of the political state to protect Christianity, the dominant faith, from the abuse of those who would deny the divinity of Christ was a form of aid to the Christian religion. It must be noted, however, that the mere presence of the laws on the statute books gives no indication of the extent of their enforcement. In early Maryland, law prescribed that blasphemers were to have their tongues cut out for the first offence, a "B" was burned into their foreheads for the second misdeed, and they were hanged for the third offense.[126] The Maryland Toleration Act of 1649 had provided that anyone who would "blaspheme God, that is, to curse him, or shall deny our Savior, Jesus Christ," shall be punishable with death, and confiscation of all his property.[127] This law continued in Maryland throughout the entire period 1776 to 1789, and, indeed, harsh blasphemy laws prevailed until 1819. Throughout the period from independence until the Bill of Rights, there was still in force a 1700 Pennsylvania law which imposed punishment upon anyone who would "wilfully, pre-meditatedly, and despitefully blaspheme, or speak lightly or profanely of Almighty God, Christ Jesus, the Holy Spirit or the Scriptures of Truth." According to the Supreme Court of that state, this was still the law in 1824.[128]

Under the influence of the tolerant spirit of the times the public attitude toward blasphemy began to mellow. At one time, anyone questioning the validity of fundamental doctrines might be accused of either heresy or blasphemy. By 1783, however, Ezra Stiles of Connecticut could depict an altogether different situation. In his sermon, "The United States Elevated to Glory and Honor," he wrote:

> [I]t begins to be a growing idea that it is mighty indifferent, forsooth, not only whether a man be of this or the other religious sect, but whether he be of any religion at all. And that truly deists, and men of indifferentism to all religion, are the most suitable persons for civil office and most proper to hold the reigns of government. . . . I wish we had not to fear that a neglect of religion was coming to be the road to preferment.[129]

Like many of his brethren, Stiles regarded Deism as a particular threat to traditional religion. However, unlike some, he did not believe that the way to meet the threat of Deism or indifferentism was to suppress religious discussion by tightening laws against blasphemy. His solution was free and open discourse:

> Religion may here [in America] receive its . . . most liberal, and impartial examination. Religious liberty is peculiarly friendly to fair and generous disquisition. Here Deism will have its full chance; nor need libertines more to complain of being overcome by any weapons but the gentle, the powerful ones of argument and truth. Revelation will be found to stand the test to the ten thousandth examination.[130]

The new attitude is probably reflected in the change of the Pennsylvania law. A 1786 revision provided

> That if any person of the age of sixteen years and upwards . . . shall profanely swear or curse by the name of God, Christ Jesus, or the Holy Ghost, every person so offending . . . shall . . . pay . . . five shillings for every profane oath or curse . . . shall be committed . . . not exceeding twenty-four hours for every such offense.[131]

As events of the "Great Revival" toward the end of the century were to prove, neither Stiles' faith nor that of the citizens of Pennsylvania had been misplaced.[132]

Sentiment frequently favored punishment of those who blasphemed the Founder of Christianity. At the end of this period, a bill to punish blasphemy was introduced in the New Hampshire Legislature. A Reverend Weldman urged that any person "speaking disrespectfully of any part of the Bible should have his tongue bored through with a hot iron."[133] John Sherburne did not consider such punishment sufficient and demanded the death penalty for all blasphemers. The proposal for such punishments was defeated largely through the efforts of William Plumer.[134] In 1788, Oliver Ellsworth of Connecticut, who represented that state in the Federal Constitutional Convention and the First Congress, and later became Chief Justice of the United States wrote that civil authority has the right to pass laws against "blasphemy and professed atheism."[135]

Aid to Religion Through Sunday Laws

From independence until the Bill of Rights, there was much interest in encouraging religion by laws intended to assure that the Sabbath day of the majority would be reserved as a day of rest with adequate time for worship services. Thus, in 1780, both Houses of the Massachusetts Assembly promised the governor that in the new Constitution of that year they would "make such additions to or amendments in [the law] as may be necessary and consistent with personal liberty, for the due observance of that day which the Supreme Being hath consecrated to his more immediate worship and service."[136] Evidence that theocratic considerations might enter into the Sunday Laws is seen by the passage of an act two years later whereby Massachusetts imposed a fine of ten shillings upon anyone who for one month without reason absented himself from church on the Lord's Day.[137] In other states, however, the trend was to replace older-type laws with laws prohibiting and punishing other than religious activities on Sundays.

The newer variety of the Sunday Law of the period is well illustrated by a New Jersey act which provided "That drunkenness, cursing, swearing or breaking the Lord's Day, by doing any ordinary work or labour thereon, excepting works of necessity and mercy, shall be punishable. . . ."[138] In the New York Senate on March 10, 1786, a special committee referred to such laws as a complement to the blasphemy laws designed to "make effectual [the] due observance of the Lord's Day." The report was presented by Phillip Schuyler, soon destined to represent New York in the Senate of the First Congress.[139]

In 1785, the same year that Virginia enacted "A Bill for Establishing Religious Freedom," James Madison presented to the Virginia legislators "A Bill for Punishing . . . Sabbath Breakers." The bill provided:

> If any person on Sunday shall himself be found labouring at his own or any other trade or calling, or shall employ his apprentices, servants or slaves in labour, or other business, except it be in the ordinary household offices of daily necessity, or other work of necessity or charity, he shall forfeit the sum of ten shillings for every such offence, deeming every apprentice, servant, or slave so employed, and every day he shall be so employed as constituting a distinct offence.[140]

This was passed by the Virginia Legislature the following year.[141] It remained the law during the time that Madison worked for the First Amendment in the Congress of the United States. Apparently such governmental accommodation to the interests of the Christian religion was deemed both good social policy and also constitutional under the state charter by James Madison and his fellow Virginians. Most other states enacted similar legislation[142] which was often enforced during the period concerned.[143]

Although probably less effective than the colonial laws punishing citizens who did not attend Sunday services of the Established Church, nevertheless, during the early period of independence, Sunday laws were state efforts to encourage "due observance of that day" and an aid to religion or to those faiths honoring it as the Sabbath.

Days of Thanksgiving to the Deity, Fasting and Prayer

During the American Revolution the public authorities frequently encouraged appeals to the Deity by officially announcing days of fasting and prayer.[144] July 20, 1775, seems to be the first day of general fast proclaimed for America. This day had been officially proclaimed by the Continental Congress as "a day of public humiliation, fasting and prayer."[145] The next year the same Congress ordered that May 17, 1776, be set aside as a day of prayer and fasting throughout the land.[146] In November of the same year, John Witherspoon, the eminent president of Princeton, was appointed chairman of a committee of the Congress to recommend a day of fasting and prayer. His proposal read: "[I]t becomes all public bodies, as well as private persons, to reverence the Providence of God. . . ." Later the president of the Continental Congress, John Jay, proclaimed

October 8, 1778, as a day of fast and prayer to "Almighty God . . . to avert the calamities."[147] The Continental Congress, furthermore, suspended its deliberations on Good Fridays.[148] When Thomas Jefferson was governor of Virginia, he issued proclamations, such as the one of November 11, 1779, appointing days "of public and solemn thanksgiving and prayer to Almighty God."[149] On April 5, 1782, Governor William Livingston of New Jersey proclaimed a day of prayer for the last Thursday in April, "thereby recommending it to the Ministers of the Gospel, of every denomination therein, to perform Divine Services."[150] Days of public prayer and thanksgiving were also promulgated by the governors of New Jersey and on November 13, 1789, the Legislature resolved to have such a proclamation "printed in handbills at the expense of the State and distributed. . . ."[151]

Although in the next century there was some unwillingness by Presidents Jefferson and Madison to use their office to issue proclamations appointing days of prayer of thanksgiving there is no evidence during the period 1776 to 1789 of objections — official or private — to setting aside days for petitioning or thanking God.

State Incorporation of Churches

It is difficult today to look upon state incorporation of a church as providing such affirmative aid to religion as to bring about an establishment.[152] But it must be recalled that the dissenting churches were having difficulties with the trustee system of maintaining their property and funds. It would seem, therefore, that an inevitable step toward disestablishment would have included conferring equal and full property-holding rights on all churches; but this was not true in many of the colonies. To understand the resistance to the grant of corporate power to a church it is necessary to recall, first, that, during the colonial period, charters were granted rarely even to business institutions;[153] second, that the corporation was a creature of the state which breathed fictitious life into it;[154] third, that frequently under an establishment, corporate status had been a special privilege granted to the state church and denied to others; fourth, that often these corporate powers had carried with them the power to tax — so that these corporations were more like a closed municipal corporation rather than a business corporation whose interest in corporate capacity is continuity of a legal existence;[155] and, last, that a church which could hold property in its own name might become an "endowed church" and acquire too much power.

Opposition to incorporation was especially strong in Virginia, where the members of the non-Anglican faiths viewed governmental incorporation of the Anglican Church as an important and distasteful aspect of an establishment. From the privileged position of the Anglicans under the establishment the citizens generalized inversely that the civil power should treat all religions alike by doing as little as possible for any of them and by forcing all to conform to one procedure.[156] This meant that the state should grant corporate status to *no* religion. Confusion over the distinction between a corporation with the power to tax, as the former parishes and possessed in the manner of a modern municipal corporation, and the private corporation seems implicit. It was probably as a result of this kind of thinking that on August 5, 1786, the General Committee of the Baptists of Virginia resolved to draw up petitions to the General Assembly praying for an end to the incorporation act.[157] The campaign bore early fruit: the same year the Virginia Legislature repealed the act incorporating the Protestant Episcopal Church.[158]

In 1792 the Legislature struck another blow at the churches by repealing the statutes which allowed unincorporated charities to receive charitable bequests.[159] The effect of the enactment was to reinstate the old legal rule that a devise or bequest was void unless the claimant could be ascertained with definiteness. Since the church was not considered a legal entity but only an association of ever changing membership, a devise or bequest to a church would fail for lack of certainty. This harsh rule of law was enforced in other jurisdictions[160] as well as in Virginia. Although the courts avoided holding that the gifts were void because they were made to a religious group, that was the practical effect of the rule. In Virginia it seems that such a policy was actually intended by the legislature. In the case of *Gallego's Executors v. Attorney General,* which involved a devise of land to the members of the Roman Catholic Church in Richmond, the president of the Virginia Court of Appeals, Henry Saint George Tucker, made a lengthy exposition of the attitude of the legislature at the time of repeal.

No man at all acquainted with [the] course of legislation in Virginia, can doubt, for a moment, [the] *decided hostility* of the legislative power to religious incorporations. Its jealousy of the possible inter-ference of religious establishments in matters of government, if they are permitted to accumulate large possessions, as the church has been prone to do elsewhere, is doubtless at the bottom of this feeling. The legislature knows . . . that wealth is power. Hence the provision in the bill of rights; hence, the solemn protest of the act on the sub-ject of religious freedom; hence, the repeal of the act incorporating the episcopal church, and of that other act which invested the trustees of religious societies with power to manage their property; hence too, in part, the law for the sale of the glebe lands; hence the tenacity with which applications for permission to take property in a corporate character (even the necessary ground for churches and graveyards) have been refused. The legislature seems to have been fearful, that the grant of any privilege, however trivial, might serve but as an entering wedge to greater demands. . . .[161]

These feelings persisted for many years in Virginia, and ultimately a ban upon legislative incorporation of "any church or religious denomination" appeared in the State's Constitution.[162] When Madison became president, this background may have influenced him to veto congressional incorporation of churches.[163]

Such absolute objections to incorporating religious bodies were limited to Virginia, although for some years after independence the states that continued their Established Churches manifested some reluctance to incorporate other faiths. Maryland was willing to confirm the Anglicans in their rights to the glebes in the Bill of Rights of 1776[164] and to grant corporate status on a grudging basis. Apparently motivated by fear of an endowed church, the thirty-fourth paragraph of the Bill of Rights had imposed a mortmain policy on transfers of property to unincorporated churches. All gifts, sales, legacies, or bequests devised for the support of religion (except where less than two acres of land were involved) were declared void unless it was made with "leave of the legislature."[165] Special charters were granted from time to time,[166] but the repeated efforts of the Roman Catholics had all ended in failure. The reason for this failure, according to John Carroll, was that sectarian politicians were attempting to confiscate ex-Jesuit properties then in the hands of trustees. These politicians contended that inasmuch as ministers of other faiths were maintained by free contributions of their flocks, so should the clergy of the Catholic Church. The land, they maintained, should, therefore, be declared escheated to the state since there was a failure of the purpose of the trust.[167] In contrast to the Virginia practice, the preamble of the 1787 Delaware law which constituted religious societies as bodies corporate and political declared: "This General Assembly, considering it their duty to countenance and encourage virtue and religion, by every means in their power, and in the most expeditious manner, desire that it may be enacted. . . ."[168]

In New York the Legislature incorporated the Reformed Protestant Dutch Church of Tappon on February 25, 1783, and on March 17, 1784, the Reformed Protestant Dutch Church of New York City.[169] Then, on April 6, 1784, the New York Legislature enacted a general law "to enable all the religious denominations in this State to appoint trustees who shall be a body corporate."[170] The significance of these general incorporation laws in the fight against establishment should not be minimized. For the first time religions other than the established Church were given legal status and legal rights. This marked the official beginning of freedom of worship for all sects. It was the 1784 New York Act that made possible the incorporation of St. Patrick's Church in New York City.[171] However, the Act of 1784 did not put "all denominations upon an equal basis by allowing any religious society to incorporate," as Spaulding has claimed.[172] There was still discrimination against a church with a hierarchical system of government, such as the Roman Catholic or Methodist. Despite repeated pleas by Catholics for incorporation of their bishop as a corporation sole with title to all property in him,[173] the New York Legislature continued to impose a congregational system of church government on Catholics by allowing a majority of the church congregation to exercise absolute control over church affairs. In the nineteenth century this situation was to lead to paralyzing controversies within the church over matters of internal discipline.[174] In contrast, Georgia readily acceded to the requests of the Methodist Church to allow incorporation of their bishop and elders as a continuing body vested with the power of carrying on church government.[175]

From 1782 through 1785 the New Jersey Legislature incorporated a considerable number of Protestant churches, including Baptist, Presbyterian, and Episcopalian.[176] Then, on March 16, 1786, the New Jersey Legislature passed a general law under the title of "An Act to incorporate certain persons as trustees in every religious society or congregation in this State, for transacting the temporal concerns thereof."[177] The New Hampshire Legislature was restrained in incorporating churches other than the state-favored Congregationalist. However, it did incorporate a Presbyterian Church in Goffstown during the post-Revolutionary period, with the proviso that all who did not register their Presbyterian membership with the town clerk were to be ratable for the Congregational ministerial charges.[178] As late as 1816, Baptist congregations were being refused incorporation, while the Congregationalist petitions seem to have been regularly honored.[179]

There was freedom of incorporation in Pennsylvania. Its 1776 Constitution guaranteed that "all religious societies or bodies of men heretofore united or incorporated for the advancement of religion or learning, or for other pious and charitable purposes, shall be encouraged and protected in the enjoyment of the privileges, immunities and estates which they were accustomed to enjoy . . . under the laws and former constitution of this state."[180] By the act of February 20, 1786, Massachusetts allowed Protestant ministers to become sole corporations so that gifts to the minister were deemed jointly made to the minister, vestry, and wardens as donees. Their successors in office were deemed the church corporation. Reflecting the Congregational influence, ministers and deacons could not pass title to church property without the consent of the church membership or of a special committee appointed for that purpose.[181] South Carolina was less precise in her requirements for passage of title, being content to rest with majority rule. All Protestant churches were allowed to incorporate under the Constitution of 1778;[182] but not until the Constitution of 1790 were Roman Catholics and Jews allowed the privilege of holding property in corporate capacity.[183]

Ministers in Public Office

In a majority of the American states between 1776 and 1789, ministers of the Gospel were able to participate in governmental affairs by sitting in the state constitutional conventions, the state conventions called to ratify the United States Constitution, and the state legislatures. Among the ministers who actively participated in affairs of state were the Reverend Francis Cummins, who was a member of the South Carolina convention that ratified the federal Constitution; the Georgia Baptist ministers, Silas and Jesse Mercer, who were active in the state constitutional conventions of 1795 and 1798; the Reverend John Witherspoon of New Jersey, who was the principal draftsman of the state's 1776 Constitution; and the Reverend David Caldwell of North Carolina, who was a member of both that state's constitutional convention of 1777 and the convention called to determine whether the federal Constitution should be ratified.

Some of this generation, however, nurtured unpleasant memories of that aspect of the English Establishment which had placed clerics in Parliament and had provided the political power of the Anglican clergy in the South, and the power of the Congregationalist divines in New England. Thomas Jefferson had been caught up in the movement to take the clergy out of politics. His draft constitution for a Virginia constitution in 1783 had provided: "Of this General Assembly, the Treasurer, the Attorney General, Register, Ministers of the Gospel . . . shall be incapable of being members."[184] Two years later he revealed his reasons for wanting to exclude clerics:

> The clergy are excluded, because, if admitted into the legislature at all, the probability is that they would form its majority. For they

are dispersed through every county in the state, they have influence with the people, and great opportunities of persuading them to elect them into the legislature. This body, tho shattered, is still formidable, still forms a *corps,* and is still actuated by the *esprit de corps.* The nature of that spirit has been severely felt by mankind, and has filled the history of ten or twelve centuries with too many atrocities not to merit a proscription from meddling with government.[185]

Nevertheless, other leaders of the American community in the post-Revolutionary period saw the disqualification of clerics for what it was: an unfair and unnecessary discrimination, inconsistent with and harmful to the democratic process.

In October, 1778, James Madison severely criticized Jefferson's draft constitution:

Does not the exclusion of Ministers of the Gospel as such violate a fundamental principle of liberty by punishing a religious profession with the privation of a civil right? Does it not violate another article of the plan itself which exempts religion from the cognizance of the Civil power? Does it not violate justice by at once taking away a right and prohibiting a compensation for it? And does it not in fine violate impartiality by shutting the door against the Ministers of one religion and leaving it open for those of every other?[186]

By 1790 Thomas Jefferson had discovered that he was wrong in earlier wanting to deny political posts to ministers. In that year he sent his felicitations to the Reverend Charles Clay in approval of his candidacy for election to the United States Congress.[187] In 1800, the year before he was elected president, Jefferson acknowledged the error of his former views:

I observe however in the same scheme of a constitution, an abridgment of the right of being elected, which after seventeen years more of experience and reflection, I do not approve. It is the incapacitation of a clergyman from being elected. The clergy, by getting themselves established by law, and ingrafted into the machinery of government, have been a very formidable engine in many countries and even in some of these United States. Even in 1783, we doubted the stability of our recent measures for reducing them to the footing of other useful callings. It now appears that our means were effectual. The clergy seem to have relinquished all pretension to privilege and to stand on a footing with lawyers, physicians, etc. They ought, therefore, to possess the same rights.[188]

There had been some states that thought it proper during 1776–1789 to deny ministers of the Gospel participation in various governmental assemblies. For example, the 1775 Virginia Convention, which met in Richmond, ordained "that all clergymen of the Church of England, and all dissenting ministers or teachers, should be incapable of being elected as a delegate, or sitting and voting in convention.[189] All told, five states denied clergymen opportunity for public service in the period immediately after independence. For example, the 1776 Constitution of Delaware made preachers or clergymen ineligible for public office.[190] The North Carolina Constitution of 1776 bluntly provided "That no clergymen, or preacher of the gospel, of any denomination, shall be capable of being a member of either the Senate, House of Commons, or Council of State, which he continues in the exercise of pastoral function."[191] Although John Witherspoon, distinguished president of Princeton, urged his Georgia friends to refrain from such a disqualification,[192] the Georgia Constitution of 1777 was drawn to provide: "No clergyman of any denomination shall be allowed a seat in the legislature."[193] The New York Constitution of 1777 also rendered ministers and priests incapable of holding any civil or military office.[194] South Carolina in its 1778 Constitution provided that "ministers of the gospel are by their profession dedicated to the service of God and the cure of souls, and ought not to be diverted from the great duties of their function." In order to encourage continued devotion to the pastoral calling, the article in the South Carolina Constitution adds: "no minister of the gospel or public preacher of any religious persuasion, while he continues in the exercise of his pastoral function and for two years after" shall be eligible to serve as a member of the government or as a representative.[195]

Citizens of the new nation soon realized the force of Madison's argument. Men such as Jefferson corrected their views. Beginning with Georgia in 1789, the states with clerical disqualifications began to remove them from the constitutions.[196]

Attitude of the American Community in General, 1776–1789

During the period immediately after the Revolution and previous to the ratification of the federal Bill of Rights, it was generally acknowledged from one end of the nation to the other that government should not be hostile to religion. Indeed, the activities of the Continental Congress indicate clearly that this body was pleased to promote the cause of religion. The publication of the entire Bible was, at that time, an enterprise so hazardous for the American press that it was necessary to secure encouragement in advance of printing. So, on September 12, 1782, the Continental Congress by formal resolution recommended for purchase the first edition of

Scriptures by John Aitken. This was just five years after the Congress had recommended the importation of twenty thousand Bibles.[197] Governmental recognition that religion is necessary for morality, and public morality for the happiness of society appears strikingly in the Northwest Ordinance passed by the Continental Congress in 1787 and reenacted two years later by the same First Congress of the United States that proposed the Bill of Rights. The ordinance states: "Religion, morality and knowledge being necessary to good government and the happiness of mankind, schools and the means of education shall be forever encouraged."[198] Furthermore, the Continental Congress resolved, on October 12, 1788, that "true religion and good morals are the only solid foundation of public liberty and happiness...."[199]

When the members of the Massachusetts Constitutional Convention of 1780 sent an address to their constituents, they indicated:

> [I]t would be an affront to the People of Massachusetts Bay to labour to convince them, that the Honor and Happiness of a people depend upon Morality; and that the Public Worship of God has a tendency to inculcate the Principles thereof, as well as to preserve a people from foresaking Civilization, and falling into a State of Savage barbarity.[200]

"It is the duty of all wise, free and virtuous governments, to countenance and encourage virtue and religion," asserted the New York Legislature in 1784.[201] Worth recalling, too, is the earlier noted statement of the Delaware Legislature of 1787 to the effect that its members considered it "their duty to countenance and encourage virtue and religion, by every means in their power, and in the most expeditious manner ...."[202]

The officers of government during this period were positively interested in the welfare of religion. Addressing both houses of the New Jersey Legislature on September 13, 1776, Governor William Livingston expressed himself thus: "May the Foundation of our Infant State be laid in Virtue of the Fear of God; and the Superstructure will rise glorious, and endure for ages. Then may we humbly expect the blessings of the most High, who divides to the Nations their inheritance and separates the Sons of Adam."[203] On October 30, 1789, the Senate of New Jersey read a message from the House of Assembly, as follows:

> Ordered that Messrs. Witherspoon, Hardenbergh, Hankinson, Swain and Benson, and such other members as choose to attend, be a Committee to join a Committee of Council if they shall agree, to appoint and consider and report their opinion on what may be proper

and competent for the Legislature to do in order to promote the Interest of Religion and Morality among all ranks of People in this State and that Mr. Hardenbergh do wait on the Council and request them to appoint a committee to join the Committee of this House for that purpose.[204]

Later that day the Senate "ordered, that Mr. Martin and Mr. Woodhull, or either of them be a committee to join the Committee of the House of Assembly to consider and report their opinion on what may be proper for the Legislature to do in order to promote the Interest of Religion and Morality, and that Mr. Ellis do wait on the House of Assembly and acquaint them therewith."[205]

When the 1784 Maryland General Assembly incorporated a Society for the Relief of Widows and Children of Protestant Clergymen, the General Assembly observed: "[T]his General Assembly are earnestly desiring to promote every pious and charitable design for the relief and assistance of the widowless and fatherless, and especially those of the respectable and useful body of clergy of all denominations,"[206] Catholics such as Daniel Carroll, then a Maryland State Senator, endorsed passage of the Act.[207] To the South the same necessity of aiding and encouraging religion was noted in gubernatorial messages. For example, Governor Lyman Hall of Georgia in 1783 addressed the Assembly as follows:

> From a view of the profligate, and wicked lives of many in the community, it appears that some laws, to restrain vice and encourage virtue, are of the highest importance to the welfare of the State. It being certain, that almost all the evils of government, originate from men of corrupt principles and abandoned manners. In addition, therefore, to wholesome laws restraining vice; every encouragement ought to be given to religion, and learned clergy, to perform divine worship, in honor of God, and to cultivate principles of religion and virtue among our citizens. For this purpose, it will be in your wisdom to lay an early foundation for endowing seminaries of learning. . . .[208]

Even the Legislature of Virginia, whose people were often, and erroneously, thought to desire an absolute divorce between church and state, was anxious to help religion during this period — so long always as it was not preferential to the Episcopalian Church. Bell writes of this Legislature, with particular reference to the period 1776 to 1780: "As far as the General Assembly was concerned, it is evident that they regarded the separation of church and state as implying no hostility to religion as such; they therefore showed a predisposition favorable to religion in such points as they assumed they safely might."[209]

Private individuals, as well as public officials, indicated the intimate connection between successful government and religion and bespoke public encouragement of the latter. The Reverend Thomas Reefe, pastor of the Presbyterian Church in Salem, South Carolina, wrote in 1785:

> I have often wondered at the absurdity of those men, who glory in the name of Patriot . . . (speaking of those in high places who wish to substitute good manners in place of religion — a type of humanism for God) and yet make it their business to ridicule religion and weaken its obligations. They acknowledge that it is a necessary restraint on the manners of the multitude, and therefore useful to government; and yet do their utmost to bring it into contempt. I know of no better way to expose the inconsistency of such men, than by comparing them to an architect, who with much cost and labor raises and adorns the superstructure, while he is pulling away the main pillars which support the fabric. Can that man be reckoned a genuine lover of his country, who endeavors to promote vice, and corrupt the morals of the people? And I must take the liberty to think, that this is the case of all those who propagate infidelity, and eradicate all sense of religion from the minds of men.[210]

Another writer, who signed himself "Americanus," warned in *The Gazette of the United States* for August 12, 1789, that "Constitutions and forms of government will little avail, without a general prevalence of religion — the cultivation of private virtue and a refinement of the moral sense."[211]

Taken as a whole, the events between 1776 and 1789 clearly indicate that the people of the states and their leaders with few exceptions favored governmental encouragement of religion as a public institution so long as this action did not lead to "an establishment" of a religion by means of exclusions and discriminatory preferences which gave the state a coercive influence over the private lives of its citizens. That the general attitude was not hostile to religion or religiously oriented activities is readily apparent from the extensive practice of state and church accommodation. It would seem that the statesmen in the First Congress would have recognized that equal protection of religious societies did not necessarily lead to "an establishment." It may be suggested that they intended to honor the traditions of "nonestablishment" accommodation by continuing them in the federal districts and the territories under the control of the Congress.

The Struggle for Equality of Political Opportunity — Efforts in the Original Constitution to Deter a National Establishment by Banning Religious Test Oaths

The religious discriminations of the colonial period were not immediately abandoned upon the attainment of independence and statehood. Among the detested aspects of a religious establishment there was the religious test. It violated the rights of conscience by requiring affirmation of certain religious doctrines in the various oaths that a person might be required to take in order to exercise fully his political rights as a citizen. It prejudiced political liberty as well by granting a political preference to the members of the state church. To the Americans of the constitutional generation, a primary attack upon the privileges of the Established Church necessarily embraced a struggle for equality of political opportunity regardless of religious belief. Many were convinced there could be no equal religious liberty under the proposed federal system if individuals were denied national public office because of their faith.

The test had been widespread in the colonies. For example, before the members elected to the 1776 Pennsylvania Constitutional Convention could take their seats they were required to subscribe to the following declaration:

> I, ——, do profess faith in God, the father, and in Jesus Christ, his eternal son, the true God, and in the Holy Spirit, one God Blessed for evermore, and do acknowledge the holy scriptures of the old and new testament, to be given by divine inspiration.[1]

Comparable restraints upon holding public office frequently appeared in the first state constitutions. The New Jersey Constitution, for example, which was framed just a few days before the procla-

92

mation of the Declaration of Independence, made clear in Article XIX the restrictive nature of its religious freedom so far as political opportunities were concerned: "[A]ll persons professing a belief in the faith of any Protestant sect . . . shall be capable of being elected into any office of profit or trust, or being a member of either branch of the Legislature, and shall fully and freely enjoy every privilege and immunity, enjoyed by others their fellow subjects."[2] This clause prompted John Carroll some years later to express regret that it may have set the tone for other state constitutions. Carroll wrote:

> The Jersey state was the first, which, in forming her new Constitution, gave the unjust example of reserving to Protestants alone the prerogatives of government and legislation. At that very time the American army swarmed with Roman Catholic soldiers. . . . They could not believe that the State, which was foremost to injure them, would continue, or that any others would imitate, her partial and iniquitous policy.[3]

The other early constitutions generally limited in some manner eligibility for public office. Thus the Delaware Constitution of 1776 required all officeholders to subscribe a declaration in words evidently patterned upon the Pennsylvania convention requirement:

> I, ——, do profess faith in God the Father, and in Jesus Christ, His only Son, and in the Holy Ghost, one God, blessed forevermore; and I do acknowledge the holy scripture of the Old and New Testament to be given by divine inspiration.[4]

When the draft of the Pennsylvania Constitution of 1776 was submitted to the public for criticism, some newspapers suggested that an addition be made that the members of the new government acknowledge that God was a rewarder of the good and punisher of the wicked; and prominent citizens lamented that the Christian religion was paid scant or little respect.[5] Perhaps, as a result of such demands, the Pennsylvania Constitution as finally adopted restricted civil rights to those who "acknowledge the being of a God,"[6] and provided further:

> And each member before he takes his seat, shall make and subscribe the following declaration, viz. I do believe in one God, the creator and governor of the Universe the rewarder of the good and the punisher of the wicked. And I do acknowledge the Scriptures of the Old and New Testament be given by Divine inspiration. And no further or other religious test shall ever hereafter be required of any civil officer or magistrate in this state.[7]

Benjamin Franklin fought earnestly against this in the convention.

but he had to content himself with such a provision that made it possible for Catholics to hold office.[8] Under such constitutional restrictions Jews, Mohammedans, and others were ineligible to hold public office.

In a number of states, Catholics were denied the opportunity to hold public office. The North Carolina Constitution of 1776 restricted officeholding to Protestants.[9] The Georgia Constitution of 1777 similarly required that "all members of the legislature shall be members of the Protestant religion."[10] So, too, legislators in South Carolina were limited to Protestants by the Constitution of 1778.[11] The New Hampshire Constitutional Convention that completed its work on June 5, 1779, proposed a "Plan of Government for the State of New Hampshire" which provided:

> 8th.   All male inhabitants of the State of lawful age, paying taxes, and professing the protestant religion shall be deemed legal voters in choosing counsellors and representatives. . . .[12]

The citizens rejected this denial of political rights to Catholics, Jews, and all others who were not Protestants.[13]

Although the Constitution of the state of New York in Article 38 did ordain "free exercise and enjoyment of religious profession and worship, without discrimination or preference,"[14] in the constitutional convention an addition to this was proposed. John Jay moved the inclusion of these words:

> Except the professors of the religion of the Church of Rome, who ought not to hold lands in or be admitted to a participation of the civil rights enjoyed by members of this State, until [they] . . . solemnly swear, that they verily believe in their consciences, that no pope, priest, or foreign authority . . . has power to absolve the subjects of this State from their allegiance to the same . . . that they . . . believe to be false and wicked the dangerous and damnable doctrine that the pope, or any other earthly authority, has power to absolve men from sins described in and prohibited by the Holy Gospel of Jesus Christ. . . .[15]

The convention rejected Jay's proposal.[16] Seven years later when the New York Legislature enacted a law establishing a university, it was provided that no one should be rendered ineligible for a professorship by a "test oath" circumscribing his freedom of religious belief.[17] However, New York legislation for many years continued to demand a test oath that rendered Catholics ineligible for public office, and it was 1806 before the first Roman Catholic, Francis Cooper, took his seat in the New York Assembly.[18]

Even in the face of increasing political liberalism, in 1820 the Supreme Court of New York ruled that one who disbelieved in the existence of a God and a future state of rewards and punishments could not be a witness in a court of justice.[19]

The constitution proposed for Massachusetts in 1778 would have provided: "No person unless of the Protestant Religion shall be Governor, Lieutenant Governor, a member of the Senate or of the House of Representatives, or hold any judiciary employment within this State."[20] The convention that had endorsed this proposal also endorsed a requirement that all officeholders take an oath that "No foreign Prince, person, prelate, state or potentate, hath or ought to have, any jurisdiction, superiority, pre-eminence, authority, dispensing or other power, in any matter, civil, ecclesiastical or spiritual within this commonwealth."[21] This subscription — based upon the English oath of supremacy — would have effectively excluded Catholics and, since the Declaration of Independence, the Anglicans. The *Journal* of the convention records that the oath was directed against those "who will not disclaim those Principles of Spiritual Jurisdiction which Roman Catholics in some countries have held."[22] This proposed constitution was rejected by the voters.[23]

The proposed 1780 Massachusetts constitution required an oath of all officeholders that they "believe the Christian religion, and have a firm persuasion of its truth," and this language was ultimately adopted.[24] However, there were individuals in the state who objected to allowing any other than Protestants to hold office. The people of Lexington demanded insertion of the word "Protestant" in the oath of office.[25] The people of Roxbury demanded this, too, as "necessary to secure the peace and tranquility of the State, as well as the promotion of that Religion which our venerable Forefathers, suffered anything but death, to establish."[26] Similarly, those in the town of Springfield indicated their opposition to the liberality of the oath. "As the People of this Commonwealth are generally, if not universally of the Protestant Reformed Religion," said their memorial, "they apprehend it would be a matter of Great Concern that any Person might ever be elected to this Office over them or their Posterity, who should not be of the Protestant Religion; and they are of Opinion this ought to be provided for in the most express terms. . . ."[27] Sixty other towns are reported to have made similar requests, and it is rather surprising that the constitutional clause permitting Catholics to take the oath of office passed. Of course, all non-Christians remained ineligible for office in Massachusetts.

The general political discriminations against Catholics, Jews, and non-Protestants did not go without protest from the new segments of the American community. Thus the inhabitants of Gorham, Massachusetts (now Maine), instructed their delegates to the 1779 State Constitutional Convention as follows:

> That no qualification be required of any officer or Ruler but merit, viz., a sufficient knowledge and understanding in matters relative to the office, and fidelity and firmness in the Cause of Liberty. Pecuniary Qualifications can never give a Good understanding or Good Heart. That no restriction be lade on any Profession of Christianity or denomination of Christians, but all Equally intitled to protection of the Laws.[28]

On December 23, 1783, the Pennsylvania Council of Censors received a memorial from a number of local Jews which stated

> That the tenth section of the frame of this government deprives the Jews of the most eminent right of freemen, by disabling them to be elected by their fellow-citizens to represent them in the General Assembly, or hold any civil office in the State, and is inconsonate with the second paragraph of the bill of rights. . . .[29]

Four years later, on September 7, 1787, another Philadelphia Jew communicated with the President and members of the Federal Constitutional Convention meeting in that city, informing them that his people

> do behold with Concern that among the laws in the Constitution of Pennsylvania their is a Clause Sect. 10 to viz — I do believe in one God the Creator and governour of the universe the Rewarder of the good and the punisher of the wicked — and I do acknowledge the scriptures of the old and New Testament to be given by a devine inspiration — to swear and believe that the new testament was given by devine inspiration is absolutely against the Religious principle of a Jew is deprived of holding any publick office or place of Government which is Contridectory to the Bill of Rights Sect. 2. . . .[30]

The writer of this letter then requested the recipients to "alter the said oath and leave out the words to viz — and I do acknowledge the scripture of the new testament to be given by devine inspiration. . . ."[31] In *The American Museum* for the same year, another interesting communication appeared which objected to the restriction of civil and political opportunities to Christians. The author, William Vans Murray, Esq., wrote:

> It is not a little surprising that where the ardor of reform is extending itself in America, from politicle revolutions to those of religion, it should act on so limited a scale, as to preclude all but christians, from the blessings of equal religious freedom, to which all men are

equally entitled. . . . There yet remains one step; when this is gained, America will be the great philosophical theatre of the World. Christians are not the only people there. There are men, besides Christians, who, while they discharge every social duty, are shut from the right of citizenship. . . . If there be a man in the Empire excluded from his rights of citizenship merely, on account of his religion, the law which excludes him, is founded in force, and is a VIOLATION OF THE LAW OF NATURE. It is vain that artful men argue from policy to the necessity of religious discrimination — of tests — capacities — and insidious qualifications.

Government is a modification of the laws of nature. These are unacquainted with the distinctions of religious opinion: and of the terms Christian, Mohamentan, Jew, or Gentile . . . they [the constitutions] will throw down every barrier erected by the despotism of the impassioned ignorance, and admit every sect whom they admit at all, to the rights of citizenship. . . .[32]

Many of the intellectual leaders of our land also recognized that it was wrong to deny men political rights because of their religious beliefs. Such Founding Fathers as Thomas Jefferson openly advocated full political rights to all, regardless of their thoughts on religion. As early as 1776 Jefferson declared: "We have no right to prejudice another because he is of another church."[33] The same year, in drafting his Bill for Religious Freedom, Jefferson wrote:

That our civil rights have no dependence on our religious opinions, any more than our opinions in physics or geometry; that therefore, the proscribing any citizen as unworthy the public confidence by laying upon him an incapacity of being called to offices of trust and emolument, unless he profess or renounce this or that religious opinion, is depriving him injuriously of those privileges and advantages to which in common with his fellow-citizens he has a natural right.[34]

In his draft of a proposed Virginia constitution seven years later, Jefferson urged the inclusion of a clause to the effect that: "The General Assembly shall not have power . . . to abridge the civil rights of any person on account of his religious beliefs. . . ."[35] In full accord with Jefferson in this matter was John Carroll who attested that throughout the American Revolution the people of all faiths had "associated into one great national Union, under the express condition of not being shackled by religious tests. . . ."[36] Bishop Carroll later told how "the Catholics evinced a desire, not less ardent than that of the Protestants, to render the provinces independent of the mother country; and it was manifest that if they joined the common cause and exposed themselves to the common danger, they should be entitled to a participation in the common blessings which crowned their efforts."[37] He added that "In 1776 the American independence was declared and a revolution effected not only in political affairs but also in those relating to religion," and that "every difficulty was removed, the Catholics were placed on a level with their fellow Christians and every political disqualification was done away."[38] In this Carroll was accurate insofar as he was speaking of conditions in Virginia, Pennsylvania, and in his own State of Maryland, but elsewhere, as has been noted, political disqualifications continued for some time.

Charles Carroll of Carrollton has also indicated that he believed there must be an end to the disqualifications from public office because of religious beliefs. In a letter to George Washington Custis, Carroll indicated:

> When I signed the Declaration of Independence I had in view not only our independence from England but the toleration of all sects professing the Christian religion and communicating to them all equal rights. . . . Reflecting as you must, on the disabilities I may truly say of the prescription of the Roman Catholics in Maryland, you will not be surprised that I had much at heart this grand design, founded on mutual charity, the basis of our holy religion.[39]

To the north, the outstanding citizen of New Hampshire, William Plumer, wrote an essay on February 18, 1782, for the *New Hampshire Gazette* of Portsmouth in which he affirmed that all men should be eligible for public office without reference to their religious opinions.[40]

Although for some time after independence a number of the states continued to disqualify from public office members of various religions, as early as 1776 there was state constitutional recognition of the right of full political equality to members of all faiths. Maryland's Declaration of Rights of that year established "That no other test or qualification ought to be required to any office of trust or profit, than such oath of support and fidelity to this state."[41] In an article in the *Columbian Magazine* of December, 1787, John Carroll lauded those states which "have done the justice to every denomination of Christians, which ought to be done to them all, of placing them on the same footing of citizenship, and conferring an equal right of participation in national privileges."[42]

It is evident from the foregoing that when the convention met in Philadelphia in 1787 to draft a constitution for the United States, there was already extensive recognition that no person should be denied federal political rights because he did not share the religious beliefs of the majority.

The first attempt to protect religious liberty was made on May 23, 1787, when Governor Charles Pinckney submitted the following proposal among others in his plan for a constitution:

> The legislature of the United States shall pass no law on the subject of religion; nor touching or abridging the liberty of the press; nor shall the privilege of the writ of habeas corpus ever be suspended, except in case of rebellion or invasion.[43]

The proposal was referred to the Committee of the Whole to consider the state of the Union, and the convention adjourned.[44] The next consideration of the clause seems to have been given on August 20, 1787. This time Pinckney proposed that "no religious test or qualification shall ever be annexed to any oath or office under the authority of the United States."[45]

The reason that Pinckney modified his first article is not known. However, it would seem that he and others had adopted the belief that the Federal Government would have no power delegated to it to deal in matters of religion. Hence, the article as originally proposed would be redundant. The context in which the article next appeared would seem to fortify this observation. Ten days later, when the convention had before it a proposal to grant Congress the power to establish the qualifications for federal office and employment, Pinckney moved to add what is now the present form of the clause in Article VI, Section Three of the Constitution: "But no religious test shall ever be required as a qualification to any office or public trust under the authority of the United States." Apparently it was thought that the power to determine the qualifications for office might carry with it by implication the power to use religion as a basis of the qualification.

Not all members of the convention thought that such assurance was necessary. Roger Sherman of Connecticut expressed the view that the article was unnecessary because the prevailing liberality was a sufficient security against exclusion from the Federal Government by means of religious tests. On the other hand, Gouverneur Morris and General Charles Cotesworth Pinckney spoke in favor of such a clause and the motion was soon agreed to *nemine contradicente*.[46] After being sent to the convention's Committee on Style, it came forth and was again approved, this time in the form in which it now appears in Article VI of the Constitution.[47]

Contemporary reports indicate that Charles Pinckney explained on the floor of the convention that his clause providing for "the prevention of religious tests [was] a provision the world will expect from you, in the establishment of a System founded on Republican

Principles, and in an age so liberal and enlightened as the present."[48]
When Luther Martin — a Maryland representative in the convention — reported to his state Legislature on November 29, 1787, on
the ban upon religious tests he stated:

> The part of the system which provides, that no religious test shall
> ever be required as a qualification to any office or public trust under
> the United States was adopted by a great majority of the convention,
> and without much debate; however, there were some members so
> unfashionable as to think, that a belief of the existence of a Deity,
> and of a state of future rewards and punishments would be some
> security for the good conduct of our rulers, and that, in a Christian
> country, it would be at least decent to hold out some distinction be-
> tween the professors of Christianity and downright infidelity or
> paganism[49]

There was some feeling of apprehension in the country at this
time, that the ban upon religious tests might be, by implication, only
an exception to a larger power in Congress; that power the American community was unwilling to concede. That this view was erro-
neous was the gist of a communication on April 10, 1788, from
James Madison to Governor Edmund Randolph of Virginia, Madison wrote:

> As to the religious test, I should conceive that it can imply at most
> nothing more than that without that exception, a power would have
> been given to impose an oath involving a religious test as a qualifica-
> tion for office. The constitution of necessary offices being given to the
> Congress, the proper qualifications seem to be evidently involved.[50]

It is interesting to note here that at the Philadelphia Constitutional
Convention, Alexander Hamilton gave James Madison a draft of a
constitution thought desirable by Hamilton. It included the clause:
"Nor shall any . . . religious test for any office or place, be ever
established by law."[51] Such a clause might have been inserted after
Hamilton had heard Pinckney's motion.

During the debates in the state conventions called to ratify the
proposed United States Constitution, there were statements by some
individuals to the effect that they looked with distaste upon the proposed ban upon religious test oaths. Thus, in the Massachusetts
Convention, Major Rusk "shuddered at the idea that Roman Catholics, Papists, and Pagans might be introduced into office and that
Popery and the Inquisition may be established in America."[52] Colonel
Jones in the same convention expressed his feeling that the leaders
in America ought to believe in God or Christ and that regardless
whether a test might have been abused in England, it would be

fortunate for the United States if our public men were those who had a good standing in the church.[53] Another delegate to the convention, Amos Singletary, feared we were giving up all our privileges because there was no provision that men in power should have any religion; though he hoped to see Christians, yet, by the Constitution, a Papist or an infidel was as eligible as they. He thought in this instance "we were giving great power to we know not whom."[54] Nevertheless, the opposite view prevailed in all the conventions. Illustrative is the statement in the Massachusetts Convention of the Congregationalist minister, Reverend Daniel Shute:

> To establish a religious test as a qualification for offices in the proposed federal Constitution, it appears to me, sir, would be attended with injurious consequences to some individuals, I mean, that some, who, in every other respect, are qualified to fill some important post in government, will be excluded by their not being able to stand the religious test; which I take to be a privation on part of their civil rights. . . . Upon the plan of a religious test, the question, I think, must be, who shall be excluded from national trusts? Whatever answer bigotry may suggest, the dictates of candor and equity, I conceive, will be, None. Far from limiting my charity and confidence to men of my own denomination in religion, I suppose, and I believe, sir, that there are worthy characters among men of every denomination — among the Quakers, the Baptists, the Church of England, the Papists; and even among those who have no other guide, in the way to virtue and heaven, than the dictates of natural religion. I must therefore think, sir, that the proposed plan of government, in this particular, is wisely constructed; that, as all have an equal claim to the blessings of the government under which they live, and which they support, so none should be excluded from them for being of any particular denomination in religion.[55]

A Baptist, the Reverend Isaac Backus, endorsed the ban upon religious tests during the same convention. His statement illustrates how that generation deemed such a ban an important weapon in the fight for disestablishment:

> I shall begin with the exclusion of any religious test. Many appear to be much concerned about it; but nothing is more evident, both in reason and the Holy Scriptures, than that religion is ever a matter between God and individuals; and therefore, no man or men can impose any religious test without invading the essential prerogatives of our Lord Jesus Christ. . . . And let the history of all nations be searched from that day (of Constantine) to this, and it will appear that the imposing of religious tests had been the greatest engine of tyranny in the world. And I rejoice to see so many gentlemen, who are now giving in their rights of conscience in this great and im-

portant matter. Some serious minds discovered a concern lest, if all religious tests should be excluded, the Congress would hereafter establish Popery, or some other tyrannical way of worship. But it is most certain that no such way of worship can be established without any religious test.[56]

Another member of the Massachusetts Convention agreed that, "had there been a religious test as a qualification for office, it would, in my opinion, have been a great blemish upon the instrument."[57]

In the Connecticut Ratifying Convention, as in the Massachusetts conclave, there were a few who still desired a religious test for national office, but the more liberal representatives prevailed. Thus, Oliver Wolcott remarked:

> I do not see the necessity of such a test as some gentlemen wish for. The Constitution enjoins an oath upon all the officers of the United States. This is a direct appeal to that God who is the avenger of perjury. Such an appeal to him is a full acknowledgment of his being and providence. An acknowledgment of these great truths is all that the gentleman contends for. For myself, I should be content either with or without that clause in the Constitution which excludes test laws. Knowledge and liberty are so prevalent in this country, that I do not believe that the United States would ever be disposed to establish one religious sect, and lay all others under legal disabilities. But as we know not what may take place hereafter, and any such test would be exceedingly injurious to the right of free citizens, I cannot think it altogther superfluous to have added a clause, which secures us from the possibility of such oppression.[58]

The concept of establishment thus meant to Mr. Wolcott federal activity "to establish one religious sect, and lay all others under legal disabilities." This was the situation to avoid. The ban upon test oaths was deemed valuable as a most significant contribution to the struggle for disestablishment. A member of the federal Constitutional Convention, and the First Congress and also briefly Chief Justice of the United States, Oliver Ellsworth wrote a series of letters in the *Connecticut Courant* from November, 1787, to March, 1788, signed "A Landholder." In these he defended the ban upon test oaths.[59]

The Virginia Convention accepted the propriety of the clause in the federal Constitution banning religious test oaths. Governor Edmund Randolph and James Madison spoke out most effectively against those who wanted to protect an establishment by utilizing religious tests. Said Governor Randolph:

> Freedom of religion is said to be in danger. I will candidly say, I once thought it was and felt great repugnance to the Constitution

for that reason. I am willing to acknowledge my apprehensions removed; and I will inform you by what process of reasoning I did remove them. The Constitution provides that ". . . but no religious test shall ever be required as a qualification to any office or public trust under the United States." It has been said that, if the exclusion of the religious test were an exception from the general power of Congress, the power over religion would remain, I inform those who are of this opinion, that no power is given expressly to Congress over religion. . . . The exclusion of religious oaths or affirmation tests is an exception from this general provision, with respect to oaths or affirmations. Although officers etc. are to swear that they will support this Constitution, yet they are not bound to support one mode of worship, or to adhere to one particular sect. It puts all sects on the same footing. A man of abilities and character, of any sect whatever, may be admitted to any office or public trust under the United States. I am a friend of a variety of sects. . . . And there are now so many in the United States that they will prevent the establishment of any one sect, in prejudice to the rest, and will forever oppose all attempts to infringe religious liberty.[60]

Governor Randolph's statement to the convention is of great import, inasmuch as it clearly indicates what the American Founding Fathers found objectionable: "The establishment of any one sect, in prejudice to the rest." Furthermore, Randolph accurately noted that an important concern of the Fathers was to protect "religious liberty" from curtailment by the new government; his remarks certainly show how the ban upon establishment was deemed necessary to accomplish this principal objective. Again, Governor Randolph threw light on what the Founding Fathers were endeavoring to outlaw, namely, practices of the new Federal Government that would force men "to support one mode of worship, or to adhere to one particular sect."

James Madison also spoke in the Virginia Convention on the matter of religious liberty. He noted:

If there were a majority of one sect, a bill of rights would be a poor protection for liberty. Happily for the states, they enjoy the utmost freedom of religion. This freedom arises from that multiplicity of sects which pervades America, and which is the best and only security for religious liberty in any society; for where there is such a variety of sects, there cannot be a majority of any one sect to oppress and persecute the rest. Fortunately for this commonwealth, a majority of the people are decidedly against any exclusive establishment. I believe it to be so in the other states. There is not a shadow of right in the general government to intermeddle with religion. Its least interference with it would be a most flagrant usurpation. I can appeal to my uniform conduct on this subject, that I have warmly supported religious freedom. It is better that this security should be depended upon from the general legislature, than from one particular state. A particular state might concur in one religious project. But the United States abound in such a variety of sects, that it is a strong security against religious persecution; and it is sufficient to authorize a conclusion that no one sect will ever be able to outnumber or depress the rest.[61]

Then Madison concluded:

[W]ere uniformity of religion to be introduced by this system, it would, in my opinion, be ineligible; but I have no reason to conclude that uniformity of government will produce that of religion. This subject is, for the honor of America, perfectly free and unshackled. The Government has no juridiction over it; the least reflection will convince us there is no danger to be feared on this ground.[62]

Like Governor Randolph, Madison underscored his major concern that religion be "free and unshackled," and that there be "a strong security against religious persecution." It was for this reason that he felt there must be a ban upon establishment. Madison openly stated that he opposed "a majority of *one* sect to oppress and persecute the rest," and the "*one* religious project." What was needed — and all that was needed according to his thinking — was constitutional assurance "that no *one* sect will ever be able to outnumber or depress the rest."

Similarly in the North Carolina Ratifying Convention there was discussion of the clause banning religious test oaths. Lancaster first indicated his concern at what it would effectuate. He stated:

As to a religious test, had the article which excludes it provided none but what had been in the states heretofore, I would not have objected to it. It would secure religion. Religious liberty ought to be provided for. . . . For my part, in reviewing the qualification necessary for a President, I did not suppose that the pope could occupy the President's chair. But let us remember that we form a government for millions not yet in existence. I have not the art of divination. In the course of four or five hundred years, I do not know it will work. This is most certain, that Papists may occupy that chair, and Mahometans may take it. I see nothing against it.[63]

Lancaster's interpretation of the ban on religious tests was certainly correct, and his forecast of its effect at least in part prophetic. The great statesman of North Carolina, James Iredell, rose to strongly support the constitutional clause banning religious test oaths, though he remarked upon the futility of such oaths:

I consider the clause under consideration as one of the strongest proofs that could be adduced, that it was the intention of those who formed this system to establish a general religious liberty in America. Were we to judge from the examples of religious tests in other countries, we should be persuaded that they do not answer the purpose for which they were intended. What is the consequence of such in England? In that country no man can be a member in the House of Commons, or hold any office under the crown, without taking the sacrament according to the rites of the Church. . . . To a man of base principles, it is made a mere instrument of civil polity. The intention was to exclude all persons from office but the members of the Church of England. Yet it is notorious that dissenters qualify themselves for office in this manner, though they never conform to the Church on any other occasion; and men of no religion at all have no scruple to make use of this qualification. It was never known that a man who had no principles of religion hesitated to perform any rite when it was convenient for his private interest. No test can bind such a one. I am therefore clearly of the opinion that such a discrimination would neither be effectual for its own purposes, nor, if it could, ought by any means be made.[64]

Shortly thereafter, Iredell added:

But it is objected that the people of America may, perhaps, choose representatives who have no religion at all, and that pagans and Mahometans may be admitted into offices. But how is it possible to exclude any set of men, without taking that principle of religious freedom which we ourselves so warmly contend for? This is the foundation on which persecution has been raised in every part of the world. The people in power were always right, and everybody else wrong. If you admit the least difference, the door to persecution is opened.[65]

A ban of individuals from posts of honor and trust solely because of their religious beliefs was such evil "discrimination" to James Iredell that it was properly outlawed. To him the ban was primarily insurance of the "principle of religious freedom."

The leaders and people of South Carolina also understood that by abolishing religious tests, the cause of religious liberty was being advanced. During debates in the House of Representatives on the question of calling a ratifying convention, the eminent Baptist, Arthur Simkins, inquired "whether Congress had a right to interfere in religion."[66] General Charles Cotesworth Pinckney, who had been in the constitutional convention that drafted the federal document, answered unequivocally that "they had no power at all," and "explained this point to Mr. Simkin's satisfaction."[67] In the ratifying convention, the chairman of the Committee on Amendments,

Reverend Francis Cummins, explained that it had always been "his duty and honor to oppose the ideas of religious establishments; or of states giving preference to any religious denomination."[68] Cummins continued:

> It would be impolite for a state to give preference to one religious order over any others in matters of state, and to dictate and prescribe in points of religion in which men from different modes of education and circumstances of one kind or other, will and must split in opinion. . . .

> The religion of the most erroneous heretic, is his religion, and as dear to him as any other man's is to him; therefore, to take it away from him by force, if such a thing was possible, would not only be to deprive him of the pleasure of his life, but also to render him irreligious, consequently less valuable to the state. Hence, I conclude that all religious denominations, whose principles do not manifestly express danger to others, thereby proving such principles not to be religious, but barbarous and imperious ought to be on equal footing as to matters of state and protection from violence of any kind.[69]

Cummins explained that the Committee on Amendments wished to amend Article VI to read that "no *other* religious test" should ever be required under the authority of the United States. This change was proposed in recognition of their understanding that the oath was actually a religious affirmation.[70] Cummins feared that the structure proposed in recognition of their understanding that the oath was of Article VI would "militate against the sacred nature of an oath." He "would not wish to see any language or phrase in a national constitution of government, tending, or in any degree seeming to tend to enervate or expunge the sacredness of an oath."[71]

The ban on the religious tests was especially significant in the growth of contemporary constitutional thought. Dieffenbach clearly seems correct in suggesting that the purpose of the American community in banning religious test oaths in the United States Constitution "was to keep the state from creating an established religion."[72] For some time after the adoption of the Constitution a number of Americans evidently believed that the full fight for a religious freedom had been won by the Article VI ban upon test oaths. Thus a writer signing only as "Foreign Spectator," writing in the *New York Daily Gazette* for June 12, 1789, observed that the proposed amendment to the Constitution suggested by South Carolina was unnecessary, in that there was no need to insert "other" between "no" and "religious" in Article VI. Said this writer: "If this amendment points out a mere inaccuracy of style, it is so far proper — an oath or affirmation being a religious test; if it means to guard against religious establishments, it is, by what has been said, superfluous."[73] Thus, too, "Americanus" writing in New York's *Gazette of the United States* on May 13, 1789, observed:

> That relief of the mind from religious thraldom, which has been productive of so many evils in other countries, and which is so completely guarded against in America, stands among the foremost of those great characteristics, which gave her form of government a preference to any one extant. . . . Here without subscribing to thirty-nine articles, which thirty-nine times in a day are frequently broken, a person can be admitted to the privileges and honors of his country.[74]

Shortly after Pennsylvania ratified the federal Constitution, a pamphlet signed by "an American Citizen" and entitled *An Examination of the Constitution for the United States of America* was published in Philadelphia. The author was Tench Coxe of Pennsylvania, former member of the Continental Congress, the Annapolis Convention, and an important pamphleteer. "[D]anger from ecclesiastical tyranny, that long standing and still remaining curse of the people — that sacrilegious engine of royal power in some countries —" wrote Coxe, "can be feared by no man in the United States."[75] On another occasion Tench Coxe eloquently expressed his happiness at the accomplishment of the framers of the federal Constitution. He wrote:

> No religious test is ever to be required of any officer or servant of the United States. The people may employ any wise or good citizen in the execution of the various duties of the government. In Italy, Spain, and Portugal, no protestant can hold a public trust. In England every Presbyterian and other person not of their established church is incapable of holding an office. No such impious deprivation of the rights of men can take place under the new federal constitution. The convention has the honour of proposing the first public act, by which any nation has ever divested itself of a power, every exercise of which is a trespass on the Majesty of Heaven.[76]

Later the Presbyterians of the East wrote to President Washington and observed: "[A]mong objections to the Federal Constitution, we never considered the want of a religious test — that grand engine of persecution in every tyrant's hand. . . ."[77] Some Americans of 1789 thought that the ban upon religious test oaths in the original constitution was sufficient to have ensured not only full religious liberty, but freedom of speech and other basic freedoms as well. For instance, "E. C.," writing in the *Gazette of the United States* on April 25, 1789, noted:

The wise and liberal citizens of INDEPENDENT AMERICA, have nobly adorned their grand federal Constitution with this glorious Inscription, FREE TOLERATION, wherein they say to the world, come, and partake with us of liberty of speaking, liberty of writing, and liberty of CONSCIENCE, and every other Liberty, consistent with those laws that equally bind the natives. . . .[78]

The firm conviction was expressed in the federal constitutional convention, in the state ratifying conventions, and ultimately in the United States Constitution that it was a denial of religious liberty and an unfortunate attribute of establishment to bar individuals from public posts because of their religious beliefs. This belief soon spread to the states which earlier had not provided such a prohibition. Thus, in the Pennsylvania Constitution of 1790, the religious oath of the 1776 Constitution was deleted in favor of a simple and civil oath to support the Constitution.[79] Nevertheless, the required belief in "the rewarder of the good and the punisher of the wicked" — as described in the 1776 Constitution's oath clause[80] — was perpetuated in another article of the 1790 Constitution. It declared that: "No person, who acknowledges the being of a God and a future state of rewards and punishments, shall, on account of his religious sentiments, be disqualified to hold any office. . . ."[81] Apparently referring to the work of the state constitutional convention, an author writing in *The American Museum,* in 1789, observed:

The revisal of the test law has at length passed by a respectable majority of the representatives of this state. This is a prelude to wiser measures; people are just awakening from delusion. The time will come (and may the day be near) when all test laws, oaths of allegiance, abjuration, and partial exclusions from civil offices, will be proscribed from this land of reason. . . . The test law in Pennsylvania has produced more disorders, by making enemies in this state, than have cursed all the union besides. . . . But what right has even the legislature to deprive any class of citizens of the benefits and emoluments of civil government?[82]

Two years later the Delaware Constitution was rewritten to provide: "No religious test shall be required as a qualification to any office, or public trust, under this State."[83] In 1790, South Carolina removed the disabilities of the test from her citizens when she proclaimed that free exercise of religious profession would henceforth be had "without discrimination or preference."[84] Georgia had removed all religious tests one year previous with this clause: "No one religious society shall ever be established in preference to another; nor shall any person be denied the enjoyment of any civil right merely on the account of his religious principles."[85]

For many years in some other states, equality of political opportunity was denied members of certain religious faiths. In both the 1784 and 1792 New Hampshire Constitutions, the principal state offices were restricted to Protestants.[86] This prevailed there until 1877. In North Carolina the law continued to be that expressed in the 1776 Constitution which provided in Article XXXII "That no person, who shall deny the being of God or the truth of the Protestant religion, or the divine authority of the old and new testaments . . . shall be capable of holding any office or place of trust or profit in the civil department within this state."[87] This clause remained in that state's constitution until 1835 at which time it was revised by substituting the word "Christian" for "Protestant." Notwithstanding the language of the earlier constitution, Thomas Burke "who publicly professed and openly avowed the Catholic faith" had been a North Carolina delegate to the Continental Congress and had been elected governor of the state in 1781.[88] Another Roman Catholic, William Gaston, held numerous elective offices and was chosen a justice of the North Carolina Supreme Court.[89] This paradoxical situation apparently resulted from an interpretation of the clause merely as an article of peace which gave no power to the legislature to impose tests since there could be no establishment of any sect in preference to another. This view was forcefully advocated by Judge Gaston. He stated:

> But what is the Protestant religion? We have not an establishment to determine the truth of that religion and pronounce on schism and heresy; this establishment is forbidden by the Constitution; the Constitution has not defined the Protestant religion, has not excluded Catholics or any other denomination *eo nomine,* and is therefore inefficient and unmeaning.[90]

A letter in *The American Museum* in 1788 lauded the clause in the New Jersey Constitution which gave Protestants all civil rights. The *Museum's* editor, Mathew Carey, answered with this comment:

> This clause falls far short of the devine spirit of toleration and benevolence that pervades other of the American Constitutions. "Every Protestant is eligible to any office or profit or trust." Are Protestants, then, the only capable or upright men in the state? Is not the Roman Catholic hereby disqualified? Why so? Will not every argument in defense of this exclusion, tend to justify the intolerance and persecutions of Europe?[91]

The New Jersey disqualification disappeared from the next state constitution in 1844. Ultimately all state denials of public office through test oaths were invalidated by decision of the United States Supreme Court.[92]

The importance of the ban on religious tests in the history of religious freedom should not be underestimated. In the colonial period the test was a fundamental way of maintaining the monopolistic political power of the establishment. Thus when measures of disestablishment were introduced in the colonial and early state legislatures, a modification of the requirements for holding political office was one of the first steps in securing equal political opportunity to the individual members of all religions. Nevertheless it should be noted that in the early days of the American states, it was still thought proper to judge the quality of a man's public character by his adherence to some religion. Hence, atheists, agnostics, nonsectarians, and non-Christians had to wait much longer to gain equal treatment in the states.

It is in this context that Charles Pinckney's proposal in the Philadelphia Convention to secure religious liberty achieves a significance far beyond the mere banning of religious tests in Article VI. It must be recalled that his measures were not actually measures of "disestablishment" because there was nothing to abolish. He was seeking to prevent *ab initio* a national establishment of religion under the new Federal Government by removing the fundamental power of the religious establishment: the ability to control the political process through interference in the claims of conscience. For this reason it seems that he and the Founding Fathers omitted from the Constitution any grant of power to the Congress to legislate on matters of religion. With the ban on religious tests they sought to cut off any argument on the power to impose tests which would be derived or implied from the power to determine the qualifications for office or positions of trust. By preventing any one sect or religion from being excluded, a minority sect could be assured of the right to participate in the democratic processes of the new government where it could thereby protect its liberty. So strongly did the Founding Fathers believe in the necessity of this measure in a nation encompassing a multiplicity of sects that they took the bold step in extending the provision even to include non-Christians and nonbelievers. Thus, when the convention adjourned in September, 1787, the Founding Fathers could return home satisfied that their intentions to protect religious liberty through a policy of equality in law had been embodied in the Constitution. The question that remained open was whether their approach to the matter would be accepted by the American people.

The Desire of the People for Religion Amendments to the United States Constitution — Proposals by the State Conventions That Ratified the Constitution

At the time they ratified the Constitution of the United States, many of the states indicated they desired amendments to safeguard their religious liberty more effectively, and in some states the conventions spelled out what they desired. Thus, to determine the intent and purpose of the religious clauses in the First Amendment, it is necessary to examine the amendments relative to religion which were proposed by the states when they ratified the Constitution. As men versed in the public affairs of the day, the members of the First Congress under the Constitution of the United States certainly attempted to honor the wishes and demands of the states for additional safeguards of religious freedom through amendments. It is impossible to believe that the senators and representatives did not pay special heed to the amendments proposed by the states, at least from their respective states. Hence, any study of the First Amendment must include the state proposals.

Rhode Island and North Carolina did not ratify the Constitution until after the Bill of Rights had been formulated by Congress and sent to the President. When it rejected the Constitution in 1788, the North Carolina Convention did not demand any additional guarantees for religious liberty, being content to adopt a declaration of principles identical with those proposed by Rhode Island,[1] as set out below. Insight to the text of the article can be gained by consulting the debates in the North Carolina Convention. When the charge was made that under the Constitution the Eastern states would have too much influence, Governor Samuel Johnston rose to the defense of the new document. He asserted:

111

When you attend to circumstances, this will have no weight. I know but two or three states where is the least chance of establishing any particular religion. The people of Massachusetts and Connecticut are mostly Presbyterians. In every other state, the people are divided very much. . . . I hope, therefore, that gentlemen will see there is no fear that any one religion shall be exclusively established.[2]

The Governor's argument persuasively indicates that the people of North Carolina were concerned with the Federal Government's setting up of a particular religion to the exclusion of all others. In language identical to that of the North Carolina declaration, the convention of Rhode Island — which ratified the Constitution on June 16, 1790 — stated that its members viewed religious liberty in the same manner. Article IV of their statement (Article XX in North Carolina) provides

That religion, or the duty which we owe to our Creator and the manner of discharging it, can be directed only by reason and conviction, and not by force and violence; and therefore all men have a natural, equal, and unalienable right to the exercise of religion according to the dictates of conscience; and that no *particular religious sect or society* ought to be *favored or established,* by law, *in preference* to others.[3]

Thus it can be readily seen that the people of Rhode Island and North Carolina equated the establishment of religion with the legal preference of one particular sect or society. To ban establishment was to forbid a favoritism toward one religious group, and had nothing to do with preventing accommodation and encouragement to all such groups.

By unanimous vote, the popular conventions of Delaware, New Jersey, and Georgia quickly ratified the Constitution of the United States. They were among the first four states to ratify.[4] These states proposed no amendments. This grouping thus supports Main's suggestion that where Federalists dominated the ratifying conventions, the Constitution was extolled as so perfect that no amendments were proposed.[5] It is quite conceivable, therefore, that it was due largely to the strength of the Federalists, rather than a lack of interest in religious liberty, that these states demanded nothing by way of amendments to that document.

Connecticut ratified the Constitution on January 9, 1788, a week after Georgia, and similarly proposed no amendments. There were some in the Connecticut Convention who desired to remedy omission of a reference to the Deity. It was, in the words of the Association of Congregational Churches, "a sinful omission . . . in not looking to God for direction, and of omitting the mention of the name of God in the Constitution . . . proposed to the people."[6] A strong reason for the absence of Connecticut's demands for religious protection is that the people believed there was no need to place a restraint on a power which the Federal Government lacked.[7] This understanding was buttressed by Oliver Ellsworth, later to be a senator from that state in the First Congress. Writing under the name of "The Landholder," Ellsworth published an article in the December 10, 1787, issue of the *Connecticut Courant* which answered the charge that there was no federal bill of rights. After agreeing that there was no declaration that preserved the liberty of the press, he went on to state: "Nor is liberty of conscience, or of matrimony or of burial of the dead; it is enough that Congress have no power to prohibit either, and can have no temptation."[8] At the close of the Connecticut Convention on January 9, 1788, Oliver Wolcott added emphasis to Ellsworth's last observation — that there was no temptation for Congress to be aggressive in this area. Connecticut's delegate to the Continental Congress for seven years, Wolcott declared: "Knowledge and liberty are so prevalent in this country, that I do not believe that the United States would ever be disposed to establish one religious sect, and lay all others under legal disabilities."[9] Thus it is evident that some delegates in Connecticut attempted to assure the people of that state that no single religious group would receive preferential treatment from the Federal Government to the disadvantage of others. Once again discrimination and prejudice are equated with the term establishment.

Massachusetts followed Connecticut by about a month in ratifying the Constitution.[10] Unlike those states which had ratified previous to it, Massachusetts demanded amendments, although none dealt with religion. There was some apprehension, though, that the Constitution — in the absence of a religious test — might be perhaps too tolerant. For example, on January 19, 1788, Singleton of Worcester County made it known that he

> thought we were giving up all our privileges, as there was no provision that men in power should have any religion; and though he hoped to see Christians, yet by the Constitution, a Papist or an infidel were so eligible as they — He thought, in this instance, we were giving great power to we know not whom.[11]

Repeating the sentiments expressed in Connecticut by Ellsworth, Theophilus Parsons said in the Massachusetts Convention: "It has been objected that we have no bill of rights. . . . Is there a single natural right we enjoy, uncontrolled by our own legislature, that

Congress can infringe? Not one."[12] Perhaps accepting Parson's opinion that the preservation of the natural rights was defined in the state constitution and was without the scope of federal power, James Winthrop suggested fourteen propositions necessary to preserve the rights of the states in a federal form of government. Writing under the name "Agrippa," in the February 5, 1788, issue of the *Massachusetts Gazette,* he suggested:

> 13.   Nothing in this constitution shall deprive a citizen of any state of the benefit of the bill of rights established by the constitution of the state in which he shall reside, and such bill of rights shall be considered as valid in any court of the United States where they shall be pleaded.[13]

Thus evidence indicates that the people of Massachusetts failed to propose a religious liberty and antiestablishment amendment because it was their understanding that the Congress simply had no such power, and that their right to freedom of religion was adequately protected by the state constitution.

The Maryland and Pennsylvania ratifying conventions[14] offered no official demands for amendments, but minorities in each state were clearly dissatisfied with the protection given religious liberty in the Constitution of the United States. Although the Maryland Convention adjourned without agreeing to desired amendments, a large number of delegates, who were prominent men of that state, demanded additional protection. One of their proposed amendments read: "That there be no National Religion established by law; but that all persons be equally entitled to protection in their religious liberty."[15] Among those who so equated an establishment of a national religion with unequal protection for religion were Samuel Chase, later justice of the United States Supreme Court, William Paca, later governor of Maryland, and the great lawyer of the times, Luther Martin.[16]

An indication that some Pennsylvanians would object to the United States Constitution as submitted can be seen in an article which appeared in the Philadelphia *Freeman's Journal* on October 24, 1787. The unknown author lamented — less than two months before Pennsylvania ratified[17] — that in the proposed constitution,

> there is no declaration, that all men have a natural and unalienable right to worship Almighty God, according to the dictates of their own consciences and understanding; and that no man ought, or of right can be compelled to attend any religious worship, or erect or support any place of worship, or maintain any ministry, contrary to, or against his own free will and consent; and that no authority can

or ought to be vested in, or assumed by any power whatever, that
shall in any case interfere with, or in any manner control, the right
of conscience in the free exercise of religious worship. . . .[18]

It is interesting to note that the above statement is almost identical
to the principal part of Article II of the Pennsylvania Constitution
of 1776.[19] This perhaps indicates that at least this author feared
that the federal power would invade those rights which had been
acknowledged in his state constitution.

Another Philadelphia newspaper, the *Independent Gazette or
Chronicle of Freedom,* printed two articles in November of 1787
which were undoubtedly read by the members of Pennsylvania's
ratifying convention. Unknown except for the signature "An Ol
Whig," one author made this comment:

> I hope and trust that there are few persons at present hardy enough
> to entertain thoughts of creating any *religious establishment* for this
> country . . . but if a majority of the continental legislatures should
> at any time think fit to *establish a form of religion* for the good
> people of this continent, with all the pains and penalties which in
> other countries are annexed to the *establishment of a national church,*
> what is there in the proposed constitution to prevent their doing so?
> Nothing, for we have no bill of rights. . . .[20]

From the above comment, it can be seen that the author equated
a religious establishment with a national church, a forced form of
religion. The second author, "Philadelphiensis," was similarly of the
opinion that the proposed Constitution was deficient along these
same lines. He asserted: "The friends of this scheme of government
may possibly attempt to say that this religious liberty is sufficiently
secured by the constitution of the state (since it was not secured
by the federal constitution). But I say not; for this is a case in which
the United States are a party. . . ."[21]

Pennsylvania's ratifying convention was composed of a representative cross section of that state's cosmopolitan religious structure,
embracing: Quakers, Roman Catholics, Lutherans, Baptists, Methodists, and others.[22] During the debate, on December 4, 1787, James
Wilson rose to answer the charge that the Constitution did not protect basic rights. With eloquent simplicity, he queried: "I ask the
honorable gentleman, what part of this system puts it in the power
of Congress to attack those rights? When there is no power to
attack, it is idle to prepare the means of defense."[23] The argument
of a man of Wilson's stature[24] probably was persuasive to the
majority in the convention, for it accepted the Constitution without
amendment. This opinion, however, was far from unanimous. At

first, many in that assemblage had demanded that "Liberty of conscience be guaranteed and that the Federal government be denied the right to abrogate or infringe any provision of a state constitution for preservation of liberty, in matters of religion."[25] The minority of the delegates finally agreed to this slightly altered version:

> The right of conscience shall be held inviolable and neither the legislative, executive or judicial powers of the United States, shall have a power to alter, abrogate, or infringe any part of the several states, which provide for the preservation of liberty in matters of religion.[26]

Among those who signed the "Reasons of Dissent" were John Smilie, John A. Hannah, and William Findley — all of whom later represented Pennsylvania in the United States Congress.[27] Buttressing the remarks of Wilson and supporting all those who rested assured that the federal Constitution gave no power to Congress to infringe the delicate rights of religion, was a pamphlet published in Philadelphia shortly after Pennsylvania ratified the Constitution. Although the article entitled "An Examination of the Constitution for the United States of America" was merely signed by "An American Citizen," the author was Tench Coxe who had been that state's representative in the Continental Congress and at the Annapolis Convention. He discussed with obvious pride the limits of the executive power in the new Constitution. Because his comment received wide attention[28] and because it focused so clearly upon exactly those features of church-state relationships which the men of the period desired expurgated from the new Constitution, it will be set out at length:

> [L]et us look at the nature and powers of the head of that country, and those of the ostensible head of ours. The British King is the great bishop or supreme head of an established church, with an immense patronage annexed. In this capacity he commands a number of votes in the house of lords by creating bishops, who, besides their great incomes, have votes in that assembly, and are judges of the last resort. These prelates have also many honorable and lucrative places to bestow, and thus from their wealth, learning, dignities, powers, and patronage, give a great lustre and an enormous influence to the crown.
>
> In America, our president will not only be without these influencing advantages, but they will be in the possession of the people at large, to strengthen their hands in the event of a contest with him. All religious funds, honors and powers, are in the gift of numberless unconnected, disunited and contending corporations, wherein the

principle of perfect equality prevails. In short, danger from ecclesiastical tyranny, that long standing and still remaining curse of the people — that sacrilegious engine of royal power in some countries can be feared by no man in the United States.[29]

The strong objection, therefore, was to the union of the power of government with one sect which resulted in unequal treatment to all religions. Thus, even those states which officially demanded no amendments can teach much about the desired relation the Federal Government was to have with religion. Because these states apparently felt assured that Congress lacked power over religious matters, the members in these states' ratifying conventions apparently felt assured that it was "idle to prepare the means of defense," and hence offered no amendments.[30] However, delegates in other states believed that the guarantees of religious liberty should be clarified.

One of the early proposals dealt directly with the third part of Article VI of the Constitution of the United States which declared that the governmental officers, "both of the United States and of the several States, shall be bound by Oath or Affirmation, to support this Constitution; but no religious Test shall ever be required as a Qualification. . . ." When the ratifying convention of South Carolina accepted the Constitution on May 23, 1788, it resolved that "the third section of the sixth article ought to be amended by inserting the word 'other' between the words 'no' and 'religious.'"[31] The purpose of South Carolina's action was simply to imply that the "Oath or Affirmation" already in Article VI was really of a religious nature.[32] That opinion received support by Rev. Nicholas Collins in the *New York Daily Gazette,* more than a year after South Carolina's proposal. Signed by "A Foreign Spectator," the article commented on the suggested amendment: "If this amendment points out a mere inaccuracy of style, it is so far proper — an oath or affirmation being a religious test; if it means to guard against religious establishments, it is . . . superfluous."[33] Roger Sherman of Connecticut termed the proposal "an ingenious thought" and felt that "had that word 'Other' been inserted, it would probably have prevented any objection on that head."[34] He then offered a rather startling solution: "it may be considered as a clerical omission and be inserted without calling a convention; as it stands the effect will be the same."[35]

Perhaps the clearest insight into the amendment which South Carolina demanded is provided in a speech made by a member of the committee which drafted the proposed amendment. It was during the debate on that very amendment that the Rev. Mr. Cummins —

a Presbyterian minister prominent in South Carolina politics from
the time of the Revolution — presented a concise but complete treatment of what was probably the popular ground swell behind South
Carolina's proposal. He began by noting that he had "always thought
it [his] duty and honor to oppose the idea of *religious establishments;*
or of states giving in state affairs *preference to any religious denominations.*"[36] Cummins expanded on his statement: "it would be
impolitic as well as unjust for a state to give the preference to one
religious order over any others in matters of state, and to dictate
and prescribe in points of religion, in which men . . . will and must
split in opinion."[37] The overriding concern, therefore, was to outlaw
legal preference to a particular favored sect.

Reverend Cummins still objected to the phraseology of the
religious test ban in Article XI. He felt that its structure in fact,
though not in appearance, militated against the sacred nature of
an oath. Then as he introduced his amendment, which was adopted
by the convention, he indicated what he was attempting to remedy
by way of the amendment. He said:

> [W]ould it not have answered all the intended purposes of the ex-
> panded hearts of the convention as to civil and religious freedom
> to have said "but no religious denominations shall ever have prefer-
> ence to another in matters of state, and all religious societies shall
> have equal liberty and protection."

> This, or something of like import, would be an everlasting security
> against persecution and dissention upon religious accounts, and at
> the same time in no degree literally or otherwise, break in upon . . .
> the sacred nature of an oath even at a civil bar.

> Mr. President. One single word of amendment would perfectly satisfy
> me here. . . .[38]

This provides strong evidence for the proposition that when the
South Carolina legislators arrived at the First Congress the following year, they brought with them the understanding that the amendment which their state had demanded was designed to stop any
attempt of the Federal Government to place religious liberty in
jeopardy through national preference of one sect over the others.

The ratifying convention of Virginia convened during June of
1788. Midway through the month, Patrick Henry brought up the
subject of religion. With that as cue, James Madison rose and devoted considerable time to expressing his view that security for
religion could be had without a bill of rights, though he did admit
that if there were "a majority of one sect, a bill of rights would be
a poor protection for liberty."[39] That was not the case, he explained;

there was freedom of religion, "because of the multiplicity of sects which pervades America, and which is the best and only security for religious liberty in any society."[40] In that manner, he felt, "no one sect will ever be able to outnumber or depress the rest."[41] It is significant that in both instances in that speech where he mentioned an establishment of religion, he prefaced it with the adjective "exclusive." Governor Randolph, who had been a member of the constitutional convention, echoed Madison's sentiments shortly thereafter in that same assemblage. He noted that "the variety of sects which abounds in the United States is the best security for the freedom of religion. No part of the Constitution . . . will justify a conclusion that the general government can take away or impair the freedom of religion."[42]

The members of the ratifying convention apparently remained unconvinced, for they demanded security through an amendment. The chairman of the amendments committee was the great jurist and law professor, George Wythe. The twentieth amendment proposed

> That religion, or the duty we owe to our Creator, and the manner of discharging it, can be directed only by reason and conviction, not by force or violence; and therefore all men have an equal, natural and unalienable right to the free exercise of religion, according to the dictates of conscience, and that no particular religious sect or society ought to be favored or established, by law, in preference to others.[43]

The first three fourths of the amendment, through the word "conscience," is a repetition of what the Virginians had included in their own Bill of Rights in 1776.[44] The addition of the ban on establishment is clearly an expression of Virginia's desire to remove the opportunity for governmental favoritism: nothing more.[45]

On June 21, 1788, the ratifying convention of New Hampshire proposed twelve amendments to the Constitution. The eleventh demand was that "Congress shall make no laws touching religion, or to infringe the rights of conscience."[46] This language is important inasmuch as it was acquiesced in by the Committee of the Whole of the House, when the First Congress discussed the proposed amendments in 1789. The people of New Hampshire might have intended that the Federal Government should refrain from enacting any law whatsoever on religion. This would seem to be the literal interpretation of the proposal. On the other hand, it is equally possible that it was intended to prohibit the Federal Government from interfering with the existing religious systems in the states. Thus the states would be free to continue established religions if they so desired. A third possible construction is that the term "touching religion" was intended to mean infringing or abridging religion. The parenthetic addition of an item may illuminate the terminology as well as buttress the third possible interpretation just mentioned. The third article of the Massachusetts Constitution of 1780 had given the legislature the power to require the towns and religious societies to provide for public worship and religious instruction and the authority to force attendance.[47] Objection to this article was voiced in the "Return of the People of Ashby in Middlesex County," in these words:

> Religious Societies as such have no voice in Chusing the Legeslature, the Legeslature therefore have no right to *make Law binding* on them as such; every religious Society as such, is interely independent on any body politick, the Legeslature therefore have no more right to *make Law binding* on them, as such, then the Court of Great Britton have to make laws binding on the Independent states of America. . . . Investing the Legeslature with authority to *make Laws binding* on religious Societs as such is inconsistant and against the piece and welfare of the State. . . . He that made us reasonable creatures . . . has laid us under the strongest Obligation to the practice of Piety, Religeon, and Morality that can possibly be conceived, & if this wont impress our minds to doe our Duty nothing will.[48]

Seemingly, therefore, this objection was posited not upon public support of religious instruction, but rather upon the concept of compulsion to instruct and attend. In short, the objection was to the state's encroachment on the rights of conscience. Viewed in this light New Hampshire's proposal — congress shall make no laws touching religion, or infringing the rights of conscience — suggests a prohibition only upon those laws which would interfere with and constrict liberty of religion. Under this, accommodation and encouragement to religion and religious freedom would not be proscribed.

Three days before the New York ratification convention convened, an essay was published in the *New York Journal,* signed by "Sidney" — the favorite pseudonym of Robert Yates. He discussed in detail most of the articles in the New York Constitution of 1777 and compared them to the proposed federal Constitution. After setting out Articles 38 and 39 of the state constitution,[49] Yates went on to explain them: "The first of those articles [free exercise and enjoyment of religion] protects us from persecution in religious matters. The other excluded the clergy from enjoying any office, civil or military."[50] He then noted that those two provisions were "passed by in silence by the framers of the new constitution; and although possibly the leaders in both have been equally adverse to a democratic system, and have had the same object, the ruin of state government, in view."[51]

The fear of federal power expressed by Yates found its way into the ratifying convention, where on July 17, 1788, it was moved to add some restraints to the proposed Constitution: "[n]o right of any kind . . . can be cancelled, abridged, restrained or modified by Congress . . . except in conformity to the powers given. . . . That among other essential rights, the Liberty of Conscience . . . cannot be cancelled, or abridged by any authority of the United States."[52] This concept was more precisely defined at the close of the convention when that assembly proposed the following amendment to the federal Constitution:

> That the people have an equal, natural, and unalienable right freely and peaceably to exercise their religion according to the dictates of conscience; and that no religious sect or society ought to be favored or established by law in preference to others.[53]

The above language is so clear as to leave no doubt — the protection demanded in the federal compact by New Yorkers was the assurance that there would be no preference. Establishment is openly equated with "a favored religion."

That the people of the several states did not desire a gulf between government and religion, but rather the abolition of a preferential treatment toward one sect, is made manifest by the proposals discussed above. One further illustration is provided by an article entitled "Remarks on the Amendments to the Federal Constitution, Proposed by the Conventions . . ." which appeared in the *New York Gazette* for June 12, 1789. Rev. Nicholas Collins, "A Foreign Spectator," wrote:

> [R]ational religion is of the highest importance, as in many respects the security and perfection of virtue. The foundation of both should be laid in a good education. This ought to be a great object in the government of every state, and with the federal government in the territory belonging to the United States. . . . Schools ought to be formed with the gradual settlement of this country, and provided with sensible teachers, who shall instruct their pupils in those capital principles of religion which are generally received, such as being the believing and attributes of God, his rewards and judgments, a future state, Ec. . . .[54]

Thus the writer of the essay revealed the climate of opinion surrounding the First Congress. The Federal Government could properly make the exercise of religious and educational liberty more meaningful by encouraging the teaching of religion in the schools. In short, the new Federal Government should not be negative or neutral, but rather it should be a positive force in promoting the liberty of its citizens, so long as it did not favor one particular religious sect beyond all others.

The Meaning of the First Amendment Establishment of Religion Clause, According to Statements of Senators and Representatives in the First Congress

Not only were the members of the first Federal Congress well aware of the demands of the state ratifying conventions — discussed in the preceding chapter — but a significant number of the men in those state conventions were also present in the first Senate and House when the First Amendment was discussed.[1] This chapter is concerned with the statements made in the United States Congress when the establishment clause was under consideration. Declarations made outside the Congress will not be considered here because it is believed that, for the proper interpretation of the First Amendment, remarks made on the floor are much more relevant and weighty than are utterances made by these same men in another context years earlier or later in their casual correspondence with friends, or when they were concerned with the desirable content of state constitutional clauses or legislation.

The congressional campaign for the protection of religious liberty opened on June 8, 1789. On that day James Madison of Virginia rose in the House of Representatives and said:

> The amendments which have occurred to me, proper to be recommended by Congress to the State Legislatures, are these: . . . Fourthly that in article 1st, section 9, between clauses 3 and 4 be inserted these clauses, to wit: The civil rights of none shall be abridged on account of religious belief or worship, nor shall any national religion be established, nor shall the full and equal rights of conscience be in any manner, or in any pretext, infringed. . . . Fifthly, that in article 1st, section 10, between clauses 1 and 2, be inserted this clause, to-wit: No state shall violate the equal right of conscience. . . .[2]

Fisher Ames, a congressman from Massachusetts in the First Congress, wrote on June 11, 1789 to Thomas Dwight: "Mr. Madison has introduced his long-expected amendments. They are the fruit of much labor and research. He has hunted up all the grievances and complaints of newspapers, all the articles of conventions, and the small talk of their debates."[3]

An essay which appeared the next day in the *New-York Gazette*, signed by "A Foreign Spectator," gives some indication of the thrust of the amendments which had been proposed by the states when they ratified the Constitution. Entitled "Remarks on the Amendments to the Federal Constitution, Proposed by the Conventions (of the states)," the article is valuable in that it perhaps reminded the legislators who were sitting in New York at that time of the demands of the state ratifying conventions. The author stated that it would be

> very unjust and pernicious to establish any religious system in the United States; but it is needless to guard against such a visionary evil. Congress cannot by any construction, claim such a power; nor will they have any inclination for it. But if, by a very wonderful chance, a majority of Congress were so bigotted, their project would not have the least probability of success, while the several great denominations are a check upon each other. . . . Besides, the people of America will hardly submit to the payment of necessary taxes; is it then likely they would pay tithe to the clergy?[4]

Thus there is a clear indication that at least this gentleman equated the attempt to "establish any religious system" with the use of tax money to support the clergy. Since there were so many sects in the individual states, the author believed it was necessary to avoid giving preferential treatment to any one faith. The writer elaborated:

> Partiality to any sect, or ill treatment of any, is neither in the least warranted by the Constitution, nor compatible with the general spirit of toleration; and equal security of civil and religious rights is therefore given to all denominations, without any formal stipulations; which, indeed, might suggest an idea, that such an equality was doubtful.[5]

It is quite reasonable to presume that at least some of the senators and representatives in the First Congress took note of this essay, particularly since it appeared only four days after Madison had introduced his proposed amendments in the House.

The following week in New York, an interesting comment appeared in the *Federal Gazette* entitled "Remarks on the first part of Amendments to the Federal Constitution moved on the eighth instant in the House of Representatives." The writer commented thus:

The next article [First Amendment] established religious liberty, and all of those political rights, which by various tricks of state have been wounded through its means, on the firmest ground. The tender, the almost sacred rights of conscience, says this inestimable article, shall by no means, on no account be abridged or interfered with. No self righteous or powerful church shall set up its impious domination over all of the rest. Every pious man may pay the Divine Author of his existence the tribute of thanksgiving and, adoration in the manner of his forefathers.

A Pennsylvanian[6]

The same article was reprinted in *The Massachusetts Sentinel* on July 4, 1789, and in other leading papers throughout the states. Thus it was probably instrumental in helping create a public understanding of the contemplated article on religious liberty.[7]

The House had not been ready on June 8 to take up the matter of the amendments. Many of the delegates felt that the business of organizing the government — revenue laws and the judiciary, in particular — ought to be completed before the long and complicated discussion of the amendments was begun. Finally, on July 21, 1789, Madison noted that "there appeared, in some degree, a moment of leisure" in the House business, and so he hoped the amendments could be further considered. The suggestion was accepted, and on that same day all of the Madisonian proposals and those proposed by the several states were referred to a select committee, consisting of Messrs. Vining of Delaware, Madison of Virginia, Baldwin of Georgia, Sherman of Connecticut, Burke of South Carolina, Gilman of New Hampshire, Clymer of Pennsylvania, Benson of New York, Goodhue of Massachusetts, Boudinot of New Jersey, and Gale of Maryland.[8] Vining was chairman of the select committee. Two days later Fisher Ames wrote to George Minot: "I hope . . . that the amendments will be more rational, and less *ad populum,* than Madison's."[9] The Select Committee of Eleven on July 28, 1789, submitted a report which was read and then laid on the table.[10]

Although summer had come to New York several weeks earlier, the congressional temper for amendments was not heated. Pierce Butler, senator from South Carolina, wrote to James Iredell, the leading North Carolina Federalist, on August 11:

I told the House you might be led, but not forced. If you wait for substantial amendments, you will wait longer than I wish you to do, speaking interestedly. A few *milk-and-water* amendments have been proposed by Mr. M., such as liberty of conscience, a free press, and one or two general things already well secured. I suppose it was done to keep his promise with his constituents, to move for alteration;

but, if I am not greatly mistaken, he is not hearty in the cause of amendment.[11]

An understanding of congressional thinking on the general relation between government and religion is important at this juncture. Thus it is worth recording that on August 7, 1789, Congress re-enacted the Northwest Ordinance which provided in part: "Religion, morality, and knowledge being necessary to good government and the happiness of mankind, schools and the means of education shall forever be encouraged."[12]

The House resolved itself into a Committee of the Whole on August 13 to discuss the amendments. With New Jersey's representative, Boudinot, in the chair, on August 15, 1789, the House again went into a Committee of the Whole to consider the wording of the fourth proposition: "Article 1. Section 9. Between paragraphs two and three insert 'no religion shall be established by law, nor shall the equal rights of conscience be infringed.'"[13] Mr. Sylvester of New York indicated he had some doubts about the propriety of the mode of expression used in the paragraph. He apprehended that it was liable to a construction different from what had been made in the committee.[14],* Mr. Vining then suggested the propriety of transposing the two members of the sentence.[15] Mr. Gerry of Massachusetts said it would read better if it stated that no religious doctrine shall be established by law.[16] Mr. Sherman indicated that the amendment was altogether unnecessary, inasmuch as Congress had no authority whatever delegated to it (in Article I of the Constitution) to make religious establishments; he would, therefore, move to have it struck out.[17] Congressman Daniel Carroll of Maryland said that as the rights of conscience are, in their nature, of peculiar delicacy, and will little bear the gentlest touch of governmental hand; and as many sects have concurred in opinion that they are not well secured under the present constitution, he was much in favor of adopting the words. He thought it would tend toward conciliating the minds of the people to the government than almost any other amendment he had heard proposed. He would not contend with the gentleman about the phraseology; his object was to secure the substance in such a manner as to satisfy the wishes of the honest part of the community.[18]

Mr. Madison then rose and said that he apprehended the amending of the words to be that Congress should not establish a religion

---

* In order to facilitate ease of reading, quotation marks have frequently been omitted from statements made on the floor of Congress. However, the remarks in most cases have been taken verbatim from the *Annals;* this explains what may appear to be stilted or awkward language.

and enforce the legal observation of it by law, nor compel men to worship God in any manner contrary to their consciences.[19] Whether the words are necessary or not, he did not mean to say, but they had been required by some of the state conventions, who seemed to entertain an opinion that under the clause of the Constitution, which gave power to Congress to make all laws necessary and proper to carry into execution the Constitution, and the laws made under it, enabled them to make such laws of such a nature as might infringe the rights of conscience, and establish a national religion. To prevent these effects he presumed the amendment was intended, and he thought it as well expressed as the nature of the language would admit.[20] This language indicates that Madison himself may have desired and believed the people wanted an amendment which would simply prevent the national government from establishing "*a* national religion" which would "compel men to worship God in any manner contrary to their consciences."

Following Madison, Mr. Huntington of Connecticut stated that he feared, with Sylvester, that the words might be taken in such latitude as to be extremely hurtful to the cause of religion. He understood the amendment to mean what had been expressed by Madison; but others might find it convenient to put another construction upon it. The ministers of their congregations to the eastward, he said, were maintained by the contributions of those who belonged to their society; the expense of building meetinghouses was contributed in the same manner. These things were regulated by bylaws. If an action was brought before a federal court on any of these cases, he feared the person who had neglected to perform his engagements could not be compelled to do it; for a support of ministers, or building of places of worship might be construed into a religious establishment. By the charter of Rhode Island, he added. no religion could be established by law; he could give a history of the effects of such a regulation; indeed, the people were now enjoying the blessed fruits of it. He hoped, therefore, the amendment would be made in such a way as to secure the rights of conscience, and a free exercise of the rights of religion, but not to patronize those who professed no religion at all.[21]

For the second time that day, in defense of his proposed amendment, Madison rose and said he thought if the word "national" was inserted before religion, it would satisfy the minds of honorable gentlemen. He believed that the people feared one sect might obtain a preeminence, or two combine together, and establish a religion to which they would compel others to conform. *He thought if the word "national" was introduced, it would point the amendment directly*

on the object it was intended to prevent.[22] Here again Madison made
it clear to his colleagues that it was "*a* national religion" that he
intended to proscribe and nothing else. What Madison desired, according to the scholar, Episcopal Bishop Stokes, was a "legal equality" among the different sects.[23]

Although he did not wish to dwell long on the subject, Mr.
Livermore of New Hampshire rose and indicated that he was not
satisfied with the proposed religious amendment. He thought it would
be better if it was altered and made to read in this manner, that
"Congress should make no laws touching religion, or infringing the
rights of conscience."[24]

The question may be asked why the word "national" was excluded.
The following suggests the answer. Elbridge Gerry of Massachusetts
indicated then that he did not like the term "national," proposed by
Madison, and he hoped it would not be adopted by the House. It
brought to his mind some observations that had taken place in the
conventions at the time they were considering the present Constitution. It had been insisted upon by those who were called Anti-
Federalists, that this form of government consolidated the Union;
the honorable gentleman's motion shows that he considers it in the
same light. Those who were called Anti-Federalists at that time
complained that they had injustice done them by the title, because
they were in favor of a federal government, and the others were
in favor of a national one; the Federalists were for ratifying the
Constitution as it stood; the others not until amendments were made.[25]

In the light of this pressure, Madison withdrew his motion for the
insertion of the word "national" before "religion." He insisted,
nevertheless, on making his point clear by observing that the
words "no national religion shall be established by law" did not
imply that the government was a national one.[26] Thereupon the
question was put on Mr. Livermore's motion, and it passed in the
affirmative, 31 to 20.[27]

The Committee of the Whole continued its work on the proposed
amendments. On August 17 the discussion proceeded to the fifth
proposition: "Article I, Section 10. Between the first and the second
paragraph, insert 'no State shall infringe the equal rights of conscience, nor the freedom of speech or of the press, nor of the right
of trial by jury in criminal cases.' "[28] Mr. Tucker of South Carolina
stated that he presumed it was offered as an amendment to the
Constitution of the United States, but it went only to the alteration of
the constitutions of the particular states. It would be much better,
he apprehended, to leave the state governments to themselves, and
not to interfere with them more than they already had; and that is

thought by many to be rather too much. He therefore moved to strike out those words.[29]

Madison "conceived this to be the most valuable amendment in the whole list."[30] He felt that if there was any reason to restrain the government of the United States from infringing upon these essential rights, it was equally necessary that they should be secured against the state governments. He thought that if they provided against the one, it was necessary to provide against the other, and was satisfied that it would be equally grateful to the people. New Hampshire's Livermore had no great objection to the sentiment, but he thought it not well expressed. He wished to make it an affirmative proposition: "the equal rights of conscience, the freedom of speech or of the press, and the right of trial by jury in criminal cases, shall not be infringed by any State."[31] Tucker's motion was then rejected, and Livermore's clause was adopted.

The House began consideration of the report of the Committee of the Whole on August 19, 1789. On the next day, Fisher Ames moved that the proposed religious amendment be altered so as to read: "Congress shall make no law establishing religion, or to prevent the free exercise thereof, or to infringe the rights of conscience." This motion was accepted by the House.[32] It is reported in the *Journal of the House* for Friday, August 21, that the third article[33] was again debated and finally agreed to in this slightly different form: "Third. Congress shall make no law establishing religion, or prohibiting the free exercise thereof, nor shall the rights of conscience be infringed. . . ."[34] This event of August 21 is not noted in the *Annals of Congress*.[35] Obviously mindful of the demand from his state's ratification convention, Tucker of South Carolina moved on August 22 to amend the Constitution by inserting the word "other" between the word "no" and the word "religious" in the third section of Article Six.[36] The House did not agree with Tucker's motion. On the same day, Congressmen Benson, Sherman, and Sedgwick were appointed to arrange the articles — including the ban on the states from infringing on the rights of conscience — for delivery to the Senate. On the twenty-fourth, the clerk of the House was ordered to present the Senate with a "fair engrossed copy of the said proposed articles of amendment with a request for concurrence."[37]

On Tuesday, August 25, 1789, there was read in the Senate the House draft for what was then referred to as the Third Article.[38] From one of the senators present that day, we learn that the assemblage took up "the amendments to the constitution sent from the House of Representatives. They were treated contemptuously by Izard (South Carolina), Langdon (New Hampshire), and Mr. Morris

(Pennsylvania). Izard moved that they should be postponed until the next session. Langdon seconded, and Mr. Morris got up and spoke angrily, but not well. They, however, lost their motion, and Monday was assigned for taking them up."[39]

It was moved in the Senate on September 3 to amend the House draft of Article Three by striking out the words "Religion or prohibiting the free Exercise thereof," and inserting "One Religious Sect or Society in preference to others."[40] This motion was defeated. A motion for reconsideration was then passed, and a motion to strike the House-proposed third Article was negated. In lieu of the suggested third Article, it was moved to adopt the following: "Congress shall not make any law, infringing the rights of conscience, or establishing any Religious Sect or Society."[41] This too was defeated. The debate continued. Another motion was defeated which would have amended the House's third Article to read: "Congress shall make no law establishing any particular denomination of religion in preference to another, or prohibiting the free exercise thereof, nor shall the rights of conscience be infringed."[42] Perhaps from exhaustion, it was then moved to accept the third Article just as it had been received from the House (to wit: "Congress shall make no law establishing religion or prohibiting the free exercise thereof, nor shall the rights of conscience be infringed"). But this met defeat also.[43] Finally it was passed in the affirmative to adopt the wording of the House, but with the deletion of the words "Nor shall the rights of conscience be infringed."[44]

On September 9, 1789, the necessary two thirds of the Senate concurred in adopting a draft proposed by the Senator from Connecticut, Oliver Ellsworth.[45] It read as follows:

> To erase from the 3rd Article the word *"Religion"* and *insert* *"articles of faith or a mode of worship"* — And to erase from the same article the words *"Thereof, nor shall the rights of conscience be infringed,"* and insert *"of Religion; or abridging the freedom of speech, or of the press."*

The proposed amendment which would have prohibited the states from infringing the rights of conscience was also "erased" in Ellsworth's draft.[46] On the tenth, the House received word of the Senate action and on September 19 the House reconsidered its proposed amendments as changed by the Senate.[47]

On September 21, 1789, the House informed the Senate it could not agree to the wording approved by the Senate and so it desired a conference.[48] Accordingly, a Committee of Conference was named, composed of Senators Oliver Ellsworth of Connecticut, Charles Carroll of Maryland, and William Paterson of New Jersey, along with Representatives James Madison of Virginia, Roger Sherman of Connecticut, and John Vining of Delaware.[49] By the twenty-fourth of that month the House had agreed to the Committee's present wording of the First Amendment:[50] "Congress shall make no law respecting establishment of religion, or prohibiting the free exercise thereof. . . ." There is no satisfactory evidence as to who is the author of this wording. As Stokes has concluded, there is no present basis for assuming that it was the work of Madison anymore than of Charles Carroll or any of the others.[51] The following day, September 25, the Senate concurred in the resolution of the House requesting the President to submit the amendments to the states, and it was then sent to the President for transmission to the state legislatures for ratification.[52]

On the same day that the Senate concurred in the amendments an interesting discussion took place in the House which is worth noting. New Jersey's Congressman Boudinot — so frequently the chairman of the Committee of the Whole during the debate on the First Amendment — announced that "he could not think of letting the session pass over without offering an opportunity to all the citizens of the United States of Joining . . . in returning to Almighty God their sincere thanks for the many blessings he had poured down upon them."[53] Thus he moved that both Houses request the President to recommend a day of "public thanksgiving and prayer, to be observed by acknowledging . . . the many signal favors of Almighty God."[54]

Perhaps with tongue in cheek, Mr. Thomas Tucker of South Carolina suggested that the people might not be quite that grateful for the new Constitution, at least not until they found it promoted their safety and happiness. Then Tucker added: "[B]ut whether this be so or not, it is a business with which Congress have nothing to do; it is a religious matter, and, as such, is proscribed to us."[55] One of the men who had been on the conference committee just a few days before, Connecticut's Roger Sherman, rose, justified the practice as "laudable" — footnoted with a reference to Holy Writ — and reported his agreement with Representative Boudinot.[56] The latter followed with further precedents from the late Continental Congress. The question was put; it passed in the affirmative.[57]

The next day, September 26, the Senate received word of the House's Resolution, affirmed it, and ordered Senators Izard and Johnson to arrange with the committee of the House (Boudinot, Sherman, and Sylvester) the delivery of the amendments to the President.[58]

Possible Interpretations of the Intention of the Framers of the First Amendment: "Congress shall make no law respecting an establishment of religion, or prohibiting the free exercise thereof."

Although men in the First Congress and contemporary writers frequently employed the word "establishment," the framers of the First Amendment did not state with perfect clarity what they intended to convey by that term. It is not difficult, however, to discover the meaning they attached to "establishment" if one considers the manner in which the term has been generally used immediately prior to the first session of the First Congress. There is no doubt that the men in Congress during the debates on the present Bill of Rights were attempting to satisfy the demands of the state ratifying conventions for alteration of the Constitution they accepted. Being elected public officials, the senators and representatives in the First Congress were undoubtedly responsive to prevailing opinions in their states. Although the Maryland Convention had adjourned hurriedly in 1788 without agreeing to amendments desired, a large number of prominent delegates to that convention[59] demanded that the federal Constitution be amended so as to read: "there shall be no National Religion established by law; but that all persons be equally entitled to protection in their religious liberty."[60] New York proposed that "no religious sect or society ought to be favored or established by law in preference to others."[61] In almost identical language, the Virginia Convention desired that "no particular religious sect or society ought to be favored or established, by law, in preference to others."[62] The phraseology of the New Hampshire demand — "no laws touching religion, or to infringe the rights of conscience" — has been discussed above. Thus it can be seen that the proposals which must have been foremost in the minds of the legislators in the First Congress indicated the popular demand for an end to preferential treatment to religions and its concomitant restriction of the right of liberty of religion.

Since it can be easily assumed that the first senators and representatives were familiar with their respective state constitutions, inspection of these constitutions is also appropriate at this juncture. It is revealing to note that in every state constitution in force between 1776 and 1789 where "establishment" was mentioned, it was equated or used in conjunction with "preference." The New Jersey Constitution of 1776, for example, ordained that "there shall be no *establishment* of any *one religious sect* in this Province, in *preference* to another. . . ."[63] It was similarly provided in North Carolina's Constitution: "there shall be no *establishment* of any *one religious church or denomination* in this State, in *preference* to any other. . . ."[64] Almost identical with Jersey's clause, the 1776 Delaware Constitution provided that "there shall be no *establishment* of any *one religious sect* in this State in *preference* to another. . . ."[65] When the New Yorkers in 1777 adopted the statutes and common law of England in force at that date, they made careful provision in their constitution to exempt by abrogation "all such parts of the said common law, and . . . statutes and acts . . . as may be construed to *establish* or maintain any *particular* denomination. . . ."[66] Again, the Massachusetts Constitution of 1780 declared that "no *subordination of any one* sect or denomination to another shall ever be *established* by law."[67] The Pennsylvania Constitution of 1790 was finally drafted after the debate in the First Congress on the First Amendment had come to a close. Thus its provisions could not have been known by the members of the Assembly. But, inasmuch as Pennsylvania's constitutional convention began only two months after the completion of the First Amendment, consideration of its provision relative to religion might indeed shed light on the matter here under survey. It declared "that no *preference* shall ever be given, by law, to any *religious establishments* or modes of worship."[68] It is highly plausible that the men in the First Congress from New Jersey, Delaware, North Carolina, New York, and Pennsylvania brought with them this same idea, namely, that "no establishment" meant "no preference."

It is not surprising to find the most vocal advocates of religious liberty to be the victims of its absence. One of these men was the Reverend Patrick Allison, first pastor of the First Presbyterian Church of Baltimore. In 1783 he objected to a contemplated bill — desired by Protestant Episcopal clergymen — which appeared to many Marylanders to favor that faith. Allison declared: "the land had been grievously disgraced and distressed by a most absurd and inquitous religious establishment"; and he continued with chagrin that "former legislatures have even dared to declare *one* Christian *denomination established* in our ill-fated land."[69] It is not unlikely that the Marylanders in the First Congress shared Allison's view of establishment: favoritism or preference given to one denomination.

There is strong evidence of concern for "establishment," pro and con, in Massachusetts. During the ratifying convention in 1788, for instance, Major Thomas Lusk of West Stockbridge passed on to the article which forbade the qualification of a religious test, and concluded by saying that "he shuddered at the idea, that Roman Catholics, Papists and Pagans might be introduced into office; and that Popery and the Inquisition may be *established* in America."[70] Thus we see the term in question equated with the use of the authority by a political-religious alliance to the detriment of those of other persuasions. Taking opposite tack vis-à-vis the absence of a religious test, the Reverend Isaac Backus — a Baptist and a delegate to the convention from Plymouth County — voiced this praise:

> And I rejoice to see so many gentlemen who are now giving into the rights of conscience, in this great and important matter. Some serious minds discover a concern lest, if all religious tests should be excluded, the Congress would hereafter *establish* Popery, or some other tyrannical way of worship. But it is most certain that no such way of worship can be *established* without any religious test. . . .[71]

In this can be seen the other objectionable facet of establishment: the coercive potential of the imposition of a particular manner of worship and articles of faith.

Both the above aspects of establishment had been denounced almost a decade before in the instructions given the delegates to the Massachusetts state constitutional convention by the people of Pittsfield: "every man has an unalienable right . . . to worship God in that manner that is agreeable to his own sentiments without control whatsoever, and that no particular *mode or sect of religion* ought to be *established,* but that every one be protected in the peaceable enjoyment of his religious persuasion and way of worship."[72]

This statement recalls an early and interesting interpretation of "establishment," which had been provided by Alexander Hamilton in 1775. In connection with a discussion of the Quebec Act,[73] Hamilton stated: "In order to do this more satisfactorily, I beg leave to adopt the definition of an established religion, by a certain writer who has taken great pains to evince the contrary: 'An established religion,' says he, *'is a religion which the civil authority engages, not only to support, but to protect.'* "[74]

The evidence accumulated is sufficiently powerful to bring into focus the term "establishment." Thus the amendments demanded by the state ratifying conventions, the phraseology of the prevailing state constitutions, and the statements of men most interested in the subject, all bear witness to the equation of establishment with preference. Simply to list the language used — no religious sect favored, no preference, no particular denomination, no subordination of one sect to another, articles of worship — is convincing support.

One of the best insights into the understanding in 1789 of the word "establishment" is provided by Representative Huntington of Connecticut in a statement made midway through the discussions in the House on the proposed religion amendment. The *Annals of Congress* reports the Congressman's remark on August 15, 1789:

"By the Charter of Rhode Island, he added, no religion could be established by law; he could give a history of the effects of such a regulation; indeed the people were now enjoying the blessed fruits of it."[75] The charter of Rhode Island, to which Huntington referred, was the colonial charter of 1663 that remained the constitutional frame for that state until 1842. Nowhere does the charter provide for a prohibition on the establishment of religion. Yet it does manifest the concern of the people of Rhode Island for religious freedom, and mentions the abuses of an established religion:

> [B]ecause some of the people and inhabitants of the same colonie cannot, in theire private opinions, conforms to the publique exercise of religion, according to the litturgy, formes and ceremonyes of the Church of England, or take or subscribe the oaths and articles made and established in that behalfe. . . . Have therefore thought ffit, and doe hereby . . . declare, That . . . noe person within the sayd colonye, at any tyme hereafter, shall bee any wise molested, punished, disquieted, or called in question, for any differences in opinione in matters of religion . . . and all . . . persons may . . . freelye and fullye and have and enjoye his and theire owne judgments and consciences, in matters of religious concernments. . . .[76]

Thus Huntington equated an establishment of religion with compulsory worship of an alien faith, and with civic and civil disabilities attending membership in a faith other than that officially recognized. In short, civil rights ought not depend on one's religious convictions. It must be made clear, however, that although "no religion could be established by law" in Rhode Island, this did not mean that the state was hostile to religion. Quite the contrary. There were many instances when the state accommodated itself with religion to achieve a happy balance. For example, the state granted lotteries and incorporated religious bodies; it permitted courthouses to be used for religious worship when church buildings were lacking; the state provided for tax exemptions for clergy, houses of worship and religiously oriented schools. While there is no evidence of the *state* providing direct payment of salary to clergy, there appears to have been a degree of local autonomy in this matter, because there were instances of *towns* hiring and financially supporting the ministry.[77]

The word "establishment," therefore, was not of a single substance, but was rather a compound — a molecule perhaps — composed of the complexities involved in a state church. Neither preferential financial aid nor imposition of civil and civic disabilities on dissenters, by itself reached the level of an established religion. But to put flesh on the bare bones of a single word is not enough. The enigmatic phrase — no law respecting an establishment of religion — must be viewed in its entirety. The intent of the men in the First Congress when they framed and adopted the phrase is difficult to ascertain, but several possible explanations can be explored.

The clause may have been intended to be synonymous with "a law respecting a religious establishment." In support of this line of interpretation, it could be noted that on August 15, during the debates in the Committee of the Whole, Congressman Roger Sherman announced that he thought the amendment unnecessary because Congress had no power "to make religious establishments."[78] The implication of this interpretation is broad. Under such a prohibition, Congress arguably would be forbidden to incorporate a church or religious institution — school or hospital — or to make any law which would in any form aid any religious organization. Conversely, Congress could not interfere with such organizations. The debates indicate, however, that the intention to equate "an establishment of religion" with "religious establishments" did not occupy the minds of the legislators.[79]

Another possible interpretation depends likewise on the precise terminology used by the men in the First Congress. The term used by the House in the text which that body sent to the Senate was "no law establishing religion." This language is broad. The term used in the final version of the amendment is "an establishment of religion." The use of the singular noun, "an establishment," had the effect of narrowing the intended prohibition. Thus constricted, the ban would only apply to laws which would in fact set up religion as an "establishment — in the full meaning of that particular term. An argument of this nature, however, is academic, inasmuch as the final text of the establishment clause contained a further modification. The word "respecting" appeared before "an establishment of religion." This would have the effect of broadening the prohibition. Thus, with this addition, not only would those laws be prohibited which would set up "an establishment," but further, even those laws which might have the effect of introducing in a substantial manner one or several of the major components of the establishment structure. In support of this line of interpretation, it could be argued that many feared that while Congress might not have the power to officially proclaim an established religion in one stroke of the legislative pen, the same undesired end might be reached by smaller steps by the quiet enactment of laws which in themselves would not amount to an establishment, but when added together might have the cumulative effect of totaling a *de facto* establishment. For example, even nonpreferential aid to religion in the form of ministers' salaries or grants for construction, of houses of worship might be considered a law "respecting" an establishment, even though such aid in itself would not constitute a full establishment.

Further support for this interpretation is supplied by the comment of Congressman Tucker of South Carolina on September 25, 1789. On that day, Boudinot moved that both Houses resolve to request the President to recommend a public day of prayer and thanksgiving to acknowledge the favors of God. Tucker stated that "it is a religious matter, and as such, is proscribed to us."[80] He perhaps thought that such congressional action would be a law "respecting" an establishment, since he undoubtedly was well aware that states such as Delaware and Pennsylvania which had no established religion frequently proclaimed days of prayer. While a public day of prayer was not an establishment in the full sense, it might have meant to Tucker a law "respecting" an establishment. Tucker's objection — if in fact his statement can be taken to have been a sincere objection rather than merely a tongue-in-cheek spoof of the previous day's debates — was overruled and the House did adopt the resolution; but there is no evidence that the men who defended the resolution, Boudinot and Sherman, said that the establishment clause did not intend to proscribe such activity. All that is reported in the *Annals* is that they relied upon statements in the Old Testament and practices in the Continental Congress. Notwithstanding, the practices of the Congress clearly demonstrate that congressionally inspired public prayers were outside the prohibition of the establishment clause. Tucker may have been teasing by his objection, as mentioned above, or he simply may have been misinformed; if the latter, instruction was quickly provided by the full membership.

Another possible interpretation of the phraseology adopted by the First Congress rests largely on the discussions in the Senate on September 3 and 9 which are related to the House-Senate conference committee in which the final text was resolved. Three times on September 3, 1789, the Senate voted down texts of the establishment clause which had referred explicitly or implicitly to prohibiting preferential treatment of a particular religion. Nevertheless, the Senate did accept the establishment wording which had been decided upon in the House: no law establishing religion. This action may indicate that the Senate desired the ban on congressional lawmaking to be broad enough to rule out the possibility of governmental aid to religion even on a nondiscrimatory basis. There can be, however, another interpretation of the Senate's action on that day. The difficulty in finding an acceptable text may not have centered around the establishment concept; rather it may have revolved around the free exercise of religion provision. In the first two proposals which were moved that day, there was no mention of the free exercise of religion. These two were defeated. The third proposal read in part: "no law establishing any particular denomination of religion in preference to another, or prohibiting the free exercise thereof. . . ."[81] The senators may have feared that this version might admit the interpretation that Congress was banned from prohibiting the free exercise of only a "particular denomination of religion in preference to another." Thus the free exercise of all religions might not be safeguarded. This text was rejected also. The clause the senators found acceptable — "no law establishing religion, or prohibiting the free exercise thereof" — left no doubt that the free exercise of religion was protected, and not just that of a particular denomination. When on September 9, the Senate adopted the text with which it entered the House-Senate conference committee, it included the provision that Congress should make no law "prohibiting the free exercise of religion." Thus, just as it may be reasonable to conclude that on September 3 the Senate desired to outlaw preferential treatment of religion, it is equally reasonable to conclude that the major concern rather was over safeguarding the exercise of all religions.

There is still another possible explanation for the action of the Senate on September 3, the effects of which may have been felt in the Senate-House conference committee discussions. Each of the three proposed texts which the Senate rejected on September 3 had a provision prohibiting Congress from making any law which would infringe the rights of conscience. The text adopted that day, however, specifically made no mention of the rights of conscience. Thus the concern of the senators on that day may have been simply to remove that phrase from the amendment, rather than to forbid nondiscriminatory aid or preference to religion. This possibility is buttressed by the fact that on September 9 when the Senate inserted "articles of faith or modes of worship" in place of establishing "religion," the provision for infringement of rights of conscience was again specifically erased.

Between the time that a conference committee was named on September 21 and the time when that committee announced agreement on the twenty-fourth, the members had to resolve the differences betwen the House and Senate versions of the religion amendment. When they entered the conference, the three House members had with them the text: "Congress shall make no law establishing religion, or prohibiting the free exercise thereof; nor shall the rights of conscience be infringed"; the senators' text read: "Congress shall make no law establishing articles of faith or a mode of worship or prohibiting the free exercise of religion." The establishment clause in the House version was considerably broader in its possible scope than the Senate version. The House proposal conceivably could prohibit Congress from making any laws establishing religion in general, while the Senate desired to ban only a small portion of such possible activity — prescribing a religious doctrine and worship. On the other hand, the House text contained a provision safeguarding the rights of conscience, a provision which the Senate had rejected twice and perhaps rejected four times. It is possible, therefore, that a compromise was made which involved these two clauses of dispute, since both Houses were agreed on the need for the free exercise of religion.

Under pressure of Senators Ellsworth, Carroll, and Paterson, the House group may have yielded on its former insistence on a provision dealing with the rights of conscience. This may have taken nimble maneuvering, since the *Annals* report that both Representatives Madison and Vining had agreed previously to the inclusion of that phrase. A *quid pro quo* on the part of the Senate was needed. It is perhaps for that reason that the Senate yielded a bit on its version of the establishment clause. The pressure probably was strong, particularly when it is remembered that Senator Ellsworth himself had drafted the text of the Senate version: articles of faith or modes of worship. Ellsworth and his brothers in the Senate had to give something in return for the House retreat. Thus, rather than prohibit merely one aspect of an established religion — observance of a faith or mode of worship made compulsory by the state — the senators perhaps agreed to go further and to forbid Congress to legislate "an establishment" in the then-accepted meaning of the term, including preferential aid and loss of civil rights for dissenters. This probably would have satisfied Madison. This was the goal which he had sought in June and August; that concept also seems to have represented the demands of his own state of Virginia which had proposed a ban on favoritism and establishment of a particular religious sect. Thus it may have been in that manner that the six men in the conference committee decided upon the adopted text: "Congress shall make no law respecting an establishment of religion, or prohibiting the free exercise thereof."

It is not surprising that when these men returned to their respective Houses of Congress their resolved view on the religion amendment was readily accepted. These men had been interested in the problem and had undoubtedly studied it more than any of the other legislators. All 3 representatives had sat on the Select Committee of the House in July which sifted through all the proposed amendments, and, in fact, Vining of Delaware had been the chairman.

Madison was responsible for introducing the subject of amendments back in June. Although the Senate records are sparse, it is known that Ellsworth drafted what had been the Senate version. Carroll and Patterson were surely very much concerned with the disposition of the religion amendment; Paterson was known to be a deeply religious and tolerant man; because he was a Catholic, Carroll knew all too well the odious effects produced when one religion was preferred, established, and favored by the state. It is doubtful that these six men were hostile to religion or that they intended by way of the religion amendment to divorce religion entirely from the national government.

The final text of the present First Amendment may be viewed in yet another manner. One reason for the establishment clause may have been to forbid the Federal Government from interfering in the manner in which the state governments dealt with religion.[82] With this line of interpretation, full view must be given to clauses other than the establishment clause, in order to place the problem in its proper context. When the three House members entered the joint conference they were aware that the Senate had rejected the proposed amendment which would have forbidden the states to infringe the rights of conscience.[83] This was the amendment termed by Madison "the most valuable amendment."[84] Further, it had been expressly changed from a negative to an affirmative proposition by Livermore during the House debates a few weeks earlier,[85] although at least Tucker of South Carolina fought against it because he feared it would interfere too much with the state governments — and that was to be avoided.[86]

The remarks of Congressman Huntington of Connecticut on August 15 lend themselves to this argument. He noted that he agreed with Sylvester that the text of the "federal amendment" might be taken in such latitude as to be very hurtful to the cause of religion.[87] At this point the proposed version was: no religion shall be established by law, nor shall the equal rights of conscience be infringed. Huntington then mentioned the financial support for ministers of the "congregations to the Eastward."[88] Since the Congress was then assembled in New York City, he was presumably referring to his home state of Connecticut, where an establishment then existed. He feared that the proposed amendment might be interpreted in a way that the federal courts[89] would refuse to compel a man to perform the engagements he had made to support religion in any particular state.[90]

Huntington then pointed to Rhode Island as an example of a state in which there was no established religion, and added that the people there were enjoying "the blessed fruits." It is possible that these last words were steeped in sarcasm, and were delivered tongue in cheek, since no love was lost between Rhode Island and the other New England states. Furthermore, since, at that time, Rhode Island was suffering substantial civil and financial unrest, the "blessed fruits" were not too palatable. Thus, in effect, Huntington may have been arguing that care should be taken to make certain that the Federal Government did not have any power to disrupt any local state establishment. Such a relationship was good for the local community, but, he would argue, it should be directed locally. On the other hand, Huntington fully agreed with Madison that on the federal level there should be no national religion.[91] He simply feared that this injunction could be taken in a manner which would damage the "cause of religion" — as it existed on the local level.

That Congress had no intention to effect great change in the church-state relationships in the states is indicated by a comparison of the texts of both the "federal" and the "state" religion amendments as they were adopted by the House. That assembly desired to restrict the Federal Government from taking action which would prohibit the free exercise of religion, infringe the rights of conscience, or construct a political relationship with religion through an establishment thereof. Contrary to the broad sweep of the "federal amendment" the "state amendment" was designed to restrict state action only where it would amount to an infringement of the rights of conscience. There was no attempt in the House to prohibit the states from refusing the free exercise of religion; there was no attempt to interfere with any state establishments. The Senate, on the other hand, wanted no restriction on the states, and on the federal level, only an injunction upon a federal prohibition of free exercise along with federal articles of faith or modes of worship.

It is possible that the reason for the Senate's rejection of the "state amendment" was that it may have feared that the amendment might have placed in the hands of the Federal Government the thin edge of a wedge with which the state establishments might have been destroyed by federal interference. The manner in which the states maintained relations with religion was a local matter, one which was without the competence of the Federal Government. Encroachment into the states' domain might be made through the "state amendment," and hence was to be avoided at all costs. Perhaps the senators felt that mention of the rights of conscience even in the "federal amendment" — as in the House version — might conceivably be expanded by the central government to sanction interference with state religions. This may have been why the Senate rejected that portion of the "federal amendment."

The House probably desired a stronger establishment clause than that which the Senate offered, since the House version was considered broader in scope than the Senate's bar merely on articles of faith or worship made compulsory by the national government.

In the House-Senate Conference, therefore, the House members may have agreed to omit the "state amendment" and the provision for the rights of conscience in the "federal amendment," in acknowledgment of the Senate's fear. A *quid pro quo* was needed. The Senate then may have agreed to stop insisting on such a narrow scope for the establishment clause: rather than prohibit merely one part of the entire establishment concept — compulsory worship and belief — it may have decided to accept a ban on the totality, an establishment. And to make absolutely certain that the Federal Government could not interfere with religion in the states, the Senate may have insisted that the injunction on making laws to effect an establishment — and so constructing a national establishment or interfering with the state establishments — should be worded in such a way as to make the scope of the prohibition apparent. Hence the word "respecting" may have been inserted to make the clause read: "make no law respecting an establishment of religion." Thus it may have been in that manner that the final text was agreed upon.

Since it is impossible to give a dogmatic interpretation of the First Amendment, and to state with any accuracy the intention of the men who framed it, all of the above-mentioned possibilities seem clothed with reasonableness. All are conjectural. When more historical evidence is found, one may be proved correct.

Ratification of the First Amendment by the States — What the People Thought They Added to the Constitution by the Establishment Clause

In the process of interpreting the United States Constitution as the great charter of American liberties, courts and students of the Document have frequently stressed that the Constitution should not be separated from the historical context in which it was created. The broad, universal language employed by the draftsmen of the Constitution to embody its fundamental principles can too often be distorted unless it is read in light of the problems facing the states at the time of ratification. This was also the belief of the Americans who were closest in point of time to its promulgation. They, too, realized that its meaning could be obscured as the passage of time dimmed memories of the struggles which had brought it into existence. Only a short time after the new system of government had been inaugurated, defenders of the Constitution found it necessary to recall to the American people their original purposes in writing it. In 1800, a mere twelve years after ratification, the first plank of the platform of the Democratic-Republican Party, which had nominated Thomas Jefferson for president, proclaimed the party's intention to maintain:

> 1. An inviolable preservation of the federal constitution, according to the true sense in which it was adopted by the States, that in which it was advocated by its friends, and not that which its enemies apprehended. . . .[1]

Thus, as Thomas Jefferson's Democratic-Republicans have indicated, part of the task of seeking the meaning of the Constitution is to determine "the true sense in which it was adopted by the States." The relevance of this method of inquiry is even stronger where the Bill of Rights is involved. The people of the states in their ratifying conventions customarily gave clear evidence of the amend-

143

ments they desired, and they also had the opportunity to determine whether their congressmen had followed such instructions by approving or disapproving the list of amendments that was recommended for ratification to the state legislatures. Therefore it would seem that subsequent acceptance or rejection of the proposed amendments would be strong evidence on the issue of what the people intended to embody in a particular amendment. Accordingly this chapter will seek to illuminate the meaning of the First Amendment religion clauses by examining the actions of the various state assemblies in ratifying or rejecting the Bill of Rights.

One of the first states to consider the proposed articles of amendment was Virginia. The Virginia Constitutional Convention had proposed an amendment guaranteeing "an equal, natural, and unalienable right to the free exercise of religion . . . and that no particular religious sect or society ought to be favored or established, by law, in preference to others."[2] When the work of the First Congress was submitted to the Virginia Legislature, fears were expressed that the proposed amendment had not encompassed the desires of the state. On November 30, 1789, the House of Delegates voted to ratify all of the articles, including the present First Amendment which was then the third one in enumeration.[3] The Senate, however, found some of the articles wanting, and on December 8 voted to postpone consideration of several articles until "the next session of Assembly, for the consideration of the people."[4] Among these articles were the present First, Sixth, Ninth, and Tenth Amendments.

On December 9, 1789, Senator Taylor reported to the House of Delegates: "The Senate have agreed to the resolutions ratifying the amendments proposed by Congress to the Constitution of the government of the United States, with several amendments, to which they desire the concurrence of this house."[5] Two days later the House of Delegates informed the Senate that it could not agree and that it desired a conference.[6] The conference was unsuccessful, and the two Houses adjourned. The bickering continued through the next two years. Not until December 15, 1791, was the matter settled when the Senate adopted the articles *in toto* without a record vote.[7]

The basic cause for the delay of ratification, as revealed by the *Journal of the Senate,* seems to have been a concern that individual and state rights might not have been sufficiently secured. Thus the objection to the present Sixth Amendment was that it did not adequately guarantee the right to a "jury of the vicinage." The novel Ninth Amendment, which had not been requested by any state, was declared to be "highly exceptionable." The danger was that it might put a burden on the state citizens to prove which specific rights they had retained, although Madison believed it would have the opposite effect. Even the Tenth Amendment was thought defective by some in its phraseology "or to the people," since "it is not declared to be the people of the respective states; but the expression applies to the people generally as citizens of the United States, and leaves it doubtful what powers are reserved to the State Legislatures. . . . Congress might, as the supreme rulers of the people, assume those rights which properly belong to the respective states, and thus gradually affect an entire consolidation."[8]

In seeking the meaning of the First Amendment the Senate objections to the third article are even more significant. The eight-member majority declared that it was "dangerous and fallacious, as it tends to lull the apprehensions of the people on these important points without affording them security." They further stated:

> The nineteenth and twentieth [articles of the Virginia Bill of Rights] hold sacred the rights of conscience, secure to every religious sect or society, the most perfect equality, and effectually guard against any religious establishments. The Third Amendment [the present First Amendment], recommended by Congress does not prohibit the rights of conscience from being violated or infringed; and although it goes to restrain Congress from passing laws establishing any national religion, they might, notwithstanding levy taxes to any amount, for the support of religion or its preachers; and *any particular* denomination of Christians might be *so favored* and supported by the General Government, as to give it *a decided advantage over others,* and in process of time render it as powerful and dangerous as it was established as the national religion of the country.[9]

This statement was signed by John Pride, John Scasbrook Wills, Stephen T. Mason, Joseph Jones, W. Russell Turner Southall, and John Pope, all members of the majority.[10]

In the search for the intentions of the Founding Fathers as embodied in the First Amendment, the statement of the Virginia Senate is probably the most revealing extant document. It indicates that the people of Virginia intended to accept only the substance of that statement of religious freedom which they had proposed in their ratifying convention. This article, taken almost verbatim from the nineteenth and twentieth articles of the Virginia Declaration of Rights, had forbidden the establishment of a particular sect or denomination in preference to others. The fear of the Virginia Senate was that the First Amendment might not encompass the Virginia ban on preferential establishment simply by a ban on laws *"respecting an establishment."*

The senators were confident that the amendment would prohibit a "national" religion, which would probably operate to exclude persons from government privileges, benefits, and services through the erection of various tests or conditions of acceptance. (In this respect the First Amendment would be a considerable improvement over the Article VI ban on religious tests which extended only to offices held "under the authority of the United States.") They were equally confident that the Federal Government might levy taxes for the support of religious institutions. What the Senate probably feared was that the same detrimental result as a national religious establishment could be brought about through preferential treatment of a sect. Thus Congress might extend a benefit only to one sect or denomination or church. No formal test or condition imposed by Congress would be required in order for a nonmember to participate in the services, benefits, or privileges. Nevertheless the operative effect would be the same, and Congress would be able "to buy up" the members of other religions through the subtle but nonetheless coercive use of the spending power. This problem had concerned the people of Virginia once before. In the *Act for Establishing Religious Freedom* they had admonished the civil government for "bribing, with a monopoly of worldly honors and emoluments, those who will externally profess and conform to it."[11] Moreover, it would seem that such an interpretation has a direct relationship to states' rights objections made against the other proposed amendments since preferential use of the spending power could readily forment religious discord among and within the states.

Although the senators' statement revealed considerable anxiety over the meaning of the amendment, their concern seems to have been dissipated. After two years they voted for the amendment, as well as for the other questioned articles, without a record of dissent. This action would seem to indicate their belief that Congress could not establish a national religion through the use of tests and ex- clusions. Congress still might spend money for religious institutions, but the ban on preferential extension of benefits and services would insure that Congress could not establish a religion through financial favoritism.

The extant record of the Delaware General Assembly does not divulge what was discussed on the floor of either the Council or the House of Delegates anent the establishment clause of what is now the First Amendment. The House agreed to this amendment on January 22, 1790, the Council concurring on January 27, 1790.[12]

An indication of what may have been in the minds of the citizens of Delaware during the time of ratification is found in the bill of rights of the Delaware constitution of 1792. Whereas in the constitution of 1776 the clause on religious liberty stated simply that "there shall be no establishment of any one religious sect in this State in preference to another,"[13] the new constitution contained an elaborate amplification of this concept of religious liberty. It recognized that it was "the duty of all men to assemble together for public worship," that "piety and morality . . . are thereby promoted," and that on this "the prosperity of the community depends." The article continued:

Yet no man shall or ought to be compelled to attend any religious worship, to contribute to the erection or support of any place of worship, or to the maintenance of any ministry, against his own free will and consent; and no power shall or ought to be vested in or assumed by any magistrate that shall in any case interfere with, or in any manner control, the rights of conscience, in the free exercise of religious worship, nor a preference be given by law to any religious societies, denominations, or modes of worship.

The article further provided:

No religious test shall be required as a qualification to any office, or public trust, under this state.[14]

Thus the people of Delaware had come to believe during the period of the ratification of the First Amendment that participation in religious exercises should be voluntary. This did not mean that the state must be blind to religion as an institution in the lives of her citizens; the morality and prosperity of the community depended upon religion. Thus the state could recognize and protect religion, provided that this official recognition was extended on a nonpreferential basis, and that this recognition was not used to invade the rights of conscience, *viz.*, the ban on religious tests.

The records of Maryland do not indicate what the legislators thought they were accepting when they ratified the First Amendment.[15] The only clue to the feeling of the people is found in later amendments to the state Constitution of 1776. In 1795 and 1798 amendments were passed which allowed Quakers, Mennonites, and others conscientiously scrupulous of taking an oath instead to make an affirmation.[16] In 1810, perhaps reflecting the fear of the Carrolls that a particular church would be established, the legislature was forbidden "to lay an equal and general tax, or any other tax, on the people of this State, for the support of religion." Churches, accordingly, could no longer have a power of appointment over public funds to be used either for the maintenance of their houses of worship and ministers or for the support of the poor within the county.[17]

New Jersey newspapers and legislative records are even more unsatisfactory than those of Maryland, and they are completely silent on what the people thought they were adopting.[18] The state constitutional provisions are not really close enough in time to the ratification to support an exact conclusion as to what the people intended to accept. It seems, however, that New Jersey was in the mainstream of American thought on religious liberty. In 1776 it was declared that "there shall be no establishment of any one religious sect in this province, in preference to one another; and that no Protestant inhabitant of this State shall be denied the enjoyment of any civil right, merely on account of his religious principles. . . ."[19] In the next constitution adopted in 1844 the reference to "Protestant inhabitant" was dropped. The new constitution provided that while no one could be deprived of the right of worshiping God "in the manner agreeable to the dictates of his conscience," neither could he be compelled "to attend any place of worship"; nor could any person be compelled to pay tithes, taxes, or other rates to maintain any church or minister "contrary to what he believes to be right, or has deliberately and voluntarily engaged to perform."[20] The constitution continued the requirement that there could be no preferential establishment of one religious sect and that there could be no religious tests.[21]

When the United States Constitution was ratified by Pennsylvania, a minority report recommended that guarantees of religious liberty be incorporated into the Constitution by amendment. These Pennsylvanians wanted no interference with the rights of conscience, which included an exemption from military duty for those who were conscientiously scrupulous of bearing arms.[22] In the Pennsylvania General Assembly that ratified the Bill of Rights there is no indication that this minority made objection to the clause of what is now the First Amendment. On November 3, 1789, the Supreme Council submitted the amendments to the Assembly. There was only slight consideration that month. Committee action was not taken until the next session, when on February 24, 1790, the legislative committee studying the proposed amendments, approved most of the measures. On March 1, 1790, an attempt to reconsider the article dealing with apportioned representation in the then proposed amendments was defeated. On March 10, 1790, the Legislature gave formal approval to the present ten amendments. In September of 1791, under a new state constitution, the Legislature approved one of the amendments that had been struck previously.[23] No statements by the committee or members of the General Assembly have survived.

The intention of the Pennsylvania Legislature may be best understood if one considers its approval of the First Amendment within the context of contemporary provisions protecting religious liberty.

Of primary importance, therefore, is the change in the religion clause of the state constitution of 1790, since the constitution was being drafted in convention during the time the Pennsylvania Assembly was considering the federal Bill of Rights.[24] The constitution of 1776 had proclaimed that men have "an unalienable right to worship God according to the dictates of their own consciences." No man could be compelled to attend any religious worship or maintain any ministry "contrary to, or against his own free will and consent." It continued: "No authority . . . shall in any case interfere with, or in any manner controul, the right of conscience in the free exercise of religious worship."[25] The new constitution repeated this declaration, but added to it a statement designed to clarify the state's position in regard to an establishment. This significant clause stated: "That no preference shall ever be given, by law, to any religious establishments or modes of worship."[26]

In approving the First Amendment the legislature of Pennsylvania seems to have intended to accept the proposition that there could be no exclusive "establishment" of religion without a preference or discrimination in favor of one or more religions to the prejudice of others. Moreover, the clause indicated that the term was associated with the imposition of a "mode of worship."

In contrast to the activity in Pennsylvania, New York proceeded to ratify the Bill of Rights almost without serious debate. The governor submitted the proposals on January 12, 1790. On the twenty-third of that month the Senate resolved itself into a committee of the whole to consider the amendments. The Senate, speaking through the chairman of the committee, Mr. Williams, announced on January 26, that it rejected the second and unanimously agreed to the remainder. Events moved rapidly from then until final passage. On February 4 Mr. Williams reported that the committee believed that a special committee should be appointed to consult with the House to consider the mode of ratification. The House proceeded to affirm the action of the Senate, sending a resolution of ratification to the Senate on the twenty-second. Finally, on February 24, 1790, the bill ratifying the amendments was reported out of the Senate committee, was agreed to, and was passed.[27]

New Hampshire quietly ratified the federal Bill of Rights on January 25, 1790. The state records are mute as to the opinions of the ratifying legislators on the congressional proposals concerning religion.[28] Apparently the legislators did not think there was any serious conflict between the present First Amendment and the New Hampshire proposed text of the amendment that Congress be denied power to make any law "touching" religion.

The failure of Connecticut to ratify the federal Bill of Rights has long been a puzzle. The legislative records are sparse, reporting only proposal and rejection. The General Assembly met in October of 1789. The proposals were submitted to both Houses which passed favorably on Proposals Three through Twelve (the present Bill of Rights), although there was some confusion over the fate of Proposal Two.[29] In the 1790 spring session the proposals were again considered; and again Proposals Three through Twelve were approved by both bodies, with the Senate accepting Proposal Two. Disagreement over the form of the amendments put a halt to further consideration.[30] The fall session brought the two Houses no closer together. The lower House at one time rejected all the proposals, but it later concurred with the Senate in tabling them until the spring session of 1791.[31] There was no action on the amendments in either session in 1791. Since the necessity of acting was removed by Virginia's ratification on December 17, 1791, no further action was necessary to put the ten amendments in force; thus Connecticut never again considered them until her ceremonial ratification in 1941.[32]

The explanation of Connecticut's failure to ratify has many facets. At that time she was still rigidly controlled by the Congregationalist oligarchy which dominated her intellectual, political, and economic life.[33] Moreover, the concept of civil liberties was not yet recognized in that state's fundamental law. There was no state constitution, except so far as the original colonial charter might serve the needs of government. Statutory law issuing from an all-powerful Legislature was the only recognized law.[34] If public comment is any indication of the contemporary feeling, the people had no vital interest in the proposed amendments to the federal Constitution. Typical of the public attitude was the action of the *Connecticut Courant* which simply printed the amendments without comment.[35] The early apathy of Connecticut citizens was noted by James Madison in a letter to John Randolph, in which he declared: "Connecticut is least inclined, though I presume not inflexibly opposed, to a moderate revision."[36] Thus it appears likely that the people of Connecticut considered that the Constitution itself had satisfied their fears concerning religious liberty — fears of legal disabilities being placed on a religious sect[37] and the lack of a mention of religion in the Constitution.[38] Upon further reflection they probably saw no need for a reference to religion.

Apathy also marked Massachusett's attitude toward the proposed federal Bill of Rights. Governor John Hancock did not formally submit the amendments to the General Court (the Legislature) until

January 14, 1790, recommending them to the court's "serious and careful attention."[39] "The seventh, eighth & ninth articles [present Amendments 5, 6, and 7]" appeared to him "to be of great consequence."[40] There were others which were "very important to that personal security, which is so truly characteristic of a free government." Inevitable disagreements arose. The Senate was willing to adopt Articles Two through Twelve. The House rejected the first two, but added number Twelve to the list of discarded articles.[41] A solution was sought by the appointment of a joint committee. The committee took a broad view of the proposals. It was not content to consider only those amendments sent from the Congress but also considered what further amendments might be necessary.[42] Religion, however, must have appeared secure to the court for the joint legislative committee report made no mention of religion.[43] The greatest concern among them seems to have been the preservation of a federal system with strong state governments. It was only natural, therefore, "that every good man will seasonably oppose a consolidation of the States, an event that must be attended with the loss of everything dear to a free, virtuous and manly people."[44]

The growing satisfaction of the people of Massachusetts with the new Constitution seems to have done away with any necessity for action on the proposed amendments.[45] Even though the amendments had been endorsed by the joint committee, no action was ever taken. Governor Hancock in his address of January 19, 1791, to the legislature remonstrated that the people of the Commonwealth had ratified the Constitution on the supposition that amendments would be forthcoming. However, no prodding would pry the amendments out of the legislature. When Thomas Jefferson asked Christopher Gore about the fate of the amendments, Gore reported: "It does not appear that the committee has ever reported the bill."[46]

Georgia was another state that failed to ratify the amendments. There is but a single cryptic statement by a joint committee of the two Houses of the Legislature to the effect that "the defective parts of the Constitution . . . cannot be effectually pointed out, but by experience. . . ."[47] The committee recommended postponement, which both the Senate and the House immediately brought about by laying the amendments on the table.[48] Nevertheless, it should be noted that Georgia's constitutional provisions reflected the American consensus on the subject of religious liberty. In the constitutions of 1777 and 1789 she had declared that all persons should have "free exercise" of their religion.[49] In 1798 she had expounded her concept as meaning: "No one religious society shall ever be established in this State, in preference to another; nor shall any person be denied the enjoyment of any civil right on account of his religious principles."[50]

In South Carolina, too, ratification of the amendments was without disagreement. In his speech of January 4, 1790, Governor Charles Pinckney submitted the proposed articles to both Houses. On the seventh of that month they were received in the House.[51] On the same day the chair appointed a committee of five, headed by Major Thomas Pinckney, and which included the ardent proponent of a bill of rights, Patrick Dollard.[52] The committee reported in favor of all twelve amendments on the next day.[53] On January 18, 1790, they were approved with no dissent recorded.[54] Action in the Senate was equally swift. The amendments were submitted on the twelfth.[55] With a similar lack of dissent, concurrence with the House came on the nineteenth, along with a rejection of New York's proposal for a second convention as "inexpedient."[56]

South Carolina's rapid acceptance of the amendments was confirmation that she believed her ideas on religion had been embodied in the new federal Constitution. These had developed from the constitution of 1778 which had hesitatingly agreed that all persons acknowledging "one God and a future state of rewards and punishments" should be "freely tolerated," and that all Protestant Christians should enjoy "equal religious and civil privileges."[57] At the convention which ratified the federal Constitution, South Carolina had endorsed Reverend Francis Cummins' concept that religious liberty meant "no preference" and "equal liberty and protection."[58] Finally, in June of 1790, five months after ratifying the First Amendment, the South Carolina state constitutional convention affirmed the belief that religious freedom demanded equality in law. The new constitution proclaimed that:

> The free exercise and enjoyment of religious profession and worship, without discrimination and preference shall hereafter be allowed within this State to all mankind . . . [and the] rights, privileges, immunities, and estates of both civil and religious societies, and of corporate bodies, shall remain as if this constitution had not been altered or amended.[59]

It is extremely difficult to determine the motives behind the actions of Rhode Island, which first rejected the Constitution and then ratified it after the Bill of Rights had been proposed. In the first rejection it is likely that the people were expressing dissatisfaction with some of the basic principles behind the structure of the new government. The reason generally assigned for the long delay in ratification is that the state was opposed to a hard money policy and a strong central government that would have resulted from the federal system. Recent appraisals have reinforced this view. Thus, as H. M. Bishop concluded, the principal objection to the Constitution was a fear of heavy land and other taxes plus fear of delegating too much power to the central government.[60]

In the town meetings in 1788–1789 some persons feared that through southern influence the Episcopal Church might be forced upon the Union and there were even some recommendations that liberty of conscience should be secured.[61] However, it does not follow from evidence of these sporadic remarks that fear of a lack of adequate safeguards for religious liberty was a controlling factor in the delay, as some writers would imply.[62]

The records concerning ratification of the Constitution and the Bill of Rights are fragmentary, giving only a bare outline of the official action. They do indicate that seven requests were made in the Rhode Island Legislature to call a convention. The eighth request for a convention was granted, but only by the margin of a tie-breaking vote cast by the governor in the Senate. The first session of the convention met in South Kingston in March of 1790. The official journal is filled with gaps and it breaks off in the middle of the discussion of the amendments. What record there is of the debates comes from the sketchy personal journals of Theodore Foster and Daniel Updike.[63] Foster's journal records the following discussion on March 4, 1790:

Mr. Marchant moves that the Amend[ments] recommend[ed] by Congress be read.

[They are read accordingly.]

Mr. Sheldon — thinks that every State ought to [be] precluded from making any law respecting Religion or abridging the Rights of Consci[ence].

Mr. Marc[han]t — says it will be dangerous to attempt such a measure — every State will.

Sheldon. If it is right that Congress should not make any Laws respecting it, no State ought to have the Right.

B. Bou[rn] Says there is no Danger of any Establish[men]t of any mode of Religion whether we wou[l]d not appoint a Chaplain.[64] The persecution in the other States of our Ancestors was an Advant[a]ge to this State — and should they persecute them it will be a means of Accession to this State.

Mr. Mar[chan]t wishes all men would agree not to establish any

Religi[on] — enough for us to keep it out of the Gen[eral] Gov[ernmen]t.

B. Bourn. Provisi[on] made by Consti[tution]. That no establish-[ment] shall not be made to [incomplete]. No danger of any of the States taking measur[es] tending — from the high[e]st practic[e] and the present General Sentiment of the World on this subject.

The Rhode Island convention then proceeded to ratify the Constitution and the Bill of Rights, with final action on the latter being taken on June 15, 1790, by the Legislature.[65] That the people of Rhode Island were satisfied with the First Amendment is indicated not only by the brevity of their remarks on it but also by their reluctance to propose any amendments on the subject of religion. They were content to adopt a statement on religious liberty which is verbatim the religious clause of the Virginia Declaration of Rights of 1776.[66] This article declared Rhode Island in favor of "no preference" and no favoritism to any "particular religious sect." This was indeed consistent with the ideas expressed during the first convention by Mr. Bourn, who had equated "establishment" with religious "persecution." Additional light may be shed on the Rhode Island statement of religious liberty by comparing it with the "Act Relative to Religious Freedom," which was passed in 1794 by the Legislature. The preamble denounced the presumption of legislators and rulers "who being themselves but fallible and uninspired men" in "setting up their own opinions and modes of thinking as the only true and infallible, and as such endeavoring to impose them on others, hath established and maintained false religions over the greatest part of the world."[67] The Act also condemned compelling "a man to furnish contributions of money for the propagation of opinions which he disbelieves." Like several of the other state laws and constitutions, it equated "teachers" of religion and "ministers." The Act declared: "[E]ven forcing him to support this or that teacher of his own religious persuasion, is depriving him of the comfortable liberty of giving his contributions to the particular pastor whose morals he would make his patterns on." The Act also discussed the relationship that religion should bear to the exercise of political and civil rights, saying

> that our civil rights have no dependence on our religious opinions; that therefore the prescribing any citizen as unworthy the public confidence, by laying upon him an incapacity of being called to offices of trust and emollument, unless he profess or renounce this or that religious opinion, is depriving him injuriously of those privileges and advantages to which . . . he has a natural right . . . to

suffer the civil magistrate to intrude his powers into the field of opinion . . . is a dangerous fallacy. . . .[68]

Finally, the Act codified its declaration of principles in the following statement:

> That no man shall be compelled to frequent or support any religious worship, place or ministry, whatsoever; nor shall be enforced, retrained, molested, or burthened in his body or goods, nor shall otherwise suffer on account of his religious opinions or beliefs; but that all men shall be free to profess, and by argument maintain, their opinions in matters of religion, and the same shall in no wise diminish, enlarge or affect their civil capacities.[69]

As the foregoing would seem to indicate, the chief concern that Rhode Island had expressed in regard to religious freedom was that the civil power might use religion to obstruct men in the exercise of their liberties. The scrupulous Mr. Bourn may have believed that the Legislature had not used a chaplain so as to avoid even the chance that the government might use religion to infringe upon civil rights. It should be noted, however, that the people of Rhode Island do not seem to have elevated Mr. Bourn's fear into a rule of conduct. As the discussion in other chapters has indicated, and as Chapter Eight will further develop, the people in Rhode Island believed in a pragmatic accommodation of the mutual interests of the church and the state. The important thing was that "opinions in matters of religion" should not be used either to grant a special privilege or to impose a civil incapacity.

North Carolina has also presented problems of historical interpretation. The charge has been made that North Carolina was dissatisfied with the provisions for religious freedom in the new Constitution.[70] One writer has claimed that North Carolina voted against the adoption of Article VI because of anti-Roman Catholic objections.[71] Because North Carolina rejected the Constitution in 1788, it would seem, therefore, that the first question to determine is whether the religious safeguard in Article VI was deemed an adequate safeguard for the liberties of the citizens of the new states. A reading of the debates and available studies on this state's role in the formation of the Union indicates that the assertions discussed *supra* are without foundation. The authority on ratification in North Carolina, Louise I. Trenholme, reports that "the all-inclusive objection to the Constitution was the delegation of power to the central government at the expense of the states and the people. . . ."[72] The concerns over a lack of protection for religious liberty and the admitting of Roman Catholics and Jews to the national government were swept away both by Federalists and Anti-Federalists. Fears of a national establishment were absolved with the arguments (1) that the government had no power to make an establishment and (2) that the multiplicity of existing sects guaranteed that no one sect could ever gain control of the Federal Government.[73] Moreover, Samuel Spencer, a leading Anti-Federalist who generally opposed the Constitution, went so far as to endorse the provisions of the sixth article, saying, "I cannot object to this part of the Constitution. I wish every other part was as good and proper."[74] When the vote was called, the measure passed without record of a dissenting vote.[75]

Further evidence that North Carolina's refusal to ratify was not due to dissatisfaction with the religion provisions of the Constitution can be seen in the recommendations of the first convention. Although the convention passed a Declaration of Rights similar to the proposed articles of amendment from Virginia and Rhode Island, which would ban preferential establishment,[76] out of twenty-six recommended amendments there is *none* on the subject of religious liberty.[77] The inference must be that the Federalists had carried their arguments that religious freedom was protected.

Ratification of the Constitution and the amendments was accomplished in December of 1789. Although records of the debates are not extant,[78] available evidence indicates that the citizens of North Carolina had swung overwhelmingly to the side of the Federalists. A bill of rights was an important factor in the change of sentiment, but it seems not to have been paramount.[79] In the first place, copies of the convention debates containing the well-reasoned Federalist arguments in behalf of the Constitution were widely circulated. In the second, commercial pressures acted to unite the agricultural interests of the back country, the heart of the Anti-Federalist camp, with the strongly Federalist mercantile interests on the coast. The rapprochement was hastened by a general dissatisfaction with the leadership of the Anti-Federalist movement.[80]

If the newspaper reports of the time can be taken as representative of the attitude of the citizens, again it seems that they were acting to confirm the views expressed in the first convention.[81] The few articles dealing with religion and religious liberty indicated a deep concern for the place of religion in the public life of the new republic.[82] The most important of these was an article by the Reverend Nicholas Collins, which had been first printed in the New York newspapers in June of 1789 and was then being widely circulated in the influential magazine, *The American Museum*.[83] Even though it concerned the proposed articles of amendment on religious liberty, it is relevant to the intentions of the people of North Carolina since it first appeared there at the time that the text of First Amendment was presented. Apparently Reverend Collins' essay was being used as an *explication du texte* of the First Amendment. The highlights of the discussion include arguments that *de facto* a multiplicity of sects would prevent an establishment, that establishment meant partiality to or ill treatment of a sect, and that purpose of any amendment must be to guarantee to every state in the union, "perfect liberty of conscience; because it is much more probable that superstition mingled with political faction, might corrupt a single state than that bigotry should infect a majority of the states in congress." His solution was that every state and the Federal Government in the territories belonging to the United States should provide a system of education "with sensible teachers, who shall instruct their pupils in the capital principles of religion, which are generally received, such as the being and attributes of God, his rewards and judgments, a future state, &c."[84] When this statement is considered in relation to the events in the first convention, it is apparent the citizens of North Carolina did not intend to embody a revolutionary principle in the First Amendment which would strip the Federal Government of power to recognize the needs of her religious citizens. To the contrary, it would seem that they had embodied a mandate for impartial accommodation of the coordinate interests of church and state.[85]

From the foregoing discussion of the ratification of the First Amendment, two basic historical facts stand out strongly: first, the necessary states ratified the amendments within a relatively short period of twenty-six months; second, there was notable lack of protest over or even comment on the content of the amendment as it was submitted to the states. Only Virginia articulated concrete objections, but these were not strong enough to prevent approval by that state. The delay in acceptance of Rhode Island and North Carolina seems to be explained by factors other than dissatisfaction with the content of the First Amendment. The failure of three states to ratify — Georgia, Connecticut, and Massachusetts — seems to have been due to the lack of a sense of necessity to modify the Constitution. It would seem, therefore, that Congress had sufficiently captured the aspirations of the states in the religion clauses of the First Amendment.

The question, then, is what had the states asked of their senators and representatives by way of alteration in the new federal Constitution. When making the inquiry, one should recall, first, that the amendments were to be safeguards *in addition* to those already implicit in the Constitution under the doctrine of delegated powers and to those explicitly stated, such as the ban on the religious test; second, that the requests for amendments were largely for equality and nonpreferential treatment in matters involving religion; and, third, that the language employed by the ratifying conventions was often directly quoted from existing state constitutional guarantees of religious liberty. Thus it appears that what was proposed and what was accepted was largely a reflection of the tolerant spirit of the times and was by no means intended to be a radical experiment in the progress of religious freedom.

The Practices of the Times as Casting Light Upon the Meaning of the Establishment Clause of the First Amendment

In seeking the meaning of the Constitution it is necessary to examine the manner in which the people of the constitutional generation lived under the new Constitution, since their actions will often reveal what they thought the provisions meant. James Madison and the United States Supreme Court both have endorsed this method. The "practices of the times," they declared, are highly relevant in determining the meaning of the Constitution.[1] Such an investigation is of critical importance when the religion clauses of the First Amendment are in issue, for as the previous chapters have indicated, not every relationship between the church and the state was to be condemned by the epithet "establishment." Often the colonies and then the states believed it desirable and proper to aid and protect the functions of religious organizations, especially where the interests of the state and the religious organization might coincide. This had most often brought about an accommodation of their mutual interests in the fields of public morality, poor relief, and education. In order to eliminate discrimination in these areas of accommodation — and the possible charge of "establishment" — the state constitutions most frequently provided that there be no preference granted to any religion but that all religions were equal before the law.

From the early days of the republic it had been the opinion of many persons that such a policy had been embodied in the First Amendment. In 1800 Thomas Jefferson's Democratic-Republican Party, which was devoted to supporting the Constitution in the "true sense in which it was adopted by the states," had proclaimed in its platform its belief in:

> 8. Freedom of religion, and opposition to all maneuvers to bring about legal ascendancy of one sect over another.[2]

This was also the considered opinion of Justice Joseph Story of the United States Supreme Court, who had observed in the first edition of his famous *Commentaries on the Constitution:*

> Indeed, the right of a society or government to interfere in matters of religion will hardly be contested by any persons, who believe that piety, religion, and morality are intimately connected with the well being of the state, and indispensable to the administration of civil justice . . . it is impossible for those, who believe in the truth of Christianity, as a divine revelation, to doubt, that it is the especial duty of government to foster, and encourage it among all the citizens and subjects.[3]

> Probably at the time of the adoption of the constitution, and of the amendment to it, now under consideration, the general, if not the universal sentiment in America was, that Christianity ought to receive encouragement from the state, so far as was not incompatible with the private rights of conscience and the freedom of religious worship. An attempt to level all religions, and to make it a matter of state policy to hold all in utter indifference, would have created universal disapprobation, if not universal indignation.[4]

And he concluded:

> The real object of the amendment was, not to countenance, much less to advance Mahometanism, or Judaism, or infidelity, by prostrating Christianity; but to exclude all rivalry among Christian sects, and to prevent any national ecclesiastical establishment, which should give to an hierarchy the exclusive patronage of the national government.[5]

Thus, according to the foremost commentator of the times on the Constitution of the United States, the religious clauses of the First Amendment were designed to prohibit the use of religion as an instrument of national civil policy by forbidding exclusive privileges to any one sect. A policy of withdrawing the power of the Federal Government to aid religion was not contemplated and would have found emphatic disapproval. It was, in short, a policy of "non-establishment" or equality in law for all religious groups.

A study of the practices of the times during the period from 1789 to 1825 substantiates the claim of Jefferson's party and Justice Story's observations. It is important to note, however, that state and federal practices may be of different significance in that what was desired in the states may not have been foreseen in those early days as a course of action by the Federal Government. Nevertheless, as Madison suggested, these practices are illuminating in the task of seeking the meaning of the First Amendment.

An inspection of the religion clauses in the state constitutions which were in effect during the period 1789–1825 discloses that the people of not a single state desired "an absolute wall of separation." What was denunciated in "establishment," according to a majority of the state constitutions, was the preference or favoritism of one sect or a combination of sects over others. The Delaware Constitution of 1776 ordained that "There shall be no establishment of any one religious sect in this State in preference to another. . . ."[6] In 1792 the people of that state reworded the clause to safeguard themselves against the possibility of a multiple establishment. The constitution of that year added to the religious liberty guarantee these words: "[N]or a preference be given by law to any religious societies, denominations, or modes of worship."[7] Like the original Delaware constitution, the New Jersey Constitution of 1776 provided: "That there shall be no establishment of any one religious sect in this Province in preference to another."[8] Religious liberty was guaranteed under the New York Constitution of 1776 "without discrimination or preference."[9] And in the North Carolina Constitution of 1776 it was ordained that "There shall be no establishment of any religious church or denomination in this State, in preference to any others."[10] Virginia's opposition to preference was expressed by a clause in its 1776 constitution to the effect that "all men are equally entitled to the free exercise of religion."[11] Somewhat similarly, the South Carolina Constitution of 1790 guaranteed religious freedom "without discrimination or preference."[12] The Pennsylvania Constitution of the same year added to its religious liberty clause the provision "that no preference shall ever be given, by law, to any religious establishments or modes of worship."[13]

Some of the state constitutions in effect during the period 1789 to 1825 also specifically incorporated the desires of the citizenry that religion be financially aided by the state. For example, the Massachusetts Constitution of 1780, which prevailed until 1833, provided:

> As the happiness of a people, and the good order and preservation of civil government, essentially depend upon piety, religion and morality . . . the legislature shall from time to time authorize *and require* the several towns and parishes . . . to make suitable provision, at their own expense for the institution of the public worship of God.[14]

The New Hampshire Constitution of 1784 stated:

> As morality and piety, rightly grounded on evangelical principles, will give the best and greatest security to government, and will lay in the hearts of men the strongest obligations to due subjection; and as

the knowledge of these, is most likely to be propagated through a society by the institution of the public worship of the Deity, and of public instruction in morality and religion; therefore, to promote those important purposes, the people of this state have a right to impower, and do hereby fully impower the legislature to authorize from time to time, the several towns, parishes, bodies-corporate, or religious societies within this state, to make adequate provision at their own expense, for the support and maintenance of public protestant teachers of piety, religion and morality.[15]

The identical provision was repeated in the New Hampshire Constitution of 1792.[16] James Madison was willing to acknowledge as late as 1832 that "it is true that the New England States have not discontinued establishments of Religion."[17] Nor were these the only states whose constitutions specifically authorized aid to religion. For example, the Maryland Declaration of Rights of 1776 empowered the Legislature to "lay a general and equal tax, for the support of the Christian religion."[18] The people of Georgia in their 1798 Constitution provided: "No one religious society shall ever be established in this State, in preference to another. . . ."[19] They added in a subsequent section:

> The arts and sciences shall be promoted, in one or more seminaries of learning; and the legislature shall, as soon as conveniently may be, give such further donations and privileges to those already established as may be necessary to secure the objects of their institution. . . .[20]

Abiding with the Charter of 1663, Rhode Island adopted no state constitution until 1842.

Because the United States Supreme Court has often indicated that contemporary state constitutional provisions are relevant in construing the United States Constitution, it is important to note that under all the foregoing state constitutions it was legally proper for the state to aid religion and religious education in the period immediately following ratification of the Bill of Rights. Indeed, there is ample evidence that the states aided religious institutions after 1789, as they had previously, by continuing:

1. To aid churches and church-related schools by the grant of lands;

2. To aid religion and religious education by providing public funds;

3. To empower churches and church-related schools to conduct lotteries;

4. To grant tax exemptions to churches and religiously oriented schools;

5. to grant legal status and powers to churches by incorporation;
6. To employ and compensate chaplains, and give public prayer;
7. to proclaim days of prayer, fast, and thanksgiving;
8. To enact and enforce laws making it a crime to blaspheme or to engage in nonreligious activities on Sunday.

Of even greater significance for an understanding of the religion clauses in the First Amendment is the fact that, like the states, the Federal Government itself was willing to aid religion and religious education in many ways. No hostility to religious institutions was ever displayed. Not only did the government of the United States under the Constitution regularly employ and compensate chaplains in the House and Senate, the armed forces, and the hospitals, but the federal Congress also thought it proper and legal to grant land to a Baptist church in Mississippi. On a number of occasions the Federal Government made funds available to religion and religious education. The practices of the years immediately subsequent to the ratification of the First Amendment demonstrate that the great majority of the American community fully accepted the idea of church-state accommodation. There is, in this period, no evidence of hostility to religion just as there was none during the first years of independence.

The Grant of Public Lands to Churches and Church-Related Schools

The Congress of the United States, in the early years of our national existence, frequently made grants of land to educational institutions, both public and private.[21] Thus the Seventh Congress set aside a township of land in 1803 in the Ohio Territory "for the purpose of establishing an academy," and there was no limitation upon the sponsorship of such academy.[22] The following year in organizing the Indiana Territory, the Eighth Congress provided that Section Sixteen in each township was to be reserved "for the support of schools," and again there was no restriction that the schools be "public."[23] This pattern was followed by the Eleventh Congress in 1811 for the Louisiana Territory[24] and by the Fifteenth Congress in 1818 for the Territory of Michigan.[25] In Alabama Territory a township was reserved in 1818 by the same Congress "for the support of a seminary of learning,"[26] and a township was set aside by the Nineteenth Congress for the same purpose in Florida Territory in 1827.[27] When Congress provided for the organization of states in the territories, it often set aside land for the use of schools, without any limitation to governmental institutions.[28] It was in 1845 that Congress for the first time limited the grant to "public schools."[29]

The understanding of our earlier congressmen that the First Amendment did not prevent federal governmental grants of land to church-related educational institutions is vividly shown by grants of land "to the amount in value of twenty-five thousand dollars" each to two denominational institutions in the District of Columbia: Columbian College in 1832[30] and Georgetown College the following year. The act granting the land to Georgetown provides:

> Be it enacted, That there shall be, and hereby are, granted to the President and Directors of Georgetown College in the District of Columbia, lots in the city of Washington, to the amount, in value, of twenty-five thousand dollars, which said lots shall be selected and valued by the commissioner of the public buildings, when requested by the said president and directors; and when the said lots shall be so selected and valued, the same shall be vested in the said corporation in fee simple. . . .[31]

In effect, these grants were donations of funds to the sectarian institutions, since the act directed the land to be sold "as soon as reasonably practicable," and the proceeds to be used "to the establishment and endowment of professorships."

Furthermore, the Congress was willing during the first year of national life to reserve and appropriate land for the encouragement of religion, and there is no reason to believe that the members of these Congresses deemed such aid inappropriate. In 1787 the Congress granted land to the Ohio Company, reserving various plots for the encouragement of religion.[32] About the same time, an indenture was executed to one John Cleeves Symmes covering land in Ohio subject to the same reservation. Then, on April 21, 1792, the Congress authorized the President to issue letters patent to the agents of the Ohio Company "with the reservations in the said indenture expressed."[33] Lastly, in 1833 the Congress of the United States authorized the State of Ohio to dispose of

> the lands heretofore reserved and appropriated by Congress *for the support of religion* within the Ohio Company's and John Cleeves Symmes' purchases, in the state of Ohio, and to invest the money arising from the sale thereof in some productive fund; the proceeds of which shall be forever annually applied, under the direction of the said legislature, *for the support of religion* within the several reserved and set apart, and for no other use or purpose whatsoever, according to the terms and stipulations of the contracts of the said Ohio Company's and John Cleeves Symmes' purchases within the United States. . . .[34]

Further evidence that the members of the early Congresses understood that the grant of government lands to churches was both desirable and constitutional is found in an 1811 bill providing for a grant of land to a Baptist church in Salem, Mississippi. That James Madison vetoed the bill[35] does not detract from the congressional conclusion of constitutionality.

The people of the various states accepted as proper the grant of public lands to religious institutions and religiously affiliated educational institutions. For example, a number of religiously owned academies in Massachusetts were given such assistance in the period from 1780 to 1800.[36] In 1790 the New York Legislature gave Columbia College and a number of academies public lands to be applied to the encouragement of literature.[37] The policy of the state during this decade was, as noted by Charles J. Mahoney, "to benefit religion and education" by land grants.[38] Rhode Island also granted lands to schools run by religious groups such as the Society of Friends.[39] The same story can be told of Pennsylvania. There, on April 9, 1791, the Pennsylvania Legislature granted 5000 acres of land to "The Society of the United Brethren for Propagating the Gospel Among the Heathen," so that "the savages may be induced to turn their minds to the Christian religion, industry and social life with the citizens of the United States."[40]

In the southern states the people were equally agreed that granting state lands to churches and church-related schools was desirable. In 1813 the South Carolina Legislature turned over lots in Columbia to the Presbyterian and Protestant Episcopal Churches for building sites.[41] On many occasions between 1791 and 1818 the same Legislature turned over to various churches and religious schools land that had, or would have, escheated to the state.[42] In Georgia a Savannah city ordinance of 1790 ordained

> that four lots be reserved and vested forever in the trustees of the Episcopal Church called Christ Church . . . that three lots be reserved and vested forever in the trustees of the Presbyterian meeting house . . . and that two lots be reserved and vested forever in the wardens of the German Lutheran Church . . . and that one lot be reserved forever in the Baptist Society and one other in the Hebrew Congregation.[43]

It is significant that during the years 1789 to 1791, when the Virginians were debating whether to ratify the First Amendment to the United States Constitution, the Virginia General Assembly allowed the Episcopal Church to retain the glebe lands which had been purchased for them in the colonial period by tax funds raised from all denominations. The *Journal of the House of Delegates* for

November 24, 1791, indicates that the House on that date tabled a memorial from the Baptists to the effect that it was unconstitutional to confirm in the Protestant Episcopal Church the glebe lands.[44] And, on December 6, 1791, when it was moved in that body to repeal the acts vesting "in the Protestant Episcopal Church glebe lands which have been purchased with money arising from taxes levied on the citizens of this commonwealth," it was voted down 77 to 48.[45] The *Journal of the House of Delegates* reports that on October 10, 1792

> A memorial and remonstrance of the general committee of the Baptists in this State, was presented and read, complaining of the laws whereby the glebe lands and other church property, purchased at the expense of the community at large before the revolution, were vested in the members of the Protestant Episcopal church only, and praying that the said laws may be repealed, and the said property applied to the public use.[46]

The memorial was presented to a committee of the whole House and nothing came of it.

In 1799 the Virginia Legislature repeated its attempt to take away the Episcopal Church glebe lands.[47] The repealing act and subsequent acts of 1801 recited in the preamble that continued possession of the land would "admit *the* church established under regal government, to have continued so." Such previous legislative enactments, the repealing statute explained, were "inconsistent with the principles of the Constitution, and of religious freedom, and manifestly tends to the re-establishment of *a* national church."[48] The repealing act and the statute attempting to turn over the confiscated land to public officials were declared invalid by the United States Supreme Court in *Terrett v. Taylor*. The fundamental consideration to the Court was that a ban on an establishment generally meant equality in law. Justice Story spoke for the unanimous Court in the following language:

> Consistent with the constitution of Virginia, the legislature could not create or continue *a* religious establishment which would have exclusive rights and prerogatives, or compel the citizens to worship under a stipulated form or discipline, or to pay taxes to those whose creed they could not conscientiously believe. But the free exercise of religion cannot be justly deemed to be restrained, by aiding with equal attention the votaries of every sect to perform their own religious duties, or by establishing funds for the support of ministers, for public charities, for the endowment of churches, or for the sepulture of the dead.[49]

In full agreement with Justice Story were Chief Justice John Marshall, Justices Bushrod Washington, William Johnson, Brockholst Livingston, Thomas Todd, and Gabriel Duvall.

Thus the Supreme Court recognized the fact that the people of the United States had not renounced their belief in the institutional value of religious societies and that their governmental assemblies might properly aid them in their work for the betterment of society, provided the governmental aid was extended on a nondiscriminatory basis. Moreover, the Court realized that the government was not called on to level all religious societies, for that would be an imposition of a legal disability on the sects and an unfair discrimination.

The Grant of Public Funds to Churches and Church-Related Educational Institutions

The practices of the times in the years following ratification of the First Amendment attest that this generation accepted as normal the use of governmental funds to encourage religion and religious education. In the manner of the Continental Congress, the Congress of the United States under the Constitution was agreeable to using public funds to see that persons had ample opportunities for exposure to religion. In 1803, for example, Thomas Jefferson as President requested and received ratification from the Senate for a treaty with the Kaskaskia Indians. This treaty provided:

> And whereas the greater part of said tribe have been baptized and received into the Catholic Church, to which they are much attached, the United States will give annually, for seven years, one hundred dollars towards the support of a priest of that religion, who will engage to perform for such tribe the duties of his office, and also to instruct as many of their children as possible, in the rudiments of literature, and the United States will further give the sum of three hundred dollars, to assist the said tribe in the erection of a church.[50]

Again, in March of 1819, the United States Congress indicated that it considered that it was proper and constitutional to appropriate $10,000 to be given to the mission boards of many denominations for work among the American Indians.[51] John C. Calhoun, as Secretary of War from 1817 to 1825, gave the mission societies thousands of dollars to christianize and educate the Indians.[52] Capable scholars have noted that up through the 1830's all the principal churches, including Congregationalists, Baptists, Methodists, Presbyterians, Moravians, Episcopalians, and Catholics, accepted such federal funds for education and apparently saw nothing amiss in the practice.[53]

The states were as willing as the Federal Government to transfer public funds for the benefit of churches and church-related schools. Most education at this time was conducted by the churches. The distinction between public and private education had not taken on "political significance."[54] Moreover, the evidence is overwhelming that these generations deemed religion and education of such value to the commonwealth that the state could properly finance them in their concurrent functions.

Edward W. Reisner concludes that this was the general situation:

> In New England almost up to the time of Horace Mann the civil control of education meant control by the Congregationalist Church with large influences residing in the local pastor. In all other states, much of the private initiative that operated in the provisions for schools was exhibited by religious organizations. . . . During this period the religious question was in no sense acute. The various states frequently made contributions to schools maintained by religious bodies, and it was a very common thing indeed for the civil authorities in the state which pretended to give free education to pauper children, to pay the tuition of such children in denominational schools.[55]

It must be observed, however, that where the state undertook to support the church itself through the public tax system there could be the opportunity for discrimination and prejudice on religious grounds. On occasion this had actually occurred in Massachusetts and the other New England states.

The Massachusetts Constitution of 1780, noted earlier, required the towns to make suitable provision for the public worship of God, and it remained in effect until 1833. The growing conservative reaction in Massachusetts discredited the extreme ideas of some of the dissenters and resulted in a new strength for orthodoxy and establishment.[56] The views of this establishment in New England were known to Thomas Jefferson in Virginia who wrote to Levi Lincoln concerning their reaction to his opposing the proclamation of days of thanksgiving: "I know it will give great offense to the New England clergy; but the advocate of religious freedom is to expect neither peace nor forgiveness from them."[57]

Throughout the period after ratification of the federal Bill of Rights, dissenters in Massachusetts continued to have difficulty securing exemption from the tax for the established Congregationalist Church. Thus, in Hampshire County in 1797, the statutory exemption was claimed by a Baptist minister who had no parish and preached throughout the country. The exemption was denied because the Baptist cleric did not qualify, according to the court, as "a settled minister."[58] The Methodists fared no better. In 1802 the Methodists of West Springfield were taxed for the repairs to the Congregationalist church despite the fact that they all possessed certificates showing they were supporting their own church. When the Methodist minister sued to collect the funds paid in by his people, the state refused to pay on the grounds that the Methodist circuit rider was not "a settled minister" within the meaning of the statute.[59] The position of the plaintiff was calculated, said the court, to "subvert the regular societies in the community."[60]

In 1809 the Baptist minister serving Middleborough and Kingston was denied the advantages of the Massachusetts statute because his society had not been incorporated and he was not the "settled minister" of the statute.[61] The following year, the case of *Barnes v. First Parish* held that only ministers of incorporated societies were eligible for tax monies collected for religion. The views of the Massachusetts community were ably expressed by the renowned Chief Justice Parsons, speaking for the Massachusetts Supreme Judicial Court:

> The second objection is, that it is intolerant to compel a man to pay for religious instruction, for which, as he does not hear it, he can derive no benefit. This objection is founded wholly in mistake. The object of public religious instruction is to teach, and to enforce by suitable arguments, the practice of a system of correct morals among the people, and to form and cultivate reasonable and just habits and manners, by which every man's person and property are protected from outrage, and his personal and social enjoyments promoted and multiplied. From these effects every man derives the most important benefits; and whether he be, or be not, an auditor of any public teacher, he receives more solid and permanent advantages from this public instruction, than the administration of justice in courts of law can give him. The like objection may be made by any man to the support of public schools, if he have no family who attend; and any man, who has no lawsuit, may object to the support of judges and jurors on the same ground; when, if there were no courts of law, he would unfortunately find that causes for lawsuits would sufficiently abound.[62]

This decision precipitated violent reaction throughout the state and was largely instrumental in the victory of the Jeffersonians at the polls in 1810. The next year a Republican Legislature passed the Religious Freedom Act repudiating the *Barnes* ruling.[63] As late as 1820, however, leaders of the state, including Daniel Webster, continued to endorse governmental aid to religion.[64]

Through all these years the plight of Catholics in Massachusetts was worse than that of any Protestant dissenters. In 1801 Father Cheverus, later first Bishop of Boston, was tried in Wiscasset for officiating at a marriage, even though the couple had also presented themselves to the local justice of the peace.[65] When a Catholic, Edward Kavanagh, brought suit before the Supreme Court of Massachusetts for relief from the ministerial taxes, he was turned down. Said the Court: "The Constitution obliges everyone to contribute to the support of Protestant ministers and them alone. Papists are only tolerated, and as long as their ministers behave well, we shall not disturb them. But let them expect no more than that."[66] Atheists, agnostics, and those who belonged to no church were similarly obligated to support the established Congregationalist Church.[67]

State funds in New Hampshire were regularly expended for Protestant church support and for education under Protestant auspices under the earlier noted constitutions of 1784 and 1792. The Constitutional Convention of 1791 had proposed an amendment which would have permitted dissenters from the Established Church to be exempt from church taxes upon filing a certificate of membership and support in another church. However, by a vote of 3993 to 994 the voters of New Hampshire rejected the proposed amendment.[68] The Legislature was unwilling to incorporate other religions and the courts were reluctant to recognize them as churches. Thus, in 1795, Christopher Erskine had sought exemption from the tax for the state church by presenting a certificate signed by an elder of the Universalist Society of Claremont. In a unanimous decision, the Supreme Court of New Hampshire ruled that the Universalists were not "a sect, persuasion or denomination" so as to benefit by the constitutional clause theoretically exempting those of other Protestant faiths from supporting the Congregationalists.[69] But a single Universalist Society was recognized in the state before 1824 — this was the Society in Portsmouth which had been incorporated in 1793.[70] As late as 1816, Baptists were being refused incorporation.[71] And the same year both Baptists and Methodists were distrained and imprisoned for failure to pay the tax for the state church.[72] It was not until the passage of the Toleration Act of 1819 that dissenters from the Established Congregationalist Church were given tax relief in New Hampshire.[73] Once Vermont was admitted into the Union in 1791, practices there were comparable to those of the parent state. Thus it was enacted in 1801 that all individuals would be taxed for the support of the state church unless they declared in writing: "I do not agree in religious opinion, with a majority of the inhabitants of this town."[74]

The people of Connecticut were agreed in using tax funds to support churches and to aid church-related education so long as there were no discriminations involved. In 1792 the Legislature appropriated a sum of $40,000 to Yale College, under the control of the Congregationalist Church.[75] The same year the General Association of (the Churches of) Connecticut appealed to the Legislature for permission to take up a collection annually for three years to help their missionary efforts in parts of New York, Vermont, Pennsylvania, and Ohio. The permission was granted and Governor Huntington issued a proclamation "that there be a contribution taken up in every congregation for the support of the Presbyterian Missions in the Western Territory." This was done over objections of Baptists who believed that they would be coerced into making contributions.[76] The following year the state disposed of public lands by sale and provided that the proceeds "be appropriated to the use and benefit of the several Ecclesiastical Societies, Churches or Congregations of all denominations in this State, to be by them applied to the support of their respective Ministers or Preachers of the Gospel, and Schools of Education."[77] Because the Congregationalist Church would have benefited most by the measure, rivalry between the sects caused generally unfavorable reaction and it was repealed in 1795 by an act diverting the proceeds solely to school uses.[78]

The discriminatory aspects of the certificate system continued to cause protest. Under this law dissenters from the Congregationalist Church were exempted from paying taxes for that church if they could produce a certificate of dissent. Under an act of May, 1791, the certificate thenceforth had to be signed by two civil officers. This made it possible, at least for the public officials who were generally members of the Congregationalist Church, to coerce dissenters by denying the certificates. The protests over this law were so forceful that in six months the Legislature repealed the act and enacted a new law allowing a dissenter to write his own certificate and file it himself with the clerk of his society. Many thought that this measure had abolished the Connecticut establishment.[79] For example, Judge Zephaniah Swift declared that this concession "levelled all distinctions, and placed all denominations of Christians equally under the protection of the law."[80] He might have been unduly optimistic, for the Baptists did not abate their outspoken opposition to the remnants of the Congregationalist establishment. They resented the discrimination inherent in the certificate system which determined a civil status according to one's religious belief, and they objected to the unfairness of being coerced to contribute to the support of Congregationalist proselytizing.[81]

In 1802 the Reverend John Leland, a Baptist minister, wrote:

"Government has no more to do with religious opinions of men than it has with the principles of mathematics. . . ." He added: "Is it just to balance the establishment against the rights guaranteed in the charter, and to enact a law which has no saving clause to prevent taxation of a Jew, Turk, Papist, Deist, Atheist, for the support of a ministry in which they would not share and which violated their conscience?"[82] The following year, the Baptists of Connecticut sent a remonstrance to the General Assembly, asserting: "[A]ll human laws which oblige a man to worship in any law-prescribed mode, time or place, or which compel him to pay taxes, or any way assist in the support of religious teachers, unless on his voluntary contract, are unjust and oppressive."[83] Notwithstanding these voices of dissent, the prejudice and discrimination of the establishment lingered in Connecticut until 1818.

Other states continued to use public funds to aid and encourage religion and education. Rhode Island, which was proud of the fact that it had no establishment, continued its policy of aiding and encouraging religion. Public education remained under the control of the churches and land was granted to schools run by religious groups, such as the Society of Friends and the Baptists.[84] In some communities even more affirmative methods were employed. Between 1718 and 1798 the town of Barrington paid the salary of the local minister. A historian of the state, Thomas Bicknell, has observed, that "as the minister was called by the town, settled by the town, paid by the town, and dismissed by the town . . . [this evidenced] all the elements of a church-state."[85] Other communities also encouraged the growth of religion among their citizens by making available the use of public buildings for religious services. The town of Bristol opened its courthouse to itinerant Methodist preachers in 1790,[86] and up until 1831 Methodists of East Greenwich used the courthouse as a regular place of worship.[87]

In the period from the ratification of the federal Bill of Rights until 1825, the state of New York gave substantial aid to existing schools, most of which, in New York City, were conducted by the churches. A 1795 act appropriated fifty thousand dollars for five years to maintain schools, many of which were church-related.[88] When this law expired in 1800, the private and church-related schools helped by it had to rely on voluntary contributions until 1806. However, some relief came in 1801 when the Legislature directed the city government to apportion the money that remained in its hands after the 1795 act. Those funds were to be divided equally among the trustees of the African schools and the trustees of the ten church denominations which maintained schools.[89] St.

Peter's Free School, the first Catholic School in New York, was added to the list in 1806 and received $1,565.78, an amount equal to that paid to each of the denominational schools in 1801.[90]

In New Jersey the problem was one of rivalry between the sects. The state Legislature was asked for financial aid by the Reverend Samuel Stanhope Smith in 1795, shortly after his election as president of Princeton College. The trustees of Princeton alleged that the college was nonsectarian and devoted to the public welfare, although the institution had been traditionally Presbyterian. The Legislature granted Princeton £600 for the library, apparatus, and repair of the buildings, but this precipitated much resentment and the members who voted for the aid were turned out at the next election.[91]

Tax funds were also available to denominational institutions in Delaware. Thus, in 1821, Newark College, a Presbyterian institution, was granted the proceeds of state taxes on stage lines and steamboats between Philadelphia and places on the Delaware.[92] The same year the Delaware Legislature provided that twenty cents per annum for each white scholar be paid by the county to "every school or schools instituted in this State, for the education of children on the Sabbath. . . ."[93] These so-called "Sabbath Schools" were, of course, denominational.

The Maryland Constitution of 1776 permitted the Legislature to enact laws aiding Christian teachers. Nevertheless, influential leaders of the state such as Archbishop John Carroll and the Reverend Patrick Allison viewed requests to the Legislature as first steps in the return of the established Episcopal Church. As a result, proponents of financial-aid bills authorized by the constitution were never able to secure a majority in the Legislature.[94] However, during the last quarter of the eighteenth century the state of Maryland gave financial assistance to Washington College and St. John's College. The former had been founded on "Principles of Religion and Virtue" and was under the special influence of the Episcopalians.[95] And, on December 27, 1791, the Maryland Legislature agreed to advance £200 for the building of a church in St. Anne's Parish, Annapolis.[96]

Practices in Georgia under the constitutions of 1789 and 1798 indicate that the people there saw no conflict between freedom from establishment and encouraging religion.[97] In the town of Augusta and in Wilkes County public lands were turned over to commissioners who used proceeds from the sale of a portion of the land to build churches and schools.[98] Returns from the remainder of the land were used to maintain the church and the minister. When an impasse arose because different denominations were contending for support of their minister, the commissioners resolved the conflict by allotting the funds and the use of the church buildings on an equal basis.[99] Under the provisions of the state constitution providing for the support of "seminaries of learning"[100] both the state Legislature and the local commissioners gave substantial aid to the establishment of schools.[101] Dominated by ministers, most of these schools were in effect denominational institutions.

North Carolina, like many of the states, had effected disestablishment in her constitution by prohibiting favoritism to any particular denomination.[102] Like Georgia, her constitution directed that education be encouraged and promoted in the state.[103] Public education was from the first closely connected with the churches which maintained an extensive system of parochial schools.[104] Their influence continued even after a state-supported system of education came into being, for the administrative effect of the act was to encourage the local community to take over the church academy and convert it to a public school supported by tax funds. As a result these schools often retained a strong denominational flavor.[105] Higher education was the exclusive concern of the state at first. However, church influence, especially that of the Presbyterians, was strong from the early beginnings. The University of North Carolina was virtually a Presbyterian seminary, for the religious forces of North Carolina expected the university to train the leaders of both the church and the state.[106] Financial support of public education was provided by an endowment fund administered by the literary board.[107] And when the churches began to establish their own colleges and seminaries of higher learning, the Legislature directed the literary board to make direct grants, low-interest loans, and scholarships available to the students at these institutions. Interest on and repayment of the loans was frequently waived by the board.[108]

As the practices of the times indicate, almost universally Americans from 1789 to 1825 accepted and practiced governmental aid to religion and religiously oriented educational institutions.

Authorization to Conduct Lotteries

Throughout the period immediately following the ratification of the First Amendment, the people of America through their state legislatures frequently aided churches and church-related schools by conferring upon them the privilege to conduct public lotteries. Because of the popularity of the lottery the privilege was tantamount to an appropriation by the legislature. The practice was followed even in Virginia.[109] It was found in Delaware also, where the Legislature of 1818 passed an act to enable the trustees of Newark Academy, a Presbyterian school, to raise $50,000 by a lottery.[110] Six years later, Middletown Academy was built by the Presbyterians with the proceeds of a lottery authorized by the same Legislature.[111]

The New Jersey Legislature frequently authorized churches to conduct lotteries in this period.[112] In 1790 that Legislature enacted "An Act Authorizing the Protestant Episcopal Church to Have a Lottery"; and it provided: "[T]hey are hereby authorized and empowered to raise by lottery, a sum not exceeding three hundred and fifty pounds, to be appropriated . . . towards repairing and completing the Church and Parsonage. . . ."[113] The same practice prevailed in Pennsylvania. On March 16, 1798, the Legislature authorized the Presbyterian congregation in the county of Montgomery to conduct a lottery to finance the erection of a schoolhouse.[114] That same day the Legislature empowered the German Episcopal Church in Greencastle to conduct a lottery for defraying the expense of finishing its building.[115] The following year the same Legislature authorized a lottery for construction of a Presbyterian meetinghouse in Mifflintown.[116]

In 1801 the Connecticut Legislature granted to the Chesire [Episcopal] Academy the right to hold a lottery to raise $15,000 to expand its library.[117] South Carolina authorized lotteries in 1809 for the Episcopal Church in Greenville, and in 1824 for St. Peter's Roman Catholic Church.[118]

Tax Exemptions

During this period it was generally understood that tax exemptions for churches and church-related schools were proper and constitutional.[119] This privilege, like the lottery, was equivalent to an appropriation of public funds. A financial burden was remitted; at the same time the remitted burden was placed equally on the remaining taxpayers. Illustratively, a 1702 Connecticut statute remained in effect through 1812 which exempted all property used "for the maintenance of the ministry of the Gospel."[120] A 1786 New York act authorized letters patent to Samuel Kirkland "in trust for any minister of the gospel, who may hereafter for the time then being be employed by the Oneida Indians to preach the gospel among them." It added that all such lands granted by letters patent should be exempted from taxes through 1793.[121] When South Carolina passed a law in 1812 imposing a tax on slaves, free Negroes, city lots and lands, stocks in trade and professions, the enactment exempted clergymen and schoolmasters.[122] The following year the

Legislature of South Carolina wrote into another general tax law a proviso: "But nothing in this Act contained shall be construed to impose any tax upon the property or estate of any religious society."[123] Also during this period Rhode Island continued its policy of exempting "all estates, real or personal, granted or appropriated to religious uses, or to the use of schools or seminaries of learning."[124]

Incorporation of Churches

The states continued to grant to churches the legal privilege of the status of incorporation. Georgia, for example, incorporated an Episcopalian and a Congregational church in 1789 and authorized the governor to grant additional charters.[125] The Second Presbyterian Church in Newark, the Society for Propagating the Gospel among the Heathen, and the Protestant Episcopal Church of St. Mary's in Burlington were chartered by New Jersey between 1790 and 1793.[126] In South Carolina as a consequence of the constitution of 1790, which provided for freedom of religious worship "without discrimination or preference," the Legislature began to grant charters to Jewish and Catholic congregations.[127] Although the Connecticut Assembly in 1795 had declined to honor an episcopal request to establish by law a "Bishop's Fund" empowered to "hold estate real and personal . . . for the benefit of the Bishop of the Episcopal Church in Connecticut," the request was honored by the Assembly four years later.[128] By controlling the incorporation of religious societies, the state of Massachusetts continued its preference of the established Congregationalist Church during this period. For example, many denials of tax exemptions to the Baptists, Methodists, Shakers, and Catholics were based on the proposition that only ministers of incorporated churches were entitled to receive the taxes paid by their parishioners.[129] Similarly, New Hampshire regularly granted requests for Congregationalists' incorporation while customarily refusing the Baptists' incorporation.[130]

The Congress of the United States emulated the states in 1811 by incorporating the Protestant Episcopal Church in the town of Alexandria in the District of Columbia. However, on February 21 of that year, President James Madison vetoed the bill,

> Because the bill exceeds the rightful authority to which governments are limited by the essential distinction between civil and religious functions, and violates in particular the article of the Constitution of the United States which declares that "Congress shall make no law respecting a religious establishment."[131]

Madison's principal objection was that Congress had interfered with the internal affairs of the church. By incorporating the church articles in the charter Congress had frozen them. The church membership would no longer be able to change them without the consent of Congress.

> The bill enacts into and establishes by law sundry rules and proceedings relative purely to the organization and polity of the church incorporated, and comprehending even the election and removel of the minister of the same, so that no change could be made therein by the particular society or by the general church of which it is a member, and whose authority it recognizes. This particular church, therefore, would so far be a religious establishment by law, a legal force and sanction being given to certain articles in its constitution and administration. Nor can it be considered that the articles thus established are to be taken as the descriptive criteria only of the corporate identity of the society, inasmuch as this identity must depend on other characteristics, as the regulations established are generally unessential and alterable according to the principles and canons by which churches of that denomination govern themselves, and as the injunctions and prohibitions contained in the regulations would be enforced by the penal consequences applicable to a violation of them according to the local law.

Madison's view that giving a church corporate status was violating the establishment ban was rigorously contested in Congress. Upon hearing of the veto, Congressman Pitkin of Connecticut declared:

> He had no idea that the Constitution precluded Congress from passing laws to incorporate religious bodies for the purpose of enabling them to hold property. He had always held the Constitution to intend to prevent the establishment of a national church, such as the Church of England, a refusal to subscribe to the tenets of which was to exclude a citizen from office.[132]

Equally at odds with the Madisonian thesis was an editorial entitled "Democratic Qualms" in the *Baltimore Federal Republican and Commercial Gazette* for February 26, 1811. The editorial states:

> What was the meaning of the Constitution in providing against a religious establishment? Does any man but Mr. Madison imagine it was to prevent the District of Columbia from engaging legal church regulations, and from exercising corporate rights in their congregations? Does the Legislature of Maryland believe it is creating a religious establishment when it is occupied in granting charters to the churches of the different sects of Christians as often as they apply?

Where all are equally protected and accommodated, where each sect
and congregation has its own establishment, modified according to
its wishes and sanctioned in that modification by law, the best security exists against 'a religious establishment' that is to say, one
preeminent establishment which is preferred and set up over the rest
against which alone the constitutional safeguard was created.[133]

Virginians continued to suspect virtually every aspect of the
church-state relationship. The slightest concession to a church, no
matter how inconsiderable or innocuous, might become an opening
wedge for the return of the hated Virginia establishment. The
atmosphere of Virginia toward churches, in the words of Judge
Henry St. George Tucker, was "decidedly hostile."[134] For this reason the state had refused to allow church incorporation even though
virtually all other states had granted the privilege to churches. The
supposed danger was that great church corporations might grow up
with a power to rival that of the state. In his later years in the
"Detached Memoranda" Madison revealed the strong influence of
his Virginia experiences when he wrote: "There is an evil which
ought to be guarded against in the indefinite accumulation of
property from the capacity of holding it in perpetuity by ecclesiastical corporations. The power of all corporations ought to be limited
in this respect. The growing wealth acquired by them never fails to
be a source of abuses."[135]

Although Madison reacted to the congressional bill as though it
were an act of the Virginia Legislature, it is important to note that
the situations were not comparable. The Federal Government had
had no previously Established Church. Thus the fact that the church
to be incorporated was Episcopal would not make the act of incorporation an act strengthening a formerly privileged church within
the federal jurisdiction. Moreover, during this time Madison's *de
facto* condition for guaranteeing religious liberty, a multiplicity of
sects, was present on the national level. This situation practically
guaranteed that no one denomination could gain an advantage over
the others in the new federal system.

The Use of Chaplains

The use of chaplains by public bodies was a common occurrence
during this time. Most Americans approved the practice. However,
some persons thought that the practice might contain the seeds of
religious persecution. For this reason James Madison believed that
the use of chaplains in Congress and the armed forces might violate
the First Amendment. In his "Detached Memoranda" or essay on

"Ecclesiastical Trusts,"[136] which was written many years after he had been president, he argued that "the danger of silent accumulations and encroachments by Ecclesiastical Bodies have not sufficiently engaged attention in the U. S." A major fear was that by giving state sanction to a religious observance the door to religious persecution would be opened. He gloomily exhorted Americans to be on guard "against every evil lurking under plausible disguises, and growing up from small beginnings. *Obsta principiis* [Resist the beginnings]." After a discussion of the similar dangers of incorporation of religious groups, he then turned to the question of chaplains:

> Is the appointment of Chaplains to the two Houses of Congress consistent with the Constitution, and with the pure principle of religious freedom?

> In strictness the answer on both points must be in the negative. The Constitution of the United States forbids anything like an establishment of a national religion. The law appointing Chaplains establishes a religious worship for the national representatives, to be performed by ministers of religion elected by a majority of them; and these are to be paid out of the national taxes. Does not this involve the principle of a national establishment applicable to a provision for a religious worship for the Constitution as well as of the Representative Body, approved by the majority and conducted by ministers of religion paid by the entire nation?

His major objection was that the existing systems of choosing chaplains operated just like an establishment to violate equal religious liberty. The tax money of persons of all faiths was being used to support the chaplains, but the ministers of minority sects had no chance of being chosen.

> The establishment of the chaplainship to Congress is a palpable *violation of equal rights,* as well as of Constitutional principles: The tenets of the chaplains elected [by the majority] shut the door of worship against the members whose creeds and consciences forbid a participation in that of the majority. To say nothing of other sects, this is the case with that of Roman Catholics and Quakers who have always had members in one or both of the Legislative branches. Could a Catholic clergyman ever hope to be appointed a Chaplain? To say that his religious principles are obnoxious or that his sect is small is to lift the evil at once and exhibit the naked deformity that religious truth is to be tested by numbers, or that the major sects have a right to govern the minor.

He reluctantly opposed army and navy chaplaincies. He recognized that the state might have a legitimate interest in seeing that the

morale of its troops was maintained, but he could not reconcile this
admittedly valid interest with his beliefs in religious liberty. In case
of doubt he preferred to adhere to his "principles."

> Better also to disarm in the same way, the precedent of Chaplainships
> for the army and navy, than erect them into a political authority in
> matters of religion. The object of this establishment is seducing; the
> motive too is laudable. But is it not safer to adhere to a right prin-
> ciple, and trust to its consequences, than confide in the reasoning,
> however specious in favor of a wrong one. Look thro' the armies
> and the navies of the world, and say whether in the appointment of
> ministers of religion, the spiritual interest of the flocks or the tem-
> poral interest of the Shepherds be most in view; whether here, as
> elsewhere the political care of religion is not a nominal more than
> a real aid. If the spirit of armies be devout, the spirit out of the
> armies will never be less so; and a failure of religious instruction and
> exhortation from a voluntary source within or without, will rarely
> happen: and if such be not the spirit of armies, the official services
> of their Teachers are not likely to produce it. It is more likely to
> flow from the labours of spontaneous zeal. The Armies of the
> Puritans had their appointed Chaplains, but without these there
> would have been no lack of public devotion in that devout age.

He also considered the possibility that the restricted freedom of
movement of the military personnel might require the appointment
of chaplains to prevent an infringement on the free exercise of
religion.[137] The army's land mobility gave its men access to local
churches; the situation of the navy was far different. But once again
he could not find room for the novel ideal among his other "principles," which had been tempered in the fires of the singular Virginia experience.

> The case of navies with their insulated crews may be less within the
> scope of these reflections. But it is not entirely so. The chance of a
> devout officer, might be of as much worth to religion, as the service
> of an ordinary chaplain [were it admitted that religion has a relative
> interest in the latter]. But we are always to keep in mind that it is
> safer to trust the consequences of a right principle, than reasonings
> in support of a bad one.

It should be noted, however, that these views were expressed many
years after Madison had been president. Evidence indicates that
these later opinions are not the same as those that he held in 1789
when the First Congress was drafting the First Amendment. During
that same session Madison participated as a member of the House
committee which organized the national chaplaincy system. Although
there was ample opportunity to dissent, no record of opposition to

the measure from the articulate Virginia Congressman has ever been discovered.[138]

There was apparently at least one other Virginian who condemned the use of chaplains, although it is always possible that the author of an unsigned article in the *Virginia Herald and Fredericksburg Advertiser* for December 24, 1789, might have been none other than Madison. The article asserted:

> I say it is not constitutional. No part of the Virginia constitution authorizes such acts, nor does the federal constitution honor them.
>
> The moment that a minister is so fixed by law as to obtain a legal claim on the treasury for religious services, that moment he becomes a minister of state and ceases to be a gospel ambassador. This is the very principle of religious establishment and should be exploded forever. If government has a right to make a law to support one religious teacher, it has the same claim to support all; and if rulers are to prescribe forms of prayer, they have the same power to establish creeds of faith. . . . If a chaplain must be employed to read prayers in the statehouse and to visit the criminals in prison, let him be paid by the free contribution of those who employ him.[139]

The American community on the whole, however, was overwhelmingly agreeable to and desirous of enjoying the services of chaplains in a variety of situations. The earlier practice of the Continental Congress of utilizing chaplains was continued by the First Congress under the Constitution of the United States. That Assembly enacted "that there shall be allowed to each chaplain of Congress, at the rate of five hundred dollars per annum during the session of Congress."[140] And, on September 19, 1789, the Treasury Department reported the following expenditures: "Chaplain of the Senate, from the 15th of April, the time of his appointment, to the 22nd of September, at the rate of five hundred dollars per annum," and "Chaplain to the House of Representatives, from 1st of May, the time of his appointment, to 22nd September, at five hundred dollars per annum, $197.21."[141] Then, on January 7, 1790, the House of Representatives adopted a resolution "that the chaplains, of different denominations, be appointed to Congress for the present session, one of each House, who shall interchange weekly."[142] The following day the House elected the Reverend William Linn to office.[143] This practice of Congress in employing and remunerating chaplains for both the Senate and House has continued through all the years. The Congress that proposed the First Amendment further enacted legislation providing for a chaplain to be attached to a new regiment of troops.[144] Again, the Second Congress provided for army chaplains to be attached to three new regiments and paid $50 per month.[145] And the succeeding Congress similarly provided chaplains for the navy.[146]

The use of chaplains was just as common in the state governments as it was in the federal. For example, when the New York Legislature was meeting in New York City early in 1790, the State Senate ordered that a committee "wait upon such gentlemen of the Clergy, in this City, as have usually attended, and request them to make such arrangements among themselves that one of them may attend daily to open the business of this Senate with prayer."[147] In Madison's own state of Virginia, the House of Delegates on October 1, 1792, at Richmond "Ordered, that the Reverend Benjamin Blagrove be appointed chaplain to this House and that he attend to read prayers every morning, at the time appointed by the standing order of the House."[148]

Days of Prayer, Fast, and Thanksgiving

In the period immediately following the adoption of the First Amendment, governmental authorities continued to proclaim days of prayer, fast, and thanksgiving. Thus, on September 24, 1789, the very day that the House accepted the report of the Conference Committee and adopted its resolution recommending the First Amendment to the states, it also adopted a resolution: "That a joint committee of both Houses be directed to wait upon the President of the United States, to request that he would recommend to the people of the United States a day of public thanksgiving and prayer, to be observed by acknowledging with grateful hearts, the many signal favors of Almighty God, especially by affording them an opportunity to establish a Constitution of government for their safety and happiness."[149] And to properly observe Good Friday, the same House adjourned on April 2, 1790.[150]

State authorities were equally agreeable to proclaiming days of prayer, fast, and thanksgiving. Thus John Jay as Governor of New York deemed it proper and constitutional to appoint a day of Thanksgiving, requesting the people to show "national gratitude and obedience to the Supreme Ruler of all nations" on November 26, 1795.[151] Governor Richard Howell of New Jersey proclaimed the same day one of thanksgiving and recommended its observance to the citizenry. "As reasonable creatures, we are bound to acknowledge our Dependence upon God . . ." the Governor said, and "entertain a reasonable hope that God in his Providence will continue his many Favors. . . ."[152] Not only did the public authorities urge upon the people such days of fast, prayer, and thanksgiving, but Connecticut in 1791 enacted a law laying a fine upon all who failed to observe days of public fast and thanksgiving.[153] The only recorded opposition came from the Episcopalians whose liturgical calendar did not always coincide with that of the Congregationalists.[154] There is no record of prosecutions under the law.

In 1802 President Jefferson refused to honor the request of the Danbury Baptist Association for proclamation of a day of fast and prayer in thanksgiving for the welfare of the new nation. Although he had previously approved such proclamations as being patriotically inspired, in this instance he declined to favor the Baptist petition. Declaring that he was acting in behalf of religious liberty, Jefferson made his famous "wall of separation" statement, which is so often quoted only in part. He stated:

> I contemplate with sovereign reverence that act of the whole American people which declared that their legislature should "make no law respecting an establishment of religion or prohibiting the free exercise thereof," thus building a wall of separation between church and state. Adhering to this expression of the supreme will of the nation *in behalf of the rights of conscience,* I shall see with sincere satisfaction to the progress of those sentiments which tend to restore man to all his natural rights. . . .[155]

What Jefferson was obviously lauding was the end of those establishment practices that had prevented full enjoyment of the natural rights of religious freedom.

James Madison was similarly reluctant to use his office as president to proclaim days of fast, prayer, and thanksgiving. "Although recommendations only," he remarked, "they imply a religious agency, making no part of the trust delegated to political rulers."[156] It is interesting to note that during the War of 1812, at the request of the Congress, Madison formally proclaimed "a day of *Public Humiliation and Prayer.*" The proclamation recommended those who might feel disposed to come together for purpose of prayer might assemble together" in "their respective religious congregations."[157] Since that time there has been no reluctance on the part of his successors to make such proclamations. "Time and custom," Professor Lynford Lardner has ably noted, "have long since overruled the beliefs of Jefferson and Madison that presidential proclamation of national days of prayer and religious observance was contrary to the Constitution."[158]

*Laws Making It a Crime to Blaspheme, to Engage in
Nonreligious Activities on Sunday*

Blasphemy laws prevailed everywhere during the period immediately following the ratification of the Bill of Rights. They were drawn in such a manner as to punish individuals who publicly used vulgar and abusive language to denounce the dominant religion of the people of the states. Although it was thought that regulation of such offensive public displays was proper, there was, of course, the danger that a simple criticism of the Christian religion could be construed as blasphemy. Hence, the laws could be used to persecute as they had been used in the colonial period. The New Jersey law of 1800 is fairly representative. It provided:

> XIX.   All impostors in religion, such as personate our Saviour Jesus Christ, or suffer their followers to worship or pay them divine honors, or terrify, or abuse the people by false denunciations of judgments, shall, on conviction, be punished for every such offense by a fine, not exceeding one hundred dollars, or an imprisonment at hard labor, not exceeding six months, or both at the discretion of the court.

> XX.   If any person shall wilfully blaspheme the holy name of God, by denying, cursing or contumeliously reproaching his being or providence, or by cursing or contumeliously reproaching Jesus Christ, or the Holy Ghost, or the Christian religion, or the holy word of God, that is, the canonical scriptures contained in the books of the Old and New Testament or by profanely scoffing at, or exposing them, or any of them to contempt and ridicule, then every person so offending shall, on conviction, be punished by a fine, not exceeding two hundred dollars, or an imprisonment at hard labor, not exceeding twelve months, or both, at the discretion of the court.[159]

Pennsylvania in 1794 enacted a law punishing those who "shall profanely swear or curse by the name of God, Jesus Christ, or the Holy Ghost" by a fine of "seventy-five cents per curse."[160] And throughout this period Pennsylvania enforced its law, imposing penalties upon anyone who should "wilfully, premeditatedly, and despitefully blaspheme, or speak lightly or profanely of Almighty God, Jesus Christ, the Holy Spirit or the Scripture of Truth."[161] The thrust of the Pennsylvania statute is indicated in a later statement by the Pennsylvania Supreme Court which declared:

> The infidel who madly rejects all belief in a Divine Essence may safely do so, in reference to civil punishment, so long as he refrains from the wanton and malicious proclamation of his opinions with intent to outrage the moral and religious convictions of a community, the vast majority of whom are christians.[162]

The Connecticut blasphemy law of 1642 still prevailed through-out the post-Bill of Rights period. It punished by whipping, fine, or imprisonment "every person who shall blaspheme against God, either of the Persons of the Holy Trinity, the Christian religion, or the Holy Scriptures."[163] In 1795 the law was reaffirmed.[164] Similarly, Maryland's severe blasphemy laws, under which individuals could be punished for denying the divinity of Christ, remained in force until 1819.[165]

The blasphemy statutes did not prevent religious debate. So free was the discussion that the deist newspaper, *The Temple of Reason,* could celebrate the equality of all beliefs including those of the deists. Like Ezra Stiles, they placed their reliance on freedom of speech:

> [F]ortunately for the Peace and Prosperity of America, *Mahometism* is as much *established by law,* there, as Christianity. The immortal framers of the Constitution, wisely thought, that in matters of reli-gion, all men have an equal right to private and public opinion; and therefore, left them all on the same level — on this level we stand; and if we show our religion to be superior to that of others, it shall be by the force of Reason, not by scurrility, deception, or persecution.[166]

The most famous blasphemy prosecution of the period occurred in New York in 1811 when a man publicly uttered: "Jesus Christ was a bastard, and his mother must be a whore." The man was indicted and convicted. In affirming the conviction and punishment of three months' imprisonment plus a fine of $500, Chief Justice Kent, speaking for the New York Supreme Court, epitomized the views of the times when he specifically ruled that punishing those who blaspheme the founder of Christianity is not an unconstitu-tional establishment of religion. Said Kent: "Such offenses (those which tend to corrupt morals and destroy good order) have always been considered independent of any religious establishment or the test of the Church."[167] The Chief Justice added:

> [T]o revile, with malicious and blasphemous contempt, the religion professed by almost the whole community, is an abuse of that right [religious liberty]. Nor are we bound, by any expressions in the constitution, as some have strangely supposed, either not to punish at all, or to punish indiscriminately the like attacks upon the religion of Mahomet or of the Grand Lama; and for this plain reason that the case assumes that we are a Christian people, and the morality of the country is deeply ingrained upon Christianity, and not upon the doctrines or worship of those imposters.[168]

Addressing himself to the constitutional ban upon establishment, Kent continued:

> Though the constitution has discarded religious establishments, it does not forbid judicial cognizance of those offenses against religion and morality which have no references to any such establishment. . . . [The New York Constitution] will be fully satisfied by a free and universal toleration, without any of the tests, disabilities or discriminations incident to a religious establishment.[169]

The Chief Justice concluded: "the framers of the constitution intended only to banish test oaths, disabilities and the burdens, and sometimes the oppressions, of church establishments; and to secure to the people of this State freedom from coercion, and an equality of right, on the subject of religion."[170] The decision not only sustains the validity of such blasphemy prosecutions, but indicates powerfully that in the mind of one of the nation's greatest legal scholars and a contemporary of those in the First Congress a ban upon establishment was intended only to secure "freedom from coercion," an end to "disabilities, burdens and oppressions," and "an equality of right."

Throughout this period Sunday laws regularly banned a variety of nonreligious activities. Typically, the Pennsylvania law of 1794 provided that:

> [I]f any person shall do or perform any wordly employment or business whatsoever on the Lord's day, commonly called Sunday, or shall use or practice any unlawful game, hunting, shooting, sport or diversion whatsoever, on the same day . . . every such person so offending .. . shall . . . pay . . . four dollars . . . or shall suffer six days imprisonment.[171]

New Jersey four years later passed "An Act for Suppressing Vice and Immorality," which provided:

> [T]hat no traveling, wordly employment or business, ordinary or servile labor or work . . . nor shooting, fishing . . . nor any interludes of plays, dancing, singing . . . or music for the sake of merriment . . . nor any other kind of playing, sports, pastimes or diversions, shall be done . . . within this State on the Christian Sabbath, or first day of the week, commonly called Sunday; and that every person . . . offending . . . shall . . . forfeit and pay to the use of the poor of the township . . . the sum of one dollar.[172]

To make sure travelers would not enjoy themselves on Sundays near churches, that same year the Pennsylvania Legislature, on April 4, authorized religious societies in Philadelphia "to extend and fasten so many chains across the streets . . . during the time of divine services . . ." and provided for a fine of $30 upon anyone who dared to remove the chains."[173] In 1822 Rhode Island forbade the sale of rum, wine, or strong liquor within one mile of any meeting being held "for the worship of Almighty God."[174] The colonial laws of Georgia compelling observance of the Sabbath remained effective throughout the eighteenth century and were at times complemented by municipal ordinances, but they seemed to have been honored largely in the breach.[175]

Although by this time most of the earlier laws compelling persons to attend religious services on Sunday had been removed from the books, there was still an occasional enactment. For instance, when in 1791 in Massachusetts a new Sunday observance law was passed, the Legislature provided for fines upon those who on that day absented themselves from religious worship.[176] Similarly, the New Jersey Act for Suppressing Vice, discussed above, further provided for a subtle method of compelling religious worship on Sunday. If a person was charged with having violated the Sabbath law in any fashion, the burden of proof then shifted to him. He had to prove that "he devotes the day to the exercise of religious worship, then such defendent shall be discharged."[177]

The "Blue Laws" indicated in this section were generally acknowledged as constitutional. For example, Chief Justice Smith, speaking for the New Hampshire Supreme Court in 1803, remarked that it did not follow from religious liberty or bans upon establishment "that a civil magistrate may not lawfully punish certain offenses against the unalterable and essential principles of natural and revealed religion . . . such as blasphemy, reviling religion, and profanation of the Sabbath."[178]

Desire of the Community for Encouragement of Religion and Morality on a Basis of Equality

The quest of the American community in the years immediately following the ratification of the First Amendment was the same as in the years 1776 to 1789: equality of all religious faiths before the law. Few believed the state should be hostile to religion. It was legislative favoritism that was opposed by the Reverend Patrick Allison, pastor of the First Presbyterian Church in Baltimore, in 1792 when it appeared the Maryland Legislature was preferring the Protestant Episcopal Church by giving funds to a church in Annapolis.[179] And it was because "all law-made subordination of one or more denominations of professing Christians to another, is productive of evil," that the Baptists of Connecticut in 1803 protested establishment of the Congregational Church in a remonstrance to the General Assembly.[180] So, too, John Adams urged that Massachusetts acknowledge equality to "all men of all religions," when he proposed in the Massachusetts Constitutional Convention of 1820 the elimination from state law of all test oaths.[181]

Throughout the land in the years 1776 to 1825 there was the consensus that the government should be concerned with the promotion of public morality, and that religion was necessary to public morality. The same First Congress that proposed the First Amendment to the Constitution readopted the Northwest Ordinance of 1787 with its memorable language that "Religion, morality, and knowledge being necessary to good government and the happiness of mankind, schools and the means of education shall be forever encouraged."[182] Schools were to be encouraged, according to these Founding Fathers, because they promoted "religion, morality, and knowledge." Presumably, according to this language, schools that most effectively produced this triad were to be particularly worthy of favor. And the states were agreed with the federal Congress that schools were to be encouraged because they promoted religion and morality. According to 1808 New Hampshire legislation, for example, the goal of the schools was the inculcation of "literature, morality, and religion."[183] To assure the reasonable probability of attaining such goals, teaching certificates in New Hampshire could normally be obtained only from ministers from 1789 to 1827.[184] Strickland tells how "in contrast to modern practice, Georgians of the early republic never thought of separating religion and education."[185]

We can recall George Washington's language in his farewell address:

> Of all the dispositions and habits which lead to political prosperity, religion and morality are indispensable supports . . . let it simply be asked where is the security for prosperity, for reputation, for life — if the sense of religious obligation desert . . . and let us with caution indulge the supposition that morality can be maintained without religion.[186]

Views of Church-State Relations Expressed Outside the Congress by Members of the First Congress and Other Prominent Men of the Times

The first federal legislators have left a legacy of expression concerning their views of religion and its relation to the state. Their statements — other than those made during the congressional debates on the First Amendment — cannot be seized upon to support authoritatively any proffered interpretation of the religion clauses of the First Amendment. Often these statements were made many years before or after the debates in Congress, or were directed at the meaning of a particular state constitutional clause which did not even faintly resemble the federal. Nevertheless, the opinions of these congressmen should be ascertained, notwithstanding their potentially delusive nature, for they will often indicate the basic philosophy of these important Americans.

Oliver Ellsworth had represented Connecticut in the Constitutional Convention, then as a senator in the First Congress, and later became Chief Justice of the United States Supreme Court. It is known that Ellsworth had been pleased to have disestablishment by the federal government to the extent achieved by the ban upon religious test oaths in the original Constitution.[1] Yet he was quite willing for the state to aid religion through laws proscribing "blasphemy and professed atheism."[2] Ellsworth indicated that he would have found acceptable a proposed preamble to the Constitution which would have declared a firm belief in the "being and perfection of the one living and true God, the creator and supreme Governour of the World."[3]

Charles Carroll of Carrollton was a Maryland senator in the First Congress of the United States. He was chairman of the Senate conferees in the Committee of Conference of the Congress that was

189

concerned with the First Amendment. Fortunately his views on desirable church-state relations can be discerned from his utterances and actions at many times. First, there can be no doubt that he was unwilling to have any government force a state religion upon the people. As early as 1773, Carroll wrote: "I am as averse to having a religion crammed down my throat as a proclamation."[4]

Second, Charles Carroll of Carrollton found obnoxious any governmental favoritism or preference to one sect over others, with the concomitant discriminations of dissenters. In 1773 he had argued that non-Anglicans were entitled to freedom of communication. When, in that year, Daniel Dulaney in his "Antillon" letters observed that Papists are distrusted by the laws and laid under disabilities," Charles Carroll responded:

> They cannot I know, ignorant as I am, enjoy any place of profit or trust, while they continue papists; but do these disabilities extend so far as to preclude them from thinking and writing on matters merely of a political nature? Antillon would make a most excellent inquisitor; he has some striking specimens of an arbitrary temper, the first requisite. He will not allow me freedom of thought or speech.[5]

Later in life, Charles Carroll wrote to George Washington Custis:

> When I signed the Declaration of Independence I had in view not only our independence from England but the toleration of all sects professing the Christian religion and communicating to them all equal rights. . . . Reflecting as you must on the disabilities I may truly say of the prescription of the Roman Catholics in Maryland, you will not be surprised that I had much at heart this grand design, founded on mutual charity, the basis of our holy religion.[6]

Throughout his life he recalled that it was the threat that one religious sect might with the aid of law become dominant and accordingly deny religious freedom to others that had to be guarded against. In 1827 Charles Carroll wrote to a Protestant minister:

> Your sentiments on religious liberty coincide with mine. To obtain religious as well as civil liberty I entered zealously into the Revolution and observing the Christian religion divided into many sects I founded the hope that no one would be so predominant as to become the religion of the State. That hope was thus early entertained because all of them joined in the same cause with few exceptions of individuals. God grant that this religious liberty may be preserved in these states to the end of time and that all believing in the religion of Christ may practice the leading principle of charity, the basis of every virtue.[7]

In federal constitutional matters as well, Charles Carroll of Carrollton wanted bans upon preference and discrimination because of religion. He approved the ban upon religious test oaths in Article Six of the United States Constitution and led the forces in Maryland in favor of ratifying this document.[8]

Third, Charles Carroll of Carrollton was probably agreed to the use of governmental funds to aid religion, so long as there was no preference given to one sect. Although it was Charles Carroll, the barrister, who was most responsible in the Maryland Convention of 1776 for the Declaration of Rights, with its provision empowering the Legislature to tax for the support of the Christian religion,[9] Charles Carroll of Carrollton was one of the committee of seven charged with the drafting of this Declaration. As Werline has noted,[10] he favored such impartial state support of religion at that time. No evidence has been brought to light to indicate that he believed the Federal Government should have been denied such expenditures.

Fourth, it is possible that Charles Carroll of Carrollton did not believe that members of the Congress should, as such, participate in religious ceremonies. In the First Congress he spoke against the proposal that Congress should, at the inauguration of President Washington, accompany him to St. Paul's Church and attend divine service.[11] Nevertheless, such antipathy is only conjectural and Carroll remained silent on the vote to attend such services. Rowland notes: "Charles Carroll, no doubt, showed good sense as well as courtesy in not further opposing a religious service advocated by a majority of his fellow Senators."[12]

Charles Carroll of Carrollton's cousin, Daniel Carroll, served as a representative from Maryland in the First Congress of the United States. He, too, was willing to utilize governmental funds to aid religion. As a Catholic he was active while a Maryland state senator in advocating passage of an act which was to provide relief for widows and children of the Protestant clergy.[13] It is interesting to note that Charles Carroll openly approved the same measure.[14] Daniel Carroll, while serving as president of the Maryland Senate, introduced a bill to "incorporate certain persons in every Christian church or congregation throughout this state."[15] His sympathy with the United States Constitution's ban upon religious test oaths can be deduced from the fact that he joined his cousin, Charles Carroll of Carrollton, in securing ratification of the federal compact in Maryland.[16] No reason has been discovered why Daniel Carroll would have intended to prevent the Federal Government, any more than Maryland, from either aiding religion without preference or incorporating the various churches. As noted in the earlier chapters, Daniel Carroll spoke enthusiastically on the floor of the First Congress for what is now the First Amendment. Humphrey has written that the Carrolls "were largely instrumental in reading into the federal Constitution a principle of religious freedom drawn from that phrase of the Declaration of Independence that 'All men are created equal and endowed by their Creator with certain inalienable rights.' "[17] It was primarily this equality of all sects before the law that all of the Carrolls demanded.

The third Carroll important in the period 1776 to 1800 was the Reverend John Carroll, who was to become the first American archbishop. Like Charles and Daniel, he wanted above all else in the American constitutions religious liberty and equality of freedom of religion for all. On November 11, 1783, he wrote to Charles Carroll of Carrollton, who was then serving in the Maryland Senate, asking him to work for the repeal of the old laws forbidding Catholics to be guardians of Protestant children. John Carroll observed:

> As this clause is inconsistent with that perfect equality of rights, which by our Constitution is secured to all Religions, I make no doubt but you will be able to obtain a general repeal of this and all other laws and clauses of laws enacting any partial regard to one denomination to the prejudice of others.[18]

In the early days of our federal Constitution, there had been suggestions in Philadelphia and New York papers that Catholics should be subordinated to Protestants in the new Constitution. In response to these, John Carroll wrote to Mathew Carey in New York on January 30, 1789. Carey had been for some time an editor of the *Columbian Magazine,* before he resigned in protest to the policy of printing letters and essays which were but thinly veiled attacks upon the Catholic citizens. John Carroll wrote:

> After having contributed in proportion to their numbers, equally at least with every other denomination to the establishment of independence, and run every risk in common with them, it is not only contradictory to the avowed principles of equality in religious rights but a flagrant act of injustice to deprive them of those advantages to the acquirement of which they so much contributed.[19]

Efforts continued to have something inserted into the federal Constitution that would prefer Protestantism. In May of 1789 a writer who signed only as "E. C." penned an essay entitled "The Importance of the Protestant Religion Politically Considered" for the *Gazette of the United States,* which was published in New York City where the First Congress was about to consider amendments to the United States Constitution. It subtly suggested that Protestantism ought to be favored by the national law. This was the sort of establishment that the Catholics naturally wanted to prevent, and the willingness of the Catholic Carrolls to insert into the Constitution the establishment ban of the First Amendment is best understood against this background. In a letter of June 10, 1789, entitled "To the Editor of the Gazette of the United States" but printed in *The American Museum* which was then under the editorship of Mathew Carey, John Carroll force-fully took issue with the thesis that Protestantism somehow deserved preference in our federal law. Writing under the name "Pacificus," John Carroll indicated:

> Every friend of the rights of conscience, equal liberty and diffusive happiness must have felt pain in seeing the attempt made by one of your correspondents to revive an odious system of religious intoler-ance. The author may not have been fully sensible of the tendency of his publication because he speaks of preserving universal tolera-tion. Perhaps he is one of those who thinks it consistent with justice to exclude certain citizens from the honors and emoluments of society merely on account of their religious opinions, provided they be not restrained by racks and forfeitures from the exercise of the religious worship which their consciences approve. If such are his views, in vain have Americans associated in one grand national union under the express condition of not being shackled by religious tests and under a firm persuasion that they were to retain, when associated every natural right not expressly surrendered. Is it pretended that they who are objects of an intended exclusion from certain offices of honor and advantage, have forfeited by any act of treason against the United States, the common rights of nature or the stipulated rights of the political society of which they form a part? This, the author has not presumed to assert. Their blood flowed as freely in proportion to their numbers to cement the fabric of independence as that of any of their fellow citizens. They concurred with perhaps greater unanimity than any other body of men in recommending a form of government from whose influence America anticipates all the blessings of justice, peace, plenty, good order and civil and reli-gious liberty. What character shall we give to a system of policy calculated for the express purpose of divesting rights legally acquired by those citizens who are not only unoffending but those whose conduct has been highly meritorious?[20]

He added:

> I am anxious to guard against the impression intended by such in-sinuations, not merely for the sake of any one profession but from an earnest regard to preserve inviolate forever in our new empire the great principle of religious freedom. The constitutions of some of our states continue still to entrench on the sacred rights of con-

science and men who have bled and opened their purses as freely in the cause of liberty and independence as any other citizens are most unjustly excluded from the advantages which they contributed to establish. But if bigotry and narrow prejudices have hitherto prevented the cure of these evils, be it the duty of every lover of peace and justice to extend them no further.

It was the opportunity for freedom of worship and the end of civil and political disabilities that John Carroll treasured most in American law. In connection with a request that the American clergy be permitted to elect their own bishop, Carroll wrote to a friend in Rome:

> You are not ignorant that in these United States our religious system has undergone a revolution, if possible, more extraordinary than our political one. In all of them free toleration is allowed to Christians of every denomination, and particularly in the states of Pennsylvania, Delaware, Maryland and Virginia, a communication of all civil rights without distinction or diminution is extended to those of our religion. This is a blessing and advantage which it is our duty to preserve and improve with the utmost prudence by demeaning ourselves on all occasions as subjects zealously attached to our government and avoiding to give any jealousies on account of any dependence on foreign jurisdiction more than that which is essential to our religion, an acknowledgment of the Pope's supremacy over the whole Christian world.[21]

After Bishop Carroll's death an interesting paper that has been attributed to him came to light and in 1830 was published. Ives concluded it had reference to the First Congress of the United States and the body's reasons for proposing the First Amendment.[22] The paper states:

1. The leading characters of the first assembly or congress were, through principle, opposed to everything like vexation on the score of religion: and as they were perfectly acquainted with the maxims of the Catholics, they saw the injustice of persecuting them for adhering to their doctrines.
2. The Catholics evinced a desire, not less ardent than that of the Protestants, to render the provinces independent of the mother country; and it was manifest that if they joined the common cause and exposed themselves to the common danger, they should be entitled to a participation in the common blessings which crowned their efforts.
3. France was negotiating an alliance with the United Provinces, and nothing could have retarded the progress of that alliance more effectually than the demonstration of any ill will against the religion which France professed.

4. The aid, or at least the neutrality of Canada, was judged necessary for the success of the enterprise of the provinces and by
placing Catholics on a level with all other Christians, the Cana-
dians, it was believed, could not but be favorably disposed towards the Revolution.[23]

However, a close reading of the language and a study of the work
of one of the Bishop's biographers, John Carroll Brent, who brought
this paper to light, seems to indicate that it was originally penned in
reference to the first Continental Congress, and not the First Congress
of the United States. It nevertheless is both interesting and valuable in
affording insight into the desires of both the Catholics of 1776–1800
and their contemporaries for religious liberty and freedom from the
kind of establishment that connoted favoritism and discriminations.

A great man of his time was William Paterson, a senator in the
First Congress of the United States from New Jersey. Between 1770
and 1772, while he was practicing law, he wrote frequently on topics
of the day. During the discussions of the threatened establishment
of an American episcopate, he sided with those who dreaded such a
move.[24] Although there is some dispute, Paterson is generally credited
with having drafted the New Jersey Constitution of 1776.[25] After
serving as governor of that state, he entered the federal judiciary.
Like so many judges of the times, Paterson frequently lectured on
religion and morality in connection with his charges to juries. There
is one account of the opening of a United States circuit court, at
which it was said: "Religion and morality were pleasingly included
and enforced as being necessary to good government, good order
and good laws. . . ." The report adds that "after the charge was
delivered, the Reverend Mr. Alden addressed the throne of Grace
in an excellent and well adapted prayer."[26]

Elias Boudinot was a representative from New Jersey in the
First, Second, and Third Congresses, and was chairman of the Committee of the Whole during its debates on the First Amendment. The
manner in which he embraced all religious faiths is indicated in a
letter to his daughter in 1777. He noted that as she grew, she would
find the "Christian World, unhappily split into a Multitude of Denominations."[27] This Presbyterian lay leader continued the epistle:
"The true Catholicism of the Scriptures will teach you to take them
all into the Arms of your Love and Charity and to look upon them
all as the Servants of the same Master."[28] In the first days of the first
Provincial Congress of New Jersey, Boudinot set the keynote: "Let
us in the First Place . . . humbly and penitently implore the Aid of
that Almighty God, whom we profess to serve — let us earnestly call

and beseech Him for Christ's sake to preside in our Councils. . . ."[29]
When Boudinot was president of the Continental Congress in 1783,
he proclaimed the first Thanksgiving Day; and then six years later,
just as the First Congress had completed work on the Amendments,
he rose to say that "[we] could not think of letting the session pass
over without offering an opportunity to all the citizens . . . in returning to Almighty God their sincere thanks for the many blessings he
had poured down upon them."[30]

One of the leaders in New Jersey's civic affairs,[31] Boudinot was
also prominent in religious affairs.[32] Thus he was persuaded to
defend religion against the attack in Paine's *Age of Reason,* and
so he published his *Age of Revelation.*[33] Boudinot was also a trustee
of Princeton College during its vigorous fund campaign, culminating
in limited financial support from the state of New Jersey in 1796.[34]
It was Elias Boudinot who stood up in the first New Jersey State
Legislature and moved "that some Minister of the Gospel be requested to attend . . . every morning . . . during the Sessions in order
to open the Meeting with Prayer humbly supplicating Almighty God
to preside over and direct our Councils. . . ."[35]

Virginia's two senators in the First Congress were Richard Henry
Lee and William Grayson: both believed that government could
give financial aid to religion. One of Lee's most memorable utterances
on this subject is in a letter to James Madison on November 26,
1784:

> I conceive that the General Assessment, and a wise digest of our
> militia laws are very important concerns; the one to secure our peace,
> and the other our morals. Refiners may weave as fine a web of reason
> as they please, but the experience of all times shows Religion to be
> the guardian of morals — And he must be a very inattentive ob-
> server in our Country, who does not see that avarice is accomplish-
> ing the destruction of religion, for want of a legal obligation to con-
> tribute something to its support. The Declaration of Rights, it seems
> to me, rather contends against forcing modes of faith and forms of
> worship, than against compelling contribution for the support of
> religion in general.[36]

Senator Grayson also believed during the 1780's in the permissibility
and propriety of the state aiding religion without preference or
discrimination.[37]

James Madison, one of Virginia's representatives in the First
Congress, was one of the leading men of that period. His views on
religious liberty and church-state relations have been the subject of
many books and articles. Accordingly, he will not be quoted as

fully as might be possible; to do so would fill volumes and would probably not cover new ground.

Madison understood that the importance of the establishment clause of the First Amendment lay in its ban on any national preference and its insistence that all sects be placed on an equal footing before national law. Writing to a friend in 1820 about the United States Constitution, Madison lauded "the perfect equality of rights which it secures to every religious sect."[38] He had always sought to stop religious favoritism. For example, when the Virginians were discussing a state constitution, Madison asked for no ban upon any "establishment," but rather proposed a clause providing, *inter alia,* that "all men are equally entitled to the full and free exercise [of religion] according to the dictates of conscience; and therefore that no man or class of men, ought, on account of religion to be invested with peculiar emoluments or privileges, nor subjected to any penalties or disabilities. . . ."[39] In 1785 Madison opposed the proposed Virginia Bill for a general assessment to aid *Christian* teachers primarily "because, the bill violates that equality which ought to be the basis of every law. . . ."[40] The bill favored the Christian sects at the expense of Jews and others; further, it opened a possibility that it would be followed by a state preference of one Christian sect over others. Madison found this particularly odious, and replied in his famous memorial and remonstrance: "Who does not see that the same authority which can establish Christianity in exclusion of all other religions may establish with the same ease any particular sect of Christians in exclusion of all other sects?"[41] No one can say for sure how Madison would have felt had the general assessment treated all the sects within the state on a fair and equal basis. Divorced of its preferential treatment of Christians, it might have been acceptable to him.

Just as he feared an exclusive establishment of one faith, so too Madison dreaded the thought of two powerful sects — such as the Anglicans and Presbyterians — merging for favor as a national religion. His reason was his basic one: it would impair the religious rights of all others. In the midst of the campaign against the proposed general assessment, he wrote to Thomas Jefferson:

> The Presbyterian clergy, have at length espoused the side of the opposition [to the bill], being moved either by a fear of their laity or a jealousy of the Episcopalians. The mutual hatred of these sects has been much inflamed by the late act incorporating the latter. I am far from being sorry for it, as a coalition between them could alone endanger our religious rights, and a tendency to such an event has been suspected.[42]

Speaking in 1788 before the Virginia Convention that ratified the Constitution of the United States, but one year before he introduced the proposed religious liberty amendment in the First Congress, Madison said: "Fortunately for this Commonwealth, a majority of the people are decidedly against any exclusive establishment. . . . A particular state might concur in one religious project but the United States abound in such a variety of sects, that it is a strong security against religious persecution, and it is sufficient to authorize a conclusion, that no one sect will ever be able to outnumber or depress the rest."[43] Later in his distinguished and long career, Madison made clear that he thought it violative of the establishment concept for the Federal Government to incorporate the Episcopal Church in the District of Columbia.[44] He similarly was of the opinion that the use of chaplains by Congress and the gift of federal land to a Baptist church in the Mississippi territory violated "the principle of national establishment."[45] In addition, Madison objected to executive proclamations of fasts and festivals.[46]

There were some, particularly in New England, who felt that the omission of a religious test oath in the United States Constitution was a serious error. John Sullivan, governor of New Hampshire from 1787 to 1790, wrote in 1788 on the absence of such a test oath: "[T]he President at least ought to be compelled to submit to it, for otherwise, says one, 'a Turk, a Rom(an) Catholic, and what is worse than all a Universal(ist), may be President of the United States.' "[47] The subsequent Chief Justice of the Massachusetts Supreme Court, Theophilus Parsons, speaking during the Massachusetts ratifying convention, felt that a religious test oath would have little effect, for one who had no fear of God would not hesitate to swear falsely. He continued: "No man is so illiberal as to wish the confining places of honour or profit to any one sect of Christians . . . the only evidence we can have of the sincerity and excellency of a man's religion is a good life."[48] Another national leader from Massachusetts, John Adams, proposed in that state's constitutional convention of 1820 that the test oath be eliminated and equality extended there to "all men of all religions."[49] That Adams believed in religious equality not just in his later life, but also in his youth, is indicated in a letter he wrote in 1776. He said that he was in favor of "the most liberal toleration of all denominations of religionists, but I hope that [the Continental] Congress will never meddle with religion further than to say their own prayers, and to fast and give thanks once a year. Let every colony have its own religion without molestation."[50] Once again, therefore, it is seen that inherent in the concept of religious freedom and equality is the absence of a national church. This notion of toleration and equality of all faiths was also expressed by another famous New Englander, Samuel Adams. During the first Continental Congress, some members objected to the use of prayers to open the sessions, on the grounds of the religious diversity among the delegates. To this Adams replied: "I am not a bigot. I can hear a prayer from a man of piety and virtue, who is at the same time a friend of his country."[51]

Like Madison, Thomas Jefferson left numerous indications which point out his sentiments on the First Amendment and the whole concept of church-state relations. For example, during the Revolution Jefferson agreed with the Congresses and other state chief executives in proclaiming days of prayer and thanksgiving. Thus, acceding to the request of the Congress, dated October 20, 1779, that December 9, 1779, be set aside as "a day of publick and solemn thanksgiving and prayer," Thomas Jefferson when governor of Virginia on November 11, 1779, gave his proclamation

hereby appointing Thursday the 9th day of December next, a day of publick and solemn thanksgiving and prayer to Almighty God, earnestly recommending to all the good people of this commonwealth, to set apart the said day for those purposes, and to the several Ministers of religion to meet their respective societies thereon, to assist them in their prayers, edify them with their discourses, and generally to perform the sacred duties of their function, proper for the occasion.

However, as President of the United States, Jefferson refused to proclaim days of fast, thanksgiving, or other religious observance. His explanation is contained in his letter of January 1, 1802, to the Danbury Baptists, in which Jefferson wrote:

Gentlemen. — The affectionate sentiments of esteem and approbation which you are so good as to express towards me, on behalf of the Danbury Baptist Association, give me the highest satisfaction. My duties dictate a faithful and zealous pursuit of the interests of my constituents, and in proportion as they are persuaded of my fidelity to those duties, the discharge of them becomes more and more pleasing.

Believing with you that religion is a matter which lies solely between man and his God, that he owes account to none other for his faith or his worship, that the legislative powers of government reach actions only, and not opinions, I contemplate with sovereign reverence that act of the whole American people which declared that their legislature should "make no law respecting an establishment of religion, or prohibiting the free exercise thereof," thus building a wall of separation between Church and State. Adhering to this expression of the supreme will of the nation on behalf of the rights of conscience, I shall see with sincere satisfaction the progress of those sentiments which tend to restore to man all his natural rights, convinced he has no natural right in opposition to his social duties.

I reciprocate your kind prayers for the protection and blessing of the common Father and Creator of man, and tender you for yourselves and your religious association, assurance of my high respect and esteem.[52]

Further explanation for Jefferson's decision is contained in a letter written in 1808 to another clergyman. There Jefferson wrote:

I consider the government of the United States as interdicted by the Constitution from intermeddling with religious institutions, their doctrines, discipline, or exercises. This results not only from the provision that no law shall be made respecting the establishment or free exercise of religion, but from that also which reserves to the States the powers not delegated to the United States. Certainly, no power to prescribe any religious exercise, or to assume authority in religious discipline, has been delegated to the General Government. It must then rest with the States, as far as it can be in any human authority. But it is only proposed that I should recommend not prescribe a day of fasting and prayer. That is, that I should indirectly assume to the United States an authority over religious exercises, which the Constitution has directly precluded them from. . . . I do not believe it is for the interest of religion to invite the civil magistrate to direct its exercises, its discipline, or its doctrine; nor of the religious societies, that the General Government should be invested with the power of effecting any uniformity of time or manner among them. Fasting and prayer are religious exercises; the enjoining them an act of discipline. Every religious society has a right to determine for itself the times for these exercises, and the objects proper for them, according to their particular tenets; and the right can never be safer than in their hands, where the Constitution has deposited it.[53]

Again, in his second inaugural address, Jefferson said:

In matters of religion, I have considered that its free exercise is placed by the constitution independent of the powers of the general government. I have therefore undertaken, on no occasion, to prescribe the religious exercises suited to it; but have left them, as the constitution found, under the direction and discipline of state or church authorities acknowledged by the several religious societies.[54]

Thomas Jefferson was not at all enthusiastic about having secular religion introduced into his University of Virginia.[55] However, he provided for the appointment of a professor of ethics who was to treat "the proof of the being of a God, the Creator, Preserver, and

Supreme Ruler of the Universe, the author of all the relations of morality, and the laws and obligations which these infer. . . ."[56] At the time of the Rockfish Gap report on education at the university on August 1, 1818, Jefferson approved of the setting aside of a room at the university "for religious worship."[57] However, on April 21, 1825, he wrote to Arthur S. Brockenbrough, indicating that he and the visitors of the university were unwilling to allow the lecture room of Pavilion No. 1 to be used by "two particular sects" for Sunday worship.[58] Jefferson in 1822 proposed to encourage various denominations to situate their theological schools near the university. They could thus "give to their students ready and convenient access and attendance on the scientific lectures of the University. . . . Such establishments would offer the further and greater advantage of enabling the students of the University to attend religious exercises with the professor of their particular sect . . . but always understanding that these schools shall be independent of the University and of each other."[59]

Jefferson, like most of his contemporaries, was willing to use public funds, and government funds specifically, to send Christian missionaries to the Indians. In 1803, for instance, he proclaimed a treaty with the Kaskaskia Indians which, in recognizing that the greater part of the tribe had already been baptized and received into the Catholic Church "to which they are much attached," provided that $100 would be given annually for seven years to a priest designated to "perform for the said tribe the duties of his office and also instruct as many of their children as possible in the rudiments of literature." In addition, the treaty provided that $300 be given to the tribe to assist it in erecting a church.[60] There were many other instances of government funds used to provide missionaries to the Indians. Leo Pfeffer, a contemporary scholar, could well conclude "that the Federal government could constitutionally finance missionary activities among the Indians."[61]

Although he was not a member of the First Congress and was the United States representative in France at that time, the views of Gouverneur Morris are important because he was such a prominent American. Sometime before September, 1791 — when the first constitution of France was accepted by the King — Morris wrote in French his "Notes on a Form of a Constitution for France." Under the heading "Principles" he provided:

. . . the State should provide for public education. . . . Religion is only solid basis of good morals; therefore education should teach the precepts of religion, and the duties of man towards God . . . provision should be made for maintaining divine worship as well as education.

But each one has a right to entire liberty as to religious opinions, for religion is the relation between God and man; therefore it is not within the reach of human authority.[62]

In the article which dealt with "Education and Worship" Morris made provision for a tithe system: "For the maintenance of worship, for providing for education, for the relief of the poor, and to defray the expenses of the hospitals, the tithe shall be collected in the manner prescribed by the legislature."[63] Granted, Morris was writing with reference to France, not America; nevertheless these statements reflect the trend of his thoughts on church-state relations.

During the debates in the North Carolina Convention which ratified the federal Constitution, Governor Samuel Johnston defended the position that under the Constitution the eastern states would not have a disproportionate amount of influence. In the course of his argument, he said:

When you attend to circumstances, this will have no weight. I know but two or three states where is the least chance of establishing any particular religion. The people of Massachusetts and Connecticut are mostly Presbyterians. In every other state the people are divided very much. . . . I hope, therefore, that gentlemen will see there is no fear that any one religion shall be exclusively established.[64]

Thus it can be seen that this prominent North Carolinian did not want the Federal Government to establish one religion to the exclusion of the others.

The Father of the Country, George Washington, has left undisputed evidence of his insistence on religious toleration and freedom. In a letter to George Mason, Washington noted that he was opposed to any kind of restraint on religious principles, but then quickly added: "[Y]et I confess, I am not among the number of those who are so alarmed at making men pay toward the support of that which they profess."[65] A further illustration of the manner in which Washington demeaned himself during his public life is provided in a reply he wrote to the Methodist bishops in the United States in 1789. There he stated: ". . . I shall always strive to prove a faithful and impartial patron of genuine, vital religion."[66] Thus, rather than a hostility or even negative neutrality, Washington demonstrated his desire to be a patron of religion, albeit impartial. Two years after the First Amendment went into effect, Washington viewed with pride the degree of religious liberty in the newly formed country. He rejoiced that:

Every person may here worship God according to the dictates of his own heart . . . equal liberty is our boast, that a man's religious tenets will not forfeit the protection of the Laws, nor deprive him of the right of attaining and holding the highest offices that are known in the United States.[67]

Virtually every important man in America in the years 1789 to 1791 was aware of the need to establish religious freedom on the national level and to insure that it would be unfettered. Some of these prominent men desired that the Federal Government should be positioned close to religion; some wanted an enormous distance between the two. Most men cast their ballot somewhere in between. For them, safeguards against a national church and federal preference for one faith over others was the vehicle best calculated to ensure religious liberty for all.

Conclusion

The events and ideas which have been presented provide no simple solution to the determination of the intention of the Founding Fathers embodied in the First Amendment. There is no one event or item of historical evidence that is definitive of the meaning of the religion clause. Even though the Founders' intent might be ascertained in regard to some church-state relationships, this could hardly be offered as the complete solution to modern problems of church and state. Perhaps the closest one may come to an answer is to ascertain a historical consensus of religious liberty and church-state relationships which will serve to illuminate rather than to control the meaning of the First Amendment. When the church-state relationships and religious liberty are placed in a historical context, it appears that the direction of the mainstream of American thought and practice was remarkably constant.

The rough contours of church-state relations appear in the early colonial period. At that time church and state were closely connected in most countries in the Western World; most governments chose and established an official religion. The American colonies generally were no exception. Typically, one of the first governmental acts of the colonists — many of whom had left their mother country to escape religious persecution — was to make provision for their own official church. This apparent paradox can be explained when it is remembered that religious freedom was understood at that time to be most meaningful where the state used its power to protect and advance the cause of religion. Thus, for example, the taxing system was utilized as an efficient means of supporting the church. Further, the civil government employed church standards to insure that good citizenship was maintained. Membership in the official church, therefore, was conclusive evidence that a person was qualified to participate in the political affairs of the community.

In the small, religiously homogeneous communities of New England, this theocratic plan of government may have worked satisfactorily at first, but the system soon began to break down as new religious sects were introduced. Thereafter, governmental attempts to maintain religious purity became the occasion for religious persecution. It became increasingly difficult to judge a person's qualifications for full citizenship according to his membership in an official church or his adherence to a particular religious doctrine: Protests were raised against such discrimination. As dissenters from the official faith were admitted to participation in the political process, a degree of disestablishment occurred. But this did not mean that the civil power could not still aid religion. In many areas the tax system continued to be used as a means of supporting the community religion. Again, as dissenters were allowed to utilize the tax system to support their own religion, the establishment began to fade.

Full religious liberty, however, had not yet been achieved by these steps, for participation in these governmental benefits was by sufferance, not by right. The state, which was still controlled by members of the Established Church, retained the power to determine the propriety of religious doctrine. Many new colonists realized that the certificate system was an invitation to use religion as a means for obtaining and maintaining political power outside the normal democratic process. This charge was also made against the royal government. In the middle and southern colonies the royal governors classified citizens according to religious belief in order to determine who should participate in the political processes and benefits of government. These attempts to gain power led to a paradoxical situation; the New England colonies — which had established the Congregationalist church — could protest against an establishment, the Anglican Church, as vigorously as a dissenting Presbyterian or Baptist in the southern colonies.

The American Revolution initiated a period of liberty which saw the success of the struggle for political equality. Religious freedom was slower in maturing. The unhappy colonial experiences were not entirely eliminated in 1776; it was difficult indeed for dissenters to uproot such long-established practices and concepts. Gradually, however, the political freedom granted to members of some religious sects necessarily brought with it a movement toward fuller religious equality. As the new state constitutions were promulgated, the constant theme was that there should be no preference or privilege allotted to any sect or denomination. Nevertheless, multiple establishments favoring Protestantism or Christianity were supported in some states. But they were only an intermediate phase in the development of religious liberty. As the nineteenth century opened they began to fade.

Although most of the state constitutions effectively disestablished the official churches, they did not prohibit church-state accommodation which continued throughout the period from 1776 to 1825. The practice of distributing public lands to churches began to diminish during the period, but land grants to church-related educational institutions continued at a steady pace. The grant of public funds followed a similar pattern. Tax exemptions for churches, church-related educational institutions, and the clergy were considered proper as they had been from the earliest colonial times. The special privilege of the public lottery was frequently authorized for support of churches and schools operated by the churches. Incorporation was granted regularly to churches of all faiths by the end of the eighteenth century, except for James Madison's anomalous 1811 veto of a congressional church incorporation bill. On occasion, public buildings were still used for religious services without protest. Chaplains as well as proclamations of days of prayer and thanksgiving were standard features of governmental life on all levels. Official statements of the times were replete with declarations that it was the duty of government to encourage "religion and morality" as being essential to the welfare of the state.

When the Federal Government was to be fashioned, new problems of religious freedom had to be faced. Whereas the object in most of the states had been to end the practices of favoritism, the goal on the federal level was to insure that discriminatory treatment never began. With the great multiplicity of sects that were within the ambit of federal power, any partiality toward one religion would have been politically unthinkable. The Philadelphia Convention understood the necessity for constitutionalizing a provision to prevent political favortism on the basis of religion. A proposal that the government make no law on the subject of religion was rejected in favor of the ban on religious tests. The advocates of limited powers probably thought that the new government had no legislative power to bring about the inherent abuses of establishment of religion except possibly by implication in or derivation from its power to prescribe the qualifications for federal office.

The ban on religious tests was warmly applauded in almost all of the ratifying conventions. Many Americans, however, thought that the acknowledged theory of limited powers might not sufficiently protect religious liberty from federal encroachments. Because they thought that the Federal Government might prejudice their liberty even without a formal test, they sought additional explicit safeguards to prevent discrimination on religious grounds. The requests were worded like the religion clauses in the state constitutions: no preference should be granted to any one religious sect or denomination. The petitions were forwarded to the First Congress and studied by the newly elected senators and representatives who finally proposed the First Amendment. The citizens of the new republic ratified the amendment almost without comment. Only in Virginia was there a suggestion that the amendment might not adequately protect religious liberty. The principal objection was that the government might discriminate among the various sects by paying the ministers of only a select group. Apparently, the proponents of the amendment were able to assure the objectors that the Virginia proposal banning preferential treatment had been encompassed, for the amendment ultimately passed without a record of further dissent.

It is not likely that the American community intended to make a revolutionary change in the general relationship between government and religion when it accepted the First Amendment. A radical step was unnecessary. The progress toward a fuller religious liberty in the preceding decades, and which was being achieved by gradual disestablishment in the states, was incorporated into the First Amendment. The desire of the people was to consolidate the gains of the past and to make certain that the new Federal Government would not invade the treasured religious freedom. The amendments proposed by the states support this, and their acceptance of the First Amendment without adverse comment tends to confirm it.

The constitutional generation realized that, as long as there are governments and churches, inevitable problems would arise out of the concurrent interests in the public welfare. But they knew that it was undesirable and impractical for the government to be hostile to or aloof from church-related activities. Such an attitude itself could endanger religious liberty. Accordingly, by the First Amendment they sought a reasonable and pragmatic solution. They sought to omit from the ambit of Federal Government any power to bring about the discriminatory consequences and specific abuses which could flow from an improper relationship of the churches and the government. The First Amendment was intended to prevent the birth of federal political persecution and financial prejudice on the basis of religion. Moreover, there seems to have been no desire to permit the Federal Government to interfere with religious practices.

Some persons, however, urged a broad view of the amendments. Perhaps Madison and Jefferson personally thought that to achieve the full protection of religious liberty, the government must have nothing to do with the subject of religion. The intentions of these great men were indeed admirable, but the American community disagreed with their means. In fairness, it must also be observed that the First Amendment was hardly the exclusive product of any one person. Subsequent interpretations of the amendment should not be controlled by the singular statements of Madison, Jefferson, the

Carrolls, or Ellsworth. Many people were vitally interested in the constitutional solution to the church-state problem; often these men had highly individualistic and divergent views of the state's relation to religion which fluctuated according to the situation. Moreover, the task of the First Congress was not to write into law the personal views of its members; rather it was to assimilate the proposals submitted by the states together with what was thought to be politically satisfactory and in the best interests of both religion and government.

An examination of the early activities of the Federal Government indicates that the people approved and welcomed its aid to church-related activities. Because of the influence of congregationalism and an awareness of the possibility of abuses, the American community probably did not desire any clergy other than chaplains to be paid directly by the Federal Government. On the other hand, church-related activities in behalf of the common good were never considered undesirable merely because they were associated with religion. It was understood that the Federal Government properly held a strong interest in them. For example, Congress provided lands for churches on the western frontier, undoubtedly because settlers would thereby be encouraged to move west and develop the land. Furthermore, in order to assimilate and pacify the Indians, the Federal Government financially supported — without preference or favoritism — mission activities of many religious organizations among the Indians. To maintain the proper moral tone in the armed forces, Congress provided military chaplains. These examples of governmental involvement in these so-called "religious" areas indicate that the men in the early Congresses took a pragmatic view of church-state relations. They did not harbor the opinion that the establishment clause required the Federal Government to be antagonistic or even neutral in matters of religion. To the contrary; they believed they had the power to accommodate and encourage the interests concurrent of religion and government.

Federal welfare legislation in the early Federal Period was minimal. It must be remembered that the idea of a "welfare state" was not then in the American mind. The individual relied more on his own initiative than on governmental support, even on the state level. Dependence on the Federal Government was virtually unthinkable. Yet, in the subjects clearly within the federal interest — Indians, the army, the frontier, the District of Columbia — Congress did not hesitate to accommodate religion where it served the public welfare and could be accomplished in a nonpreferential manner. Governmental involvement in these areas of admitted federal interest was not only permissible, but also desirable.

Thus, when the American community proposed, discussed, and accepted the First Amendment, the intention seemingly was not to remove from the Federal Government the power to aid and cooperate with the public services of the various religious groups. There was undoubtedly faith that subsequent generations of Americans would be able to utilize the power of the Federal Government to promote the concurrent interests of government and religion under First Amendment norms that were reasonable, pragmatic, and just.

Notes

INTRODUCTION

[1] *McCulloch v. Maryland,* 17 U.S. (4 Wheat.) 316, 406 (1819).
[2] *Slaughter House Cases,* 83 U.S. (16 Wall.) 36, 67 (1872).
[3] *Reynolds v. United States,* 98 U.S. 145, 162 (1878).
[4] *Everson v. Board of Education,* 330 U.S. 1, 8 (1947).
[5] *Reid v. Covert,* 354 U.S. 1, 30 (1957).
[6] Speech in the Fourth Congress, April 6, 1796, in *Writings of James Madison* (Gaillard Hunt, ed.; New York, 1900–1910), VI, 272. [Hereinafter cited as Hunt.]
[7] Letter to Thomas Ritchie, September 15, 1821; Hunt, IX, 71–72.
[8] Letter to Henry Lee, June 25, 1824; Hunt, IX, 190–192.
[9] Letter to M. L. Hurlbert, May, 1830; Hunt, IX, 370–375.
[10] Conrad Henry Moehlman, *The Wall of Separation Between Church and State* (Boston, 1951), p. 113.
[11] Norman Sykes, *Church and State in England in the XVIIIth Century* (Hamden, Conn., 1962), p. 321.
[12] 1685, 25 Car. II, c. 2.
[13] 1676, 16 Car. II, c. 4.
[14] William Anderson. "The Intention of the Farmers: A Note on Constitutional Interpretation," *American Political Science Review,* II (1955), p. 340.
[15] Richard H. Barry, *Mr. Rutledge of South Carolina* (New York, 1942), p. 397.
[16] One should bear in mind the *caveat* of Justice Frankfurter on construing amendments according to speeches made in Congress: "Remarks of a particular proponent of the Amendment [the Fourteenth], no matter how influential are not to be deemed part of the Amendment. What was submitted for ratification was his proposal, not his speech." *Adamson v. California,* 332 U.S. 46, 64 (1947).

CHAPTER ONE

[1] Carl Bridenbaugh, *Miter and Sceptre* (New York, 1962), pp. 56, 338. See Chapter Two, nn. 1–2, and accompanying text.
[2] Sanford Cobb, *The Rise of Religious Liberty* (New York, 1902), p. 175.
[3] Goldwin Smith, *History of England* (New York, 1957), pp. 217–218.
[4] Charles R. Beazley, "The Religious Struggle," *Social England* (New York, 1902), III, 593–596; Charles H. Metzger, *Catholics in the American Revolution* (Chicago, 1962), p. 1.
[5] Beazley, "The Coming of the Reformation," *op. cit.,* III, 33; Smith, *op. cit.,* p. 221.
[6] H. J. Laski, *Foundations of National Sovereignty* (New York, 1921), pp. 233–234.
[7] G. Smith, *op. cit.,* p. 217 ff.
[8] William Blackstone, *Commentaries on the Laws of England,* ed. Thomas Cooley (4 vols.; 3rd ed.; Chicago, 1884), IV, pp. 52–53.
[9] 1661, 13 Charles II, st. 2, c. 1; 1673, 25 Charles II, c. 2; 1678, 29 Charles II, c. 9.

¹⁰ Even the high churchmen could be excluded. In the nonjuror controversy, members of the Anglican clergy who adhered to the doctrine of the divine rights of kings refused to take an oath to support the Hannoverian monarch. Norman Sykes, *Church and State in England in the XVIIIth Century* (Hamden, Conn., 1962), pp. 285–288; H. J. Laski, *Political Thought in England from Locke to Bentham* (New York, 1920), p. 66.

¹¹ *E.g.,* 1487, 3 Henry VII, c. 1; 1529, 21 Henry VIII, c. 20; 13 Charles II, st. 1, c. 12.

¹² Theodore F. T. Plucknett, *A Concise History of the Common Law* (4th ed.; London, 1948), pp. 175, 181–183, 413.

¹³ A. L. Smith, "New Era in Church and State," *Social England* (New York, 1902), III, p. 43.

¹⁴ Sykes, *op. cit.,* p. 41.

¹⁵ *Ibid.,* pp. 150–151, 176.

¹⁶ *Colonial Records of North Carolina,* ed. W. L. Sanders (10 vols.; Raleigh, N. C., 1886–1890, II, p. 207. [Hereinafter cited: *C.R.N.C.*]

¹⁷ *South Carolina Statutes at Large,* ed. Thomas Cooper (I–VI) and David McCord (VII–XII) (Columbia, S. C. 1836–1841), II, 282. [Hereinafter cited: *South Carolina Statutes.*]

¹⁸ *C.R.N.C.,* pp. 867–882; *South Carolina Statutes,* II, p. 282 ff.; G. E. Howard, *An Introduction to Local Constitutional History of the United States* (Baltimore, 1899), pp. 128, 131–133.

¹⁹ Robert L. Meriwether, *The Expansion of South Carolina, 1729–1765* (Kingsport, Tenn., 1940), p. 85.

²⁰ Cobb, *op. cit.,* p. 93; William B. Hesseltine and David L. Smiley, *The South in American History* (Englewood Cliffs, N. J., 1960), p. 33.

²¹ *Ibid.,* p. 171.

²² *Ibid.,* pp. 210–211.

²³ *Colonial Records of the State of Georgia,* ed. Allen D. Candler (Vols. 1–19, 21–26) (Atlanta, 1904–1916), XVIII, pp. 158–172. [Hereinafter cited: *C.R.Ga.*]

²⁴ Reba S. Strickland, *Religion and the State in Georgia in the Eighteenth Century* (New York, 1939), pp. 104–105.

²⁵ *Ibid.*

²⁶ Barnett A. Elzas, *Jews of South Carolina* (Charleston, S. C., 1903), p. 25; Meriwether, *op. cit.,* pp. 205–226.

²⁷ David Ramsey, *History of South Carolina,* 2 vols. (Newberry, S. C., 1958; reprint ed., Spartanburg, S. C., 1960), II, p. 11.

²⁸ Leonard W. Labaree, ed., *Royal Instructions to the British Colonies,* 2 vols. (New York, 1935), *e.g.,* II, pp. 482–512; Leonard W. Labaree, *Royal Government in America* (New York, 1938), p. 115.

²⁹ *C.R.N.C.,* IV, p. 357.

³⁰ Bridenbaugh, *op. cit.,* p. 120.

³¹ Edward McCrady, *History of South Carolina,* 4 vols. (New York, 1901), I, 434.

³² Frederick Dalcho, *History of Protestant Episcopal Church in South Carolina to the Year 1808* (Charleston, 1820), p. 63. Emphasis added.

³³ *South Carolina Gazette,* April 16, 1744. Emphasis added.

³⁴ *New York Mercury,* July 9, 1753; Bridenbaugh, *op. cit.,* p. 152.

³⁵ Letter of Cotton Mather to Mr. Rhodin of Glasgow, June 6, 1715, quoted by George Howe, *History of the Presbyterian Church in South Carolina* (Columbia, 1870), pp. 129, 176, 219.

³⁶ Hugh T. Lefler and Albert R. Newsom, *History of a Southern State, North Carolina* (Chapel Hill, N. C., 1954), p. 123.

³⁷ Stephen B. Weeks, "The Church and State in North Carolina," *Johns Hopkins Studies,* XI (Baltimore, 1893), pp. 234–235.

³⁸ Bridenbaugh, *op. cit.,* p. 143.

³⁹ Strickland, *op. cit.,* p. 95.

⁴⁰ Metzger, *op. cit.,* p. 5.

41 Bridenbaugh, *op. cit.*, p. 48.

42 Metzger, *op. cit.*, p. 273.

43 Strickland, *op. cit.*, p. 81.

44 *E.g.*, Charter of Georgia (1732), Francis N. Thorpe, *The Federal and State Constitutions, and Colonies Now or Heretofore Forming the United States of America*, 7 vols.; 59th Congress, 2nd Session, H. Doc. No. 357 (Washington, 1909), II, 773. [Hereinafter cited as Thorpe.]

45 Strickland, *op. cit.*, p. 180.

46 *Virginia Statutes at Large*, ed. Henning, VII, 35 [hereinafter cited: Hening's *Statutes*]; *cf. C.R.N.C.*, II, 884. *South Carolina Statutes*, II, 131.

47 Ray A. Billington, *Protestant Crusade* (New York, 1952), p. 9.

48 *Ibid.;* Ramsey, *op. cit.*, pp. 1, 2, claims that early settlers feared a popish successor to the English throne.

49 Strickland, *op. cit.*, p. 81. In South Carolina the Indian trade was often interfered with by the French in the Mississippi Valley. See, Meriwether, *op. cit.*, pp. 13–14, 185, 189–190; Knox Mellon, Jr., "Christian Priber and the Jesuit Myth," *South Carolina Historical Mag.*, LXI, 75, 1961.

50 Robert H. Lord, John E. Saxton, Edward Thorrington, *History of the Archdiocese of Boston in the Various Stages of its Development, 1604 to 1943*, 3 vols. (New York, 1944), I, pp. 33, 214.

51 Metzger, *op. cit.*, pp. 6, 8.

52 *Ibid.*, p. 25.

53 14 Geo. III, c. 83. Emphasis added.

54 Metzger, *op. cit.*, p. 42, citing *The Votes and Proceedings of the Freeholders and Inhabitants of the Town of Boston* (Boston, 1772), p. 4.

55 *Georgia Gazette*, December 14, 1774.

56 Thorpe, VI, pp. 3241–3242, emphasis added; *cf.* Georgia Act of Provincial Congress, July, 1775, denounces the Quebec Act as "little short of full establishment" of a religion which is injurious to the rights of the sovereign and mankind. *Revolutionary Records of Georgia* (Atlanta, 1908), I, 241, 243, 265. Some even feared a "popish plot" to restore the Stuarts. *American History Researches* (October, 1880), VI, pp. 163–169. See n. 48 *supra*.

57 Sykes, *op. cit.*, p. 41.

58 *Ibid.*, pp. 76, 150–151.

59 Cobb, *op. cit.*, p. 175.

60 *South Carolina Statutes*, II, p. 242; Wallace, *op. cit.*, I, p. 146. See Arthur L. Cross, *The Anglican Episcopate in the American Colonies* (New York, 1902), pp. 46–47.

61 *Colonial Laws of New York*, 5 vols. (Albany, N. Y., 1894–1896), IV, p. 57.

62 Strickland, *op. cit.*, pp. 106–107.

63 Cobb, *op. cit.*, p. 88. Francis H. Simkins, *A History of the South* (New York, 1953), p. 53. See Cross, *op. cit.*, pp. 5–6, 139 ff.; see also, Hesseltine and Smiley, *op. cit.*, p. 33.

64 Strickland, *op. cit.*, p. 83.

65 *Ibid.*, p. 85.

66 McCrady, *op. cit.*, I, 404–408, 430–434. The colonial governor in South Carolina possessed extraordinary ecclesiastical power. In 1765 Governor Bull excommunicated a colonist for failing to answer the governor's summons! This was tantamount to outlawry in the colonial period. Ramsey, *op. cit.*, II, 13. And in that colony John Rutledge, later Chief Justice of the United States, once sought to convert the church vestry into an ecclesiastical court. When he was unable to collect a debt owing his client in the court of law, he petitioned the vestry to expel the debtor on the grounds that failure to pay a just debt was immoral. See Richard Barry, *Mr. Rutledge of South Carolina* (New York, 1942), pp. 146–147.

67 *South Carolina Statutes*, II, p. 288.

68 *C.R.N.C.*, VI, pp. 10, 81, 223; VII, p. 103.

[69] Lefler and Newsome, *op. cit.*, p. 123. Cross, *op. cit.*, pp. 130–132.

[70] Bridenbaugh, *op. cit.*, pp. 117–120.

[71] Schism Act, 12 Anne c. 7 (1711).

[72] C. L. Raper, *The Church and Private Schools of North Carolina* (Greensboro, N. C., 1898), p. 7; Strickland, *op. cit.*, p. 93.

[73] Strickland, *op. cit.*, pp. 92–93.

[74] Meyers, *op. cit.*, p. 10.

[75] Edward M. Connors, *Church-State Relationships in Education in the State of New York,* dissertation (Catholic University of America, 1951), Introduction, p. xiv.

[76] Bridenbaugh, *op. cit.*, p. 68.

[77] Joseph H. Crooker, *Winning of Religious Liberty* (Boston, 1918), p. 209.

[78] Nelson R. Burr, *Education in New Jersey, 1630–1871* (Princeton, 1947), pp. 77–78.

[79] The governor's instructions imposed what were essentially the terms of the English Schism Act (*supra,* n. 71), *e.g.,* the instructions to Governor Burrington in 1730, *C.R.N.C.,* III, 110, 111.

[80] *C.R.N.C.,* IX, 250.

[81] *Ibid.,* IX, 596, 665; Weeks, op. cit., p. 243.

[82] Weeks, *op. cit.*, p. 243.

[83] Letter of September 9, 1771, quoted by David Duncan Wallace, *Life of Henry Laurens* (New York, 1915), p. 179. (Emphasis added.) The dislike of monopoly in South Carolina is evidenced by a 1765 proposal for providing schools and a college. Although lip service to the establishment was paid by requiring the headmaster to be of the Anglican religion, other teachers were free to choose their own creed. Officiating clergymen were barred from being either a headmaster or a teacher Gertrude Foster, "Documentary History of Education in South Carolina," 13 vols., unpublished dissertation (University of South Carolina, 1934), I, pp. 267, 282.

[84] Leah Townsend, *South Carolina Baptists* (Florence, S. C., 1935), p. 274.

[85] Howard, *op. cit.*, pp. 31, 35, 36, 43.

[86] Cobb, *op. cit.*, p. 284.

[87] Thorpe, III, pp. 1880–1881.

[88] Howard, *op. cit.*, pp. 128, 131; Strickland, *op. cit.*, pp. 109–110; Wallace, *History of South Carolina,* I, p. 258.

[89] Howard, *op. cit.*, pp. 118–120.

[90] *Ibid.,* p. 123.

[91] *South Carolina Statutes,* II, pp. 684–685 (1716).

[92] *Ibid.,* III, p. 555.

[93] *Ibid.,* IV, 9–10, 301, 408; IV, pp. 49, 144–145; James B. Ramage, *Local Government and Free Schools in South Carolina* (Baltimore, Md., 1883), p. 12.

[94] *C.R.N.C.,* I, 558, 568–569; Howard, *op. cit.*, pp. 131–132.

[95] *C.R.Ga.,* XVIII, 258–272; Strickland, *op. cit.*, pp. 110, 104–105.

[96] Strickland, *op. cit.*, 104.

[97] Sykes, *op. cit.*, p. 321.

[98] Blackstone, *op. cit.*, IV, pp. 52–53.

[99] E. B. O'Callaghan, *Documentary History of the State of New York,* 4 vols. (Albany, N. Y., 1849–1851), III, p. 1007.

[100] *Ibid.,* III, 1008–1009, 1011–1012.

[101] McCrady, *op. cit.*, I, 406–408.

[102] *South Carolina Statutes,* II, 131; Wallace, *op. cit.*, I, pp. 154, 258.

[103] Wallace, *History of South Carolina,* I, 284–285.

[104] *C.R.N.C.,* VII, 241.

[105] *C.R.N.C.,* VII, 241.

[106] *Ibid.,* VIII, 202, 217–218, 221, 503.

[107] Davis' *Revisal,* II, 315, ed. 1765; cf. ed. 1773, p. 434.

[108] Weeks, *op. cit.*, p. 240.

[109] Cobb, *op. cit.*, p. 397.

[110] *Pennsylvania Records,* IV, 629; X, 42.

[111] Oscar I. Janowsky, ed., *The American Jew* (New York, 1942), pp. 11, 12; Elzas, *op. cit.*, p. 25; Alexander C. Flick, ed., *History of New York State* (New York, 1937), IX, 215–216.

[112] Hugh F. Rankin, "Criminal Trial Proceedings in the General Court of Colonial Virginia," *The Virginia Magazine of History and Biography*, LXXVII, No. 1 (January, 1964).

[113] Blackstone, *op. cit.*, IV, p. 51.

[114] Conventicle Act, 1664, 16 Charles II, c. 4; Blackstone, *op. cit.*, IV, 51–59.

[115] Blackstone, *op. cit.*, IV, 63.

[116] Cobb, *op. cit.*, p. 285.

[117] *South Carolina Statutes*, II, 66–69, 106, 396–399.

[118] *Laws of Maryland*, c. 1, 13, 16 (1723); Kilty ed., *Laws of Maryland*, 2 vols. (Annapolis, 1799), 16.

[119] Hening's *Statutes*, p. 358.

[120] Cobb, *op. cit.*, 90, 92.

[121] *Ibid.*, p. 99.

[122] Bruce E. Steiner, "The Catholic Brents of Virginia," *The Virginia Magazine of History and Biography*, LXX, No. 4 (October, 1962), pp. 381–409.

[123] Irving Kull, ed., *History of New Jersey* (New York, 1930), p. 337.

[124] C. J. Hoadley and Leonard W. Labaree, eds., *Public Records of the State of Connecticut* (Hartford, 1894–1951), XIII, 360. [Hereinafter cited as *Connecticut Records.*]

[125] Quoted as Allen Nevins, *The American States During and After the Revolution 1775–1789* (New York, 1924), p. 430.

[126] Thorpe, V, 2783.

[127] Hening's *Statutes*, I, 532 (1659); I, 269 (1642).

[128] *E.g., Laws of the Colony of Massachusetts*, pp. 121–125 (1656).

[129] Cobb, *op. cit.*, pp. 180–194.

[130] *Ibid.*, pp. 195–197.

[131] Samuel G. Arnold, *History of Rhode Island and Providence Plantation*, 2 vols. (New York: 1860), II, 490–491.

[132] Cobb, *op. cit.*, p. 260.

[133] *Connecticut Records*, II, 546; Cobb, *op. cit.*, pp. 260–261.

[134] Cobb, *op. cit.*, p. 177.

[135] Patrick J. Dignan, *History of the Legal Incorporation of Catholic Church Property in the United States, 1784–1932* (New York: 1935), p. 50.

[136] Cobb, *op. cit.*, p. 398; Lord, *et al., op. cit.*, I, 33, 214.

[137] *Ibid.*, p. 177.

[138] *South Carolina Gazette*, November 21, 1774.

[139] Metzger, *op. cit.*, p. 174.

[140] Richard Walsh, *Charleston's Sons of Liberty* (Columbia, S. C., 1959), pp. 71–72; McCrady, II, 23–25. But *cf.*, Meriwether, *op. cit.*, pp. 152–153. Catholic settlers were freely admitted to the colony although they were not eligible for grants of land from the legislature unless they renounced their religion.

[141] Strickland, *op. cit.*, pp. 80–81.

[142] *Ibid.*, p. 43.

[143] *Ibid.*, pp. 41–43.

[144] *Ibid.*, pp. 82–83.

[145] *Ibid.*, pp. 76–78.

[146] *Ibid.*, p. 78.

[147] State exempting statutes are collected in the case of *United States v. MacIntosh*, 42 F. 2d 845, 847–848 n. 1 (2d Cir. 1931). For state constitutional provisions, see, *e.g.*, Thorpe, VI, 371 (Vermont); *ibid.*, V, 2637 (New York); *ibid.*, V, 3083 (Pennsylvania); also Rhode Island Act of January 7, 1740; *Records of the State of Rhode Island and Providence Plantations in the Northeast* (Bartlett, ed.), VIII, 122–123, 135–136, 151–152, 189, 204.

[148] Weeks, *op. cit.*, p. 249, n. 2.

149 *C.R.Ga.,* XIII, 335, 339, 346, 355, 364, 367, 414, 625, 655, 692; XVIII, 308, 443, 494; *C.R.N.C.,* III, 298, 584; *South Carolina Statues,* II, 177, 200, 280, 649.

150 *Eg.,* Swan's *Revisal,* 108, 111, 346, 348, ed. 1752; *Davis' Revisal,* II, 121, 133, ed. 1765; *South Carolina Statutes at Large,* II, 177, 200, 280, 649.

151 Thorpe, V, 2783.

152 *C.R.N.C.,* VII, 43.

153 *Georgia Gazette,* May 10, 1769; *cf.* protest by inhabitants of the fork between the Broad and Saluda Rivers in South Carolina, *South Carolina Gazette,* March 27–April 3, 1762.

154 Isaac Backus, *A History of New England, with Particular Reference to the Denomination of Christians Called Baptists* (Boston, 1887), II, 203–204. See also II, 200, for petition to the Continental Congress for equal rights, discussed in Chapter Two, *infra.*

155 Address of the Reverend William Tennant to the House of Assembly, November 11, 1777, Charleston, January, 1778. (Microfilm, American State Records.)

156 Wallace, *op.cit.,* I, 354. See Meriwether, *op. cit.,* p. 85, explaining that the settlers had originally petitioned for an Established Church in order to obtain representation in the Colonial Assembly.

157 Weeks, *op. cit.,* p. 253.

158 *C.R.N.C.,* VIII, 202, 217, 218, 503.

159 Townsend, *op. cit.,* p. 274; Howe, *op. cit.,* pp. 219–220, citing letters of South Carolina Huguenots. Books for the Charleston Public Library were purchased only if they favored the Anglican Church. *Ibid.,* 163. Richard Hooker, ed., *The Carolina Backcountry on the Eve of the Revolution* (Chapel Hill, 1953), p. xvi; Meyer, *op. cit.,* p. 10; Meriwether, *op. cit.,* pp. 40, 47, 84.

160 *C.R.N.C.,* X, 241.

161 Joseph F. Thorning, *Religious Liberty in Transition* (New York, 1931), p. 27; *cf.* Samuel Eliot Morison, *History of the Constitution of Massachusetts* (Boston, 1917), p. 24.

162 Province Laws, I, 62–63.

163 Thorpe, III, 1880–1881.

164 Meyer, *op. cit.,* p. 13; Acts of the Privy Council, 1720–1745, pp. 58, 59, 121.

165 Meyer, *op. cit.,* 14–15; Province Laws, II, 459–460, 477, 495–496, 543–544, 619–620, 714–715.

166 Bridenbaugh, *op. cit.,* pp. 11–12, citing Ezra Stiles, *Discourse on the Christian Union.*

167 *Records of the Colony of Connecticut,* VII, 107.

168 *Ibid.,* VIII, 237, 257.

169 *Ibid.*

170 Cobb, *op. cit.,* p. 298.

171 Meyer, *op. cit.,* p. 10.

172 Nn. 59 and 150, *supra.*

173 Strickland, *op. cit.,* p. 24.

174 *Ibid.,* p. 126.

175 *Ibid.*

176 *Ibid.,* p. 114.

177 *Ibid.,* p. 183; *cf.* George Howe, *History of the Presbyterian Church in South Carolina* (Columbia, 1870).

178 N. 148 *supra;* McCrady, *op. cit.,* II, 444; Wallace, *op. cit.,* I, 230.

179 Cobb, *op. cit.,* pp. 100–107.

180 H. J. Eckenrode, *Separation of Church and State in Virginia* (Richmond, 1910), p. 37.

181 Cobb, *op. cit.,* pp. 376–377.

182 *Ibid.,* pp. 388–389.

183 *Ibid.,* p. 392.

184 *Ibid.,* p. 397.

185 N. 137, *supra.*

[186] Cobb, *op. cit.,* p. 277.

[187] *Documentary History of New York,* III, 1012–1027.

[188] *South Carolina Statutes,* II, 234.

[189] McCrady, *op. cit.,* II, 444.

[190] Howe, *op. cit.,* pp. 176, 129, 219.

[191] N. 31, *supra.*

[192] Howe, *op. cit.,* pp. 176, 129, 219.

[193] *C.R.N.C.,* X, 241.

[194] *Ibid.*

[195] *Ibid.*

[196] Cobb, *op. cit.,* 92; Hesseltine and Smiley, *op. cit.,* p. 34.

[197] *Documentary History of New York,* pp. 1007–1012.

[198] Strickland, *op. cit.,* pp. 68, 122–123.

[199] *Ibid.,* p. 99.

[200] Weeks, *op. cit.,* pp. 243.

[201] Swann's *Revisal,* pp. 127–130 (ed., 1752).

[202] Weeks, *op. cit.,* p. 246; Davis' *Revisal,* p. 350 (ed., 1773) (Newbern, N. C., 1773).

[203] Iredell's *Revisal,* p. 354 (Edenton, N. C., 1791).

[204] Howe, *op. cit.,* p. 129; Bridenbaugh, *op. cit.,* pp. 143–144.

[205] Davis' *Revisal,* II, 279 (ed., 1765).

[206] Strickland, *op. cit.,* pp. 126–127. Frink should be contrasted with the Reverend Charles Woodmason of South Carolina who never took the fees. Hooker, ed., *op. cit.,* pp. 43, 91.

[207] Strickland, *op. cit.,* pp. 80, 82.

[208] *Ibid.,* p. 127.

[209] *Ibid.*

[210] E. H. Abrahams, "The Early History of the Sheftalls of Georgia," *American Jewish Society Publication,* No. 17 pp. 172–173.

[211] Ramsey, *op. cit.,* II, 11, 16.

[212] Dignan, *op. cit.,* p. 39.

[213] *Ibid.,* pp. 31–32.

[214] *Ibid.,* pp. 27–28, 38–39.

[215] Bridenbaugh, *op. cit.,* p. 260.

[216] *Georgia Gazette,* May 10, 1769.

[217] Weeks, *op. cit.,* p. 245.

CHAPTER TWO

[1] Carl Bridenbaugh, *Mitre and Sceptre* (New York, 1962), p. 47.

[2] See Daniel J. Boorstin, *The Genius of American Politics* (Chicago, 1953), pp. 77–73.

[3] Francis B. Simkins, *A History of the South* (New York, 1953), p. 90. It is interesting to note the view of George Rogers that an "establishment" is a retreat by a defeated aristocracy:

"In Western Europe a defeated aristocracy has usually retreated into an 'Establishment.' The French aristocrats with the rise of the bourgeoise sought refuge in their chateaux, in the army, and in the church. The English aristocrats have had their country houses, colleges, and clubs, as well as crack regiments. The rice aristocrats of South Carolina built their own 'establishment' of plantations, select societies, and a church."

Evolution of a Federalist: William Loughton Smith of Charleston (1758–1812)

(Columbia, S. C., 1962), p. 382. It is apparent that this "establishment" faded rapidly in the face of the tide of democracy that engulfed the state in 1776. After the Constitution of 1778 the South Carolina "establishment" was one of "social enjoyment." See *ibid.,* pp. 382–391; also discussion of "disestablishment" in South Carolina in 1777 *infra* this chapter.

4 John M. Mecklin, *The Story of American Dissent* (New York, 1934), p. 268.

5 Mark D. Howe, *Cases on Church and State in the United States* (Boston, 1952 ed.), p. 4.

6 *Journal of House of Delegates,* November 19, 1776; William T. Thom, "The Struggle for Religious Liberty in Virginia; The Baptists," *John Hopkins University Studies,* No. 18 (Baltimore, 1900), pp. 534–535. This was passed by the House, *Journal of the House of Delegates,* December 5, 1776.

7 *Papers of Thomas Jefferson* (Boyd ed.; Princeton, 1952), I, 532.

8 Hening's *Statutes,* IX, 164; H. J. Eckenrode, *Separation of Church and State in Virginia* (Richmond, 1910), p. 53.

9 Hening's *Statutes,* X, 197.

10 *Ibid.,* XII, 984; Kenneth B. Umbreit, *Founding Fathers* (N. Y., 1941), p. 57.

11 *Papers of Thomas Jefferson* (Boyd ed.; Princeton, 1952), VI, 289. [Hereinafter cited as Boyd].

12 Cited in Saul K. Padover, *The Complete Jefferson* (1943), p. 113.

13 H. J. Eckenrode, *op. cit.,* p. 77.

14 R. B. Semple, *History of the Rise and Progress of the Baptists in Virginia* (Beale ed., Richmond, 1894), p. 98.

15 Article XXIX, Constitution of 1776; Thorpe, VI, 3247.

16 Reverend William Tennant, "Address of the Reverend William Tennant to the House of Assembly, November 11, 1777" (Charleston, 1778), American State Records Series, Library of Congress (microfilm). Emphasis added.

17 Article XIII; Thorpe, VI, 3251.

18 Article XXXVIII; Thorpe, VI, 3255.

19 *Candid Animadversions on a Petition Presented to the General Assembly of Maryland by the Reverend William Smith and Reverend Thomas Gates* (Baltimore, 1783), pp. 3, 4, 8, 21, in Rare Manuscript Room, New York Public Library.

20 Article XXXIII; Thorpe, III, 1689.

21 Section 2.

22 *Pennsylvania Constitution,* 1777, *Declaration of Rights,* Art. II.

23 *The Fundamental Constitution for the Province of East Jersey in America, anno domini* 1683, § XVI, in Thrope, V, 2579–2580.

24 Section XVIII; Thorpe, V, 2597.

25 Section XXXVIII; Thorpe, V, 2637.

26 Section XXXV; Thorpe, V, 2635.

27 *Laws of New York,* 1784, c. 33, April 17, 1784.

28 Article LVI; Thorpe, II, 784.

29 Article IV, § 5; Thorpe, II, 789.

30 Article XXIV; Thorpe, V, 2793.

31 *Connecticut State Records,* I, 232; Thorning, *Religious Liberty in Transition* (Washington, 1931), p. 95.

32 The law was entitled "An Act for Securing the Rights of Conscience," and in full it stated: "No persons professing the Christian religion, who soberly dissent from the worship and ministry established by law, and attend worship by themselves, shall incur a penalty by not attending the established worship; that Christians of other denominations, who attend and help maintain worship according to their consciences shall not be taxed for the support of other worship; that those who do not belong to any other society are to be taxed for the support of the State Church; and that all Protestant dissenters shall have liberty to use the same powers for maintaining their respective societies, as belongs to societies established by law." *Connecticut State Records,* I, 11; quoted in Edward F. Humphrey, *Nationalism and Religion in America* (Boston, 1924), pp. 495–496.

[33] New Hampshire Constitution of 1784, Article VI; Thorpe, IV, 2444.

[34] Joseph F. Haynes, *The Struggle for the Constitution in Massachusetts, 1775–1780* (M.S. thesis, Harvard University, Cambridge, 1891), p. 245.

[35] Jacob C. Meyer, *Church and State in Massachusetts, 1740–1833* (Cleveland, 1930), pp. 101–102.

[36] *Ibid.*

[37] Massachusetts Archives, CLVI, 393; Robert J. Taylor, *Massachusetts Colony to Commonwealth* (Chapel Hill, 1901), Doc. 23, p. 63.

[38] Sanford H. Cobb, *The Rise of Religious Liberty in America* (New York, 1902), p. 500.

[39] Jacob C. Meyer, *op. cit.*, pp. 121–123.

[40] *Ibid.*, pp. 121–123.

[41] *Ibid.*, p. 118 and note.

[42] *Ibid.*, p. 113.

[43] Harry A. Cushing, *History of the Transition From Provincial to Commonwealth Government in Massachusetts* (New York, 1896), p. 266.

[44] Humphrey, *op. cit.*, pp. 331–333; Anson P. Stokes, *Church and State in the United States,* 3 vols. (New York, 1950), I, 530.

[45] Meyer, *op. cit.*, pp. 134–136; Thorning, *op. cit.*, p. 41.

[46] *Journals of the Continental Congress,* IV, 152; March 20, 1776.

[47] Act for Establishing Religious Freedom (1785); Hening's *Statutes,* XII, 84; Boyd, II, 545.

[48] Boyd, I, 530.

[49] *Ibid.*, 363.

[50] Thorpe, VII, 3814.

[51] *Journal of the House,* December 5, 1776, quoted in Humphrey, *op. cit.*, p. 379.

[52] Article XXXIII; Thorpe, III, 1689.

[53] Section 2.

[54] Section II; Thorpe, V, 3082.

[55] Theodore G. Tappert and John W. Doberstein, trans., *The Journals of Henry Melchior Muhlenberg,* 3 vols. (Philadelphia, 1942), Vol. II, pp. 720–721.

[56] Semple, *op. cit.*, p. 85.

[57] Eckenrode, *op. cit.*, p. 46.

[58] Mark D. Howe, *op. cit.*, p. 5.

[59] *Journal of the House of Delegates,* October 16, 1776; Thom, "The Struggle for Religious Freedom in Virginia; The Baptists," *Johns Hopkins Univ. Studies,* No. 18 (1900), p. 533.

[60] *Journal of the House of Delegates of Virginia,* October 22, 1776.

[61] *Ibid.*, November 1, 1776.

[62] Rough draft of Jefferson's "Resolution for Disestablishing the Church of England," in Boyd.

[63] The Madison proposal failed. Irving Brant, "Madison: On the Separation of Church and State," *William and Mary Quarterly,* VIII (Jan., 1951), p. 6.

[64] Section 4; Thorpe, VII, 3813.

[65] *Journal of the House of Delegates of Virginia,* May, 1784, p. 21; H. J. Eckenrode, p. 77.

[66] Hunt, II, 186 ("The Memorial and Remonstrance"); see also Padover, *op. cit.*, p. 301.

[67] Kate M. Rowland, *Life and Correspondence of Charles Carroll* (New York and London, 1898), I, 358.

[68] Leo J. McCormick, *Church-State Relationships in Education in Maryland* (Washington, D. C., 1942), pp. 45–46.

[69] John C. Brent, *Biographical Sketch of the Most Reverend John Carroll* (Baltimore, 1843), p. 142.

[70] Baltimore Cathedral Archives, Special A-G 2; Peter K. Guilday, *Life and Times of John Carroll* (New York, 1922), I, 112.

[71] Peter K. Guilday, *op. cit.*, I, 114.

[72] Joseph Gurn, *Charles Carroll of Carrolton* (New York, 1932), pp. 129–130.

[73] Address of the Reverend William Tennant, n. 16 *supra*.

[74] Article XXXVIII, Constitution of 1778; Thorpe, VI, 3255.

[75] *Proceedings of the Constitutional Convention of Delaware on August 27, 1776* (reprinted, Wilmington, 1927), p. 34. Thorpe, I, 567.

[76] Thorpe, V, 2793.

[77] *C.R.N.C.*, IX, 1014; Weeks, "Church and State in N. C.," p. 255.

[78] Iredell's *Revisal*, p. 354. In Georgia the Executive Council had reaffirmed the colonial marriage in 1778 (Rev. Records of Ga., II, 88–89). In 1785 all ministers or justices of the peace were allowed to perform the marriage ceremony. (*A Digest of the Laws of the State of Georgia ... to the year 1798*, Robert and George Watkins, eds. [Philadelphia, 1800], pp. 314, 414–415.

[79] Iredell's *Revisal*, p. 369.

[80] *Elliot's Debates on the Federal Constitution* (Philadelphia, 1907), IV, 194.

[81] Joseph F. Thorning, *Religious Liberty in Transition* (Washington, 1931), p. 95.

[82] Reprinted in *American Museum*, IV (1788), 495.

[83] W. Spaulding, *New York in the Critical Period 1783–1789* (New York, 1932), p. 89.

[84] Article XXXVIII; Thorpe, V, 2637.

[85] Article XXXV; Thorpe, V, 26, 36; Cobb, *op. cit.*, p. 501.

[86] William Jay, *Life of John Jay* (New York, 1833), I, 69.

[87] *Laws of New York in 1784*, c. XXXIII (April 17, 1784).

[88] (Boston, 1780) in Rare Manuscript Room, New York Public Library.

[89] Elliot's *Debates*, 544; *Records of the Federal Convention of 1787* (Farrand ed.), III, 310 [hereinafter cited as Farrand]; Arthur T. Prescott, *Drafting the Federal Constitution* (Baton Rouge, La., 1941), p. 533; Hunt, IX, 4; Stokes, *op. cit.*, p. 533.

[90] N. 89, *supra*.

[91] Elliot's *Debates*, III, 204; see also, *ibid.*, III, 469.

[92] Quoted by William W. Sweet, *Religion in the Development of American Culture 1765–1840* (New York, 1952), p. 120.

[93] Chapter XXXVIII; Thorpe, VI, 3255.

[94] Article XIX; Thorpe, V, 2597.

[95] The Fifth Article of the rejected Constitution would have read: "The future Legislature of this State shall make no Laws to infringe the Rights of Conscience, or any other of the natural unalienable Rights of men, or Contrary to the Laws of God, or against the Protestant Religion." *New Hampshire Provincial and State Papers*, XI, Appendix.

[96] Article VI; Thorpe, IV, 2444; Cobb, *op. cit.*, p. 499.

[97] Quoted in Thorning, *op. cit.*, pp. 156–157.

[98] Joseph M. Ives, *The Ark and the Dove* (New York, 1936), p. 356.

[99] Ives, *op. cit.*, p. 389 ff.; Wilfrid Parsons, *The First Freedom* (Baltimore, 1948), pp. 31–32.

[100] Cobb, *op. cit.*, p. 501.

[101] Article XXXIII; Thorpe, III, 1689.

[102] *Acts of the Maryland Legislature (1781)*, c. XIX.

[103] Mathew P. Andrews, *History of Maryland* (Garden City, N. Y., 1926), p. 450.

[104] *Journal of Council of Censors of Pennsylvania*, First Session, December 23, 1783.

[105] Hunt, I, 143 ff.

[106] Cobb, *op. cit.*, p. 496.

[107] Irving Brant, "Madison: On the Separation of Church and State," VIII, *William and Mary Quarterly*, #1 (3d Ser.), January, 1951, p. 7, see also Saul K. Padover, *The Complete Madison* (New York, 1953), p. 301.

[108] N. 105, *supra*. It is interesting to compare Madison's use of the "three pence" allusion in his "Memorial and Remonstrance" which was written in 1785, eight years after Reverend Tennant had spoken before the South Carolina House of Assembly. When the Assembly proposed to keep the establishment "as a matter of

religious superiority, without taxing other religious denominations," Reverend Tennant replied that the cost was incidental, the primary objection to an establishment was its abridgment of natural rights:

"But they seem to forget, that every reason for which they desire the superiority by establishment, operates as an abridgment of Religious Liberty ... let it be remembered, that there are many Dissenters in this State, who care but little for the money that it costs them to support the Church of England. They value much more their religion, their unalienable rights, than the expense. Sir! you very well know, that *it was not the Three Pence on the Pound of Tea* that roused all the virtue of America. It is our birthright that we prize. It is a full and undiminished freedom in the exercise of our judgment, in all religious matters that we value and esteem." (Emphasis added.)

[109] John T. Ellis, "Church and State: An American Tradition," *Harpers Magazine,* CCVII (November, 1953), p. 63, @ 84. See n. 107, *supra.*

[110] Eckenrode, *op. cit.,* p. 107.

[111] Quoted in William T. Thom, "The Struggle for Religious Freedom in Virginia; the Baptists," *Johns Hopkins Univ. Studies,* No. 18 (Baltimore, 1900), p. 552.

[112] John M. Mecklin, *The Story of American Dissent* (New York, 1934), p. 268.

[113] *Ibid.,* p. 268.

[114] Charles F. James, *Documentary History of the Struggle for Religious Liberty in Virginia* (Lynchburg, 1900), p. 227 ff.

[115] Ellis, *op. cit.,* p. 63. It should be recalled that the dangers of a preferential establishment were as great as that of the exclusive Anglican Establishment. See Chapter One, n. 159 and accompanying text. Events during the period of Carroll's statement tend to confirm his apprehension. It was at this time that sectarian politicians attempted to confiscate lands belonging to certain Roman Catholic religious institutions. See Chapter Three, nn. 164–167 and accompanying text.

[116] Address of the Reverend William Tennant, n. 16, *supra.*

[117] Article XXXVIII; Thorpe, VI, 3255.

[118] *Ibid.*

[119] Address of the Reverend William Tennant, n. 16, *supra.*

[120] Article XXXVIII; Thorpe, VI, 3255.

[121] Articles XII, XIII; Thorpe, VI, 3250–3252. It was during the period of drafting of the Constitution of 1778 that the infamous tarring and feathering of two men occurred because of the charge of "popery."

[122] Article XIII; Thorpe, VI, 3251.

[123] Barnett Elzas reports that Jews apparently voted and held office during this period despite the tests. *Jews of South Carolina* (Charleston, 1903), p. 25.

[124] Article I, Sects. 4, 6, 8; Article VIII; Thorpe, VI, 3258–3259, 3264.

[125] Joseph H. Crooker, *The Winning of Religious Liberty* (Boston, 1918), p. 209.

[126] Article 22; Thorpe I, 566.

[127] William Jay, *op. cit.,* I, 82.

[128] *Annals of Congress,* I, 730.

[129] *Davis v. Beason* 133 U.S. 333, 242 (1889).

[130] Quoted by Humphrey, *op. cit.,* pp. 331–333.

[131] Ives, *op. cit.,* pp. 351–352; Guilday, *op. cit.,* I, 172.

[132] Section 16; Thorpe, VII, 3814.

[133] *Writings of Thomas Jefferson,* Paul L. Ford, ed., 10 vols. (New York, 1892–1899), I, pp. 53–54. [Hereinafter cited as Fond.] Quoted by Humphrey, *op. cit.,* pp. 378–379.

[134] *Journals of the House of Delegates for Virginia,* November 14, 1778.

[135] *Journals of Henry Melchior Muhlenberg,* II, 740–741.

[136] Article XVIII; Thorpe, V, 2597.

[137] *American Museum,* IV (1788), 495.

[138] Article XXXIII; Alfred S. Niles, *Maryland Constitutional Law* (Baltimore, 1915), p. 2; Cobb, *op. cit.,* p. 503.

[139] Edward I. Devitt, S.J., ed., "Letters of Father Joseph Mosley, S.J., and Some

Extracts from His Diary 1757–1786," *Records of the American Catholic Historical Society of Philadelphia* (Philadelphia, 1906), XVII, 305.

140 John Carroll, *An Address to the Roman Catholics of the United States of America* (Annapolis, 1784), 115.

141 Section 3; 1 *Delaware Code Annotated,* 81 (1953).

142 Thorpe, I, 534, 537; Thorning, *op. cit.,* p. 132.

143 Quoted in Jared Sparks, *Life of Gouverneur Morris,* 3 vols. (Boston, 1932), I, 124.

144 Jay, *op. cit.,* XI, 82.

145 Thorning, *op. cit.,* p. 16.

146 Taylor, *op. cit.,* Doc. 33, pp. 73–74.

147 *Boston Gazette,* September 6, 1779.

148 J(oseph) E(dward) A(dams) Smith, *History of Pittsfield, Massachusetts,* 2 vols. (Boston, 1869–1876), I, pp. 366–367; Taylor, *op. cit.,* Doc. 48, p. 118.

149 Massachusetts Archives, CLX, 288; Taylor *op. cit.,* Doc. 49, p. 120.

150 *Journals of Henry Melchior Muhlenberg,* III, 647.

CHAPTER THREE

1 *Journal of the House of Delegates of Virginia,* October 24, 1776.

2 Hening's *Statutes* IX, 164 (1776).

3 *Acts of General Assembly* (1784), c. XXV (1789) (Hampden-Sydney College); LXVIII (Randolph Academy).

4 Section XXXVIII; Thorpe, VI, p. 3255.

5 *South Carolina Statutes,* V, 357 (1799); VI, 95 (1818).

6 Reba Carolyn Strickland, *Religion and the State in Eighteenth Century* (New York, 1939), pp. 167–173.

7 Sherman M. Smith, *Relation of the State to Religious Education in Massachusetts* (New York, 1926), pp. 114–119.

8 Henry G. Welbon, "History of Christian Education in Delaware" (unpublished M.A. thesis, Library, University of Delaware, 1937), p. 116.

9 Pennsylvania, *Statutes at Large,* XII, 221–225 (1785–1787) (Act of April 7, 1786).

10 *Ibid.,* 479–483 (Act of March 28, 1787).

11 *Ibid.,* 391–398 (Act of March 10, 1787).

12 Pennsylvania, *Statutes at Large,* XIII, c. MCCXCI (1787–1790).

13 *Ibid.,* c. MCDXXXIX.

14 *Laws of New York* (May 5, 1786), c. 67.

15 M. Louise Greene, *Development of Religious Liberty in Connecticut* (New York, 1905), p. 360.

16 *Journals of the Continental Congress,* XXXII, 276.

17 16C. *Ibid.* XXXIII, 399–400.

18 Madison's behavior here is in sharp contrast to the pedantic attitude he took in 1811 in vetoing incorporation of churches and grant of land to churces. See Chapter Eight, *infra,* for a full discussion. Edward W. Reisner, *Nationalism and Education Since 1789* (New York, 1922), pp. 342–343, suggests that Congress' benevolence may have been used by a real-estate promoter, Manessah Cutler, as a device for increasing the value of his land. He also attributes motives of self-interest to the Congress in increasing the value, since funds from the sale would be used to pay off the national debt.

19 Edward F. Humphrey, *Nationalism and Religion in America* (Boston, 1924), p. 389.

20 H. J. Eckenrode, *Seperation of Church and State in Virginia* (Richmond, 1910), p. 77.

21 *Journal of the House of Delegates of Virginia,* May 15, 27; Nov. 4, 12, 1784.

22 Humphrey, *op. cit.,* p. 391.

23 Hunt, II, pp. 58–59.

24 John M. Mecklin, *The Story of American Dissent* (New York, 1934), pp. 274–275.

25 Hunt, II, p. 132.

26 *Ibid.*

27 W. F. Thom, "The Struggle for Religious Freedom in Virginia: The Baptists," *Johns Hopkins Univ. Studies,* No. 18 (Baltimore, 1900), pp. 552–554; Irving Brant, "Madison on the Separation of Church and State," *William and Mary Quarterly,* VIII, January, 1951), p. 7.

28 Thom, *op. cit.,* p. 554.

29 *Letters of Richard Henry Lee,* ed. Ballagh (1914), II, p. 304.

30 Humphrey, *op. cit.,* p. 401.

31 Hunt, II, 183; Mecklin, *op. cit.,* pp. 270, 273.

32 *Acts of General Assembly,* c. XCVI (1787), c. LIII (1790).

33 Leo J. McCormick, *Church-State Relationships in Education in Maryland* (1942), pp. 45–46; Charles A. Barker, *The Background of the Revolution in Maryland* (1940), p. 25.

34 Article XXXIII; Thorpe, III, 1689; see Alfred S. Niles, *Maryland Constitutional Law* (Baltimore, 1915) p. 3.

35 Proceedings of the *Convention of the Province of Maryland* (1836), p. 307; Albert W. Werline, *Problems of Church and State in Maryland During the 17th and 18th Centuries* (1948), pp. 158, 196.

36 John T. Scharf, *History of Maryland,* 3 vols. (Baltimore, 1879), II, 551.

37 Werline, *op. cit.,* p. 178, citing *Maryland Gazette,* January 20, 1785.

38 John T. Ellis, "Church and State: An American Catholic Tradition," *Harpers Magazine,* CCVI (November, 1953), p. 64.

39 Patrick Allison, *Candid Animadversions on a Petition Presented to the General Assembly of Maryland by the Reverend William Smith and Reverend Thomas Gates* (Baltimore, 1783), p. 22.

40 Werline, *op. cit.,* pp. 178–179.

41 Allan Nevins, *The American States During and after the Revolution: 1775–1789* (New York, 1924), p. 430.

42 Laws of Maryland, c. 37, s 19 (1784); McCormick, *op. cit.,* p. 48.

43 *Maryland Session Laws,* 1788, c. XVI.

44 McCormick, *op. cit.,* pp. 48, 53, 78, 86.

45 *Journal of General Assembly of Georgia,* January 21, 1784.

46 *Ibid.,* February 21, 1785.

47 Reba C. Strickland, *op. cit.,* p. 166.

48 J. Dinan, "Religion in America 1776–1876," *North American Review* CXXII, 9.

49 Thorpe, III (1889), Art. III.

50 *Massachusetts Acts of 1786,* c. 10, § 3.

51 Sanford H. Cobb, *The Rise of Religious Liberty in America* (New York, 1902), p. 500.

52 Sherman M. Smith, *Relation of the State to Religious Education in Massachusetts* (Syracuse, 1926), pp. 114–119.

53 Cobb, *op. cit.,* p. 501.

54 *Hartford, Connecticut Courant,* September 11, 1788.

55 *The American Museum* (1789), V.

56 Thomas W. Bicknell, *The History of Rhode Island and Providence Plantations,* 2 vols. (New York, 1920), II, 590.

57 Irving Berdine Richman, *Rhode Island — A Study in Separatism* (Boston,

1905), p. 164. Edward Field, ed., *History of Rhode Island,* 3 vols. (Boston, 1902), II, 260, 326.

⁵⁸ Henry Jackson, *An Account of the Churches of Rhode Island* (Providence, 1854), p. 71.

⁵⁹ *The American Museum* (1787), I, 326–329.

⁶⁰ David Ramsay, *History of South Carolina,* 2 vols. (Charleston, 1809), II, 23–28.

⁶¹ *Ibid.,* II, 25–26.

⁶² Welbon, *Christian Education in Delaware,* p. 101, citing *Laws of Delaware,* February 3, 1821.

⁶³ Edgar W. Knight, *Twenty Centuries of Education* (New York, 1940), pp. 231, 246; Reisner, *op. cit.,* p. 346.

⁶⁴ Reisner, *op. cit.,* p. 362.

⁶⁵ N. 41, *supra.*

⁶⁶ See Chapter One.

⁶⁷ Knight, *op. cit.,* pp. 233–234; Reisner, *op. cit.,* p. 360.

⁶⁸ Reisner, *op. cit.,* pp. 352–354, 364.

⁶⁹ *Ibid.,* p. 364. It may also be suggested that the state constitutions and statutes which forbade the use of the taxing system to pay any "teachers of religion" referred simply to ministers or preachers who instructed pupils in religious doctrine in seminaries for the professional training of ministers or perhaps in the Sunday or church schools, which were solely connected with the evangelical or proselytizing interests of the churches. See Chapter Two.

⁷⁰ *Journals of Congress,* X, 106; XVI, 162–163; William W. Sweet, *Religion in the Development of American Cultures 1765–1840* (New York, 1952), p. 241.

⁷¹ John Hall, *History of the Presbyterian Church in Trenton* (New York, 1859), p. 263.

⁷² *Ibid.,* p. 261.

⁷³ Humphrey, *op. cit.,* p. 421.

⁷⁴ *Journal of the Continental Congress,* IV, pp. 267–269; Humphrey, *op. cit.,* pp. 421–422.

⁷⁵ *History of New York State,* IX, p. 168.

⁷⁶ Carl Zollman, *American Civil Church Law* (1917 ed., St. Paul), p. 239.

⁷⁷ 66 *Connecticut Rev.,* 1702.

⁷⁸ *Acts and Resolves of 1781,* c. 16.

⁷⁹ Sherman M. Smith, *op. cit.,* p. 218.

⁸⁰ Charles Carroll, *Three Centuries of Democracy,* 2 vols. (New York, 1932), II, 959.

⁸¹ *Ibid.,* I, 553; Field, *op. cit.,* III, 238.

⁸² Field, *op. cit.,* III, 232.

⁸³ Hening's *Statues,* IX, p. 351; Bell, *op. cit.,* p. 156.

⁸⁴ *South Carolina Acts of Assembly* (1788), P.L. 435.

⁸⁵ *State Gazette of South Carolina,* April 19, 1787.

⁸⁶ *Ibid.,* April 12, 1787.

⁸⁷ *Georgia Gazette,* April 2, 1789.

⁸⁸ *Acts of The General Assembly,* c. XC (1787); c. LXVIII, LXXIV (1789); *Journal of the Senate,* December 2, 1791.

⁸⁹ Manuscripts (First Presbyterian Church of Elizabethtown; November 25, 1784), New Jersey State Library; New Jersey Manuscripts, Vol. I (St. Peter's Church of Perth Amboy; April 16, 1785), New Jersey Historical Society; Manuscripts (Protestant Episcopal Church of Perth Amboy; May 1787 and Protestant Episcopal Church of New Brunswick; May 17, 1786), New Jersey State Library.

⁹⁰ Journal of *Proceedings of New Jersey Legislative Council* (1787), Entry of March 15, 1786.

⁹¹ *Pennsylvania Statutes at Large* (1787–1790), XIII, c. MCDXIX, passed March 27, 1789; c. MDXX, passed April, 1790, c. MCDLX, passed September 29, 1789.

⁹² *Connecticut State Records,* VI, 334.

[93] *Ibid.,* VII, 51.

[94] Thomas Weston, *History of Town of Middleboro, Massachusetts* (1906), p. 96.

[95] Carroll, *op. cit.,* I, 421; Field, *op. cit.,* II, 140.

[96] Carroll, *op. cit.,* I, 421; Richman, *op. cit.,* p. 165; Josiah Quincy, *History of Harvard University* (Boston, 1840), ii, 162, 273.

[97] Anson Phelps Stokes, *Church and State in the United States,* 3 vols., (New York, 1950), II, 25–26.

[98] William W. Sweet, *op. cit.* (p. 50).

[99] *Journals of the Continental Congress* (Washington ed., 1828), I, 26. The second Continental Congress resolved on their opening day, May 10, 1775, "That Mr. Duche be requested to open the Congress with prayers tomorrow morning." *Journals of the Continental Congress,* II, p. 12. The same Congress resolved on June 7, 1775, that the coming July 20 be observed "as a day of humiliation, fasting and prayer." *Journals of the Continental Congress,* II, 81.

[100] *Journals of Continental Congress,* VI, 886–887; Humphrey, *op. cit.,* p. 413.

[101] *Journals of Continental Congress,* IV, 351.

[102] *Ibid.,* VI, 1033.

[103] *Ibid.,* IV, 811.

[104] Hall, *Presbyterian Church in Trenton,* pp. 302–303.

[105] *Ibid.,* pp. 277–278.

[106] *Acts of the General Assembly of New Jersey,* CCXL (1784) (Act of January 6, 1781).

[107] *Journal of the Votes and Proceedings of the Convention of New Jersey at Burlington* (1776), June 28, 1776.

[108] Werline, *op. cit.,* p. 146.

[109] *Minutes and Proceedings of the Convention of the State of Pennsylvania,* July 17, 1776.

[110] Bell, *op. cit.* (Philadelphia, 1930), pp. 155–156.

[111] *Journal of the Proceedings of the Convention of the State of New York* (1788), June 17, 1788.

[112] *New York Daily Gazette,* July 14, 1789.

[113] *Records of the Colony of Rhode Island and Province Plantations in New England, 1636–1792* (Bartlett ed.; Providence, 1856–1865), 10 vols., IX, 264, 615.

[114] Hall, *op. cit.,* p. 261 n.

[115] *Journal of the Votes and Proceedings of the Convention of New Jersey at Burlington* (1776), June 11–12, 1776.

[116] *Ibid.,* December 13, 20, 1787; *History of Trenton: 1679–1929* (Princeton, 1929), I, 197.

[117] Hall, *op. cit.,* p. 286.

[118] *Ibid.,* p. 287.

[119] *Resolution of the New Jersey Assembly,* November 30, 1789.

[120] Cobb, *op. cit.,* p. 504.

[121] *Writings of James Madison,* ed. Gaillard Hunt, IX, 449.

[122] *Ibid.,* III, 310–312.

[123] *Ibid.*

[124] Madison noted in his *Journal* that Mr. Williamson observed: "The true cause of the omission could not be mistaken. The convention had no funds." Farrand, I, 452. In a letter to Thomas Grimke on January 6, 1834, James Madison alluded to the "proposition of Doctor Franklin in favor of a religious service in the Federal Convention. The proposition was received and treated with the respect due to it; but the lapse of time which had preceded, with considerations growing out of it, had the effect of limiting what was done, to a reference of the proposition to a highly respectable Committee. This issue of it may be traced in the printed Journal. The Quaker usage, never discontinued in the state and the place where the Convention held its sittings, might not have been without an influence as might also, the discord of religious opinions with the Convention as well as among the Clergy of the Spot." Farrand, III, 531, Appendix A, CCCXCIII.

[125] *Ibid.*

[126] Edward L. Israel, "Maryland's Laws Governing Religion" (unpublished manuscript in Enoch Pratt Library, Baltimore, undated), p. 2.

[127] Mathew Page Andrews, "Separation of Church and State in Maryland," *Catholic History Review,* XXI (April, 1935), pp. 164, 166.

[128] *Updegraph v. Commonwealth,* 11 Sergeant & Rawle, 394, 404 (Pa., 1824).

[129] Quoted in G. A. Koch, *Republican Religion* (New York, 1933), pp. 240–241.

[130] *Ibid.*

[131] *Pennsylvania Statutes at Large,* XII, 313–322, Act of September 25, 1786.

[132] See Chapter Eight. Koch, *op. cit.,* XII, XV; Herbert M. Morriss, *Deism in Eighteenth Century America* (New York, 1960), p. 8. One of the interesting features of the Deist movement is that virtually none of the Founding Fathers were substantially associated with it. Apparently they believed that it was impolitic. Morais, *op. cit.,* p. 99. See Chapter Eight.

[133] Joseph F. Thorning, *Religious Liberty in Transition* (Washington, D. C., 1931), pp. 157–158.

[134] *Ibid.*

[135] Ford, *Essays on the Constitution of the United States* (1892), p. 171.

[136] *Independent Chronicle of Boston,* November 16, 1780.

[137] Cited in Sherman M. Smith, *op. cit.,* p. 75.

[138] *New Jersey Acts of 1790* (passed at Perth Amboy), June 12, 1790.

[139] *Journal of the Senate of New York* (1777–1795), March 10, 1786.

[140] Boyd, II, 555.

[141] *Acts of 1786,* c. LIV; Hening's *Statutes at Large,* XII, 337.

[142] William G. Torpey, *Judicial Doctrines of Religious Rights in America* (Chapel Hill, 1948), pp. 51–58.

[143] *E.g., Muzzy v. Wilkins,* 1 Smith's Reports, 10 (N.H., 1803).

[144] Claude H. Van Tyne, *The Loyalists in the American Revolution* (1929), pp. 208–209.

[145] *Journals of the Continental Congress,* II, 81, 87, 192.

[146] *Journals of Melchior Muhlenberg,* II, 270.

[147] Quoted in Anson P. Stokes, *op. cit.,* I, 300.

[148] *New Jersey Gazette,* March 31, 1779, Vol. II, No. 69.

[149] *Papers of Thomas Jefferson,* ed. Boyd (1951), III, 178.

[150] *New Jersey Gazette,* April 10, 1782.

[151] *Resolution of the New Jersey Assembly,* November 13, 1789.

[152] Leo Pfeffer, *Church, State, and Freedom* (Boston, 1953), pp. 123–124.

[153] Davis A. McFarland, *Corporations in the Days of the Colony* (Cambridge, Mass., 1894), cited by Edward J. Dignan, *Catholic Church Property* (New York, 1935), p. 50. Joseph S. Davis, "American Charters to Business Corporation, 1781–1800," *Harvard Economic Studies,* 1917, XVII, 332–345.

[154] Dignan, *op. cit.,* pp. 49–50; Hannis Taylor, *The Origin and Growth of the English Constitution,* 2 vols. (Boston, 1898), II, 154.

[155] The concept of the corporation has often plagued legal as well as nonlegal thinkers. See Pollock and Maitland, *History of the English Law* (2nd ed.; Cambridge, 1923), I, 494–495, 505, 507–508; George C. Rogers, Jr., *Evolution of a Federalist: William Loughton Smith of Charleston (1758–1812)* (Columbia, 1962), p. 130. Prior to disestablishment the privilege of incorporation was granted only to four philanthropic organizations, which provided schools and a hospital. Public services were carried on by the parishes and by unincorporated business associations. *E.g., South Carolina Statutes at Large,* VIII, 106–113. After the 1778 disestablishment placed all persons seeking corporate status on an equal footing, there was a substantial increase in the number of municipal and public service corporations. *E.g., ibid.,* VIII, 165, 218, 227, 235.

[156] Dignan, *Catholic Church Property,* pp. 50–51; George J. Bayles, "American Ecclesiology," *Annual Report of the American Historical Society,* 1900 (Washington, 1901), I, 136.

[157] Semple, *op. cit.,* p. 98; Thom, *op. cit.,* p. 551.

[158] *Acts of General Assembly,* c. XII (1786); Hening's *Statutes at Large,* XII, 266.

[159] *Gallego's Executor's v. Attorney General,* 30 Va. (3 Leigh.), 450 (1832).

[160] E.g., *Trustees of the Philadelphia Baptist Association v. Hart's Executors,* 4 U. S. (4 Wheat.) 1 (1819) (Per Marshall, C. J.). *Overruled by Vidal v. Girard's Executors,* U. S. (2 How.) 127 (1844) (Per Story, J.).

[161] 30 Va. (3 Leigh.), 450, 477–478 (1832). Emphasis added.

[162] *Virginia Constitution* (1850), Art. IV, Sec. 32; Thorpe, VII, 3842.

[163] Irving Brant, "Madison: On the Separation of Church and State," *William and Mary Quarterly,* VIII (No. 1; 3rd Ser.; January, 1951), p. 18.

[164] Thorpe, III, 1689.

[165] *Ibid.,* III, 1690. In North Carolina in the first part of the nineteenth century there was strong oppositon to the incorporation of the denominational colleges, Wake Forrest (Baptist) and Davidson (Presbyterian). After a lengthy public controversy the two colleges were incorporated, but severe restrictions on the amount of property that they could hold were placed in the charter. This limit caused Davidson College to lose a large portion of a legacy in 1856. See Luther L. Gobbel, *Church-State Relationships in Education in North Carolina Since 1776* (Durham, N. C., 1938), pp. 30–36, esp. p. 35, explaining the fear of an endowed church as motivating the legislature policy.

[166] Dignan, *op. cit.,* p. 54.

[167] Letter to Cardinal Antonelli, March 13, 1786. Peter K. Guilday, *The Life and Times of John Carroll* (New York, 1922), I, 169.

[168] *Laws of the State of Delaware: 1700–1797* (1797), II, p. 878 ff.

[169] *Laws of New York:* 1783, c. 17, February 25, 1783; 1784, c. 9, March 17, 1784.

[170] *Ibid.,* 1784, c. 18, April 6, 1784.

[171] Ernest W. Spaulding, *New York in the Critical Period 1783–1789* (New York, 1932), p. 34.

[172] *Ibid.,* p. 33.

[173] A corporation sole is an entity composed of one person and his sucessors in office. The advantage in such a system is that title to the property held by the organization can pass to the successor without the formal necessity of a deed or a will. 18 *Corpus Juris Secundum,* "Corporations," §§ 15, 16 (1939).

[174] *Laws of the State of New York,* eds. Samuel Jones and Richard Varick (New York, 1789), I, 104–109; *Laws . . . of New York, 1812–1813* (Albany, 1813), II, 214, 216; Dignan, *op. cit.* (New York, 1935), pp. 63–66.

[175] Strickland, *op. cit.,* p. 173.

[176] *Journal of the Proceedings of the Legislative Council of New Jersey,* entries dated: November 6, 1782; November 2, 1784; November 3, 1785; November 5, 1785; and November 7, 1785.

[177] Hall, *op. cit.,* pp. 284–285. A similar act was passed November 24, 1789.

[178] *Laws of New Hampshire,* IV, 368–370.

[179] Thorning, *op. cit.,* p. 161 ff.

[180] Pennsylvania Constitution of 1776, § 45; Thorpe, V, 3091.

[181] *Laws of the Commonwealth of Massachusetts: 1780–1807* (Boston, 1807), I, 282–283.

[182] Thorpe, VI, 3235–3257.

[183] See Chapter Eight.

[184] Boyd, VI, 1297–1298.

[185] To Francois Jean de Chastellux, September 2, 1785; Boyd, *op. cit.,* VIII, 470.

[186] "Madison's Observations on Jefferson's Draft of a Constitution for Virginia," October 1788; Boyd, VI, 311; Hunt, V, 288.

[187] Letter to Jeremiah Moore, August 14, 1800; Ford, VII, 454–455, *cf.* IX, 145. At one time Jefferson would have also made ministers ineligible to serve as a "visitor" in his bill for establishing a system of public education in 1817. The provision was stricken in committee and Jefferson acquiesced. For a thorough treatment of the bill and the ensuing controversy over Thomas Cooper at the University of

Virginia, see Robert M. Healey, *Jefferson on Religion in Public Education* (New Haven, 1962), pp. 227–245, and notes.

188 Ford, V, 142; VI, 110–111.
189 Hening's *Statutes at Large,* IX, 57.
190 *Delaware Constitution of 1776,* Art. 29; Thorpe I, 567–568.
191 Article XXXI; Thorpe, V, 2793.
192 Stokes, *Church and State,* I, 302.
193 *Georgia Constitution of 1777,* Art. LXII; Thorpe, II, 785.
194 Article XXXIX; Thorpe, V, 2637.
195 Article XXI; Thorpe, VI, 3253.
196 Delaware Constitution (1792); Thorpe, I, 570; New York Constitution (1846); Thorpe, V, 2656–2659; II, 785.
197 John Hall, *History of the Presbyterian Church in Trenton* (New York, 1859), p. 329.
198 *U. S. Stat.,* c. 8 (August 7, 1789).
199 *Journals of the Continental Congress,* XII, 1001.
200 Massachusetts Archives, CCLXXVI, Taylor, *op. cit.,* Doc. 51, p. 125.
201 *Laws of New York* (April 6, 1784), c. 18.
202 *Laws of the State of Delaware: 1700–1797* (1797), II, p. 878.
203 *Journal of the Proceedings of the Legislative Council of New Jersey,* September 13, 1776.
204 *Ibid.,* October 30, 1789.
205 *Ibid.,* p. 18.
206 *Laws of Maryland* (1784), c. LXXVIII.
207 Mary V. Geiger, *Daniel Carroll, Framer of the Constitution* (Washington, 1943), p. 83.
208 *Georgia Executive Council Journal* (1783–1784), cited in Strickland, *op. cit.,* p. 176.
209 Bell, *op. cit.,* p. 157.
210 *The American Museum* (1790), VIII,
211 *The Gazette of the United States,* August 12, 1789.

CHAPTER FOUR

1 *Proceedings Relative to Call the Conventions of 1776 and 1790* (Harrisburg, 1825), p. 39 (June 21, 1776).
2 *American Charters, Constitutions and Organic Laws* (Thorpe ed.; Washington, 1909), V, 2597 [hereinafter cited as Thorpe].
3 Supplement to the December, 1787, issue of the *Columbian Magazine,* quoted in Peter K. Guilday, *The Life & Times of John Carroll* (New York, 1922), I, 113.
4 Article 22; Thorpe, I, 566.
5 Theodore G. Tappert and John W. Doberstein, trans., *The Journals of Henry Melchior Muhlenberg,* II, 740–741.
6 Declaration of Rights, Art. II; Thorpe, V, 3082.
7 Section 10; Thorpe, V, 3085.
8 Sanford H. Cobb, *Rise of Religious Liberty in America* (New York, 1902), p. 503.
9 Article XXXII; Thorpe, V, 2793.
10 Article VI; Thorpe, II, 779.
11 Articles III, XII, XIII; Thorpe, VI, 3249, 3250, 3251. South Carolina further proclaimed that no person or society would be "freely tolerated" unless the following declaration was made:
"1st. That there is one eternal God, and future state of rewards and punishments.

2d. That God is publicly to be worshipped.

3d. That the Christian religion is the true religion.

4th. That the holy scriptures of the Old and New Testaments are of divine inspiration, and are the rule of faiths and practice.

5th. That is lawful and the duty of every man being thereunto called by those that govern, to bear witness to the truth. And that every inhabitant of this State, when called to make an appeal to God as witness to the truth, shall be permitted to do it in that way which is most agreeable to the dictates of his conscience...."
(*Constitution of South Carolina (1778)*, Thorpe, VI, 3255–3256.)
This test strongly reflected the influence of Locke's *Fundamental Constitutions (1669)*, §§ 95, 100; Thorpe, V, 2783–2784.

12 Joseph F. Thorning, *Religious Liberty in Transition* (Washington, 1931), pp. 147–148.

13 *Ibid.*

14 Thorpe, V, 2637.

15 Jared Sparks, *The Life of Gouverneur Morris* (Boston, 1832), I, 124; Anson P. Stokes, *Church and State in the United States* (New York, 1950), I, 405.

16 *Ibid.*

17 *Laws of New York, 1784*, c. 51, May 1, 1784.

18 Guilday, *op. cit.*, I, 247–248; Stokes, *op. cit.*, I, 406.

19 *Jackson, ex. dem. Tuttle v. Gridley*, 18 Johnson 98 (N. Y., 1820).

20 Article XXIX, quoted in Thorning, *op. cit.*, 16.

21 *Journal of the Convention* (Boston, 1832), p. 218.

22 *Ibid.*

23 Thorning, *op. cit.*, 18.

24 Chapter VI, Art. I; Thorpe, III, 1908.

25 Harry A. Cushing, *History of the Transition from Provincial to Commonwealth Government in Massachusetts* (New York, 1896), p. 268.

26 *Ibid.*

27 Massachusetts Archives, CCLXXVI, p. 66, quoted in Robert J. Taylor, *Massachusetts, Colony to Commonwealth* (Chapel Hill, 1961), pp. 155–156.

28 *Ibid.*, CLX, p. 288, quoted in Taylor, *op. cit.*, p. 120.

29 "A Memorial of Rabbi Gershom Seixas, of the Synagogue of Jews at Philadelphia, Simon Nathan, et al., in behalf of themselves and their brethren, the Jews residing in Philadelphia," *Journal of Council of Censors*, p. 20. This was read and "ordered, to lie on the table." Prior to the instant memorial, on December 4, 1783, the Council had resolved itself into a committee of the whole to consider "whether there is a necessity of amending any article of the Constitution which may be defective." The report, voted upon on January 19, 1784, made no mention of this objectionable section. It might be noted that the president of the Council was Frederick A. Muhlenberg, who was later to become the Speaker of the House of Representatives in the First Congress when the First Amendment was proposed. Among the other Censors were Thomas Fitzsimmons and Thomas Hartley, both of whom represented Pennsylvania in the same First Congress.

30 Farrand, III, pp. 78–79.

31 *Ibid.*

32 *The American Museum (1787)*, II, 245–246.

33 Boyd, I, 546.

34 Hening's *Statutes*, XII, 84.

35 Saul K. Padover, *The Complete Jefferson* (New York, 1950), p. 113.

36 Joseph Gurn, *Charles Carroll of Carrollton* (New York, 1932), pp. 129–130.

37 J. Moss Ives, *The Ark and the Dove* (New York, 1936), p. 100.

38 *Ibid.*

39 Quoted by John G. Shea, *History of the Catholic Church in America*, 4 vols. (New York, 1892), III, 421.

40 William Plumer, Jr., *Life of William Plumer* (Boston, 1857), pp. 50–51; Thorning, *op. cit.*, 154–155.

[41] Article XXXV; Thorpe, III, 1690.

[42] John Tracy Ellis, "Church and State: An American Catholic Tradition," *Harpers Magazine,* CCVII (November, 1953), p. 64.

[43] Elliot's *Debates,* V, 131. The Pinckney draft had been the object of considerable historical controversy. Irving Brant, *James Madison, the Father of the Constitution* (New York, 1950), pp. 27, 29, 132, severely criticizes Pinckney's claim to originality, but Richard Alden, *The South in the Revolution, 1763–1789* (Baton Rouge, 1955), p. 379, describes Pinckney as "a man of ability." A sympathetic treatment of the Pinckney plan is found in G. C. Nott, *The Mystery of the Pinckney Draft* (New York, 1908). For an extensive bibliography, see A. J. Bethea, *The Contribution of Charles Pinckney to the Formation of the Union* (Richmond, 1937). The most recent comprehensive review of the controversy surrounding the Pinckney draft is found in the articles of Professor S. S. Ulmer. After an exhaustive analysis of the literature and documents involved he concludes that the Pinckney Plan contributed substantially to the formation of the Constituion. "James Madison and the Pinckney Plan," 19 *S.C.L.Q.,* 415 (1957); "Charles Pinckney; Father of the United States Constitution," 10 *S.C.L.Q.,* 225 (1958).

[44] Elliot's *Debates,* V, 132.

[45] Farrand, II, 335, 342.

[46] *Ibid.,* pp. 342, 468. Madison, however, reports that North Carolina voted "No" and that Maryland was divided on the whole article that included the test oath ban. *Madison's Notes on the Debates in the Federal Convention,* Hunt and Scott, eds. (New York, 1920), p. 495.

[47] Farrand, II, 579; "But no religious test shall ever be required as a qualification to any office or public trust under the United States."

[48] *Ibid.,* III, 122.

[49] *Ibid.,* 227.

[50] *Ibid.,* 297.

[51] Hunt, III, 206.

[52] Elliot's *Debates,* II, 118.

[53] *Ibid.,* 119.

[54] *Ibid.,* II, 44.

[55] *Ibid.,* 118–119.

[56] *Ibid.,* 148–149.

[57] *Ibid.,* 120.

[58] *Ibid.,* 202.

[59] Paul L. Ford, *Essays on the Constitution of the United States* (Brooklyn, 1892), pp. 168–171.

[60] Elliot's *Debates,* III, 204.

[61] *Ibid.,* 330.

[62] *Ibid.,* 93.

[63] *Ibid.,* IV, 212.

[64] *Ibid.,* 193.

[65] *Ibid.,* 194.

[66] *Ibid.,* 300.

[67] *Ibid.*

[68] *City Gazette or Daily Advertiser of Charleston,* May 26, 1788. This important speech has been strangely omitted from the standard editions of the debates, including Elliot and Millar.

[69] *Ibid.*

[70] Stokes, *op. cit.,* I, 610.

[71] N. 68, *supra.*

[72] Albert C. Dieffenbach, *Religious Liberty* (New York, 1927), p. 131.

[73] *New York Daily Gazette,* June 12, 1789.

[74] *Gazette of the United States* (New York City), May 13, 1789.

[75] Paul L. Ford, *Pamphlets on the Constitution of the United States* (Brooklyn, 1888), p. 137.

[76] *The Pennsylvania Gazette,* October 24, 1787.
[77] *The Federal Gazette and Philadelphia Evening Post,* December 16, 1789.
[78] *Gazette of the United States* (New York City), April 25, 1789.
[79] Article VIII; Thorpe, V, 3099.
[80] Frame of Government, § 10, Thorpe, V, 3085.
[81] Article IX, § 4; Thorpe, V, 3100. This clause was first reported by the committee of the convention on December 23, 1789. Then, on February 19, 1790, the convention discussed that section in an interesting fashion. A motion was made to adopt the following section in lieu of the one reported by the committee: "As civil society is instituted for the purposes of enforcing a discharge of the relative duties and preventing the violences of men toward each other, so the great author of their existence can alone determine the truths of religious opinions, therefore no power shall be assumed of depriving a citizen of the privilege of serving his country, in office, on account of his religious belief." This motion was defeated, 6 to 55. It was then moved to postpone the reported section to introduce the following: "No religious test shall ever be required as a qualification to any office or public trust under this constitution." This, too, was rejected, by a vote of 11 to 47. The following two motions were introduced and likewise rejected: "to insert after the word 'God' the following: 'the rewarder of the good and punisher of the wicked,' and to strike out the words 'and a future state of rewards and punishments; "to strike out the words 'who acknowledges the being of a God and a future state of rewards and punishments.' " Finally, the convention voted to adopt the report of the committee.
[82] *The American Museum* (1789), V. 157.
[83] Article I, § 2; Thorpe, I, 568.
[84] Article VIII; Thorpe, VI, 3264.
[85] Section 10; Thorpe, II, 800.
[86] Section 29; Thorpe, IV, 2479.
[87] Thorpe, V, 2793.
[88] Stephen B. Weeks, "Church and State in North Carolina," *Johns Hopkins University Studies* (1893), XI, 264 ff.
[89] *Ibid.,* 265–266.
[90] *Proceedings and Debates of the Convention of North Carolina Called to Amend the Constitution of the State, which Assembled at Raleigh, June 4, 1835* (Raleigh, N. C., 1836), p. 264; Weeks, *op. cit.,* pp. 263–266. The general view of the convention was that such a declaration in behalf of religion served as articles of peace to protect the religion from defilement. See *Proceedings and Debates of the Convention . . . 1835, supra,* at pp. 222, 223, 259, 267. Some members of the convention feared an importation of Roman Catholic tyranny. *Ibid.,* 222–223, 242, 254. Attempts at total abrogation failed because "to strike out this Article about Deists, would be a sort of declaration in favor of Deism." *Ibid.,* pp. 303–312, 325, 331, esp. at 327.
[91] *The American Museum* (1788), IV, p. 495.
[92] *Torcaso v. Watkins* 367 U.S. 488 (1961).

CHAPTER FIVE

[1] Elliot's *Debates,* IV, 244.
[2] *Ibid.,* 199.
[3] *Ibid.,* I, 334; IV, 244. Note that this statement is identical to the religious amendment proposed by the Virginia ratifying convention. See *infra,* p. 119. (Emphasis added.)

4 Delaware, December 7, 1787; Pennsylvania, December 12, 1787; New Jersey, December 18, 1787; Georgia, January 2, 1788.

5 Jackson Turner Main, *The Anti-Federalists* (Chapel Hill, 1961), p. 255.

6 *Records of the General Association of the Congregational Churches in Connecticut,* p. 126. Cited in Anson Phelps Stokes, *Church and State in the United States* (New York, 1950), I, 606. [This work is hereinafter cited as Stokes.]

7 Another reason is supplied by Stokes: "It is due to the fact that New England Congregationalism was so identified historically with the established Churches in Massachusetts and Connecticut that most of its leaders were not strong advocates of freedom at the time." Stokes, I, 356.

8 *Connecticut Courant* of December 10, 1787. Reprinted in Paul Leicester Ford, ed., *Essays on the Constitution* (Brooklyn, 1892), pp. 163–164. [This work is hereinafter cited as Ford, *Essays.*]

9 Elliot's *Debates,* II, 202.

10 Massachusetts ratified on February 6, 1788.

11 Elliot's *Debates,* II, 44.

12 *Ibid.,* 93.

13 *Massachusetts Gazette* for February 5, 1788. Reprinted in Ford, *Essays,* p. 119.

14 Maryland ratified on April 28, 1788; Pennsylvania on December 12, 1787.

15 Elliot's *Debates,* II, 553.

16 *Ibid.*

17 Pennsylvania ratified the Constitution on December 12, 1787.

18 *Freeman's Journal,* October 24, 1787. Quoted in MacMaster and Stone, *Pennsylvania and the Federal Constitution* (Lancaster, Pa., 1808), p. 589.

19 In full, Article II read: "That all men have a natural and unalienable right to worship Almighty God according to the dictates of their own consciences and understanding: And that no man ought or of right can be compelled to attend any religious worship, or erect or support any place of worship, or maintain any ministry, contrary to, or against, his own free will and consent: Nor can any man, who acknowledges the being of a God, be justly deprived or abridged of any civil right as a citizen, on account of his religious sentiments or peculiar mode of religious worship: And that no authority can or ought to be vested in, or assumed by any power whatever, that shall in any case interfere with, or in any manner control, the right of conscience in the free exercise of religious worship." Thorpe, V, 3082.

20 *The Independent Gazette or Chronicle of Freedom,* November 1, 1787. (Emphasis added.)

21 *Ibid.,* November 28, 1787.

22 "The two Morrises and Jared Ingersoll were Episcopalians, Thomas Mifflin was a Quaker, Thomas Fitzsimmons was a Roman Catholic, Benjamin Franklin, raised as a Congregationalist, was a nominal Episcopalian but thought as a Deist. There were also Moravians, Lutherans, Baptists, a Huguenot Calvinist and a German Reformer, but most were Presbyterians. A Lutheran minister, Frederick Augustus Conrad Muhlenberg, was the president of the convention." William W. Sweet, *Religion in the Development of American Culture, 1765–1840* (New York, 1952), p. 89.

23 Elliot's *Debates,* II, 455.

24 James Wilson was a delegate to the Continental Congress, 1775–1778, 1782–1783, 1785–1787. He also was at the Constitutional Convention and signed the Constitution. An outstanding jurist, his lectures on constitutional law at the College of Philadelphia were accepted as authoritative by the American community.

25 MacMaster and Stone, *Pennsylvania and the Federal Constitution* (Lancaster, Pa., 1808), p. 482. Of the 14 dissenters whose religion is ascertainable, "5 were Presbyterian, 3 were German Lutherans or Reformed, one was a Moravian and one, Abraham Lincoln, was a Congregationalist." William W. Sweet, *Religion in the Development of American Culture, 1765–1840,* pp. 89–90.

²⁶ *The Reasons of Dissent* (Philadelphia, 1787), reprinted in *The American Museum*, II, (v), 536–553.

²⁷ A list of those who signed the "Reasons for Dissent" appears in MacMaster and Stone *op. cit.*, p. 482. Smilie was in the third and sixth Congresses; Hannah in the fifth and sixth; and Findley in the third, fourth, and fifth Congresses.

²⁸ While in newspaper form, it also appeared in Charleston's *City Gazette or the Daily Advertiser*, December 6, 1787, and in Boston's *Independent Chronicle*. It was also reprinted in the Debates of the Massachusetts ratifying convention, at pp. 335–339.

²⁹ Paul L. Ford, ed., *Pamphlets on the Constitution of the United States* (Brooklyn, 1888), p. 137.

³⁰ It should be noted that Anti-Federalist agitation in Pennsylvania continued after the state's ratifying convention and culminated in the Harrisburg Convention on September 3, 1788. There they demanded a new general convention and proferred twelve desired amendments. None of the amendments specifically dealt with religious liberty, but sufficient protection was probably thought to have been provided by their First Amendment's strong states' rights position. See Elliot's *Debates*, II, 542–546; David M. Matteson, ed., *Formation of the Union Under the Constitution* (Washington, 1941), pp. 281–282.

³¹ Elliot's *Debates*, I, 325.

³² Stokes, I, 610.

³³ *New York Daily Gazette*, June 12, 1789. Reprinted in *The American Museum*, V, 303 (Oct., 1789).

³⁴ *New Haven Gazette*, December 4, 1788.

³⁵ *Ibid.*

³⁶ *City Gazette or Daily Advertiser*, May 26, 1788. (Emphasis added.)

³⁷ *Ibid.*

³⁸ *Ibid.*

³⁹ Elliot's *Debates*, III, 330.

⁴⁰ *Ibid.*

⁴¹ *Ibid.*

⁴² *Ibid.*, 469.

⁴³ *Ibid.*, 659.

⁴⁴ Thorpe, VII, 3814, § 16.

⁴⁵ This establishment clause, claims Irving Brant, "furnished a loophole for financial support of all churches." Brant, "Madison on Separation of Church and State," *Wm. & Mary Q., VIII* (Jan., 1951), p. 13.

⁴⁶ Elliot's *Debates*, I, 326. It is interesting to note, however, that the phraseology of New Hampshire's proposal does not appear in that state's constitution of 1784 or 1792. On the contrary, provision was made in Article VI of each constitution for "public worship of the Deity, and of public instruction in morality and religion," and for the support of the ministry. That article concluded with this declaration: "and no subordination of any one sect or denomination to another shall ever be established by law." Thorpe, IV, 2454, 2471–2472.

⁴⁷ The provision read in part: "the legislature shall, from time to time, authorize and require, the several towns, parishes, precincts, and other bodies politic, or religious societies, to make suitable provision, at their own expense, for the institution of the public worship of God, and for the support and maintenance of public Protestant teachers of piety, religion, and morality, in all cases where such provision shall not be made voluntarily. And the people of this commonwealth . . . invest their legislature with authority to enjoin upon all the subjects an attendance upon the instructions of the public teachers, aforesaid, at stated times and seasons, if there be any on whose instructions they can conscientiously and conveniently attend." Article III, *Massachusetts Constitution* (1780) Thorpe, III, 1889–1890.

⁴⁸ Massachusetts *Archives*, CCLXXVII, 3; quoted in Robert J. Taylor, ed., *Massachusetts, Colony to Commonwealth* (Chapel Hill, 1961), pp. 151–152, Document 54.

[49] "XXXVIII. And whereas we are required, by the benevolent principles of rational liberty, not only to expel civil tyranny, but also to guard against that spiritual oppression and intolerance wherewith the bigotry and ambition of weak and wicked priests and princes have scourged mankind, this convention doth further, in the name and by the authority of the good people of this State, ordain, determine, and declare, that the free exercise and enjoyment of religious profession and worship, without discrimination or preference, shall hereafter be allowed, within this State, to all mankind: Provided, That the liberty of conscience, hereby granted, shall not be so construed as to excuse acts of licentiousness, or justify practices inconsistent with the peace or safety of this State.

"XXXIX. And whereas the ministers of the gospel are, by their profession, dedicated to the service of God and the care of souls, and ought not to be diverted from the great duties of their function; therefore, no minister of the gospel, or priest of any denomination whatsoever, shall, at any time hereafter, under any pretence or description whatever, be eligible to, or capable of holding any civil or military office or place within this State." Thorpe, V, 2636–2637.

[50] *New York Journal,* June 14, 1788. Reprinted in Ford, *Essays,* p. 313.

[51] *Ibid.*

[52] *Journal of the Proceedings of the Convention of the State of New York, Held at Poughkeepsie.*

[53] Elliot's *Debates,* I, 328.

[54] *New York Daily Gazette,* June 12, 1789; *The American Museum,* V, 303 (Oct., 1789).

CHAPTER SIX

[1] For example, among the members of the First Congress who had served in their state ratifying conventions were: both senators from Massachusetts and Connecticut, five out of the six representatives from Maryland, and three of South Carolina's five representatives.

[2] *Annals of Congress,* I, 433–434. It can be recalled that the previous year the Virginians demanded an amendment to the United States Constitution to the effect "that no particular religious sect or society ought to be favored or established by law, in preference to others." Jonathan Elliot, *Debates on the Federal Constitution* (Philadelphia, 1907) III, 659. They had every right to anticipate that Madison would seek to advance this sort of provision.

[3] Seth Ames, *Works of Fisher Ames* (Boston, 1854), I, 52–53.

[4] *New York Daily Gazette,* June 12, 1789.

[5] *Ibid.*

[6] *Federal Gazette,* 18 June 1789.

[7] It might also be noted that in the *Gazette of the United States,* there appeared a running debate between "E. C." and "Pacificus" (John Carroll) on May 9th, June 10th, and June 13th, 1789, on the subject of religious toleration. In essence, it was resolved that there should be no preference, no "distinguishing favors" for one sect or denomination. Although this discussion is not exactly on point — the First Amendment — it may be relevant to indicate the feelings of the community; and, inasmuch as the Congress was sitting in that city at that time, the thoughts expressed might very well have been read and absorbed by the men who framed the establishment clause.

[8] *Annals of Congress,* I, 660, 665.

⁹ Ames, *Works*, I, p. 65.

¹⁰ *Annals*, pp. 672–673.

¹¹ Griffith J. McRee, *James Iredell* (New York, 1857), II, 265 (italics in the original).

¹² Statutes 1789, C. VIII, August 7, 1789: *Documents of American History* (Henry Steele Commager ed: New York, 1949), 131.

¹³ *Annals*, p. 729.

¹⁴ *Ibid., New Jersey Journal and Political Intelligence*, August 26, 1789.

¹⁵ *Annals*, p. 729.

¹⁶ *Ibid.*, p. 730.

¹⁷ *Ibid.*

¹⁸ *Ibid.*

¹⁹ This statement was noted by Mr. Justice Reed, dissenting in McCollum: "The phrase 'an establishment of religion' may have been intended by Congress to be aimed only at a state church. When the First Amendment was pending in Congress in substantially its present form, 'Mr. Madison, he apprehended. . . .'" *McCollum v. Bd. of Ed.*, 333 U. S. 203, 244 (1948). Reed went on to "indicate his inclination to accept the argument that the principal promoter of the amendment by no means interpreted it to inhibit Congress from encouraging religion." F. Wm. O'Brien, *Justice Reed and the First Amendment* (Washington, 1958), p. 132.

²⁰ *Annals*, p. 730.

²¹ *Ibid.*, pp. 730–731.

²² *Ibid.*, p. 731.

²³ Anson Phelps Stokes, *Church and State in the United States*, 3 vols. (New York, 1950), I, 548.

²⁴ Livermore's suggestion was modeled after a proposal by his own state's ratifying convention that "Congress shall make no laws touching religion, or infringing the rights of conscience." Elliot's *Debates*, I, 326.

²⁵ *Annals*, p. 731. Typical of the "states' rights" sentiment in Massachusetts during the time referred to by Mr. Gerry, is a proposal by James Winthrop, writing under the name of "Agrippa," in the February 5, 1788, issue of the *Massachusetts Gazette*. He suggested to the Massachusetts ratifying convention fourteen propositions necessary to preserve the rights of the States in a Federal Government. The thirteenth read: "Nothing in this constitution shall deprive a citizen of any state of the benefit of the bill of rights established by the constitution of the state in which he shall reside, and such bill of rights shall be considered as valid in any court of the United States where they shall be pleaded." Reprinted in Paul L. Ford, *Essays on the Constitution* (Brooklyn, 1892), p. 119.

²⁶ *Annals*, p. 731.

²⁷ *Ibid.*

²⁸ *Ibid.*, p. 756.

²⁹ *Ibid.*

³⁰ *Ibid.*

³¹ *Ibid.*

³² *Ibid.*, p. 766.

³³ It is interesting to note that in the *Annals* report of August 20 the amendment is numbered "The Fourth." Yet, the report in the *House Journal* for the next day refers to the same article as the third. *Journal of the House of Representatives* (New York, 1789), p. 107; *Journal of the House of Representatives* (Cales & Seaton, Washington, 1826), p. 85.

³⁴ *Journal of the House* (1789), p. 107; (1826), p. 85.

³⁵ *Annals*, pp. 767–773.

³⁶ See *supra*, Chapter Five, for the South Carolina proposal.

³⁷ *Annals*, p. 778.

³⁸ *Senate Journal for the First Session of the First Congress of the United States* (New York, 1789), p. 104; *Journal of the First Session of the Senate* (Gales & Seaton, Washington, 1820), p. 63.

[39] *Journal of William Maclay* for August 25, 1789, ed. by Edgar S. Maclay (New York, 1890), p. 134.

[40] *Senate Journal* (1789), p. 116; (1820), p. 70.

[41] *Ibid.*

[42] *Ibid.*, (1789), p. 117; (1820), p. 70.

[43] *Ibid.*

[44] *Ibid.*

[45] "Mr. Ellsworth's draft amending Articles to the Constitution, dated September 9, 1789" from the records of the United States Senate, in the National Archives. See also *Senate Journal* (1789), p. 129; (1820), p. 77.

[46] *Senate Journals, op. cit.*

[47] *Annals*, pp. 889, 904.

[48] There is some confusion as to whether the House informed the Senate or whether the Senate so informed the House. The *Annals* report that the Senate sent a message to the House stating that the Senate would recede from their "third amendment to the Constitution of the United States; and do insist on the other amendments to the said articles disagreed to by the House; and that they have agreed to a conference on this subject." *Annals*, p. 904. It was apparently after that that the House resumed consideration of the amendments, noted agreement and disagreement and finally appointed managers of the conference. The *House Journal*, however, reverses the order. It reports that the House first considered the amendments, noted the agreement and disagreement and then resolved that a conference be desired with the Senate. *Journal of the House* (1789), p. 146; (1826), p. 116. The notation of the message from the Senate in which it agreed to recede from the third amendment appears later that day. *Journal of the House* (1789), p. 147; (1826), p. 117. The House had indicated that it disagreed to the 1st, 3rd, 5th, 6th, 7th, 9th, 10th, 11th, 14th, 15th, 17th, 20th, 21st, 22d, 23d, and 24th amendments as proposed by the Senate. *Senate Journal* (1789), p. 141; (1820), pp. 83–84.

[49] *Annals*, p. 905; *Senate* and *House Journals, op. cit.*, n. 48.

[50] On that day the House resolved to "recede from their disagreements to all the amendments (mentioned in note 48); provided that the two articles, which, by the amendments of the Senate, are now proposed to be inserted as the third and eighth articles, shall be amended. . . ." *Annals*, p. 913. The two articles were the present First and Sixth Amendments. See also *Journal of the House* (1826), pp. 121–122. Senator Ellsworth reported to the Senate on that same day. He referred to the change in the third Article as the "fifth amendment" and the eighth Article change as "the fourteenth amendment." *Senate Journal* (1820). Therefore, the "third amendment" discussion noted in footnote 48 did not deal with the religion clauses in the third Article.

[51] Stokes, *op. cit.*, I, 548.

[52] *Annals*, p. 88. *Senate Journal* (1789), pp. 150–151; (1820), p. 88.

[53] *Annals*, p. 914.

[54] *Ibid.*

[55] *Ibid.*, p. 915.

[56] *Ibid.*

[57] *Ibid.; Journal of the House* (1789), p. 155; 1826, p. 123.

[58] *Annals*, p. 90; *Senate Journal* (1789), p. 154; (1820), p. 90.

[59] Among those present who believed in preventing a national religion were: William Paca, later governor of the State; Samuel Chase, later justice of the U. S. Supreme Court; John F. Mercer; Jeremiah T. Chase; John Love; Charles Ridgely; Edward Cockey; Nathan Cromwell; Charles Ridgely of Wm., Luther Martin; Benjamin Harrison; and William Pinckney. Elliot's *Debates*, II, 553.

[60] *Ibid.*

[61] Elliot's *Debates*, I, 328.

[62] *Ibid.*, 659.

[63] Article XIX; Thorpe, V, 2597 (emphasis added).

64 *Constitution of North Carolina* (1776); Article XXXIV; Thorpe V, 2793 (emphasis added).

65 Article 29; Thorpe, X, 567 (emphasis added).

66 *Constitution of New York* (1777); Article XXXV; Thorpe V, 2635–2636 (emphasis added).

67 Part First, Article III, *Massachusetts Constitution* (1780); Thorpe, III, 1890.

68 *Constitution of Pennsylvania* (1790); Article IX, § 3; Thorpe, V, 3100 (emphasis added).

69 Patrick Allison, *Candid Animadversions on a Petition Presented to the General Assembly of Maryland by the Reverend William Smith and Reverend Thomas Gates* (Baltimore, 1783), pp. 22, 29. Rare Manuscript Room, New York Public Library. Emphasis added.

70 *Debates and Proceedings in the Massachusetts Convention held in the Year 1788* (Boston, 1856), p. 251; Elliot, *op. cit.*, II, 148. Emphasis added.

71 Elliot's *Debates*, II, 148–149; February 8, 1788. Emphasis added.

72 Quoted in Robert J. Taylor, *Massachusetts, Colony to Commonwealth* (Chapel Hill, 1961), p. 118. Emphasis added.

73 The Quebec Act is treated *in extenso* in Chapter One, *supra*.

74 "Remarks on the Quebec Bill," in *The Works of Alexander Hamilton,* John C. Hamilton ed., 2 vols. (New York, 1850–1851), II, 131. Emphasis added.

75 *Annals,* p. 730.

76 Thorpe, VI, 3212–3213.

77 Authority for these facts is found in Chapters Three and Nine.

78 *Annals,* p. 730.

79 See also *Bradfield v. Roberts,* 175 U. S. 291, 20 S. Ct. 121 (1899), where the Supreme Court dismissed by strong implication the argument that congressional aid to a District of Columbia hospital under the auspices of a religious order of the Roman Catholic Church violated the ban on Congress making a law respecting a religious establishment. The Court stated that that phrase was not synonymous with that used in the Constitution: a law respecting an establishment of religion.

80 *Annals,* p. 915.

81 *Journal of the Senate* (1789), pp. 116–117; (1820), p. 70.

82 For a discussion of this possibility, see Snee, "Religious Disestablishment and the Fourteenth Amendment," *1954 Wash. Univ. L. Q.* 391 (1954); see also Sutherland, "Establishment According to Engel," 76 *Harv. L. Rev.* 25, 28, 41 (1962).

83 See *supra,* n. 45.

84 *Annals,* p. 755.

85 *Ibid.*

86 *Ibid.*

87 *Ibid.,* p. 730

88 *Ibid.*

89 The federal judiciary had not yet been organized; the Judiciary Act was considered by Congress after it had completed its work on the amendments. This perhaps explains Huntington's misguided notion of federal court jurisdiction.

90 *Annals,* p. 730.

91 *Ibid.*

CHAPTER SEVEN

[1] *American State Papers Bearing on Sunday Legislation,* William Addison Blakely, ed. (Washington, D. C., 1911), p. 166.

[2] Elliot's *Debates,* III, 659.

[3] *Journal of the House of Delegates of Virginia for 1789* (Virginia State Library, Richmond), p. 90.

[4] *Journal of the Senate of Virginia for 1789* (Virginia State Library, Richmond), p. 51.

[5] *Journal of the House of Delegates,* p. 79.

[6] *Ibid.,* p. 97.

[7] *History of the Formation of the Union Under the Constitution* (David M. Matteson, ed., Washington, D. C., 1941), p. 324 [hereinafter cited as Matteson].

[8] *Journal of the Senate,* pp. 62–64.

[9] *Ibid.,* p. 51. (Emphasis added.)

[10] *Ibid.,* p. 62.

[11] *Minutes of the Council of Delaware 1776–1792* (Dover, 1928), p. 1188.

[12] Hening's *Statutes,* 454.

[13] Article 29. Thorpe, I, 567.

[14] Article I; Section 1; Thorpe, I, 568.

[15] The proposed amendments had been sent by the governor to the House on November 9, 1789. Three days later the committee to which they had been referred reported favorably, and on the twenty-fifth the House approved what is now the First Amendment. Five days later the Senate concurred. Matteson, *op. cit.,* pp. 317–318.

[16] Thorpe, III, 1702, extending provisions of Article XXXV; *ibid.,* 1690.

[17] *Ibid.,* 1695, reversing provisions of Article XXXIII; *ibid.,* 1689.

[18] Based on an extensive search of newspapers and legislative records from *August, 1789,* through *December, 1789,* available at the Library of Congress.

[19] Thorpe, V, 2598 and 2637.

[20] *Ibid.,* 2599; Chapter One, *supra.*

[21] *Ibid.*

[22] Chapter Five, *supra.*

[23] Matteson, *op. cit.,* pp. 318–319.

[24] Thorpe, V, 3092. November 24, 1789–February 26, 1790. Formally proclaimed September 2, 1790.

[25] Declaration of Rights, Article II; Thorpe, V, 3082.

[26] Article IX, Section 3; *Ibid.,* V, 3100.

[27] *Journal of the Senate of New York, 1775–1795.* There is nothing to indicate that the New York Legislature in ratifying the First Amendment believed that it was accepting anything directly opposed to its own views on religious liberty. The New York constitution of 1777 had declared in favor of liberty of conscience that was in keeping with the safety of the state. Thorpe, V, 2637. This policy excluded Roman Catholics from political rights, but no other denomination had been laid under a disability. Chapter One, *supra.* Consistent with the general American attitude of the times, there are indications of a softening even in New York of the policy of excluding sects because of their imagined dangers to the public safety. Shortly after the Bill of Rights had been adopted a Mr. Brown of New York wrote in the *Federal Gazette:*

"I am an anxious friend of Religious liberty, and love to see all denominations of christians dwell together in unity. . . . I find in the legislature, executive, and Judical departments of the Federal government and the state governments, there are several persons of each of the following societies — German Lutherans, the German Reformed Church, Protestant Episcopalians, being the same as the Church of England, English, Scotch, and Irish Presbyterians, Independent's or Congregationalists,

Quakers, Baptists, and Roman Catholics, seceders from the Scotch Church, Duty Presbyterians or the Church of the Netherlands, French Huguenots, and Moravians, and I am sure there are others which I do not remember . . ." (*Federal Gazette,* March 20, 1790).

New York's lately awakened spirit of tolerance took some time to manifest itself in definite political reform. It is known, for example, that the first Catholic did not sit in the New York Legislature for nearly sixteen years. Chapter Four, *supra.* Moreover, it was not until 1821 that New York undertook to revise her constitution to bring it in line with the prevailing concept of freedom. In the constitution of that year the "religious profession and worship without discrimination or preference shall be forever allowed in this State to all mankind" (Thorpe, VI, 2648).

[28] Matteson, *op. cit.,* p. 318.

[29] *Ibid.,* p. 327.

[30] Thomas H. Le Duc, *Connecticut and The First Ten Amendments,* Sen. Doc. 96, 75th Congress (Washington, D. C., 1937), p. 2.

[31] Matteson, *op. cit.,* p. 327.

[32] *Ibid.;* Le Duc, *op. cit.,* p. 31.

[33] Le Duc, *op. cit.,* p. 1.

[34] *Ibid.*

[35] *Connecticut Courant,* October 12, 1789. Le Duc declared that he scanned papers and found no mention of the First Amendment, *op. cit.,* p. 4, n. 9.

[36] April 12, 1789. Hunt, V, 346.

[37] Statement by Oliver Wolcott; Elliott's *Debates,* II, 202. See Le Duc, *op. cit.,* p. 6.

[38] Chapter Five, *Supra.*

[39] *House Journal,* X, 153; Jacob C. Meyer, *Church and State in Massachusetts from 1740 to 1783* (Cleveland 1930), pp. 9–10.

[40] *House Journal,* X, 153.

[41] Matteson, *op. cit.,* p. 395.

[42] *Senate Journal,* pp. 10, 192; *House Journal,* pp. 10, 218.

[43] See Meyer, *op. cit.,* pp. 14–15.

[44] *Report of the Committee of the General Court on Further Amendments.* Massachusetts Archives, Senate Miscellaneous Documents No. 1145 of 1790. Cited, also, by Meyers, *op. cit.,* pp. 25–29. esp. @ 25; Matteson, *op. cit.,* p. 326.

[45] Matteson, *op. cit.,* p. 327; *Massachusetts Centinel,* February 6, 1790.

[46] Letter from Christopher Gore to Thomas Jefferson, August 18, 1791, pp. 8–9, cited in Denys P. Myers, *Massachusetts and the First Ten Amendments to the Constitution,* 74th Congress, 2nd Session, Senate Doc. 81, Washington, D. C.

[47] Matteson, *op. cit.,* p. 328. The only item bearing on religious freedom appearing in the newspapers during the constitutional period is the following article from the *August Chronicle and Gazette:* June 13, 1789:

"Charleston, March 17. A great number of Protestant settlers in the province of New Orleans have been recently obliged to quit that place. . . . Governor Mayo received a preemptory mandate from his court ordering all Protestants to leave. . . The rigour of the mandate was a little softened, by allowing all Protestant settlers to remain there who were there in 1782. A gentleman, who was unfortunately one of those who were prescribed by this, of an enlarged train of thinking, being unwilling to leave a harvest of shining dollars, waited upon the Governor with an offer, that he was willing to qualify himself as a member of the Roman Catholic church, and a subject of the King of Spain. His Excellency politely complimented him on the fervancy of his allegiance, and observed, that it was an easy business, being nothing more to make an affidavit — that his parents were Catholics, and subjects of Spain — that he was educated in the same principles and allegience, which had uniformly supported, and meant to continue such during his life. This pill being bitter to swallow, and hard to digest, was declined, and the applicant left New Orleans, not without casting many a *longing, lingering* look behind."

[48] *Ibid.*

49 Article LVI (1777); Thorpe, II, 784; Article IV, Section S (1789), *Ibid.*, 789.

50 Article IV, Section 10; *Ibid.*, 801.

51 *Journal of the House of Representatives,* 1790 (South Carolina Archives, Columbia), p. 13.

52 *Ibid.*, p. 15.

53 *Ibid.*, p. 18.

54 *Ibid.*, pp. 75–78.

55 *Journal of the Senate,* 1790 (South Carolina Archives, Columbia), p. 13.

56 *Ibid.*, p. 42.

57 Article XXXVIII; Thorpe, VI, 3255.

58 *City Gazette or Daily Adverister,* May 26, 1788. See Chapter Six, *supra.*

59 Article VIII, Section 1; Thorpe, VI, 3264.

60 H. M. Bishop, "Why Rhode Island Opposed the Federal Constitution," *Rhode Island Hist.,* VIII (1949), pp. 36, 38, 39.

61 Frank Greene Bates, *Rhode Island and the Formation of the Union* (New York, 1898), pp. 165–176.

62 Pfeffer, *Church and State and Freedom* (Boston, 1953), p. 112; R. Freeman Butts, *The American Tradition in Religion and Education* (Boston, 1950), p. 72.

63 Robert C. Cotner ed., *Theodore Foster's Minutes of the Convention . . . at South Kingston, Rhode Island, in March, 1790,* Appendix 93–98 (Providence, 1929); Daniel Updike, *Journal of the Convention,* in William R. Staples, *Rhode Island in the Continental Congress* (Providence, 1870), pp. 650–655, 659–674.

64 Updike's version is "We have even refused the accepting chaplain." *Quaere:* Could this passage be read: "Whether *or not* we would appoint a chaplain"?

65 Matteson, *op. cit.,* p. 319.

66 Section 16; Thorpe, VII, 3814.

67 Charles Carroll, *Rhode Island, Three Centuries of Democracy,* 2 vols. (New York, 1932), I, 470 (text of entire act is set out).

68 *Ibid.*

69 *Ibid.*

70 N. 62, *supra.*

71 Stokes, *op. cit.,* I, 524.

72 Louise Irby Trenholme, *Ratification of the Federal Constitution in North Carolina* (New York, 1932), p. 243.

73 Elliot's *Debates,* IV.

74 *Ibid.*, V. 200.

75 *Ibid.*

76 *Ibid.*, V, 244. See, Article XXIV of the Constitution of 1776: "No establishment of any one religious church in preference to any other," and statements of various members regarding equality. *Ibid.*, 193, 194, 199, 208; also Chapter Four, *supra.*

77 Davie wrote to James Madison, June 10, 1789, to the effect that the "farrago" of amendments borrowed from Virginia did not represent the wishes of the people and were proposed in the heat of the convention without consideration. Department of State, Bureau of Rolls and Library, *Documentary History of the Constitution, 1786–1870* (Washington, 1894–1905), V, 175, 177, 181.

78 Only the bare outlines of procedure have been preserved. *State Records of North Carolina,* XXII, pp. 41–42. See Hugh T. Leflar and Albert R. Newsome, *History of North Carolina* (Chapel Hill, 1951), p. 612. Trenholme, *op. cit.,* pp. 237–240.

79 Trenholme, *op. cit.,* pp. 229, 243.

80 *Ibid.*, pp. 140, 152–156, 162, esp. 201, 204–213, 221, 225, 242.

81 Trenholme endorses the validity of this method. *Ibid.*, pp. 237–240.

82 *Fayettville Gazette,* September 14, 21; October 12, 1789.

83 V, 303 (October, 1789).

84 *Ibid.*

[85] Statements made in later North Carolina constitutional conventions tend only to confirm that state's original position. For example, in the convention of 1835, the question of religion arose when it was proposed to remove the requirements for office of a profession of the Protestant religion. Speaking in behalf of the change, Weldon Edwards agreed with with James Iredell, Samuel Johnson, and Samuel Spencer: *"Legal* religion and political liberty are incompatible.... To blend Religion and Politics would have the effect to open the door wide to a union of Church and State.... The only true way to keep Religion and Politics apart ... [is] to confer no particular privileges on any one sect ... to extend equal protection to all." *Proceedings and Debates of Convention of North Carolina Called to Amend the Constitution of the State, Which Assembled at Raleigh, June 4, 1835* (Raleigh, 1836), pp. 215–217 (italics in original).

CHAPTER EIGHT

[1] See Introduction, *supra.*

[2] *American State Papers Bearing on Sunday Legislation,* William Addison Blakely, ed. (Washington, D. C., 1911), p. 166.

[3] Joseph Story, *Commentaries on the Constitution of the United States* (Boston, 1833), III, § 1865.

[4] *Ibid.,* § 1868.

[5] *Ibid.,* § 1871.

[6] Article 29, Thorpe, I, 567.

[7] Article I, § 1; Thorpe, I, 568.

[8] *Ibid.*

[9] Article XXXVIII; Thorpe, V, 2637.

[10] Article XXXIV; Thorpe, V, 2793.

[11] Section 16; Thorpe, VII, 3814.

[12] Article VIII, § 1; Thorpe, VI, 3264.

[13] Article IX, § 3; Thorpe, V, 3100.

[14] Part the First, Article III; Thorpe, III, 1889. (Emphasis added.)

[15] Article VI; Thorpe, IV, 2454, Note that "teachers" probably meant "ministers" or preachers. See Chapters Three, Seven, esp. n. 69.

[16] Article VI; Thorpe, IV, 2471.

[17] *Writings of James Madison,* Hunt, ed.; 9 vols. (New York, 1900–1910), IX, 486.

[18] Article XXXIII; Thorpe, III, 1688.

[19] Article IV, § 10; Thorpe, II, 801.

[20] Article IV, § 13; Thorpe, II, 801.

[21] David S. Hill and William A. Fisher, *Federal Relation to Education* (Washington, 1931), Part II, pp. 23–24; see also, Edward H. Reisner, *Nationalism and Education Since 1789* (New York, 1922), pp. 342–343.

[22] 2 Statutes at Large 226 (1803).

[23] 2 Statutes at Large 279 (1804).

[24] 2 Statutes at Large 621 (1811).

[25] 3 Statutes at Large 430 (1818).

[26] 3 Statutes at Large 467 (1818).

[27] 4 Statutes at Large 201 (1827).

[28] *E.g.,* Alabama, 3 Statutes at Large 491 (1819); Mississippi, 3 Statutes at Large 485 (1819); Louisiana, 4 Statutes at Large 244 (1827); Arkansas, 5 Statutes at Large 58 (1836).

[29] 5 Statutes at Large 788 (1845) (Florida).

³⁰ 4 Statutes at Large 603–604 (July 14, 1832).

³¹ 6 Statutes at Large 538 (March 2, 1833).

³² See I Statutes at Large 257.

³³ I Statutes at Large 257 (April 21, 1792).

³⁴ 4 Statutes at Large 618–619 (emphasis added).

³⁵ Madison said on February 28, 1811, that he vetoed the bill "Because the bill in reserving a certain parcel of land of the United States for the use of said Baptist Church comprises a principle and precedent for the appropriation of funds of the United States for the use and support of religious societies, contrary to the article of the Constitution which declares that 'Congress shall make no law respecting a religious establishment.' " *Writings of James Madison,* Hunt, ed. (New York, 1900–1910), VIII, 133.

³⁶ Sherman M. Smith, *The Relation of the State to Religious Education in Massachusetts* (Syracuse, 1926), 114.

³⁷ *Laws of New York State* (New York, 1790), Vol. III, c. XXXVIII.

³⁸ Charles J. Mahoney, *The Relation of the State to Religious Education in Early New York, 1633–1825* (Washington, 1941), 92; see, Reisner, *op. cit., pp.* 362–364, and discussion in Chapter Three, *supra.*

³⁹ *History of Rhode Island,* Edward Field, ed., 3 vols. (Boston, 1902), II, 260, 326; see Rhode Island "Act for Establishing Religious Liberty," Chapter Seven, n. 69, *supra.*

⁴⁰ Pennsylvania, *Statutes at Large* (1791–1793) (Harrisburg, 1909), c. MDLVII, pp. 71–73.

⁴¹ Joseph Brevard, *An Alphabetical Digest of the Public Statue Law of South Carolina* (Charleston, 1814), III, Title 7, §§ 49–41, p. 35.

⁴² *South Carolina, Statutes,* V, 357 (December 21, 1799); VI, 246 (December 18, 1824).

⁴³ *Georgia Gazette,* September 30, 1790.

⁴⁴ *Journal of the House of Delegates of Virginia,* November 24, 1791.

⁴⁵ *Ibid.,* December 6, 1791.

⁴⁶ *Ibid.,* October 10, 1792.

⁴⁷ H. J. Eckenrode, *Separation of Church and State in Virginia* (Richmond, 1910), 147–152.

⁴⁸ See *Terret v. Taylor,* 13 U.S. (9 Cranch) 43, 49 (1815) (emphasis added).

⁴⁹ *Ibid.,* (Emphasis added).

⁵⁰ Charles Kappler, *Indian Affair — Law and Treaties,* Vol. 2, p. 67; see William W. Sweet, *Religion in the Development of American Culture 1765–1840* (New York, 1952) 242; see also Costanzo, "Federal Aid to Education and Religious Liberty," 36 *U. Det. L.J.* 1, 15 (1958).

⁵¹ R. Pierce Beaver, "Church, State and the Indians," *Journal of Church and State,* IV (1962), 23–24.

⁵² Martha L. Edwards, "A Problem of Church and State in the 1870's," *Mississippi Valley Historical Review,* XI (June: 1924), 39.

⁵³ Sweet, *op. cit.,* p. 242; Beaver, *op. cit.,* pp. 23–24; and Edwards, *op. cit.,* p. 39.

⁵⁴ Reisner, *op. cit.,* p. 362.

⁵⁵ *Ibid.,* p. 364.

⁵⁶ Joseph F. Thorning, *Religious Liberty in Transition* (New York, 1931), 49, 50, 81; Jacob C. Meyer, *Church and State in Massachusetts From 1740–1833* (Cleveland, 1930), 133–159 *passim.*

⁵⁷ Quoted by Thorning, *op. cit.,* p. 53.

⁵⁸ *Massachusetts Historical Society Collections* (First Series), V, 48–49.

⁵⁹ Meyer, *op. cit.,* p. 148.

⁶⁰ *Ibid.,* n. 39.

⁶¹ *Ibid.,* p. 154.

⁶² *Barnes v. First Parish,* 6 Mass. 400 (1810); discussed in Meyer, *op. cit.,* p. 154; and Thorning, *op. cit.,* p. 60.

⁶³ Thorning, *op. cit.,* p. 61.

[64] Evarts B. Greene, *Religion and the State: The Making and Testing of an American Tradition* (New York, 1941), 91.

[65] Thorning, *op. cit.,* p. 52, n. 87.

[66] *Ibid.,* p. 52.

[67] Sanford H. Cobb, *The Rise of Religious Liberty in America* (New York, 1902), 500.

[68] Charles B. Kinney, *Church and State: The Struggle for Separation in New Hampshire, 1630–1900* (New York, 1955), 128.

[69] Thorning, *op. cit.,* p. 165.

[70] *Laws of New Hampshire,* VI, 105; Kinney, op. cit., p. 95.

[71] Issac Hill, editorial in *New Hampshire Patriot,* March 5, 1816; Kinney, *op. cit.,* p. 99.

[72] Kinney, *op. cit.,* pp. 98–99.

[73] Thorning, *op. cit.,* pp. 166–172.

[74] Edward F. Humphrey, *Nationalism and Religion in America* (Boston, 1924), p. 498.

[75] M. Louise Greene, *The Development of Religious Liberty in American* (Boston, 1905), 380–381.

[76] M. Greene, *op, cit.,* pp. 385–387.

[77] *Connecticut State Records,* VIII, 100.

[78] *Ibid.,* 237–239.

[79] *Connecticut Archives, Ecclesiastical Affairs* (Second Series), I, 2–3.

[80] Zephaniah Swift, *System of the Laws of the State of Connecticut* (Wyndham, Conn., 1795), I, 144.

[81] M. Greene, *op. cit.,* p. 388.

[82] John Leland, *The Rights of Conscience Inalienable . . . Or the High Flying Churchman* (New London, Conn., 1902), 10, 17; see also Abraham Bishop, *Proofs of a Conspiracy Against Christianity and the Government of the United States* (Hartford, 1802), quoted by M. Greene, *op. cit.,* p. 425.

[83] Single-page broadside, in Rare Manuscript Room, New York Public Library.

[84] Field, *op. cit.,* II, 260–326.

[85] Thomas W. Bicknell, *The History of Rhode Island and Providence Plantations,* 2 vols. (New York, 1920), II, 590.

[86] Field, *op. cit.,* II, 182.

[87] *Ibid.,* 185.

[88] *Laws of the State of New York Passed at 18th Session of Legislature* (New York, 1795), c. 75, 50–51 (April 9, 1795).

[89] *Laws of New York* (1801), c. 189.

[90] Edward M. Connors, *Church-State Relationships in Education in the State of New York* (Washington, 1951), p. xv.

[91] Nelson R. Burr, *Education in New Jersey* (Princeton, 1947), 137.

[92] Frank Welbon, *History of Christian Education in Delaware* (unpublished M.A. thesis, University of Delaware Library, 1937), p. 101.

[93] *Laws of Delaware* (1821 , c. LXV (February 3, 1821).

[94] John Tracy Ellis, "Church and State: An American Tradition," *Harpers Magazine,* CCVII, p. 64 (Nov., 1953).

[95] Leo J. McCormick, *Church-State Relationships in Education in Maryland* (Washington, 1942), pp. 48, 65.

[96] *Journal of the House,* December 27, 1791.

[97] Strickland, *op. cit.,* pp. 164, 176–177.

[98] *Ibid.,* pp. 168–174.

[99] *Ibid.,* p. 171.

[100] *Georgia Constitution* (1798), Article 4, Sec. 13; Thorpe, II, 800.

[101] Strickland, *op. cit.,* p. 177.

[102] North Carolina Constitution (1776), Article XXXIV; Thorpe, V, 2793.

[103] Article XLI; Thorpe, V, 2794.

[104] L. J. Sherrill, *Presbyterian Parochial Schools* (New Haven, 1932), p. 2; L. L.

Goebel, *Church-State Relationships in Education in North Carolina Since 1776* (Durham, 1938), pp. 12–14, 172–176.

105 The Baptist State Convention in 1842, in supporting a system of public school education, urged that "our free schools should receive the special attention of the ministering bretheren." *Ibid.,* p. 179. The first superintendent of education was the prominent Presbyterian, C. H. Wiley, who ran the new schools after the parochial pattern. *Ibid.,* pp. 180–185; Sherrill, *op. cit.,* p. 2.

106 Goebel, *op. cit.,* pp. 15–17, 22.

107 *Ibid.,* pp. 32, n. 125; 176, n. 21; 186.

108 M. C. S. Noble, Jr., *A History of the Public School in North Carolina* (Chapel Hill, 1939), p. 247. Attempts to provide financial aid for elementary and secondary education failed because of a hatred of taxation, sparsely settled areas, a lack of communications, the pressures of slavery, and the belief that public aid smacked of charity. C. L. Coon, *The Beginnings of Public Education in North Carolina: A Documentary History, 1790–1840* (Raleigh, 1908), I, xxi.

109 *Acts of General Assembly,* 1791, c. LXIX: 1796, c. LXXVIII: Sadie Bell, *The Church, the State and Education in Virginia* (Philadelphia, 1930), 157.

110 Frank Welbon, *op. cit.,* p. 101.

111 *Ibid.,* p. 116.

112 *E.g.,* Acts of June 10, 1790 (for Presbyterian Churches at Princeton and Newton); June 11, 1790 (for Protestant Episcopal Church at Perth Amboy); November 17, 1791 (for Protestant Episcopal Church in New Brunswick); and May 22, 1793 (for Presbyterian Church in Bridgetown).

113 *Acts of the Assembly of the State of New Jersey* (New Brunswick, 1790), c. CCCIX, June 12, 1790.

114 *Pennsylvania Statutes at Large, 1798–1801* (Harrisburg, 1911), Vol. XVI, c. MCMLXXVI, 47–49.

115 *Ibid.,* c. MCMLXXVII.

116 *Ibid.,* c. MMXIX.

117 Cited in Sister Mary Paul Mason, *Church-State Relationships in Education in Connecticut, 1633–1953* (Washington, 1953), p. 89.

118 *South Carolina Statutes,* V, 601 (December 19, 1809); VI, 246 (December 16, 1824).

119 Sherman M. Smith, *The Relation of the State to Religious Education in Massachusetts* (Syracuse, 1926), 218; Carl Zollman, *American Civil Church Law* (St. Paul, 1917), 237–285.

120 *Connecticut Revised Statutes,* Title 56, § 3.

121 *Laws of New York,* c. 67, May 5, 1786.

122 *South Carolina Statutes at Large* (Columbia, 1840), V, 626, 652, 680, 703 (1812).

123 *Ibid.,* 703 (December 18, 1813).

124 *An Act for Regulating the Assessing and Collecting of Taxes,* § 27, *Public Laws of the State of Rhode Island and Providence Plantations* (Providence, 1798), pp. 407–419.

125 Strickland, *op. cit.,* p. 173.

126 Acts of June 3, 1790; November 2, 1791; May 28, 1793.

127 Article VIII, Section 1; Thorpe, VI, 3264; *South Carolina Statutes at Large,* VIII, 161 (February 19, 1791) (Roman Catholic Church of Charleston); VIII, 456 (December 29, 1837) (Roman Catholic Church of Columbia); *Acts of Assembly 1791,* 1 Faust 139 (Beth Eloihim Jewish Congregation).

128 Mason, *op. cit.,* pp. 32–33.

129 *Massachusetts Historical Society Collections* (First Series), V, 48–49; *Barnes v. First Parish* (1810), 6 Mass. 400; Meyer, *op. cit.,* p. 154; Thorning, *op. cit.,* p. 60.

130 Issac Hill, *New Hampshire Patriot* (editorial), March 5, 1816.

131 *Writings of James Madison,* Hunt, ed. (New York 1900–1910), VIII, pp. 132–133.

132 *Annals of Congress,* XXII, 984; *National Intelligencer,* February 23, 1811.

133 *Baltimore Federal Republican and Commercial Gazette,* February 26, 1811.

134 *Gallego's Executors v. Attorney General,* 30 Va. (3 Leigh.) 450 (1832).

135 See note 136, *infra.*

136 *American State Papers on Freedom in Education,* Blakely, ed. (Washington, 1943), 168–170; *William and Mary Quarterly,* 3rd Ser., III, October, 1946, pp. 534–536; 37 *N.Y.U.L. Rev.,* 995 (1962).

137 This idea has also been discussed by Professor Wilbur Katz, "Freedom of Religion and State Neutrality," 20 *U. Chi. L. Rev.* 426, 431 (1953). A more elaborate treatment can be found in the student comment: "Black Muslims in Prison: Of Muslim Rites and Constitutional Rights," 62 *Colum. L. Rev.* 1488 (1962).

138 *Annals of Congress,* I, 18, 19.

139 *Virginia Herald and Fredericksburg Advertiser,* Fredericksburg, Va., December 24, 1789.

140 *U. S. Stats.,* I, 70.

141 *New Jersey Journal & Political Intelligencer,* October 28, 1789, November 4, 1789.

142 *Annals of Congress,* I, 932.

143 *Ibid.,* 1043.

144 *U. S. Stats.,* I, 223.

145 *Ibid.,* 241.

146 *Ibid.,* 350.

147 *Journal of the New York Senate, 1777–1795,* January 18, 1790.

148 *Journal of the House of Delegates,* October 1, 1792.

149 *Annals of Congress,* I, 914–915.

150 *Ibid.,* II, 1519.

151 William Jay, *Life of John Jay* (New York, 1833), I, 385–386.

152 *New Jersey State Gazette,* IV, . . . No. 12, November 24, 1795.

153 *Connecticut State Records,* VII, 313.

154 Richard J. Purcell, *Connecticut in Transition, 1775–1818* (Washington, 1918), 55 ff.

155 Saul K. Padover, *The Complete Jefferson* (New York, 1943), 518–519 (italics added). For a complete discussion of the meaning of the "wall of separation," see, generally, Robert M. Healey, *Jefferson on Religion in Public Education* (New Haven, 1962), pp. 128–140.

156 *American State Papers on Freedom in Religion,* Blakely, ed. (Washington, 1943), 168–170.

157 *Annals of Congress,* XXVII, 2673–2674.

158 Lynford A. Lardner, "How Far Does the Constitution Separate Church and State?" *American Political Science Review,* XLV (1951), 115.

159 *Revised Laws of New Jersey* (1800), cc. XIX, XX.

160 *Pennsylvania Statutes at Large 1682–1801,* XV, 111.

161 *Updegraph v. Commonwealth,* 11, Sergeant and Rawle, 393 (Pa., 1824).

162 *Specht v. Commonwealth,* 8 Barr, 312, 322 (Pa. St. 1848).

163 *General Statutes of Connecticut, 1642–1821,* § 1323; *Revision of 1888,* § 1535.

164 Zephaniah Swift, *System of the Laws of the State of Connecticut* (Hartford, 1795), II, 320–321.

165 Edward L. Israel, "Maryland's Laws Governing Religion" (unpublished paper in Enoch Pratt Library, Baltimore, undated), p. 2.

166 November 8, 1800, quoted in Koch, *op. cit.,* pp. 85–86.

167 *People v. Ruggles,* 8 Johnson, 290, 294 (N. Y., 1811).

168 *Ibid.,* 295.

169 *Ibid.,* 296.

170 *Ibid.,* 269–297.

171 *Pennsylvania Statutes at Large 1682–1801* (Harrisburg, 1911), XV, 110.

172 *Laws of New Jersey,* revised (New Brunswick, 1800) (Act of March 16, 1798).

173 *Pennsylvania Statutes at Large, 1682–1801* (Harrisburg, 1911), XVI, 106–107.

174 Field, *op. cit.,* I, 307.

175 Strickland, *op. cit.,* p. 174.
176 Meyer, *op. cit.,* p. 138.
177 *Laws of New Jersey,* revised (New Brunswick, 1800) (Act of March 16, 1798).
178 *Muzzy v. Wilkins,* 1 Smith 1, 10 (N. H., 1803).
179 Writings as "Vindex" on November 5, 1792, pamphlet in Rare Manuscript Room, New York Public Library.
180 Single-page broadside in Rare Manuscript Room, New York Public Library.
181 Evarts Greene, *op. cit.,* p. 91.
182 *Journals of Congress* (1823 ed.), IV, 753; readopted by the First Congress of the United States. *Statutes of 1789,* c. 8 (August 7, 1789).
183 Kinney, *op. cit.,* pp. 152–153.
184 *Ibid.*
185 Strickland, *op. cit.,* p. 176.
186 Matteson, *op. cit.,* pp. 569–570.

CHAPTER NINE

1 Paul L. Ford, *Essays on the Constitution of the United States* (Brooklyn, 1892), 168–171.
2 *Ibid.*
3 *Ibid.,* pp. 195, 208.
4 Quoted in Allan Nevins, *The American States During and After the Revolution, 1775–1789* (New York, 1924), p. 430.
5 Moss Ives, *The Ark and the Dove* (New York, 1936), 310.
6 *Ibid.,* 399.
7 *Ibid.*
8 *Ibid.,* 381.
9 *Records of the Convention of Maryland* (Annapolis, 1776), entry of November 2, 1776; Sister Grace Marie Carey, S.S.N.D., "Charles Carroll, The Barrister" (unpublished M.A. thesis, Catholic University of America, Washington, 1953), pp. 54–55.
10 Albert W. Werline, *Problems of Church and State in Maryland* (South Lancaster, Mass., 1948), 158.
11 Kate Mason Rowland, *The Life of Charles Carroll of Carrollton* (New York, 1898), II, 118.
12 *Ibid.,* 118–119.
13 Mary V. Geiger, *Daniel Carroll, Framer of the Constitution* (Washington, 1943), 83.
14 *Ibid.*
15 *Ibid.,* 83–84.
16 Ives, *op. cit.,* p. 381.
17 Edward F. Humphrey, *Nationalism and Religion in America* (Boston, 1924), 238–239.
18 Thomas M. Field, ed., *Unpublished Letters of Charles Carroll of Carrollton* (New York, 1902), 159–160.
19 Peter K. Guilday, *The Life and Times of John Carroll* (New York, 1922), I, 114.
20 Ives, *op. cit.,* pp. 389–391.
21 *Ibid.,* p. 352.
22 *Ibid.,* p. 400.

[23] John Carroll Brent, *Biographical Sketch of Most Reverend John Carroll, First Archbishop of Baltimore* (Baltimore, 1843), 68–69.

[24] Gertrude S. Wood, *William Paterson* (Fairlawn, N. J., 1933), 19.

[25] *Ibid.*, 26–27.

[26] *The U. S. Oracle of the Day*, May 24, 1800, quoted in Horace W. Fuller, *The Green Bag; An Entertaining Magazine for Lawyers*, Vols. 1–26 (Boston, 1889–1914), II, 264.

[27] George A. Boyd, *Elias Boudinot* (Princeton, 1952), 45.

[28] *Ibid.*

[29] J. J. Boudinot (ed.), *Life, Public Service, Addresses and Letters of Elias Boudinot* (Boston, 1896), I, 19.

[30] *Ibid.*, p. 173.

[31] In the First Congress, for example, "Messrs. Cadwalader, Schureman and Sinnickson had been mere shadow figures in Congress, whereas Boudinot had been ranked among the leaders." *Ibid.*, p. 192.

[32] He was president of the General Assembly of the Presbyterian Church at the time of his death. *Ibid.*, p. 265.

[33] Elias Boudinot, *Age of Revelation* (Philadelphia, 1801), quoted by George A. Boyd, *Elias Boudinot* (Princeton, 1952), 253–254.

[34] George A. Boyd, *op. cit.*, p. 265.

[35] J. J. Boudinot, *op. cit.*, p. 21. One of the most tender insights into the great spirit of charity that was Boudinot's comes by way of his letter to the son of the Presbyterian minister, the Reverend James Caldwell, whom the Marquis de LaFayette had taken back to France for his education. Young Caldwell had previously indicated that he contemplated a change of faith, to Catholicism. In return, Boudinot said: "Do not suppose that I am so void of Christian Charity or so ignorant of the Principles and Practices of thousands of the Roman Church as to suppose that a man may not, under the influence of them, lead a life of holiness and devotion to God — NO — I am satisfied that the grace of God is not confined to Sect or Party." *Ibid.*, Vol. II, p. 33. (Young Caldwell remained a Presbyterian.) It cannot be said that Boudinot harbored any dislike for religion or religious toleration.

The Boudinot statement indicates that difficulty of determining the views of many of these men. For example in one of his few recorded statements on the subject of religion, Ralph Izard, one of the senators from South Carolina in the First Congress, gave only a slight indication that he was against a church-state system which would become the basis for political action. Writing from Geneva in 1777, Izard noted the Swiss experience: "[T]he differences of religious opinions, makes the Cantons jealous of each other, and refuse to incorporate their allies with themselves, least one party or other should get advantage by it. This may prove fatal to them at some time or other." Comparing that with the American situation. Izard noted: "Our country had no such cause for jealousy and disunion, and, therefore, I hope in God, she may guard against the fatal effects of them." *Correspondence of Ralph Izard, 1774–1804* (New York, 1844), p. 12. *The Letters of Benjamin Hawkins* Savannah, 1916), contain no mention of religion.

[36] Irving Brant, "Madison: On the Separation of Church and State," *William and Mary Quarterly* #1 (3d ser.), VIII, Jan., 1951, p. 16.

[37] *Ibid.*

[38] Letter of August, 1820, to Jacob de la Motta. Hunt, IX, 29–30.

[39] *Ibid.*, I, 41.

[40] *Ibid.*, II, p. 186. See Chapter Seven, n. 65.

[41] *Ibid.* See Sanford H. Cobb, *Rise of Religious Liberty in America* (New York, 1902), 496.

[42] Hunt, II, 163–164.

[43] *Ibid.*, V, 176.

[44] James D. Richardson, *A Compilation of the Messages and Papers of The Presidents* (Washington, 1896), I, 490.

[45] Irving Brant, *op. cit.*, pp. 12, 22.

46 Letter to Edward Livingston, July 10, 1822. Hunt, IX, 98, 100.

47 "The Belknap Papers," Massachusetts Historical Society *Collections,* 6th Series, Vol. IV (1891), p. 393.

48 *Debates and Proceedings of the Convention of 1788,* pp. 190–191.

49 Evarts B. Greene, *Religion and the State* (New York, 1941), 91.

50 John Adams, *Works,* ed. Henry Adams, IX, 402. Cited by Stokes, I, 513.

51 Sweet, *op. cit.,* p. 50.

52 *Writings of Thomas Jefferson* (Libscomb and Bergh, eds., Washington, D. C., 1903), Vol. 16, pp. 281–282, cited at times as Memorial ed.; Saul K. Padover, *The Complete Jefferson* (New York, 1943), pp. 518–519.

53 *Jefferson's Writings* (Monticello ed., 1905), Vol. IX pp. 428–430.

54 *Writings of Thomas Jefferson* (Ford ed.), VIII, 344.

55 Gilbert Chinard, *Thomas Jefferson, The Apostle of Americanism* (Ann Arbor, 1957), p. 511.

56 Philip Alexander Bruce, *History of the University of Virginia,* 4 vols. (New York, 1920), II, 365; Stokes, *Church and State,* I, 337; Albea Godbold, *The Church College of the Old South* (Durham, 1944), 178–179.

57 Bruce, II, 366, 369; Stokes, I, 337; Godbold, 179.

58 Original letter at the University of Virginia; published in whole in Stokes II, pp. 633–634.

59 Jefferson's statement on "Freedom of Religion at the University of Virginia" is set forth in full in J. M. O'Neill, *Religion and Education Under the Constitution* (New York, 1949), Appendix D; Bruce, II, 367–369; Stokes, I, 337.

60 *Indian Affairs,* ed. by Charles Kappler (Washington, D. C., 1903), (Vol. II, p. 67.

61 Leo Pfeffer, *Church, State, and Freedom* (Boston, 1953), p. 509.

62 Jared Sparks, *The Life of Gouverneur Morris,* 3 vols. (Boston, 1832), III, 481, 483.

63 *Ibid.,* 488–498.

64 Jonathan Elliott, *Debates on the Federal Constitution* 2 ed. (Philadelphia, 1907), IX, 199.

65 Letter to Mason in 1785, quoted in Humphrey, *op. cit.,* p. 401.

66 Quoted in Stokes, I, 496.

67 A letter to the "New Church in Baltimore," January 27, 1793, quoted in Stokes, *op. cit.,* p. 497.

Bibliography

BOOKS

Adams, Charles Francis, ed., *Works of John Adams.* 10 vols. Boston, 1850–1856.
———— *Life of John Adams.* 2 vols. Philadelphia, 1874.
Adams, James Truslow, *New England in the Republic, 1776–1850.* Boston, 1926.
Alden, Richard C., *The South in the American Revolution.* Baton Rouge, 1955.
Allison, Patrick, *Candid Animadversions on a Petition Presented to the General Assembly of Maryland by the Reverend William Smith and Reverend Thomas Gates.* Baltimore, 1783.
Ames, Fisher, *Works* (with a memoir by J. T. Kirkland). Boston, 1809.
———— Manuscript. Correspondence. Dedham Historical Society.
Ames, Herman V., "The Proposed Amendments to the Constitution, 1789–1889." *Annual Report, American Historical Association.* Vol. II. Washington, 1897.
Ames, Seth, ed., *Works of Fisher Ames.* 2 vols. Boston, 1854.
Amory, Thomas Coffin, *Life of James Sullivan: with Selections from his Writings.* 2 vols. Boston, 1859.
———— *The Military Services and Public Life of Major General John Sullivan.* Albany, 1868.
Arnold, Samuel Greene, *History of the State of Rhode Island and Providence Plantations.* 2 vols. New York, 1860.
Austin, James T., *Life and Letters of Elbridge Gerry.* 2 vols. Boston, 1828–1829.

Backus, Isaac, Diary manuscript. Baptist Library, Boston.
———— *A Letter to a Gentleman in the Massachusetts General Assembly Concerning Taxes to Support Religious Worship.* Boston, 1771.
———— *Seasonable Plea for Liberty of Conscience.* Boston, 1770.
———— *A History of New England. With Particular Reference to the Denomination of Christians called Baptists.* Edited with notes by David Weston. 2 vols. Newton, Mass., 1871.
———— *Church History of New England from 1620 to 1804.* Philadelphia, 1844.
Bacon, Leonard, *Sketch of the Life and Public Services of James Hillhouse.* New Haven, Conn., 1860.
Baldwin, Alice M., *The New England Clergy and the American Revolution.* Durham, N. C., 1928.
Ballagh, James, ed., *Letters of Richard Henry Lee.* 2 vols. New York, 1914.
Bancroft, George, *History of the United States.* 4 vols. Boston, 1864.

—————— *History of the Formation of the Constitution of the United States.* 2 vols. New York, 1889.

Barker, Charles A., *The Background of the Revolution in Maryland.* New Haven, 1940.

Barlow, Joel, *Political Writings.* New York, 1796.

Barnett, Elzas, *Jews of South Carolina.* Charleston, 1903.

Barry, Richard H., *Mister Rutledge of South Carolina.* New York, 1942.

Bartlett, J. R., ed., *Records of the Colony of Rhode Island and Providence Plantations in New England, 1636–1792.* 10 vols. Providence, 1856–1865.

Bass, Robert, *The Life of Thomas Sumter.* New York, 1961.

Bates, Frank Green, *Rhode Island and the Formation of the Union.* New York, 1898.

Bates, M. Searle, *Religious Liberty: An Inquiry.* New York: International Missionary Council, 1945.

Beard, Charles A., *An Economic Interpretation of the Constitution.* New York, 1943.

—————— *Rise of American Civilization.* 2 vols. New York, 1929–1931.

Beardsley, E. E., *Life and Times of William Samuel Johnson.* 2 ed. New York, 1886.

Beasley, Charles R., "The Religious Struggle." *Social England.* 3 vols. New York, 1902.

Belknap, Jeremy, *History of New Hampshire.* Dover, N. H., 1831.

Bell, Sadie, *The Church, the State and Education in Virginia.* Philadelphia, 1930.

Bentley, William, *The Diary of William Bentley.* Salem, Mass., 1905–1907.

Beth, Loren P., *The American Theory of Church and State.* Miami, Fla., 1958.

Bethea, Andrew J., *The Contribution of Charles Pinckney to the Formation of the American Union.* Richmond, 1937.

Bicknell, Thomas W., *The History of Rhode Island and Providence Plantations.* 2 vols. New York, 1920.

Billington, Ray A., *The Protestant Crusade.* New York, 1952.

Biographical Directory of the American Congress, 1774–1916. Washington, 1961.

Bishop, Abraham, *Proofs of a Conspiracy Against Christianity and the Government of the United States; Exhibited in Several Views of the Church and State in New England.* Hartford, 1802.

Black, H. C., *Handbook of American Constitutional Law.* 4 ed. St. Paul, 1910.

Black, Jeremiah S., *Essays and Speeches.* New York, 1885.

Blackstone, William, *Commentaries on the Laws of England,* ed. Thomas Cooley. 4 vols. 3 ed. Chicago, 1884.

Blakely, William Addison, ed., *American State Papers Bearing on Sunday Legislation.* Washington, 1911.

—————— *American State Papers On Religious Freedom.* Washington, 1943.

Blau, Joseph L., *Cornerstones of Religious Freedom in America.* Boston, 1949.

Blum, Virgil C., S.J., *Freedom of Choice in Education.* New York, 1958.

Boorstin, Daniel J., *The Genuis of American Politics.* Chicago, 1953.

Boudinot, Elias, *Age of Revelation.* Philadelphia, 1801.

Boudinot, J. J., ed., *Life, Public Services, Addresses and Letters of Elias Boudinot.* Boston, 1896.

Boutell, Lewis, *Life of Roger Sherman.* Chicago, 1896.

Bouton, Nathaniel, *et al.*, eds., *Documents and Records Relating to . . . New Hampshire. New Hampshire Provincial and State Papers*. 30 vols. Concord, N. H., 1867–1910.

Boyd, George A., *Elias Boudinot*. Princeton, 1952.

Boyd, Julian, ed., *The Papers of Thomas Jefferson*. 6 vols. Princeton, 1950.

Bradley, Cyrus P., *Biography of Isaac Hill of New Hampshire*. Concord, N. H., 1835.

Brady, Joseph H., *Confusion Twice Compounded: the First Amendment and the Supreme Court*. South Orange, N. J., 1955.

Brant, Irving, *James Madison, Father of the Constitution*. New York, 1950.

Brent, John C., *Biographical Sketch of Most Rev. John Carroll, First Archbishop of Baltimore*. Baltimore, 1843.

Bridenbaugh, Carl, *Mitre and Sceptre*. New York, 1962.

Brown, W. G., *The Life of Oliver Ellsworth*. New York, 1905.

Brush, E. H., *Rufus King and His Times*. New York, 1926.

Burr, Nelson R., *Education in New Jersey, 1630–1871*. Princeton, 1947.

Butts, R. Freeman, *The American Tradition in Religion and Education*. Boston, 1950.

Bryce, James, *The American Commonwealth*. 3 ed. New York, 1903.

Candler, Allen D., ed., *Colonial Records of the State of Georgia*. Vols. 1–19, 21–26. Atlanta, 1904–1918.

Carroll, Charles, *Rhode Island — Three Centuries of Democracy*. 2 vols. New York, 1932.

Chauncey, Charles, *Salvation for All Men*. Boston, 1782.

———— *The Accursed Thing Must Be Taken Away from Among a People*. Boston, 1778.

———— *The Only Compulsion Proper to be Made Use of in the Affairs of Conscience and Religion*. Boston, 1739.

Chinard, Gilbert, *Honest John Adams*. Boston, 1933.

Chipman, Daniel, *Memoir of Thomas Chittenden*. Middlebury, Vt., 1849.

Chipman, Nathaniel, *Sketches of the Principles of Government*. Rutland, Vt., 1793.

Clark, Samuel A., *History of St. John's Church, Elizabethtown*. Elizabethtown, N. J., 1857.

Clune, Mary Catherine, "Joseph Hawley's Criticism of the Constitution of Massachusetts," *Smith College Studies in History*, Vol. III, No. 1, 1927.

Cobb, Sanford H., *The Rise of Religious Liberty in America*. New York, 1902.

Cogley, John, *Religion in America*. New York, 1958.

Coleman, Kenneth, *The American Revolution in Georgia, 1763–1789*. Athens, 1958.

Commager, Henry Steele, ed., *Documents of American History*. New York, 1949.

Connors, Edward M., *Church-State Relationships in Education in the State of New York*. Washington, 1951.

Cooley, Thomas M., *General Principles of Constitutional Law in the United States*. Boston, 1898.

———— *Constitutional Limitations*. Boston, 1883.

Coon, C. L., *The Beginnings of Public Education in North Carolina: A Documentary History, 1790–1840*. Raleigh, 1908.

Corwin, Edward S., *A Constitution of Powers in a Secular State*. Charlottesville, 1951.
—— *Liberty Against Government*. Baton Rouge, 1948.
—— *The Constitution and What It Means Today*. Princeton, 1954.
Cotner, Robert C., *Theodore Foster's Minutes of the Convention . . . at South Kingston, Rhode Island, in March, 1790*. Providence, 1929.
Coulter, E. Merton, *A Short History of Georgia*. Chapel Hill, 1933.
Crocker, Joseph H., *Winning of Religious Liberty*. Boston, 1918.
Crowl, Philip A., *Maryland During and After the Revolution*. Baltimore, 1943.
Curtis, George Ticknor, *Constitutional History of the United States . . . to the Close of the Civil War*. 2 vols. New York, 1889.
Cushing, Harry Alonzo, *History of the Transition from Provincial to Commonwealth Government in Massachusetts*. New York, 1896.
—— ed., *The Writings of Samuel Adams*. 4 vols. New York, 1904–1908.
Cussingham, Charles E., *Timothy Dwight, 1752–1817, A Biography*. New York, 1942.

Dalcho, Frederick, *History of Protestant Episcopal Church in South Carolina to the Year 1808*. Charleston, 1820.
Dawson, Christopher, *Religion in the Modern State*. New York, 1936.
Department of State, Bureau of Rolls and Library, *Documentary History of the Constitution of the United States of America, 1786–1870*. 2 vols. Washington, 1894–1905.
Dexter, Franklin B., ed., *The Literary Diary of Ezra Stiles*. 3 vols. New York, 1901, III.
Dieffenbach, Albert C., *Religious Liberty*. New York, 1927.
Dignan, Patrick J., *History of the Legal Incorporation of Catholic Church Property in the United States*. New York, 1935.
Douglas, Elisha P., *Rebels and Democrats*. Chapel Hill, 1855.
Dumbauld, Edward, *The Bill of Rights and What It Means Today*. Oklahoma, 1953.
Dwight, Theodore, *History of Connecticut*. New York, 1841.
Dwight, Timothy, *Travels in New England and New York*. 4 vols. New Haven, 1831.
—— *The Duty of Americans at the Present Crisis, July 4, 1798*.

East, Robert A., "The Massachusetts Conservatives in the Critical Period," in Richard B. Morris, ed., *The Era of the American Revolution*. New York. 1939.
Eckenrode, Hamilton J., *Separation of Church and State in Virginia*. Richmond, 1910.
Ehler, Sidney Z., and Morrall, John B., *Church and State Through the Centuries*. London, 1954.
Eisenman, Nathaniel J., *The Ratification of the Federal Constitution by the State of New Hampshire* (mimeographed). Washington, 1938.
Elliot, Jonathan, ed., *The Debates in the Several State Conventions on the Adoption of the Federal Constitution — Together with the Journal of the Federal Constitution — Together with the Journal of the Federal Convention* (and other papers). 5 vols. Washington, 1859.
Elwyn, John Langdon, "Some Account of John Langdon." *New Hampshire State Papers*, II, ed. A. S. Batcheldor. 1891.
Elzas, Barnett A., *Jews of South Carolina*. Charleston, 1903.

Farrand, Max, ed., *Records of the Federal Convention of 1787*. 4 vols. New Haven, Conn., 1911–1937.

Field, Edward, ed., *State of Rhode Island and Providence Plantations at the End of the Century: A History*. 3 vols. Boston, 1902.

Field, Thomas M., ed., *Unpublished Letters of Charles Carroll of Carrolton*. New York, 1902.

Fitzpatrick, John C., ed., *The Writings of George Washington*. 39 vols. Washington, 1931–1944.

Flick, Alexander C., ed., *History of New York State*. 10 vols. New York, 1937.

Forbes, Harritte M., *England Diaries, 1602–1800*. Topsfield, Mass., 1923.

Force, Peter, ed., *American Archives*, 4th series, 6 vols.; 5th series, 3 vols. Washington, 1837–1857.

Ford, Paul Leicester, ed., *Bibliography and Reference List of the History and Literature Relating to the Adoption of the Constitution of the United States, 1787–1788*. Brooklyn, N. Y., 1896.

———— *Essays on the Constitution of the United States, Published During Its Discussion by the People, 1787–1788*. Brooklyn, N. Y., 1892.

———— *Pamphlets on the Constitution. Published During Its Discussion by the People, 1787–1788*. Brooklyn, 1888.

Ford, Worthington C., "The Federal Constitution in Virginia, 1787–1788." *Proceedings of the Massachusetts Historical Society*. 2nd Series, Vol. XVII. 1903.

———— ed., *Letters of Joseph Jones*. Washington, 1889.

Foster, Gertrude, "Documentary History of Education in South Carolina." Unpublished Ph.D. dissertation, University of South Carolina. 13 vols. 1934.

Foster, Theodore, *Minutes of the Convention Held at South Kingston, Rhode Island, in March, 1790, Which Failed to Adopt the Constitution of the United States*, ed. Robert C. Cotner. Providence, 1929.

Foster, W. E., "Theodore Foster," Rhode Island Historical Society, *Collections*. Vol. VII. 1885.

Fox, Dixon Ryan, and Krout, John A., *The Completion of Independence*. New York, 1944.

Frederick, Carl J., *Constitutional Government and Democracy: Theory and Practice*. Boston, 1950.

Frothingham, Louis Adams, *A Brief History of the Constitution and Government of Massachusetts*. Cambridge, Mass., 1916.

Gabel, Richard J., *Public Funds for Church and Private Schools*. Washington, 1937.

Geiger, Mary V., *Daniel Carroll: Framer of the Constitution*. Washington, 1943.

Gerry, Ellbridge, *Observations on the New Constitution and on the Federal and State Conventions. By a Columbian Patriot*. Boston, 1778.

Gewehr, W. M., *The Great Awakening in Virginia*. Durham, N. C., 1930

Goebel, Luther L., *Church-State Relationships in Education in North Carolina Since 1776*. Durham, 1938.

Goodman, Abram Vossen, *American Overture: Jewish Rights in Colonial Times*. Philadelphia, 1947.

Greene, Evarts B., *Religion and the State: The Making and Testing of An American Tradition*. New York, 1941.

Greene, George W., *Life of Nathaniel Greene.* 3 vols. New York, 1867.

Greene, M. Louise, *The Development of Religious Liberty in Connecticut.* Boston and New York, 1905.

Gregg, Alexander, *History of the Old Cheraws.* Columbia, S. C., 1925.

Gregorie, Anne King, *Thomas Sumter,* Columbia, 1931.

Grigsby, Hugh Blair, *The History of the Virginia Federal Convention of 1788, With Some Account of the Eminent Virginians of That Era Who Were Members of the Body.* 2 vols. Richmond, 1890–1891.

Groce, G. C., *William Samuel Johnson: A Maker of the Constitution.* New York, 1937.

Guilday, Peter K., *The Life and Times of John Carroll.* 2 vols. New York, 1922.

Gurn, Joseph, *Charles Carroll of Carrollton.* New York, 1932.

Hall, John, *History of the Presbyterian Church in Trenton.* New York, 1859.

Hamilton, John C., ed., *The Works of Alexander Hamilton.* 7 vols. New York, 1850–1851.

Hammond, Otis G., *Letters and Papers of Major-General John Sullivan, Continental Army.* Concord, N. H., 1934.

Harding, Samuel Bannister, *The Contest Over the Ratification of the Federal Constitutions in the State of Massachusetts.* New York, 1896.

Harlow, R. V., *Samuel Adams, Promoter of the American Revolution.* New York, 1923.

Hart, A. B., ed., *Commonwealth History of Massachusetts.* New York, 1927–1930.

Hart, Ann Clark, *Abraham Clark, Signer of the Declaration of Independence.* San Francisco, 1923.

Hawkins, Benjamin, *Letters of Benjamin Hawkins.* Savannah, Ga., 1916.

Healey, Robert M., *Jefferson on Religion in Public Education.* New Haven, 1962.

Henry, William W., *Patrick Henry: Life, Correspondence and Speeches.* 3 vols. New York, 1891.

Hesseltine, William B., and Smiley, David L., *The South in American History.* Englewood Cliffs, N. J., 1960.

Hill, David S., and Fisher, William A., *Federal Relationships to Education.* Washington, 1931.

Hoadley, C. J., and Labaree, L. W., ed., *Public Records of the State of Connecticut.* 8 vols. Hartford, 1894–1951.

Hooker, Richard, ed., *The Carolina Backcountry on the Eve of the Revolution.* Chapel Hill, 1953.

Howard, G. E., *An Introduction to Local Constitutional History of the United States.* Baltimore, 1899.

Howard, Leon, *The Connecticut Acts.* Chicago, 1942.

Howe, George, *History of the Presbyterian Church in South Carolina.* Columbia, 1870.

Howe, Mark D., *Cases on Church and State in the United States.* Boston, 1952.

Humphrey, Edward Frank, *Nationalism and Religion in America.* Boston, 1924.

Hunt, Gaillard, ed., *The Writings of James Madison.* 9 vols. New York, 1900–1910.

Hunt, Gaillard, and Scott, James Brown, ed., *The Debates in the Federal Convention of 1787 Which Framed the Constitution of the United States of America.* New York, 1920.

Israel, Edward L., "Maryland's Laws Governing Religion." Unpublished manuscript in Enoch Pratt Library. Baltimore, n.d.

Ives, J. Moss, *The Ark and the Dove.* New York, 1936.

Jackson, Henry, *An Account of the Churches of Rhode Island.* Providence, 1854.

James, Charles F., *Documentary History of the Struggle for Religious Liberty in Virginia.* Lynchburg, 1900.

Jameson, J. Franklin, ed., "Letters of Stephen Higginson, 1783–1804." *American Historical Association Annual Report of 1896.* Vol. I.

———— "Studies in the History of the Federal Convention of 1787." *American Historical Association Annual Report for the Year 1902.* Washington, 1903.

Janowsky, Oscar I., ed., *The American Jew.* New York, 1942.

Jay, William, *Life of John Jay.* New York, 1833.

Jensen, Merrill, *The New Nation.* New York, 1950.

Johnson, Allen, *Readings in American Constitutional History.* Boston, 1912.

Johnson, Alvin W., and Yost, Frank H., *Separation of Church and State in the States.* Minneapolis, 1948.

Johnston, Alexander, *The Genesis of a New England State, Connecticut.* Baltimore, 1833, revised edition, 1903. (Also Johns Hopkins University Studies in History.)

———— *Connecticut: A Study of a Commonwealth Democracy.* Boston, 1887, revised edition 1903.

Jones, Charles C., *The History of Georgia.* 2 vols. Boston, 1883.

Kauper, Paul G., *Frontiers of Constitutional Liberty.* Ann Arbor, 1956.

Kerwin, Jerome, *Catholic Viewpoint on Church and State.* New York, 1960.

King, Charles T., ed., *The Life and Correspondence of Rufus King.* 6 vols. New York, 1894–1900.

Kinney, Charles B., *Church and State: the Struggle for Separation in New Hampshire, 1630–1900.* New York, 1955.

Knight, Edgar W., *Twenty Centuries of Education.* New York, 1940.

Koch, Adrienne, *Jefferson and Madison.* New York, 1950.

Koch, G. Adolph, *Republican Religion.* New York, 1933.

Konvitz, Milton R., *Fundamental Liberties of a Free People: Press, Assembly, Religion, Speech.* New York, 1957.

Labaree, Leonard W., *Royal Government in America.* New York, 1958.

———— ed., *Royal Instructions to the British Colonies.* 2 vols. New York, 1935.

Laski, Harold, *Foundations of National Sovereignty.* New York, 1921.

———— *Political Thought From Locke to Bentham.* New York, 1920.

Lauer, Paul E., *Church and State in New England.* (Johns Hopkins University Studies in History and Political Science.) Baltimore, 1892.

LeDuc, Thomas H., *Connecticut and the First Ten Amendments.* Senate Doc. 96, 75th Congress, 1st Session. Washington, 1937.

Leflar, Hugh T., and Newsome, Albert R., *History of North Carolina.* Chapel Hill, 1951.

Leland, John, *The Rights of Conscience Inalienable . . . Or the High Flying Churchman.* New London, Conn., 1902.

Libby, Orin Grant, *The Geographical Distribution of the Vote of the Thirteen*

States on the Federal Constitution, 1787–1788. Madison, Wis., 1894.

Lingley, Charles B., *The Transition in Virginia From Colony to Common-wealth*. New York, 1910.

Lodge, Henry Cabot, "A Memoir of Culeb Strong." *Massachusetts Historical Society, Proceedings*. Boston, 1879.

——— *Life and Letters of George Cabot*. Boston, 1877.

Lord, Arthur, "Some Objections Made to the State Constitution, 1789." *Massachusetts Historical Society, Proceedings*. Boston, 1917.

Lord, Robert H., Saxton, John E., and Thorrington, Edward, *History of the Archdiocese of Boston in the Various Stages of Its Development, 1604 to 1943*. 3 vols. New York, 1944.

Maclay, Edgar S., *Journal of William Maclay, 1789–1791*. New York, 1890.

MacMaster and Stone, *Pennsylvania and the Federal Constitution*. Lancaster, Pa., 1808.

Mahoney, Charles J., *The Relation of the State to Religious Education in Early New York, 1633–1825*. Washington, 1941.

Main, Jackson Turner, *The Anti-Federalists*. Chapel Hill, 1961.

Mann, Herman, *Annals of Dedham, 1635–1847*. Dedham, Mass., 1847.

Manning, William, *Key of Liberty*, ed. Samuel Eliot Morison. Billerica, Mass., 1922.

Mason, Sister Mary Paul, *Church-State Relationships in Education in Connecticut, 1633–1953*. Washington, 1953.

Matteson, David H., *History of the Formation of the Union Under the Constitution*. Washington, 1941.

Maynard, Theodore, *The Story of American Catholicism*. New York, 1941.

Mayo, Lawrence S., *John Langdon of New Hampshire*. Concord, N. H., 1937.

Mays, David J., *Edmund Pendleton, 1720–1803*. 2 vols. Cambridge, 1952.

McCormick, Leo J., *Church-State Relationships in Education in Maryland*. Washington, 1942.

McCrady, Edward, *History of South Carolina*. 4 vols. New York, 1901.

McLaughlin, Andrew C., *A Constitutional History of the United States*. New York, 1935.

McMaster, John Bach, *History of the People of the United States*. 8 vols. New York, 1883–1913.

McRee, Griffith J., *James Iredell*. 2 vols. New York, 1857.

Mecklin, John M., *The Story of American Dissent*. New York, 1934.

Meigs, William M., *The Growth of the Constitution in the Federal Convention of 1787*. Philadelphia, 1900.

Mendenhall, Harlan G., *Presbyterianism in Perth Amboy*. Perth Amboy, N. J., 1903.

Meriwether, Robert L., *The Expansion of South Carolina, 1729–1765*. Kingsport, Tenn., 1940.

Metzger, Charles H., *Catholics in the American Revolution*. Chicago, 1962.

Meyer, Jacob C., *Church and State in Massachusetts From 1740 to 1833*. Cleveland, 1930.

Millar, M. F. X., and Ryan, John A., *The State and the Church*. New York, 1936.

Miller, J. C., *Sam Adams*. Boston, 1936.

Miller, Samuel, *Brief Retrospect of the Eighteenth Century*. 2 vols. New York, 1803.

Miller, Victor C., *Joel Barlow, Revolutionist*. Hamburg, Germany, 1932.

Moehlman, Conrad Henry, *The Wall of Separation Between Church and State.* Boston, 1951.

Morais, Herbert M., *Deism in Boston, 1951. Eighteenth Century America.* New York, 1960.

Morison, Samuel Eliot, *Life and Correspondence of Harrison Gray Otis.* 2 vols. Boston, 1913.

——— *History of the Constitution of Massachusetts.* Boston, 1917.

——— "The Struggle Over the Adoption of the Constitution of Massachusetts, 1780," *Massachusetts Historical Society, Proceedings.* Boston, 1917.

Morris, Richard B., "Insurrection in Massachusetts," ed. Daniel Aaron. *America in Crisis.* New York, 1952.

Morse, Anson Ely, *The Federalist Party in Massachusetts.* Princeton, 1909.

Morse, James K., and Morse, Jedediah, *A Campion of New England.* New York, 1939.

Murray, John Courtney, S.J., *We Hold These Truths.* New York, 1960.

Myers, Denys P., *Massachusetts and the First Ten Amendments to the Constitution.* 74th Congress, 2nd Session, Senate Doc. 181. Washington, D. C.

Nevins, Allan, *The American State During and After the Revolution, 1775–1789.* New York, 1924.

Niles, Alfred S., *Maryland Constitutional Law.* Baltimore, 1915.

Noble, M. C. S., Jr., *A History of the Public School in North Carolina.* Chapel Hill, 1939.

Nott, G. C., *Mystery of the Pinckney Draft.* New York, 1908.

O'Brien, F. William, S.J., *Justice Reed and the First Amendment.* Washington, 1958.

O'Callaghan, E. B., *Documentary History of the State of New York.* 4 vols. Albany, N. Y., 1849–1851.

O'Neill, James, *Religion and Education Under the Constitution.* New York, 1949.

——— *Catholicism and American Freedom.* New York, 1952.

Padover, Saul K., *The Complete Jefferson.* New York, 1950.

——— *The Complete Madison.* New York, 1953.

Parsons, Theophilus, Jr., *Memoirs of Chief Justice Parsons with Notices of Some of His Contemporaries.* Boston, 1859.

Parsons, Wilfrid, *The First Freedom: Considerations on Church and State in the United States.* New York, 1948.

Patterson, Bennet B., *The Forgotten Ninth Amendment.* Indianapolis, 1955.

Patterson, Caleb B., *The Constitutional Principles of Thomas Jefferson.* Austin, 1953.

Patterson, James W., "Ratification of the Constitution of the United States by the State of New Hampshire." *New Hampshire Historical Society, Proceedings, 1888–1895.*

Pfeffer, Leo, *Church, State, and Freedom.* Boston. 1953.

Pierce, Bradford K., and Hale, Charles, eds., *Debates and Proceedings in the Convention of the Commonwealth of Massachusetts, Held in the Year 1788, and Which Finally Ratified the Constitution of the United States,* Boston, 1856.

Plucknett, Theodore F. T., *A Concise History of the Common Law.* 4 ed., revised. London, 1948.

Plumer, William, Jr., *Life of William Plumer*. Boston, 1857.
Pollock, Frederick, and Maitland, Frederic, *History of the English Law*. 2 ed., revised. Cambridge, England, 1923.
Pound, Roscoe, *Interpretations of Legal History*. New York, 1923.
Purcell, Richard Joseph, *Connecticut in Transition. 1775–1818*. Washington, 1918.

Quincy, Edmund, *Life of Joseph Quincy*. Boston, 1874.
Quincy, Josiah, *History of Harvard University*. 2 vols. Boston, 1840.

Ramage, James B., *Local Government and Free Schools in South Carolina*. Baltimore, Md., 1883.
Ramsey, David, *History of South Carolina*. 2 vols. Newberry, S. C., 1858; reprinted edition, Spartanburg, S. C., 1960.
Paper, C. L., *The Church and Private Schools of North Carolina*. Greensboro, N. C., 1898.
Reisner, Edward W., *Nationalism and Religion Since 1789*. New York, 1922.
Richardson, James D., *A Compilation of the Messages and Papers of the Presidents*. 20 vols. New York, 1917.
Richman, Irving Berdine, *Rhode Island — A Study in Separatism*. Boston, 1905.
Robinson, William A., *Jeffersonian Democracy in New England*. New Haven, 1915.
Rogers, George C., *Evolution of a Federalist, William Loughton Smith of Charleston*. Columbia, S. C., 1962.
Rommen, Heinrich, *The State in Catholic Thought*. St. Louis, 1945.
Rowland, Kate Mason, *The Life of George Mason*. 2 vols. New York, 1892.
———— *The Life of Charles Carroll of Carrollton*. New York, 1898.
Russell, William T., *Maryland, the Land of Sanctuary*. Baltimore, 1907.
Rutland, Robert A., *The Birth of the Bill of Rights, 1776–1781*. Chapel Hill, 1955.

Sanders, W. L., ed., *Colonial Records of North Carolina*. 10 vols. Raleigh, N. C.
Saye, A. B., *A Constitutional History of Georgia*. Athens, 1948.
Schaff, Philip, *America: A Sketch of Its Political, Social, and Religious Character*. Cambridge, 1961.
———— *The Progress of Religious Freedom*. New York, 1889.
———— *Church and State in the United States*. Washington, 1888.
Schaper, William A., "Sectionalism and Representation in South Carolina." *Annual Report of the American Historical Association for 1900*. Vol. I. Washington, 1901.
Scharf, John T., *History of Maryland*. 3 vols. Baltimore, 1879.
Sellers, Horace B., *The Constitution and Religious Education*. Boston, 1950.
Semble, R. B., *History of the Rise and Progress of the Baptists in Virginia*. Beale edition, Richmond, 1894.
Shea, John Gilmary, *The History of the Catholic Church in the United States*. 4 vols. New York, 1886–1892.
Sherril, L. J., *Presbyterian Parochial Schools*. New Haven, 1932.
Shoemaker, E. C., *Noah Webster, Pioneer of Learning*. New York, 1936.
Simkins, Francis B., *A History of the South*. New York, 1953.
Slade, William, ed., *Vermont State Papers*. Middlebury, 1823.
Smith, Goldwin, *History of England*. New York, 1957.

Smith, Sherman M., *The Relation of the State to Religious Education in Massachusetts.* Syracuse, 1926.
Snow, Charles M., *Religious Liberty in America.* Washington, 1914.
Spalding, Henry, S.J., *Catholic Colonial Maryland.* Milwaukee, 1932.
Sparks, Jared, *The Life of Gouverneur Morris.* 3 vols. Boston, 1832.
Spaulding, Ernest W., *New York in the Critical Period, 1783–1789.* New York, 1932.
Stackpole, Everett S., *History of New Hampshire.* 4 vols. New York, 1916.
Staples, William, *Rhode Island in the Continental Congress.* Providence, 1870.
Stevens, Charles E., *Sources of the Constitution.* New York, 1942.
Stokes, Anson Phelps, *Church and State in the United States.* 3 vols. New York, 1950.
Story, Joseph, *Commentaries on the Constitution of the United States.* Boston, 1833.
Strickland, Reba Carolyn, *Religion and the State in Eighteenth Century New York.* New York, 1939.
Sweet, William W., *The Story of Religion in America.* New York, 1930.
———— *Religion on the American Frontier, The Baptists, 1783–1830.* New York, 1931.
———— *Religion in Colonial America.* New York, 1942.
Swift, Zephaniah, *System of the Laws of the State of Connecticut.* Hartford, 1795.
Sykes, Norman, *Church and State in England in the XVIIIth Century.* Hemden, Conn., 1962.

Tansill, C. C., ed., *Documents Illustrative of the Formation of the Union of the American States.* 69th Congress, 1st Session, H. Doc. 398. Washington, 1927.
Tappert, Theodore G., and Doberstein, John W., trans., *The Journals of Henry Melchior Muhlenberg.* 3 vols. Philadelphia, 1924.
Taylor, Hannis, *The Origin and Growth of the English Constitution.* 2 vols. Boston, 1898.
Taylor, Robert J., *Western Massachusetts in the Revolution.* Providence, 1954.
———— ed., *Massachusetts, Colony to Commonwealth.* Chapel Hill, 1951.
Tennant, William, Rev., *Address of the Reverend William Tennant to the House of Assembly, November 11, 1777.* Pamphlet. January, 1778. American State Records Series (microfilm).
Thayer, V. T., *The Attack Upon the American Secular School.* Boston, 1951.
———— *Religion in Public Schools.* New York, 1947.
Thom, W. F., *The Struggle for Religious Freedom in Virginia: The Baptists.* (Johns Hopkins University Studies, No. 18.) Baltimore, 1900.
Thorning, Joseph Francis, *Religious Liberty in Transition.* Washington, 1931.
Thornton, Mary Lindsey, *A Bibliography of North Carolina.* Chapel Hill, 1958.
Thorpe, Francis N., *The Constitutional History of the United States.* 3 vols. Chicago, 1901.
———— *The Federal and State Constitutions, Colonial Charters, and Other Organic Laws of the States, Territories, and Colonies Now or Heretofore Forming the United States of America.* 7 vols. Washington, 1909.
Todd, C. B., *Life and Letters of Joel Barlow.* New York, 1886.
Torpey, William George, *Judicial Doctrines of Religious Rights in America.* Chapel Hill, 1948.

Trenholme, Louise Irby, *Ratification of the Federal Constitution in North Carolina.* New York, 1932.

Trumbull, J. Hammond, *Historical Notes of the Constitutions of Connecticut, 1639 to 1918.* Hartford, 1901.

Trumbull, Jonathan, *Jonathan Trumbull, Governor of Connecticut.* Boston, 1919.

—————— "The Trumbull Papers." *Massachusetts Historical Society, Collections.* 7 ser., II, III. 1902.

Tyler, Moses Coit, *Three Men of Letters: George Berkeley, Timothy Dwight, and Joel Barlow.* New York, 1895.

Upton, Richard Francis, *Revolutionary New Hampshire, An Account of Social and Political Forces Underlying the Transition from Royal Province to American Commonwealth.* Hanover, N. H., 1936.

Van Doren, Carl, *The Great Rehearsal.* New York, 1951.

Van Tyne, Claude, *The Loyalists in the American Revolution.* New York, 1929.

Walker, Joseph B., *A History of the New Hampshire Convention of the Investigation, Discussion, and Decision of the Federal Constitution.* Boston, 1888.

Wallace, David Duncan, *Life of Henry Laurens.* New York, 1915.

—————— *History of South Carolina.* 3 vols. New York, 1934.

Walsh, Correa W., *The Political Science of John Adams.* New York, 1915.

Walsh, James J., *Education of the Founding Fathers of the Republic.* New York, 1935.

Walsh, Richard, *Charleston's Sons of Liberty.* Columbia, S. C., 1959.

Walter, E. P., ed., *Records of the Council of Safety and the Governor and Council of the State of Vermont 1775–1836.* 8 vols. Montpelier, 1873–1880.

Ward, Leo R., C.S.C., *Religion in All the School.* Notre Dame, 1960.

Warfel, Harry, *Noah Webster, Schoolmaster to America.* New York, 1936.

Warren, Charles, "Elbridge Gerry, James Warren, Mercy Warren and the Ratification in Massachusetts," *Massachusetts Historical Society, Proceedings,* LXIV, 1930–1932.

Webster, Noah, *Collection of Papers on Political, Literary and Moral Subjects.* New York, 1843.

Weeks, Stephen B., "The Church and State in North Carolina" *John Hopkins Studies,* XI. Baltimore, 1893.

Welbon, Henry G., "History of Christian Education in Delaware." Unpublished M.A. thesis, University of Delaware, 1937.

Wells, W. V., *The Life and Public Services of Samuel Adams.* 3 vols. Boston, 1865.

Werline, Albert W., *Problems of Church and State in Maryland During the 17th and 18th Centuries.* South Lancaster, Mass., 1948.

Weston, Thomas, *History of Town of Middleboro, Massachusetts.* Boston and New York, 1906.

Whipple, Leon, *The Story of Civil Liberty in the United States.* New York, 1927.

Wingate, C. E. L., *Life and Letters of Paine Wingate.* 2 vols. Medford, Mass., 1933.

Wood, Gertrude, *William Paterson.* Fairlawn, N. J., 1933.

Zollman, Carl, *American Civil Church Law*. New York, 1917.
———— "The Relation of Church and State." *Studies in Religious Education.*
Ed. by Latz and Crawford, 1931.
Zunder, Theodore A., *The Early Days of Joel Barlow*. New Haven, 1934.

STUDIES AND PERIODICALS

Abrahams, E. H., "The Early History of the Sheftalls of Georgia," *American Jewish Society Publication*, No. 17.
Andrews, Mathew Page, "Separation of Church and State in Maryland," *Catholic History Review*, April, 1935.
Beaver, R. Pierce, "Church, State and the Indians," *Journal of Church and State*, IV, 1962.
Bishop, H. M., "Why Rhode Island Opposed the Federal Constitution, *"Rhode Island History*, VIII, 1949.
"Black Muslims in Prison: Of Muslim Rites and Constitutional Rights," 62 *Colum. L. Rev.* 1488 (1962).
Brant, Irving, "Madison: On the Separation of Church and State," *William and Mary Quarterly*, VIII (No. 1; 3rd Ser.; January, 1951).
Cahn, Edmond, "The 'Establishment of Religion' Puzzle," 36 *N.Y.U.L.Rev.* 1274 (1961).
———— "On Government and Prayer," 37 *N.Y.U.L.Rev.* 981 (1962).
Costanzo, "Federal Aid to Education and Religious Liberty," 36 *U.Det.L.J.* 1 (1958).
Crowl, Philip A., "Anti-Federalism in Maryland, 1787–1788," *William and Mary Quarterly*, IV (No. 4; 3rd Ser.; October, 1947).
Davis, Joseph S., "American Charters to Business Corporations, 1781–1800," *Harvard Economic Studies*, 1917, XVII, 332–345.
Dawson, Christopher, "Education and the State," *Commonweal*, LXV, January, 1957.
Diman, Jeremiah, "Religion in America 1776–1786," *North American Review*, CXXII, 1876.
Edwards, Martha L., "A Problem of Church and State in the 1870's" *Mississippi Valley Historical Review*, XI, No. 1, June, 1924.
Ellis, John T., "Church and State: An American Catholic Tradition," *Harpers Magazine*, CCVII, November, 1953.
Ford, Paul L., "Pinckney's Draft of the Constitution," *The Nation*, LX, June, 1895.
Gillett, Rev. E. H., "The Development of Civil Liberty in Connecticut," *Historical Magazine, 2nd Series*, IV, 1868.
Hackett, William H., "The Circuit for the New Hampshire District One Hundred Years Ago," *The Green Bag*, Vol. II, 1890.
Hartogenesis, B. H., "Denial of Equal Rights to Religious Minorities and Non-Believers in the United States," 39 *YaleL.J.* 659 (1930).
Herberg, Will, "The Sectarian Conflict over Church and State," *Commentary*, November, 1952.
Jameson, J. Franklin, "Studies in the History of the Federal Convention," *American Historical Review*, IX, July, 1904.
Jensen, Merrill, "Democracy and the American Revolution," *Huntington Library Quarterly*, XX, 1957.
Katz, Wilbur, "Freedom of Religion and State Neutrality," 20 *U.Chi.L.Rev.* 426 (1953).

Lander, Ernest M., "South Carolinians at the Philadelphia Convention, 1787," *South Carolina Historical Magazine,* LVII, July, 1956.

Lardner, Lynford, "How Far Does the Constitution Separate Church and State?" *American Political Science Review,* XLV, 1951.

McCrady, Edward, "Education in South Carolina Prior to and During the Revolution," Publications of the South Carolina Historical Society. Charleston, 1883.

McLaughlin, Andrew C., "Outline of Pinckney's Plan," *The Nation,* LXXVII, April, 1904.

McRee, Griffeth J., "Warren-Adams Settlers," *Massachusetts Historical Society Collections,* LXXII 1917; LXXIII, 1925.

Mellon, Knox, Jr., "Christian Prober and the Jesuit Myth," *South Carolina Historical Magazine,* LXI, 1961.

Myer, Agnes, "The School, the State, and the Church," *Atlantic Monthly,* November, 1948.

Morison, Samuel Eliot, "Elbridge Gerry, Gentlemen Democrat," *New England Quarterly,* January, 1929.

Murray, John Courtney, "Separation of Church and State," *America Magazine,* LXXVI, December, 1946.

———— "Dr. Morrison and the First Amendment," *America Magazine,* LXXXVIII, March, 1948.

Schaff, Philip, "Church and State in the United States," *Papers of the American Historical Association,* II, 1888.

Silving, Helen, "The Oaths," 68 *Yale L.J.* 1329, 1527 (1959).

Smith, A. L., "New Era in Church and State," *Social England,* New York, 1902.

Snee, Joseph, "Religious Disestablishment and the Fourteenth Amendment," 1954 *Wash.Univ.L.Q.* 391 (1954).

Statement of Protestant Leaders (June, 1948), *Crisis and Christianity,* July, 1948.

Steiner, Bruce E., "The Catholic Brents of Virginia," *Virginia Magazine of History and Biography,* LXX, October, 1962.

———— "Connecticut's Ratification of the Federal Constitution," *Proceedings of the American Antiquarian Society, N. S.,* XXV, 1915.

Sutherland, Arthur, "Establishment According to *Engel,*" 76 *Harv.L.Rev.* 25 (1962).

Sweet, William Warren, "The Colonial Environment and Religious Liberty," *Church History,* January, 1935.

"The Thacher Papers," *Historical Magazine,* XVI, 1869.

Ulmer, S. S., "James Madison and the Pinckney Plan," 9 *S.C.L.Q.* 415 (1957).

———— "Charles Pinckney: The Father of the United States Constitution," 10 *S.C.L.Q.* 225 (1958).

Wallace, David Duncan, "Historical Background of Religion in South Carolina," *South Carolina Historical and Genealogical Magazine,* XXVII, November, 1916.

Newspapers and Magazines

CONNECTICUT NEWSPAPERS:
American Mercury (Hartford)
Connecticut Courant (Hartford)
Connecticut Gazette (New London)

New Haven Chronicle (New Haven)
Connecticut Journal (New Haven)
New Haven Gazette (New Haven)
Middlesex Gazette (Middletown)
Norwich Packet (Norwich)
Weekly Monitor (Lichfield)
DELAWARE NEWSPAPERS:
Delaware Gazette
GEORGIA NEWSPAPERS:
Georgia Gazette (Savannah)
MARYLAND NEWSPAPERS:
Baltimore Federal Republican and Commercial Gazette (Baltimore)
Maryland Gazette
MASSACHUSETTS NEWSPAPERS:
American Herald (Boston)
Berkshire Chronicle (Berkshire)
Boston Gazette (Boston)
Cumberland Gazette (Portland)
Essex Journal (Salem)
Falmouth Gazette and Weekly Advertiser (Portland)
Hampshire Chronicle (Springfield)
Hampshire Gazette (Northampton)
Hampshire Herald (Springfield)
Independent Chronicle (Boston)
Massachusetts Centinal (Boston)
Massachusetts Spy (Worcester)
Salem Mercury (Salem)
Western Star (Stockbridge)
NEW HAMPSHIRE NEWSPAPERS:
New Hampshire Mercury (Portsmouth)
New Hampshire Patriot
New Hampshire Spy (Portsmouth)
NEW JERSEY NEWSPAPERS:
New Jersey Gazette
New Jersey Journal & Political Intelligencer
New Jersey State Gazette
NEW YORK NEWSPAPERS:
Federal Gazette
Gazette of the United States
New York Daily Gazette
New York Mercury
National Intelligencer
PENNSYLVANIA NEWSPAPERS:
The Federal Gazette and Philadelphia Evening Post
Freeman's Journal
Independent Gazette or Chronicle of Freedom
Pennsylvania Gazette
RHODE ISLAND NEWSPAPERS:
Providence Gazette
U. S. Chronicle (Providence)

SOUTH CAROLINA NEWSPAPERS:
  City Gazette or Daily Advertiser (Charleston)
  South Carolina Gazette (Charleston)
VIRGINIA NEWSPAPER::
  Alexandria Gazette (Alexandria)
  Virginia Gazette and Weekly Advertiser
  Virginia Herald and Fredericksburg Advertiser
OTHER:
  The American Museum (Philadelphia)

Historical Collections

American History Researches, October.
Correspondence of Ralph Izard, 1774–1804, New York, 1844.
"Letters of William Plumer, 1786–1787," Colonial Society of Massachusetts, *Transactions,* II, 1906–1907.
Manuscripts First Presbyterian Church of Elizabethtown, New Jersey State Library.
Manuscripts Protestant Episcopal Church of New Brunswick, New Jersey State Library.
Manuscripts Protestant Episcopal Church of Perth Amboy, New Jersey State Library.
Manuscripts St. Peter's Church of Perth Amboy, New Jersey Historical Society.
Massachusetts Historical Society Collections (First Series).
Records of the General Association of the Congregational Churches in Connecticut, Revolutionary Records of Georgia, Atlanta, 1908.
"The Belknap Papers," *Massachusetts Historical Society Collections* (Sixth Series).

Records of Federal Conventions and Legislative Sessions

The Debates and Proceedings in the Congress of the United States, Annals of the Congress of the United States, 1789–1824, 42 vols., Washington, 1834–1856, I–III.
House Judiciary Committee Report, 33rd Congress, Ist Session, March, 1854, Document 124.
Journals of the Continental Congress, 1774–1789, 34 vols., Washington, 1904–1937.
Journal of the First Session of the Senate, Washington, 1820.
Journal of the House of Representatives, New York, 1789.
Journal of the House of Representatives, Washington, 1826.
Senate Journal for the First Session of the First Congress of the United States, New York, 1789.
Senate Judiciary Committee Report, 32nd Congress, 2nd Session, 1853.

STATE JOURNALS AND RECORDS

Connecticut Archives, Ecclesiastical Affairs, Second Series.
Connecticut State Records.
Debates and Proceedings in the Convention of the Commonwealth of Massachusetts Held in the Year 1788, and Which Finally Ratified the Constitution of the United States, Boston, 1856.
Journal of Connecticut Legislature.

Journal of the Convention for Framing a Constitution of Government in the State of Massachusetts Bay, 1779–1780, Boston, 1832.
Journal of the House, The Maryland Legislature, 1787–1795. Microfilm Reading Room, Library of Congress.
Journal of the House of Delegates of Virginia, 1780–1800, in Archives, Virginia State Library, Richmond.
Journal of the House of Representatives, New York, 1789.
Journal of the House of Representatives of South Carolina for 1790, South Carolina Archives, Columbia.
Journal of Massachusetts Legislature.
Journal of New Hampshire.
Journal of the Proceedings of the Convention of the State of New York, 1788.
Journal of Proceedings of the Convention of the State of New York, Held at Poughkeepsie.
Journal of Proceedings of New Jersey Legislature Council, 1877.
Journal of Rhode Island.
Journals of the Convention which Assembled in Concord to Revise the Constitution of New Hampshire, 1791–1792, Concord, 1793.
Journal of the Senate of New York, 1777–1795.
Journal of the Senate of Virginia, 1780–1800, in Archives, Virginia State Library, Richmond.
Journal of Vermont.
Journal of the Votes and Proceedings of the Convention of New Jersey at Burlington, 1776
Minutes of the Council of Delaware, 1776–1792, Dover, 1928.
Proceedings of the Convention of the Province of Maryland, 1836.
Proceedings and Debates of Convention of North Carolina Called to Amend the Constitution of the State, Which Assembled at Raleigh, June 4, 1835, Raleigh, 1836.
Proceedings Relative to Call the Conventions of 1776 and 1790, Harrisburg, Pa., 1825.
Records of the Convention of Maryland, Annapolis, 1776.
Report of the Committee of the General Court on Further Amendments, Massachusetts Archives, Senate Miscellaneous Document 1145 of 1790.

Cases and Briefs

Adamson v. California, 332 U.S. 46 (1947).
Barnes v. First Parish, 6 Mass. 401 (1810).
Bradfield v. Roberts, 175 U.S. 291 (1899).
Doremus v. Board of Education, 5. N.J. 435 (1950), *appeal dismissed,* 342 U.S. 429 (1952).
Everson v. Board of Education, 330 U.S. 1 (1947).
Gallego's Ex'rs v. Attorney General, 30 Va. (3 Leigh.) 450 (1832).
Jackson, ex. dem. Tuttle v. Grindley, 18 Johnson's Reports 98 (N.Y. 1820).
McCulloch v. Maryland, 4 U.S. (4 Wheat.) 316 (1819).
McCollum v. Board of Education, 333 U.S. 203 (1948).
Muzzy v. Wilkins, 1 New Hampshire Reports 10 (1803).
People v. Ruggles, 8 Johnson (N.Y.), 290 (1811).
Reid v. Covert, 354 U.S. 1 (1957).
Reynolds v. United States, 98 U.S. 145 (1878).
Runkel v. Winemiller, 4 H. and McH. 429 (Md. 1799).

The Slaughterhouse Cases, 83 U.S. 36 (1872).

Specht v. Commonwealth, 8 Pa St. (Barr) 312 (1848).

Terret v. Taylor, 13 U.S. (9 Cranch) 43 (1815).

Torcaso v. Watkins, 367 U.S. 488 (1961).

Trustees of the Philadelphia Baptist Association v. Hart's Ex'rs, 4 U.S. (4 Wheat.) 1 (1819).

United States v. MacIntosh, 42 F.2d 845 (2d Cir. 1931).

Updegraph v. Commonwealth, 11 Pa. (Sergeant & Rawle) 393 (1824).

Vidal v. Girard's Ex'rs, U.S. (2 How.) 127 (1844).

Brief of the Appellee, *McCollum v. Board of Education,* # 90, Supreme Court of the United States, Oct. Term (1947).

STATUTES

Acts of the Assembly of the State of New Jersey (New Brunswick, 1790).

Brevard, Joseph, *An Alphabetical Digest of the Public Statute Law of South Carolina,* Charleston, 1814.

Colonial Laws of New York, 5 vols., Albany, N. Y., 1894–1896.

Connecticut Revised Statutes, 1888.

General Statutes of Connecticut, 1642–1821.

Hening's *Statutes at Large of Virginia.*

Laws of Maryland, 1723.

Laws of Maryland (Kilty, ed.), 2 vols., Annapolis, 1799.

Laws of New York State, New York, 1790.

Laws of the State of Delaware, 1787–1821, Library of the University of Delaware, Newark.

Laws of the State of New York, 1812–1813.

Laws of the State of New York Passed at 18th Session of Legislature, New York, 1795.

Maryland General Assembly, Session Laws, 1785–1795, Microfilm Reading Room, Library of Congress.

New Jersey Acts of 1790 (passed at Perth Amboy).

Pennsylvania Statutes at Large, 1682–1801, Harrisburg, 1911.

Public Laws of the State of Rhode Island and Providence Plantations, Providence, 1798.

Revised Laws of New Jersey, New Brunswick, 1800.

South Carolina Acts of Assembly for 1799, Faust edition, Columbia, 1799.

South Carolina Statutes at Large, ed. Thomas Cooper (I–VI) and David McCord (VII–XII), Columbia, S. C., 1838–1841.

United States Statutes at Large.

Index

267